COMPUTER SCIENCE, TECHNOLOGY AND APPLICATIONS

PEER-TO-PEER NETWORKS AND INTERNET POLICIES

COMPUTER SCIENCE, TECHNOLOGY AND APPLICATIONS

Additional books in this series can be found on Nova's website under the Series tab.

Additional E-books in this series can be found on Nova's website under the E-book tab.

COMPUTER SCIENCE, TECHNOLOGY AND APPLICATIONS

PEER-TO-PEER NETWORKS AND INTERNET POLICIES

DIEGO VEGROS

AND

JAIME SÁENZ

EDITORS

Nova Science Publishers, Inc.

New York

NOTICE TO THE READER

The Publisher has taken reasonable care in the preparation of this book, but makes no expressed or implied warranty of any kind and assumes no responsibility for any errors or omissions. No liability is assumed for incidental or consequential damages in connection with or arising out of information contained in this book. The Publisher shall not be liable for any special, consequential, or exemplary damages resulting, in whole or in part, from the readers' use of, or reliance upon, this material. Any parts of this book based on government reports are so indicated and copyright is claimed for those parts to the extent applicable to compilations of such works.

Independent verification should be sought for any data, advice or recommendations contained in this book. In addition, no responsibility is assumed by the publisher for any injury and/or damage to persons or property arising from any methods, products, instructions, ideas or otherwise contained in this publication.

This publication is designed to provide accurate and authoritative information with regard to the subject matter covered herein. It is sold with the clear understanding that the Publisher is not engaged in rendering legal or any other professional services. If legal or any other expert assistance is required, the services of a competent person should be sought. FROM A DECLARATION OF PARTICIPANTS JOINTLY ADOPTED BY A COMMITTEE OF THE AMERICAN BAR ASSOCIATION AND A COMMITTEE OF PUBLISHERS.

Additional color graphics may be available in the e-book version of this book.

LIBRARY OF CONGRESS CATALOGING-IN-PUBLICATION DATA

ISBN 978-1-60876-287-3
Peer-to-peer networks and Internet policies / editors, Diego Vegros and Jaime Sáenz.
     p. cm.
 Includes bibliographical references and index.
 ISBN 978-1-60876-287-3 (hardcover)
 1. Peer-to-peer architecture (Computer networks)--Government policy. 2. Internet--Social aspects. 3. Internet research.
I. Vegros, Diego. II. Sáenz, Jaime, 1950-
 TK5105.525.P446 2009
 004.6'52--dc22
                         2009044318

Published by Nova Science Publishers, Inc. ✦ New York

CONTENTS

PREFACE

Peer-to-peer (P2P) systems are distributed systems consisting of interconnected nodes, able to self-organize into network topologies with the purpose of sharing resources such as content, CPU cycles, storage and bandwidth. Many of the largest IT companies including HP, Microsoft and IBM have invested considerable resources in such P2P applications. It has been proven as a most successful way to produce large scale, reliable, and cost-effective applications. The authors review several incentive mechanisms that have been proposed to stimulate cooperation towards achieving a resilient storage. Moreover, this book deals with a teaching course for network literacy. It includes the necessary skills for people to live in a networked information society. Also included in this book is information on P2P content distribution systems and infrastructures by identifying their non-functional properties, and determining the way in which these non-functional properties depend on, and are affected by various design features. Other chapters in this book present a Bayesian game to detect intruders in ad hoc networks, describe the quickly emerging social behavior of online user-generated video, examine the phenomenon of internet addiction, and explore the process of quality e-development, a continuing professional training (CPT) which affects faculty learning.

Peer-to-peer (P2P) has proven as a most successful way to produce large scale, reliable, and cost-effective applications, as illustrated for file sharing or VoIP. P2P storage is an emerging field of application which allows peers to collectively leverage their resources towards ensuring the reliability and availability of user data. Providing assurances in both domains requires not only ensuring the confidentiality and privacy of the data storage process, but also thwarting peer misbehavior through the introduction of proper security and cooperation enforcement mechanisms.

Misbehavior may consist in data destruction or corruption by malicious or free-riding peers. Additionally, a new form of man-in-the-middle attack may make it possible for a malicious peer to pretend to be storing data without using any local disk space. New forms of collusion also may occur whereby replica holders would collude to store a single replica of some data, thereby defeating the requirement of data redundancy. Finally, Sybil attackers may create a large number of identities and use them to gain a disproportionate personal advantage.

The continuous observation of peer behavior and monitoring of the storage process is an important requirement to secure a storage system. Observing peer misbehavior requires appropriate primitives like proofs of data possession, a form of proof of knowledge whereby the holder interactively tries to convince the verifier that it possesses the very data without actually retrieving them or copying them at verifier's memory. The authors present a survey of such techniques and discuss their suitability for assessing remote data storage.

Cooperation is key to deploying P2P storage solutions, yet peers in such applications are confronted to an inherent social dilemma: should they contribute to the collective welfare or misbehave for their individual welfare? In Chapter 1 the authors review several incentive mechanisms that have been proposed to stimulate cooperation towards achieving a resilient storage.

The effectiveness of such incentive mechanisms must be validated for a large-scale system. The authors describe how this can be assessed with game theoretical techniques. In this approach, cooperation incentive mechanisms are proven to be effective if it is demonstrated that any rational peer will always choose to follow mechanism directives whenever it interacts with another peer. The authors finally illustrate the validation of cooperation incentives with one-stage and repeated cooperative and non cooperative games and evolutionary games.

The computer laws of Colombia and Peru take a similar hybrid perspective in terms of technological neutrality. They recognize the legal validity of all types of electronic signatures, but show a preference for the digital signature by including detailed rules regarding Certification Authorities ("CA") and Public Key Infrastructure ("PKI"), two concepts only associated with the digital signature. In contrast, the U.S. approach is that of technological permissiveness—a legal recognition of all types of electronic signatures with no preference shown toward any of them. Accordingly, the U.S. law does not mention CA's or PKI because that would have been indicative of favoritism toward the digital signature. That is the essential difference between U.S. law and that of Colombia and Peru—the latter's statutes contain extensive coverage of CA's and PKI.

Colombia's statute covers both E-commerce contracts and electronic signatures, but Peru has enacted two separate statutes pertinent to those topics. Colombian law allows an electronic document to comply with a statutory requirement for production of an original paper document or a requirement for storage of a document, but Peru's statute does not mention those statutory requirements. Colombia covers carriage contracts, but Peru does not. Peru creates Registration Agents ("RA"), essentially clerks of CA's who are authorized to perform ministerial duties, but may not issue certificates or maintain a repository of them; Colombia does not mention RA's. The Colombian statute and the U.S. model law contain a list of exclusions from coverage, but the Peruvian statute does not. In Chapter 2, the author recommends that: Colombia should enact a comprehensive computer crimes law; Peru should eliminate the position of RA and use CA's alone; the U.S. should eliminate its wills exclusion and join Colombia and Peru in granting the digital signature most-favored status among electronic signatures; Colombia and Peru should enact E-government statutes and should explicitly claim long-arm jurisdiction in their E-commerce statutes; and all three nations should enact more stringent consumer protections for E-commerce buyers and should establish Information Technology Courts.

The integration of a variety of environmental, hydrographic, meteorological, and oceanographic data collected from the Gulf of Mexico (GOM) will become a valuable resource for the public, local government officials, scientists, natural resource managers, and educators. Due to the nature of the schematic heterogeneity, domain diversification, and unstable availability of the Internet-based data, a new framework is proposed in Chapter 3, and being developed to integrate and retrieve results from the underlying data sources to answer user queries.

The framework is a peer-to-peer based system, called GDS (the Gulf of Mexico Dataspace), which exploits a hybrid method to handle a user's query. To be more specific, the current data is searched and retrieved on demand in real time from the Internet while the historical data is returned from the data archives created by employing a client-server grid architecture, integrated rule-oriented data system (iRODS). In the framework, a peer represents the data sources from an application domain, and peers share information with each other through the attribute mapping and JXTA communication technique. In addition, spatial features, such as partonomic, distance, topological relations, and directional relations between data sources, are utilized and developed to facilitate the data retrieval and integration of spatial-related data from the GOM.

Chapter 4 presents a Bayesian game to detect intruders in ad hoc networks. The authors use game theory techniques to model the interactions among nodes of an ad hoc network where each node plays a game among other neighboring nodes in the network and identifies potential attackers in peer-to-peer approach.

Chapter 5 deals with a teaching course for network literacy. The authors define network literacy as the ability to access, evaluate, and use digital information on the Internet, as well as to create digital information for dissemination on the Internet. It includes necessary skills for people to live in a networked information society.

In higher education all students, regardless of their major, need to learn how to use information on the Internet for solving their problems. Since students have been exposed to various kinds of information on the Internet before reaching college or university, they appear to have enough network literacy skills. In fact, many of them have adequate skills in the functional dimension, but not in the problem-solving dimension. They lack attitudes and skills that are necessary to evaluate information quality and to communicate effectively.

The authors designed a course for network literacy and developed teaching materials to cultivate skills and utilize the Internet effectively for solving problems. The course is composed of four units: (1) understanding what we can do with the Internet and basic technical knowledge about computer networks; (2) communication via e-mail; (3) critical evaluation of Web pages, including Web logs (blogs); (4) creation and evaluation of Web pages. In this chapter the authors provide checklists that were developed as teaching materials for the following purposes: to send e-mail for successful communication, to read Web pages critically, and to plan and evaluate original Web pages. These checklists guide students to effective learning.

The style and functions of information on the Internet have evolved with amazing speed. We can access new tools and contents on new Internet services, such as blog systems and social network systems. However, the appearance of new tools and services has not changed the core literacy skills that should be learned: how to evaluate information from the Internet and how to communicate over the Internet. In order to solve problems encountered at school, at work, and at home, it is essential for students to learn these skills in courses on network literacy. This course was originally designed for students of college or university; however, it can be applied in all disciplines and professions for people who did not study it in school.

Online education is used for a variety of purposes in higher education. Two such purposes are the improving of one's performance over time and the elucidation of one's professional development for others in the context of online teaching and learning. Relying on data from some online staff development courses delivered in universities, Chapter 6 explores online faculty learning through the lens of staff development theory. This theoretical perspective emphasizes the universities' quality assurance contexts and offers an empirical examination of the ways that faculty members learn curriculum and teaching capacities (CTC) in online staff development programs. At the core of this analysis is the contention that faculty members interprets and responds to quality teaching. Finally, this chapter highlights the points deemed important when designing, implementing and evaluating Internet training courses.

The success of companies such as Myspace and YouTube have focused attention on online companies that are quickly building their business model on participative media, leveraging a set of new social-based technologies, dubbed "Web 2.0". Chapter 7 describes the quickly emerging social behavior of online user-generated *video*. Five clear findings stand out: a) Participative media is already widespread, even it is still biased socio-demographically in favor of young males; b) Participation is fostered mostly by the desire to fame, and to a lesser extent financial incentives; c) On top of those drivers, social network aspects stand as critical drivers of the growth of user-generated video; d) Online video users limit themselves to 2 to 3 sites; e) Users of online videos are keen to have a more comprehensive offering than UGC video alone- this includes conventional TV shows as well as premium content such as movies.

Taking together, those findings lead to the conjecture that the market for online video will quickly evolve to a concentrated number of destination sites, aggregating all types of content.

Peer-to-peer (P2P) systems are distributed systems consisting of interconnected nodes, able to self-organize into network topologies with the purpose of sharing resources such as content, CPU cycles, storage, and bandwidth. Content distribution systems are designed for the sharing of digital media and other data between users. P2P content distribution systems range from relatively simple direct file-sharing applications, to more complicated systems that create a distributed storage medium for securely and efficiently publishing, organizing, indexing, searching, updating, and retrieving data. P2P systems can function, scale, and self-organize in the presence of a highly transient population of nodes and network and computer failures, without the need for a central server administration. This characteristic is mainly attributed to the network organization and location and routing algorithms. In this respect, two general categories of systems can be identified: the unstructured systems and the structured (or DHT-based) systems. Both category systems are complementary and satisfactory solutions. This chapter focuses on P2P content distribution systems and infrastructures by identifying their non-functional properties, and determining the way in which these non-functional properties depend on, and are affected by various design features. The main nonfunctional characteristics include provisions for security, anonymity, fairness, increased scalability, and performance, as well as resource management, and organization capabilities. Finally, Chapter 8 discusses open research problems, directions, and opportunities.

As the context and content of psychological research changes, so too do the ethical decisions faced by researchers. The Internet continues to grow in popularity and as it does so, more and more people are turning to it in order to seek information, advice and psychological support (Coulson, Malik, & Mo, 2007). The Internet has therefore become an invaluable resource for recruiting research participants, especially for studies that require recruitment of clinical or hard to find populations. Indeed, the prevalence of topic specific websites, online message boards and e-mail lists, provides researchers with a ready-made sampling frame that they can utilize to access participants who are interested, affiliated and connected to the topic under investigation (Griffiths, 2001; Murray & Fisher, 2002; Szabo, Frenkl, & Caputo, 1996). As in 'offline' research, a range of qualitative approaches can be employed which include: online surveys, online interviews (both 'synchronous' and 'asynchronous'), online focus groups and online observational studies, (whereby the behavior of people using chat rooms or message boards is analysed).

However, the expansion of the online research milieu brings with it new ethical challenges particularly in terms of consent and privacy and confidentiality. As a consequence, a number of authors have written about practical and ethical considerations with regard to online research (Coulson et al., 2007; DeLorme, Zinkhan, & French, 2001; Eysenbach & Till, 2001; Rodham & Gavin, 2006). Furthermore, the British Psychological Society (2007) has recently published guidelines for conducting research online which are intended to be a supplement to the existing ethical code of conduct for British psychologists, whereas other professional bodies specifically mention the issue of online research within their statement of ethical practice (e.g., British Sociological Association, 2002). The British Psychological Society (BPS) guidelines, however, do not address the ethical and methodological challenges posed by so-called Web 2.0. How do researchers deal with the changing trends in Internet use, which now include multi-author and multi-media sites such as Facebook, Myspace and Youtube? How can decisions about public and private spaces, informed consent, or anonymity be addressed in online environments containing several layers of text, image and audio-visual input from multiple sources across multiple, linked sites?

Over the last few years, the authors have built up a body of research utilising the Internet as a means of collecting data (e.g. Adams, Rodham & Gavin, 2005; Hadert & Rodham, 2008; Rodham, Gavin & Miles, 2007; Gavin, Duffield, Brosnan, M., Joiner, Maras, & Scott, 2007; Gavin, Rodham & Poyer, 2008; Rodham, McCabe & Blake, 2009; Whitty & Gavin, 2001). In Chapter 9, the authors draw upon their experience as online qualitative researchers and offer a commentary on the ethics of conducting online research.

As discussed in Chapter 10, Internet is one of the major inventions of 20th century. For most users, Internet is at the same time a way of communication, a convivial and powerful workspace and a recreational activity. Internet therefore became essential to the daily lives of more than one billion people [1]. In 1982, the word *Internet* made its appearance and the web became accessible to the public in the 90's. Its almost unlimited possibilities, in the field of the communication and the diffusion of knowledge, make it a very popular tool. Internet quickly rapidly became essential in the professional sphere as a powerful tool of transferring and sharing data and in the privacy of homes as an essential need to open up to the world and knowledge. A majority of specialists estimates that between 6% and 8% of Internet users would be dependent. Nevertheless, as the phenomenon is still too recent, the national and world prevalence of cyber addiction still seems difficult to quantify [2].

Whereas the benefits are undeniable, some people to suffer the consequences of excessive use. This problem is often underestimated but some of them swear by the web. These compulsive Internet users can be described as "'connection addicts'". Their abusive use of Internet is at the origin of a new disease called the cyber addiction. Other subjects do not have an addictive relation to the web but suffer from an excessive involvement in the cyber life. They reduce their interest for relations in the "real world" and prefer on-line activities.

Their abuse of the web leads them to a new form of "cocooning". Cocooning can be described as the feeling of being so well at home that one hardly wants to go out even for vital needs.

As explained in Chapter 11, Peer-to-Peer (P2P) network based technologies facilitate a distributed community of users to share their digital or computer processing resources. Every node, or peer, that is a part of the network can potentially contribute resources to other peers. Consequently P2P networks have many advantages over centralized networks, such as: (a) inherent scalability, (b) no single point of failure, and (c) self-administration capabilities. P2P technology-based applications have recently become increasingly popular with both businesses and individual users in the Internet era. Some common P2P applications include content delivery networks (CDN) such as Amazon Cloud Front (http://aws.amazon.com/cloudfront/), collaboration technologies such as Groove (www.groove.net), digital content distribution services such as Joost (www.joost.com), among others. Many of the largest IT companies including HP, Microsoft, and IBM have invested considerable resources in such P2P applications. In this article the authors review some related research on P2P networks and discuss its characteristics and applications. Given the inherent advantages of decentralized P2P networks, the authors believe that it provides a useful methodology for organizations to effectively manage their computing resources.

Chapter 12 presents the NCTUns simulation/emulation tool for researchers to evaluate the performances of real-life P2P applications such as BitTorrent. By using a unique simulation methodology, NCTUns directly uses the real-life network protocol stacks in the Linux operating system for realistic network simulations and enables any real-life network application to be executed on a node in a simulated network. These unique capabilities enable researchers to evaluate the performances of real-life P2P applications such as BitTorrent on accurately-simulated networks. In this chapter, the authors present the architecture of NCTUns, its simulation methodology, its unique capabilities, its detailed usages, and its scalability in real-life P2P application researches. More information about NCTUns is available at http://NSL.cs.nctu.edu.tw/nctuns.html.

In: Peer-to-Peer Networks and Internet Policies   ISBN: 978-1-60876-287-3
Editors: Diego Vegros and Jaime Sáenz, pp. 1-39   © 2010 Nova Science Publishers, Inc.

Chapter 1

PEER-TO-PEER STORAGE:
SECURITY AND PROTOCOLS

Nouha Oualha[a] and Yves Roudier[b]
EURECOM, Sophia Antipolis, France

Abstract

Peer-to-peer (P2P) has proven as a most successful way to produce large scale, reliable, and cost-effective applications, as illustrated for file sharing or VoIP. P2P storage is an emerging field of application which allows peers to collectively leverage their resources towards ensuring the reliability and availability of user data. Providing assurances in both domains requires not only ensuring the confidentiality and privacy of the data storage process, but also thwarting peer misbehavior through the introduction of proper security and cooperation enforcement mechanisms.

Misbehavior may consist in data destruction or corruption by malicious or free-riding peers. Additionally, a new form of man-in-the-middle attack may make it possible for a malicious peer to pretend to be storing data without using any local disk space. New forms of collusion also may occur whereby replica holders would collude to store a single replica of some data, thereby defeating the requirement of data redundancy. Finally, Sybil attackers may create a large number of identities and use them to gain a disproportionate personal advantage.

The continuous observation of peer behavior and monitoring of the storage process is an important requirement to secure a storage system. Observing peer misbehavior requires appropriate primitives like proofs of data possession, a form of proof of knowledge whereby the holder interactively tries to convince the verifier that it possesses the very data without actually retrieving them or copying them at verifier's memory. We present a survey of such techniques and discuss their suitability for assessing remote data storage.

Cooperation is key to deploying P2P storage solutions, yet peers in such applications are confronted to an inherent social dilemma: should they contribute to the collective welfare or misbehave for their individual welfare? We review several incentive mechanisms that have been proposed to stimulate cooperation towards achieving a resilient storage.

The effectiveness of such incentive mechanisms must be validated for a large-scale system. We describe how this can be assessed with game theoretical techniques. In this approach, cooperation incentive mechanisms are proven to be effective if it is demonstrated

---

[a] E-mail address: oualha@eurecom.fr
[b] E-mail address: roudier@eurecom.fr

that any rational peer will always choose to follow mechanism directives whenever it interacts with another peer. We finally illustrate the validation of cooperation incentives with one-stage and repeated cooperative and non cooperative games and evolutionary games.

I. Introduction

Self-organization has first emerged, in the late 90's, as specialized systems and protocols to support peer-to-peer (P2P) file sharing. It became very popular thanks to services like Napster [70], Gnutella [34], KaZaA [46] and Morpheus [66], and particularly to the legal controversy regarding their copyrighted contents. Since then, the popularity of P2P systems has continued to grow such that self-organization is now regarded as a general-purpose and practical approach that can be applied to designing applications for resource sharing. Resources in this context may include the exchange of information, processing cycles, packet forwarding and routing, as well as cache and disk storage. In this sense, self-organization, as revealed in P2P, is being increasingly used in several application domains ranging from P2P telephony or audio/video streaming to ad hoc networks or nomadic computing. P2P storage services have more recently been suggested as a new technique to make use of the vast and untapped storage resources available on personal computers. P2P data storage services like Wuala [97], AllMyData Tahoe [3], and UbiStorage [93] have received some highlight. In all of these, data is outsourced from the data owner place to several heterogonous storage sites in the network, in order to increase data availability and fault-tolerance, to reduce storage maintenance costs, and to achieve a high scalability of the system.

A Case for P2P Storage

Innovation and advancement in information technology has spurred a tremendous growth in the amount of data available and generated. This has generated new challenges regarding scalable storage management that must be addressed by implementing storage applications in a self-organized and cooperative form. In such storage applications, peers can store their personal data in one or multiple copies (replication) at other peers. The latter, called *holders*, should store data until the owner retrieves them. Such P2P storage aims at maintaining a reliable storage without a single point of failure, although without the need for an expensive and energy-consuming storage infrastructure as offered by data centers. Peers volunteer for holding data within their own storage space on a long term basis while they expect a reciprocal behavior from other peers.

P2P storage has been presented as a solution for data backup ([49] and [55]) as well as for a new generation of distributed file systems ([81], [44], and [86]). P2P storage aims at a free and more importantly more resilient alternative to centralized storage, in particular to address the fact that storage can still be considered as a single point of failure. Additionally, P2P storage may also be attractive in wireless ad-hoc networks or delay-tolerant networks (DTNs), notably since mobility introduces a store-carry-and-forward paradigm ([96]) to deliver packets despite frequent and extended network partitions. The cooperative storage of other nodes' messages until their delivery to their destination thus might become an important feature of such networks. Context- or location-based services may also benefit from P2P storage. Desktop teleporting ([28], [90]) for instance aims at the dynamic mapping of the desktop of a user onto a specific location. Teleporting may make use of the storage offered by surrounding nodes at the new user location. Location-aware information delivery ([71], [5], [6], [57]) is another context-aware application. Each reminder message is created with a location, and when the intended recipient arrives at that location, the message is delivered. The remainder message may be stored at nodes situated nearby the location context rather than at the mobile node.

Though the self-organization introduced by P2P storage promises to produce large scale, reliable, and cost-effective applications, it exposes the stored data to new threats. In particular, P2P systems and, even more so, P2P storage systems may be subject to selfishness, a misbehavior whereby peers may discard some data they promised to store for other peers in order to optimize their resource usage. Maliciousness in the P2P context woult simply consist in peers destroying the data they store in order to reduce the quality of service of the system. Because of the high churn and dynamics of peers, checking that some data have been stored somewhere is quite more complex than checking that a route has been established with another node in multi-hop MANETs for instance. In addition, such verifications cannot be instantaneous but have to be repeatedly performed. All these problems contribute to the difficulty of properly determining the actual availability of data stored onto unknown peers. Countermeasures that take into account the fact that users have full authority on their devices should be crafted to prevent them from cheating the system in order to maximize the benefit they can obtain out of peer cooperation.

Security Objectives

A P2P storage application takes advantage of the existing and spare disk space at peers allowing the latter to leverage their collective power for the *common good*. While the fundamental premise of this is voluntary storage resource sharing among individual peers, there is an inherent tension between individual rationality and collective welfare that threatens the viability of these applications. This behavior, termed *free riding*, is the result of a social dilemma that all peers confront and may lead to system collapse in *the tragedy of the commons* [29]: the dilemma for each peer is to either contribute to the common good, or to free ride (shirk).

Achieving secure and trusted P2P storage presents a particular challenge in that context due to the open, autonomous, and highly dynamic nature of P2P networks. We argue that any effort to protect the P2P storage system should ensure the following goals.

Confidentiality and Integrity of Data

Most storage applications deal with personal (or group) data that are stored somewhere in the network at peers that are not especially trusted. Data must thus be protected while transmitted to and stored at some peer. Typically, the confidentiality and the integrity of stored data are ensured using usual cryptographic means such as encryption methods and checksums.

Anonymity

Anonymity can be a requirement for some type of storage applications that aim at preventing information censorship for instance; however it may not be a targeted objective for all of them. Anonymity may refer to the data owner identity, the data holder identity, or the detail of their interaction. Anonymity permits to avoid attacks whereby the data of a given user are specifically targeted in order to destroy them from the system. Systems that seek to provide anonymity often employ infrastructures for providing anonymous connection layers, e.g., onion routing [18].

Identification

Within a distributed environment like P2P, it is possible for the same physical entity to appear under different identities, particularly in systems with highly transient populations of peers. This problem may lead to attacks called "Sybil attacks" [45], and may also threaten mechanisms such as data replication that rely on the existence of independent peers with different identities. Solutions to these attacks may rely on the deployment of a trusted third party acting as a central certification authority, yet this approach may limit anonymity. Alternatively, P2P storage may be operated by some authority controlling the network through the payment of membership fees to limit the introduction of fake identities. However, that approach reduces the decentralized nature of P2P systems and introduces a single point of failure or slows the bootstrap of the system if payment involves real money. Without a trusted third party, another option is to bootstrap the system through penalties imposed on all newcomers: an insider peer may only probabilistically cooperate with newcomers (like in the P2P file sharing application BitTorrent [58]), or peers may join the system only if an insider peer with limited invitation tickets invites them [26]. The acceptable operations for a peer may also be limited if the connection of too many ephemeral and untrustworthy identities is observed [37]. This option however seems to be detrimental to the scalability of the system and it has even been shown that this degrades the total social welfare [59]. Social networks may also partially solve the identification issue.

Access Control

Encryption is a basic mechanism to enforce access control with respect to read operations. The lack of authentication can be overcome by the distribution of the keys necessary for accessing the stored data to a subset of privileged peers. Access control lists can also be assigned to data by their original owners through the use of signed certificates. Capability-based access control can be also employed like in [67]. Delete operations have to be especially controlled because of their potentially devastating end result.

Scalability

The system should be able to scale to a large population of peers. Since most of the important functions of the system are performed by peers, the system should then be able to handle growing amounts of control messages for peer and storage resource management and an increased complexity in a graceful manner. The system may also be clustered into small groups with homogeneous storage needs which may reduce the load over peers.

Data Reliability

The common technique to achieve data reliability relies on data redundancy at several locations in the network. The data may be simply replicated at a given redundancy factor. The redundancy factor should be maintained during the entire duration of the data storage. The rejuvenation of the data may be carried out either in a periodic or event-driven fashion. For instance, in the latter approach, one or multiple new replicas should be generated whenever a certain number of replicas have been detected as destroyed or corrupted. Other redundancy schemes may be used instead of merely replicating the data into identical copies; for instance erasure coding provides the same level of data reliability with much lower storage costs.

Long-term Data Survivability

The durability of storage in some applications like backup is very critical. The system must ensure that the data will be permanently conserved (until their retrieval by the owner). Techniques such as data replication or erasure coding improve the durability of data conservation but these techniques must be regularly adjusted to maximize the capacity of the system to tolerate failures. Generally, the employed adaptation method is based on frequent checks over the data stored to test whether the various fragments of a data are held by separate holders. Moreover, cooperation incentive techniques must be used to encourage holders to preserve the data they store as long as they can.

Data Availability

Any storage system must ensure that stored data are accessible and useable upon demand by an authorized peer. Data checks at holders allow the regular verification of this property. The intermittent connectivity of holders can be tolerated by applying a "grace period" through which the verifiers tolerate no response from the checked holder for a given number of challenges before declaring it non cooperative.

The rest of this chapter especially details how to achieve the last three objectives above: high reliability, availability, and long-term durability of data storage in the context of a large scale P2P storage system. These three objectives are often ignored in P2P file sharing applications which rather follow best effort approaches. Performing periodic cryptographic verifications makes it possible to evaluate the security status of data stored in the system and to design an adapted cooperation incentive framework for securing data storage in the long run.

II. Trust Establishment

In P2P systems, peers often must interact with unknown or unfamiliar peers without the help of trusted third parties or authorities to mediate the interactions. As a result, peers trying to establish trust towards other peers generally rely on cooperation as evaluated on some period of time. The rationale behind such trust is that peers have confidence if the other peers cooperate by joining their efforts and actions for a common benefit. P2P systems are inherently large scale, highly churned out, and relatively anonymous systems; volunteer cooperation is thus hardly achievable. Building trust in such systems is the key step towards the adoption of this kind of systems and relies on providing some assurance on the effective cooperative behavior of peers.

Trust between peers can be achieved in two essential ways that depend on the type and extent of trust relationships among peers and that reflect the models and trends in P2P systems (the used taxonomy is depicted in Figure 1). Static trust based schemes rely on stable and preexisting relationships between peers, while dynamic trust is relying on a realtime assessment of peer behavior.

Other taxonomies have been proposed. [82] classifies cooperation enforcement mechanisms into trust-based patterns and trade-based patterns. Obreiter et al. distinguish between static trust, thereby referring to pre-established trust between peers, and dynamic trust, by which they refer to reputation-based trust. They analyze trade-based patterns as being based either on immediate or on deferred remuneration. Other authors describe cooperation in self-organized systems only in terms of reputation based and remuneration based approaches. Trust establishment, a further step in many protocols, easily maps to reputation but may rely on remuneration as well. In this work, we adhere to the existing classification of cooperation incentives in distinguishing between reputation-based and remuneration-based approaches.

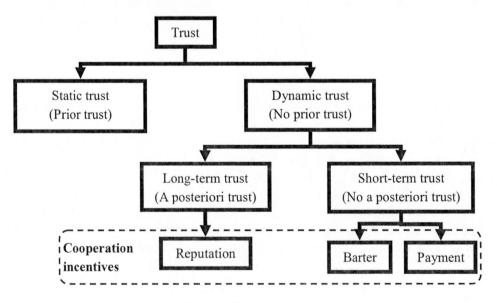

Figure 1. Trust taxonomy.

A. Static Trust

Peers may have prior trust relationships based for example on existing social relationships or a common authority. In friend-to-friend (F2F) networks, peers only interact and make direct connections with people they know. Passwords or digital signatures can be used to establish secure connections. The shared secrets needed for this are agreed-upon by out-of-band means. Turtle [14] is an anonymous information sharing system that builds a P2P overlay on top of pre-existent friendship relations among peers. All direct interactions occur between peers who are assumed to trust and respect each other as friends. Friendship relations are defined as commutative, but not transitive.

[43] proposes a F2F storage system where peers choose their storage sites among peers that they trust instead of randomly. Compared to an open P2P storage system, the proposed approach reduces the replication rate of the stored data since peers are only prone to failure not to departure or misbehavior. However, the approach is more applicable to certain types of storage systems like backup since it provides data durability not generally data availability: peers may not often leave the system but they me be offline. F2F-based approaches ensures the cooperation of peers which results in enhanced system stability and reduces administrative overhead; even though these approaches does not help to build large scale systems with large reserve of resources.

B. Dynamic Trust

The P2P storage system may rely on the cooperation of peers without any prior trust relationships. The trust is then established during peer interactions through cooperation incentive mechanisms. Peers trust each other either gradually based on reputation or explicitly through bartered resources or payment incentives. The lack of prior trust between peers allows building open large scale systems that are accessible to the public. Storage systems with cooperation incentives perhaps result in more overhead than with prior trust based approaches; but however the reliability of the stored data is increased since data will be generally stored in multiple copies at different worldwide locations rather than confined at one or limited number of locations.

Peers choose to contribute or not to the storage system. The evaluation of each peer behavior allows determining the just incentives to stimulate its cooperation. In their turn, such incentives guide the peer in adapting its contribution level. The peer chooses the best strategy that maximizes its utility gained from the system: it compensates the cost incurred due to its potential contribution with the incentives received in support for its cooperation. With such a cyclic process, the system dynamically reaches the status of "full" cooperation between peers (thus resembling a system with static trust).

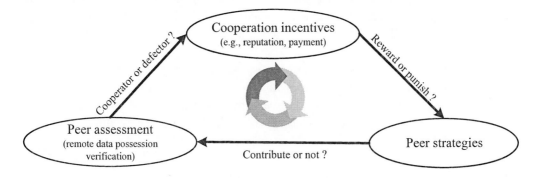

Figure 2. The feedback loop of dynamic trust.

Figure 2 depicts the feedback loop illustrating the correlation between peer assessment, cooperation incentives, and peer strategies.

1. Peer Assessment

Inciting peers to cooperate can only be achieved provided peer behavior is correctly assessed. Therefore, cooperation incentive mechanisms should comprise verification methods that measure the effective peer contributions in the P2P system.

An evaluation of the peer behavior can be performed at different timescales. An immediate evaluation of the peer behavior is only possible if the peer contribution occurs atomically like in packet forwarding application ([85] and [52]). Otherwise, peer evaluation is deferred to the completion of the peer contribution as in data storage. This constitutes a problem for storage applications where misbehaviong peers are left with an extensive period of time during which they can pretend to be storing some data they have in fact destroyed.

Periodic peer evaluation can be achieved through proof of knowledge protocols that have been called interchangeably remote data possession verifications, remote integrity verifications, proofs of data possession [33], or proofs of retrievability [8]. Such protocols are used as an interactive proof between the holder and the verifier or possibly the owner, in which the holder tries to convince the verifier that it possesses these very data without actually retrieving them. Interaction is based on challenge-response messages exchanged between the holder and the verifier. Verification of the holder's response is permitted through some information kept at the verifier side.

2. Cooperation Incentives

Peer behavior assessment forms the basis of an efficient cooperation incentive mechanism. From such evaluation, well-behaved peers will be rewarded with incentives while ill-behaved peers will be punished. Incentives may consist in exchanging identical resources (Barter), or in conferring good reputation to the well behaved peer, or in providing well behaved peers a financial counterpart for their cooperation.

Barter based approaches do not require the interacting peers to have any preset trust relationships. They rather rely on a simultaneous and reciprocal behavior. The exchange of resources takes place if both peers cooperate with each other; otherwise there is no exchange.

Reputation relies on the evaluation of the past behavior of a peer for deciding whether to cooperate with it. Reputation then builds a long-term trust between peers based on a statistical history of their past interactions. This allows going beyond barter-based approaches (direct reciprocity) by permitting to several peers to indirectly reciprocate to the behavior of the observed peer.

In contrast to reputation-based approaches, payment-based incentives constitute an explicit and discrete counterpart for cooperation and provide means to enforce a more immediate form of penalty for misconduct. Payment based approaches make it possible to secure short-term interactions between peers without relying neither on prior trust nor on some long-term history.

III. Remote Data Possession Verification

Self-organizing data storage must ensure data availability on a long term basis. This objective requires developing appropriate primitives for detecting dishonest peers free riding on the self-organizing storage infrastructure. Assessing such a behavior is the objective of data possession verification protocols. In contrast with simple integrity checks, which make sense only with respect to a potentially defective yet trusted server, verifying the remote data possession aims at detecting voluntary data destructions by a remote peer. These primitives have to be efficient: in particular, verifying the presence of these data remotely should not require transferring them back in their entirety; it should neither make it necessary to store the entire data at the verifier. The latter requirement simply forbids the use of plain message integrity codes as a protection measure since it prevents the construction of time-variant challenges based on such primitives.

A. Requirements

We consider a self-organizing storage application in which a peer, called the data *owner*, replicates its data by storing them at several peers, called data *holders*. The latter entities agree to keep data for a predefined period of time negotiated with the owner.

Peer behavior might be evaluated through the adoption of a routine check through which the holder should be periodically prompted to respond to a time-variant challenge as a proof that it holds its promise. Enforcing such a periodic verification of the data holder has implications on the performance and security of the storage protocol, which must fulfill requirements reviewed under the following two subsections.

1. Efficiency

The costs of verifying the proper storage of some data should be considered for the two parties that take part in the verification process, namely the verifier and the holder.

Storage Usage

The verifier must store a meta-information that makes it possible to generate a time-variant challenge based on the proof of knowledge protocol mentioned above for the verification of the stored data. The size of this meta-information must be reduced as much as possible even though the data being verified is very large. The effectiveness of storage at holder must also be optimized. The holder should store the minimum extra information in addition to the data itself.

Communication Overhead

The size of challenge response messages must be optimized. Still, the fact that the proof of knowledge has to be significantly smaller than the data whose knowledge is proven should not significantly reduce the security of the proof.

CPU Usage

Response verification and its checking during the verification process respectively at the holder and at the verifier should not be computationally expensive.

2. Security

The verification mechanism must address the following potential attacks which the data storage protocol is exposed to:

Detection of Data Destruction

The destruction of data stored at a holder must be detected as soon as possible. Destruction may be due to generic data corruption or to a faulty or dishonest holder.

Collusion-Resistance

Collusion attacks aim at taking unfair advantage of the storage application. There is one possible attack: replica holders may collude so that only one of them stores data, thereby defeating the purpose of replication to their sole profit.

Denial-of-Service (DoS) Prevention

DoS attacks aim at disrupting the storage application. DoS attacks may consist of flooding attacks, whereby the holder may be flooded by verification requests. The verifier may also be subject to similar attacks. They may also consist of Replay attacks, whereby a valid challenge or response message is maliciously or fraudulently repeated or delayed so as to disrupt the verification.

Man-in-the-Middle Attack Prevention

The attacker may pretend to be storing data to an owner without using any local disk space. The attacker simply steps between the owner and the actual holder and passes challenge-response messages back and forth, leaving the owner to believe the attacker is storing its data, when in fact another peer, the actual holder, stores the owner's data. The replication may again be disrupted with this attack: since the owner may run the risk of storing the data in two replicas at the same holder.

B. Verification Protocols

The verification protocol is an interactive check that may be formulated as a proof of knowledge [2] in which the holder attempts to convince a verifier that it possesses some data, which is demonstrated by correctly responding to queries that require computing on the very data.

The security of P2P storage applications has been increasingly addressed in recent years, which has resulted in various approaches to the design of storage verification primitives. The literature distinguishes two main categories of verification schemes: probabilistic ones that rely on the random checking of portions of stored data and deterministic ones that check the conservation of a remote data in a single, although potentially more expensive operation. Additionally, some schemes may authorize only a bounded number of verification operations conducted over the remote storage; yet the majority of schemes are designed to overcome this limitation.

Memory Checking

A potential premise of probabilistic verification schemes originates from memory checking protocols. A memory checker aims at detecting any error in the behavior of an unreliable data structure while performing the user's operations. The checker steps between the user and the data structure. It receives the input user sequence of "store" and "retrieve" operations over data symbols that are stored at the data structure. The checker checks the correctness of the output sequence from the structure using its reliable memory (noninvasive checker) or the data structure (invasive checker) so that any error in the output operation will be detected by the checker with high probability. In [54], the checker stores hash values of the user data symbols at its reliable memory. Whenever, the user requests to store or retrieve a symbol, the checker computes the hash of the response of the data structure and compares it with the hash value stored, and it updates the stored hash value if the user requested to store a symbol. The job of the memory checker is to recover and to check responses originating from an unreliable memory, not to check the correctness of the whole stored data. With the checker, it is possible to detect corruption of one symbol (usually one bit) per user operation.

Authenticator

The work of [65] better comprehends the remote data possession problem. It extends the memory checker model by making the verifier checks the consistency of the entire document in encoded version in order to detect if the document has been corrupted beyond recovery. The authenticator encodes a large document that will be stored at the unreliable memory and constructs a small fingerprint that will be stored at the reliable memory. Using the fingerprint, the authenticator verifies whether from the encoding it is possible to recover the document without actually decoding it. The authors of [65] propose a construction of the authenticator where there is a public encoding of the document consisting of index tags of this form: $t_i = f_{seed}(i \ o \ y_i)$ for each encoded value bit y_i having f_{seed} a pseudorandom function with *seed* taken as secret encoding. The authenticator is repeatedly used to verify for a selection of random indices if the tags correspond to the encoding values. The detection of document corruption is then probabilistic but improved with the encoding process of the document. Moreover, the query complexity is proportional to the number of indices requested. [77] proposes a similar solution to [65] but that achieves open verifiability i.e., the task of verifying data can be handed out to the public. The index tags are formulated as chunk signatures that the verifier keeps their corresponding public key. Signatures are indeed generated by the data owner; though the role of the verifier can be carried out by this latter or any peer that possesses the public key.

Provable Data Possession

The PDP (Provable Data Possession) scheme in [33] improves the authenticator model by presenting a new form of fingerprints $t_i=(hash(v\|i) \cdot g^{y_i})^d \bmod N$, where $hash$ is a one-way function, v a secret random number, N an RSA modulus with d being a signature key, and g a generator of the cyclic group of $\mathbb{Z}_N^*$. With such homomorphic verifiable tags, any number of tags chosen randomly can be compressed into just one value by far smaller in size than the entire set, which means that communication complexity is independent of the number of indices requested per verification.

Proof of Retrievability

The POR protocol (Proof of Retrievability) in [8] explicitly expresses the question of data recovery in the authenticator problem: if the unreliable data passes the verification, the user is able to recover the original data with high probability. The protocol is based on verification of sentinels which are random values independent of the owner's data. These sentinels are disguised among owner's data blocks. The verification is probabilistic with the number of verification operations allowed being limited to the number of sentinels.

Compact Proofs of Retrievability

[39] improves the POR protocol by considering compact tags (comparable to PDP) that are associated with each data chunk y_i having the following form: $t_i = \alpha y_i + s_i$ where α and s_i are random numbers. The verifier requests random chunks from the unreliable memory and obtains a compact form of the chunks and their associated tags such that it is able to check the correctness of these tags just using α and the set $\{s_1, s_2, ...\}$ that are kept secret.

Remote Integrity Check

Remote Integrity Check of [22] alleviates the issue of data recovery and rather focuses on the repetitive verification of the integrity of the very data. The authors described several schemes some of them being hybrid construction of the existing schemes that fulfill the later requirement. For instance, the unreliable memory may store the data along with a signature of the data based on redactable signature schemes. With these schemes, it is possible to derive the signature of a chunk from the signature of the whole data, thus allowing the unreliable memory to compute the signature of any chunk requested by the verifier.

Data Chunk Recovery

The majority of the probabilistic verification schemes require the recovery of one or multiple (in plain or compacted form) data chunks. For example, in the solution of [55], the owner periodically challenges its holders by requesting a block out of the stored data. The response is checked by comparing it with the valid block stored at the owner's disk space. Another approach using Merkle trees is proposed by Wagner and reported in [84]. The data stored at the holder is expanded with a Merkle hash tree on data chunks and the root of the tree is kept by the verifier. It is not required from the verifier to store the data, on the contrary of [55]. The verification process checks the possession of one data chunk chosen randomly by the verifier that also requests a full path in the hash tree from the root to this random chunk.

Algebraic Signatures

The scheme proposed in [92] relies on algebraic signatures. The verifier requests algebraic signatures of data blocks stored at holders, and then compares the parity of these signatures with the signature of the parity blocks stored at holders too. The main drawback of the approach is that if the parity blocks does not match, it is difficult (depends on the number of used parity blocks) and computationally expensive to recognize the faulty holder.

Incremental Cryptography

First step toward a solution to the deterministic verification problem comes from incremental cryptographic algorithms that detect changes made to a document using a tag, a small secret stored at a reliable memory that relates to the complete stored document and that is quickly updatable if the user makes modifications. [63] proposes several incremental schemes where the tag is either an XORed sum of randomized document symbols or a leaf in a search tree as a result of message authentication algorithm applied to each symbol. These schemes provide tamper-proof security of the user document in its entirety; although they require recovering the whole data which is not practical for remote data verification because of the high communication overhead.

Deterministic Remote Integrity Check

The first solution described in [98] allows the checking of the integrity of the remote data, with low storage and communication overhead. It requires pre-computed results of challenges to be stored at the verifier, where a challenge corresponds to the hashing of the data concatenated with a random number. The protocol requires small storage at the verifier, yet they allow only a fixed number of challenges to be performed. Another simple deterministic approach with unlimited number of challenges is proposed in [32] where the verifier like the holder is storing the data. In this approach, the holder has to send the MAC of data as the response to the challenge message. The verifier sends a fresh nonce (a unique and randomly chosen value) as the key for the message authentication code: this is to prevent the holder peer from storing only the result of the hashing of the data.

Storage Enforcing Commitment

The SEC (Storage Enforcing Commitment) scheme in [84] aims at allowing the verifier to check whether the data holder is storing the data with storage overhead and communication complexity that are independent of the length of the data. Their deterministic verification approach uses the following tags that are kept at the holder along with the data: $PK=(g^x, g^{x^2}, g^{x^3}, ..., g^{x^n})$ where PK is the public key (stored at the holder) and x is the secret key (stored at the verifier). The tags are independent of the stored data, but their number is equal to two times the number of data chunks. The verifier chooses a random value that will be used to shift the indexes of tags to be associated with the data chunks when constructing the response by the holder.

Homomorphic Hash Functions

The second solution described in [98] requires little storage at the verifier side and no additional storage overhead at the holder side; yet makes it possible to generate an unlimited number of challenges. The proposed solution (inspired from RSA) has been also proposed by Filho and Barreto in [19]. It makes use of a key-based homomorphic hash function H. A construction of H is also presented as $H(m)=g^m \mod N$ where N is an RSA modulus and such that the size of the message m is larger than the size of N. In each challenge of this solution, a nonce is generated by the verifier which the prover combines with the data using H to prove the freshness of the answer. The prover's response will be compared by the verifier with a value computed over $H(data)$ only, since the secret key of the verifier allows the following operation (d for data, and r for nonce): $H(d + r) = H(d) \times H(r)$. The exponentiation operation used in the RSA solution makes the whole data as an exponent. To reduce the computing time of verification, Sebé et al. in [25] propose to trade off the computing time required at the prover against the storage required at the verifier. The data is split in a number m of chunks $\{d_i\}_{1 \le i \le m}$, the verifier holds $\{H(d_i)\}_{1 \le i \le m}$ and asks the prover to compute a sum function of the data chunks $\{d_i\}_{1 \le i \le m}$ and m random numbers $\{r_i\}_{1 \le i \le m}$ generated from a new seed handed by the verifier for every challenge. Here again, the secret key kept by the verifier allows this operation: $\sum_{1 \le i \le m} H(d_i + r_i)= \sum_{1 \le i \le m} H(d_i) \times H(r_i)$. The index m is the ratio of tradeoff between the storage kept by the verifier and the computation performed by the prover. Furthermore, the basic solution can be still improved as described in [22]; though the verification method is probabilistic. The holder will be storing tags of $t_i = g^{y_i + s_i}$ where s_i is a random number kept secret by the verifier. The holder periodically constructs compact forms of the data chunks and corresponding tags using time-variant challenge sent by the verifier. The authors of [22] argue that this solution achieves a good performance.

C. Delegable Verification Protocol

Self-organization addresses highly dynamic environments like P2P networks in which peers frequently join and leave the system: this assumption implies the need for the owner to delegate data storage evaluation to third parties, termed *verifiers* thereafter, to ensure a periodic evaluation of holders after his leave. The need for scalability also pleads for distributing the verification function, in particular to balance verification costs among several entities. Last but not least, ensuring fault tolerance means preventing the system from presenting any single point of failure: to this end, data verification should be distributed to multiple peers as much as possible; data should also be replicated to ensure their high availability, which can only be maintained at a given level if it is possible to detect storage defection.

1. Delegability

The authenticator and the memory checker perform verifications on behalf of the user; though they are considered as trusted entities within the user's platform. None of the presented schemes considers distributing the verification task to other untrusted peers; they instead rely on the sole data owner to perform such verifications. In a P2P setting, it is important that the owner delegates the verification to other peers in the network in order to tolerate the intermittent connection of peers and even the fact that a single point of verification constitutes a single point of failure. Some of the schemes presented above may allow delegating verification provided that the verifier is not storing any secret information because it may otherwise collude with the holder. Additionally, the amortized storage overhead and communication complexity should be minimized for this purpose. To our knowledge, [78] is the first work to suggest delegating the verification task to multiple peers selected and appointed by the data owner. This approach relies on elliptic curve cryptography primitives., The owner derives from the data to be stored a public and condensed verification information expressed as $(d \bmod N_n) \times P$ where N_n is the order of the elliptic curve and P is a generator. The interactive proof of knowledge exchange between the verifier and the holder is based on the hardness of the elliptic curve discrete logarithm problem [72]. Such a verification protocol can be further refined by considering data chunks instead of a data bulk in analogy to [25]. The objective in this case is to limit the computation overhead required from the holder. A revised verification protocol is described in more detail in the following sub-section.

The main characteristics of the discussed verification protocols are summarized in Table 1.

2. Example

The following presents a secure and self-organizing verification protocol exhibiting a low resource overhead. This protocol was designed with scalability as an essential objective: it enables generating an unlimited number of verification challenges from the same small-sized security metadata.

a. Security Background

The deterministic verification protocol relies on elliptic curve cryptography ([72], [94]). The security of the protocol is based on two different hard problems. First, given some required conditions, it is hard to find the order of an elliptic curve. Furthermore, one of the most common problems in elliptic curve cryptography is the Elliptic Curve discrete logarithm problem denoted by ECDLP.

Thanks to the hardness of these two problems, the deterministic verification protocol ensures that the holder must use the whole data to compute the response for each challenge. In this section, we formalize these two problems in order to further describe the security primitives that rely on them.

Elliptic Curves over $\mathbb{Z}_n$

Let n be an odd composite square free integer and let a, b be two integers in $\mathbb{Z}_n$ such that $\gcd(4a^3 + 27b^2, n) = 1$ ("gcd" means greatest common divisor).

Table 1. Comparison of existing verification protocols (variable n and m respectively correspond to data size and the number of chunks)

	Detection	Delega-tion	Efficiency		
			Storage at verifier	CPU at holder	Communi-cation overhead
[8]: POR	Probabilistic Bounded	No	$O(1)$	$O(1)$ hash transformation	$O(1)$
[54]: Memory checker	Probabilistic Unbounded	No	$O(m)$	$O(n/m)$ chunk fetching	$O(n/m)$
[65]: Authenticator	Probabilistic Unbounded	No	$O(1)$	$O(n/m)$ chunk fetching	$O(n/m)$
[77]: based on signatures	Probabilistic Unbounded	Yes	$O(1)$	$O(n/m)$ chunk fetching	$O(n/m)$
[33]: PDP	Probabilistic Unbounded	Possible	$O(1)$	$O(n/m)$ exponentiation	$O(1)$
[39]: Compact proofs of retrievability	Probabilistic Unbounded	No	$O(1)$	$O(n/m)$ exponentiation	$O(1)$
[22]: based on redactable signatures	Probabilistic Unbounded	Possible	$O(1)$	$O(\log(n))$ signature construction	$O(\log(n))$
[22]: RSAh solution	Probabilistic Unbounded	No	$O(1)$	$O(n/m)$ exponentiation	$O(1)$
[55]: Data chunk recovery	Probabilistic Unbounded	No	$O(n)$	$O(1)$ simple comparison	$O(1)$
Wagner in [84]: based on Merkle-hash tree	Probabilistic Unbounded	Possible	$O(1)$	$O(\log(n))$ hash transformation	$O(\log(n))$
[92]: based on algebraic signatures	Probabilistic Unbounded	Possible	$O(1)$	$O(n/m)$ signature validation	$O(1)$
[98]: pre-computed challenges	Deterministic Bounded	No	$O(1)$	$O(n)$ hash transformation	$O(1)$
[63]: Incremental cryptography	Deterministic Unbounded	Possible	$O(1)$	$O(n)$ fetching	$O(n)$
[32]: MAC based	Deterministic Unbounded	No	$O(n)$	$O(n)$ hash transformation	$O(1)$
[84]: SEC	Deterministic Unbounded	No	$O(1)$	$O(n/m)$ exponentiation	$O(1)$
[98], [19]: RSA solution	Deterministic Unbounded	Possible	$O(1)$	$O(n)$ exponentiation	$O(1)$
[25]: RSA solution with data chunks	Deterministic Unbounded	Possible	$O(m)$	$O(n/m)$ exponentiation	$O(1)$
[78]: ECC based	Deterministic Unbounded	Yes	$O(m)$	$O(n/m)$ point multiplication	$O(1)$

An elliptic curve $E_n(a, b)$ over the ring $\mathbb{Z}_n$ is the set of the points $(x, y) \in \mathbb{Z}_n \times \mathbb{Z}_n$ satisfying the equation: $y^2 = x^3 + ax + b$, together with the point at infinity denoted O_n.

Solving the Order of Elliptic Curves

The order of an elliptic curve over the ring $\mathbb{Z}_n$ where $n=pq$ is defined in [Koyama et al. 1991] as N_n = lcm ($\#E_p(a, b)$, $\#E_q(a, b)$) ("lcm" for least common multiple, "#" means order of). N_n is the order of the curve, i.e., for any $P \in E_n(a, b)$ and any integer k, $(k \times N_n + 1)P = P$.

If (a = 0 and $p \equiv q \equiv 2$ mod 3) or (b = 0 and $p \equiv q \equiv 3$ mod 4), the order of $E_n(a, b)$ is equal to N_n=lcm(p+1, q+1). We will consider for the remainder of the paper the case where a = 0 and $p \equiv q \equiv 2$ mod 3. As proven in [47], given N_n = lcm($\#E_p(a, b)$, $\#E_q(a, b)$) = lcm(p + 1, q + 1), solving N_n is computationally equivalent to factoring the composite number n.

The Elliptic Curve Discrete Logarithm Problem

Consider K a finite field and $E(K)$ an elliptic curve defined over K. ECDLP in K is defined as: given two elements P and $Q \in K$, find an integer r, such that $Q = rP$ whenever such an integer exists.

b. Protocol Description

This sub-section introduces an improved version of the protocol described in [78] whereby the computation complexity at the holder is reduced. In the proposed version and in comparison to the version of [78], the data is split into m chunks, denoted $\{d'_i\}_{1 \leq i \leq m}$, and the verifier stores the corresponding elliptic curve points $\{T_i = d'_i P\}_{1 \leq i \leq m}$. We assume that the size of each data chunk is much larger than $4k$ where k is the security parameter that specifies the size of p and q and thus also the size of an elliptic curve point in $\mathbb{Z}_n$ ($n=pq$), because the verifier must keep less information than the full data.

The verification protocol is specified by four phases (see Figure 3): Setup, Storage, Delegation, and Verification. The owner communicates the data to the holder at the storage phase and the meta-information to the verifier at the delegation phase. At the verification phase, the verifier checks the holder's possession of data by invoking an interactive process. This process may be executed an unlimited number of times.

-   *Setup:* The phase is performed by the owner. From a chosen security parameter k (k > 512 bits), the owner generates two large primes p and q of size k both congruent to 2 modulo 3, and computes their product $n = pq$. Then, it considers an elliptic curve over the ring $\mathbb{Z}_n$ denoted by $E_n(0, b)$ where b is an integer such that gcd(b, n)=1, to compute a generator P of $E_n(0, b)$. The order of $E_n(0, b)$ is N_n = lcm(p+1, q+1). The parameters b, P, and n are published and the order N_n is kept secret by the owner.
-   *Storage:* The owner personalizes the data d for its intended holder using a keyed encryption function f_s, then splits the personalized data $d'= f_s(d)$ into m chunks of the same size (the last chunk is padded with zeroes): $\{d'_i\}_{1 \leq i \leq m}$. The data chunks are then sent to the holder.
-   *Delegation:* The owner generates meta-information to be used by the verifier for verifying the data possession of one holder. The owner generates the curve points $\{T_i = d'_i P \in E_n(0, b)\}_{1 \leq i \leq m}$ sent to the verifier.

- *Verification:* The verifier generates a random number r and a random seed c (size of $c > 128$ bits). Then, it sends $Q=rP$ and the seed c to the holder. Upon reception of this, the holder generates m random numbers $\{c_i\}_{1\leq i\leq m}$ from the seed c (it is possible to generate the random numbers as $c_i=c^i$ for each i, or using a random number generator function). Then, it computes the point $R = \sum_{1\leq i\leq m} c_i d'_i Q$ that is sent to the verifier. To decide whether holder's proof is accepted or rejected, the verifier generates the same m random numbers $\{c_i\}_{1\leq i\leq m}$ from the seed c and checks if R is equal to $r(\sum_{1\leq i\leq m} c_i T_i)$.

	Owner		**Holder**
Storage	Compute $d'=f_s(d)$ Split d' in m chunks: $\{d'_i\}_{1\leq i\leq m}$ send $\{d'_i\}_{1\leq i\leq m}$ ⟶	$\{d'_i\}_{1\leq i\leq m}$	Store $\{d'_i\}_{1\leq i\leq m}$
	Owner		**Verifier**
Delega-tion	Compute for each i in $[1, m]$: $T_i=(d'_i \bmod N_n)P$ send $\{T_i\}_{1\leq i\leq m}$ ⟶	$\{T_i\}_{1\leq i\leq m}$	Store $\{T_i\}_{1\leq i\leq m}$
	Verifier		**Holder**
Verifi-cation	Generate a random number r and seed c Compute $Q = rP$ Send c, Q ⟶ Generate $\{c_i\}_{1\leq i\leq m}$ from seed c ⟵ If $R = r(\sum_{1\leq i\leq m} c_i T_i)$ then "accept" else "reject"	c, Q R	Generate $\{c_i\}_{1\leq i\leq m}$ from seed c Compute $R = \sum_{1\leq i\leq m} c_i d'_i Q$ Send R

Figure 3. Delegable verification protocol.

c. Security Analysis

This section analyzes the completeness and the soundness of the deterministic protocol that are the two essential properties of a proof of knowledge protocol [2]: a protocol is complete if, given an honest claimant and an honest verifier, the protocol succeeds with overwhelming probability, i.e., the verifier accepts the claimant's proof; a protocol is sound if, given a dishonest claimant, the protocol fails, i.e. the claimant's proof is rejected by the verifier, except with a small probability.

Theorem 1- The proposed protocol is complete: if the verifier and the holder correctly follow the proposed protocol, the verifier always accepts the proof as valid.

Proof: Thanks to the commutative property of point multiplication in an elliptic curve, we have for each i in $[1, m]$: $d'_i rP= rd'_i P$. Thus, the equation: $\sum_{1\leq i\leq m} c_i d'_i rP = r(\sum_{1\leq i\leq m} c_i d'_i P)$. □

Theorem 2- The proposed protocol is sound: if the claimant does not store the data, then the verifier will not accept the proof as valid.

Proof: If the holder does not store the data chunks $\{d'_i\}_{1\leq i\leq m}$, it may try first to collude with other holders storing the same data. However, this option is not feasible since data stored at each holder is securely personalized during the storage phase. Since f_s is a keyed encryption function and the key s is secret, no peer except the owner can retrieve the original data d from

d'. The other way to generate a correct response without storing the data relies on only storing $\{d'_i P\}_{1 \leq i \leq m}$ (which is much smaller than the full data size) and retrieving r from the challenge rP in order to compute the correct response. Finding r is hard based on ECDLP. The last option for the holder to cheat is to keep $\{d'_i \bmod N_n\}_{1 \leq i \leq m}$ instead of d' (whose size is very large). The holder cannot compute N_n based on the hardness of solving the order of $E_n(0, b)$. Thus, if the response is correct then the holder keeps the data correctly. □

d. Performance Analysis

In the proposed protocol, challenge-response messages mainly each consist of an elliptic curve point in $\mathbb{Z}_n^2$. Message size is thus a function of the security factor k (size of $n \approx 2k$). Reducing communication overhead then means decreasing the security parameter.

The verification protocol requires the verifier to store a set of elliptic curve points that allows producing on demand challenges for the verification. Finally, the creation of proof and its verification rely on point multiplication operations.

The number of data chunks m can be used to fine tune the ratio between the storage required at the verifier and the computation expected from the holder: when increasing m, the verifier is required to keep more information for the verification task, but at the same time the holder is required to perform one point multiplication operation using much smaller scalars.

Assessing the actual state of storage in a P2P storage application represents the first step towards efficiently reacting to misbehavior and cooperation incentives rely on peer evaluations. The use of verification protocols should make it possible to detect and isolate selfish and malicious peers, and ultimately punish these peers through cooperation incentive mechanisms.

Table 2. Summary of resource usage of the delegable verification protocol (variable n and m respectively correspond to data size and the number of chunks)

	Storage usage	Computation complexity	Communication overhead
At holder	$O(n)$	$O(n/m)$	(upstream) $O(1)$
At verifier	$O(m)$	$O(1)$	(upstream) $O(1)$

IV. Cooperation Incentives

Cooperation enforcement is a central feature of P2P systems, and even more so self-organizing systems, to compensate for the lack of a dedicated and trusted coordinator and still get some work done. However, cooperation to achieve some functionality is not necessarily an objective of peers that are not under the control of any authority and that may try to maximize the benefits they get from the P2P system. Cooperation incentive schemes have been introduced to stimulate the cooperation of such self-interested peers. They are diverse not only in terms of the applications which they protect, but also in terms of the features they implement, the type of reward and punishment used, and their operation over time. Cooperation incentives are classically classified into barter-based, reputation-based, and remuneration-based approaches.

A. Bartering

Cooperation incentives may be cheaply built on a tit-for-tat (TFT) strategy ("give and ye shall receive"). The peer initially cooperates, and then responds likewise to the opponent's previous action: if the opponent previously cooperated, the peer cooperates; otherwise, the peer defects. TFT is demonstrated to be an evolutionary stable strategy (ESS) in game theory jargon: this strategy cannot be invaded (or dominated) by any alternative yet initially rare strategy.

In the Cooperative Internet Backup Scheme [55], each peer has a set of geographically-separated partner peers that collectively hold its backed up data. In return, the peer backs up a part of its partners' data. To detect free-riding, each peer periodically evaluates its remote data. If it detects that one of its partners dropped the data, the peer establishes a backup contract with a different partner. Since the scheme relies on identical and immediate resource exchanges, peers must be able to choose partners that match their needs and their capabilities and that ensure similar uptimes. To this end, a central server tracks peers and their partners. Decentralized methods of finding partners in a Gnutella-like flooding approach are also suggested although not evaluated in [55].

However, TFT is not perfect as illustrated by the P2P file sharing protocol BitTorrent [13]. In BitTorrent, unchoking a peer means that the peer is accepted to upload files for it. Peers follow a TFT strategy by unchoking peers that provide the highest throughput for them, and besides that they use an optimistic unchoking strategy to discover potentially better trading peers. However this strategy of (probabilistically) cooperating with newcomers blindly can be exploited by whitewashers (peers that repeatedly join the network under new identities to avoid the penalty imposed on free-riders). [58] describes the design of BitTyrant, a selfish client that demonstrates that BitTorrent incentives don't build robustness. The reason is that TFT is no longer an evolutionary stable strategy in the presence of whitewashers.

B. Reputation

Reputation relies on the evaluation of a peer's past behavior for deciding whether to cooperate with the peer. Cooperation may be reciprocated even in the absence of its beneficiary and evaluator (indirect reciprocity).

Direct vs. Indirect Reputation

Reputation generally only relies on a partial assessment of the behavior of peers, which might delay the detection of free-riders. This situation is rendered even worse in P2P storage applications, since storage is not an instantaneous operation and data are vulnerable throughout their entire storage lifetime. Group-based architecture have been suggested (e.g., [75]) as a way to enable peers to quickly know the behavior of their group fellows. The analytical model in [75] compares direct reputation whereby peers use only the results of verifications they perform themselves using direct observations to compute reputation with indirect reputation where these results are disseminated. This model demonstrates that the direct reputation approach for observing peer behavior outperforms indirect reputation in terms of correctness and exposure if the group of peers is of modest size. However, indirect reputation is more effective in an open system with a large population of peers that have asymmetric interests as shown in [61].

The direct reputation approach does not require propagating any information as opposed to indirect reputation which generates communication overhead and may even require centralization. However, it is possible to implement a decentralized indirect reputation for example on top of a distributed-hash-table (DHT) or by disseminating information to other peers similarly to routing protocols.

Resistance to Bashing

Another challenging issue in dynamic systems like P2P is the vulnerability of a reputation system to peer bashing. Reputation bashing is made possible with two types of attacks: peer collusion and Sybil attacks. Peers may collude in order to advertise their quality more than their real values ("ballot stuffing") thus increasing their reputation at other peers. Such an objective can also be achieved through a Sybil attack: if peers are able to generate new identities at will, they may use some of them to increase the reputation of the rest of their made-up identities.

Techniques to completely eliminate Sybil attacks can only be provided by trusted certification as proven by Douceur [45]. In this way, trusted devices associated in a secure fashion to peers can be used to eliminate such attacks (as discussed in [88]). However, an attacker may still buy multiple devices and then acquire multiple identities although at a high cost. Without a trusted infrastructure, Sybil attacks can only be mitigated.

To overcome the collusion problem, [31] proposes to add a "reliability" measure to the estimate of the reputation. The rating measure L becomes:

$$L = \alpha \times R + (1 - \alpha) \times (1 - G)$$

where R is the estimated reputation, G is the Gini coefficient that describes the amount of inequality in the distribution of transactions among a peer's entire partner set, α being a weight parameter. The Gini coefficient illustrates the idea that a reputation estimate is considered as less reliable if a significant fraction of transactions are performed with a small subset of the peer's partner set.

[61] addresses the same problem of peer collusion throught the application of the maxflow algorithm on the graph constructed from peers considered as vertices and the services they receive as directed edges. The maxflow algorithm gives the maximum feasible flow from a source peer to a destination peer. The cost of the maxflow algorithm increases with the number of peers examined in the graph.

The two approaches above are still trading off the number of peers examined in the algorithms with the efficiency of the detection. Sybil mitigation can also be achieved by making the newcomer pay with computational or bandwidth or storage abilities, such as for example crypto-puzzles [95] or testing peer IP address. Other techniques like SybilGuard [37] rely on prior trust relationships, e.g., real-world friendship between peers to detect Sybil attackers. [26] even enhances the SybilGuard approach by controlling the number of peer invitations that a group member possesses. In a similar fashion, [76] suggests that peers taking part in any transaction be simply chosen in a random fashion. Peer service requests are directed to a randomly chosen peers although the latter can choose to cooperate with the requesters based on their reputation.

In most of the approaches above, the costs are only paid once by Sybil attackers and can be then amortized during the rest of the system operation. As discussed in [15], such costs can be periodically paid by repeatedly performing resource testing on peers thus confining the potential return on investment of Sybil attackers to a limited time slot. It should be noted though that all these approaches, which aim at limiting Sybil attacks without trusted infrastructure, are scalable compared with certification-based approaches. Still, they incur a huge cost overhead not only on Sybil attackers but also on honest newcomers, which may undermine their practicality and adoption in P2P applications. Furthermore, [60] shows that imposing a penalty on all newcomers significantly degrades system performance when the peer churn rate is high.

C. Payment

Payment is a way to foster cooperation in exchange of some token that can be exchanged later on for some service. This approach introduces economic mechanisms that can regulate the usage of storage or bandwidth related resources, for instance. Payment brings up new requirements regarding the fairness of payment itself [68], which in general translate to a more complex and costly implementation than for reputation mechanisms. In particular, payment schemes require a trusted environment including trusted entities such as banks. These entities may be involved in the transaction, in which case the payment scheme can be deemed centralized. On the contrary, some schemes are decentralized and require banks to be contacted only to resolve payment litigations. The latter approach is more appropriate to ensure the maximum degree of self-organization to the P2P network.

Fair Exchange and Payment

Achieving an effective implementation of payment-based mechanism depends upon the realization of a protocol that enforces the fair exchange of the payment (credits) against some task: according to [69], "*a fair exchange protocol can then be defined as a protocol that ensures that no player in an electronic commerce transaction can gain an advantage over the other player by misbehaving, misrepresenting or by prematurely aborting the protocol*". Fair exchange may be enforced through a trusted third party (TTP) that may be used online or opportunistically. Tamperproof modules (TPMs), secure operating systems, or smart cards may also be employed to carry out a fair exchange protocol in a distributed fashion.

In a P2P network, TTPs may be represented as super-peers that play the same role as an online TTP but in a distributed fashion. FastTrack [42]is an example of such an architecture which is used in P2P networks like KaZaA [46], Grokster [36], and iMesh [40]. These networks have two-tier hierarchy consisting of ordinary nodes (ONs) in the lower tier and super-nodes (SNs) in the upper tier. In P2P file sharing networks, SNs keep track of ONs and other SNs and act as directory servers during the search phase of files. One way of implementing a payment scheme is to use super-peers distributed within the P2P network. These super-peers then provide neutral platforms for performing an optimistic fair exchange protocol. The use of such an infrastructure of trusted peers, that would not necessarily need to be related with the payment authority, may be rendered feasible by the deployment of other infrastructures like content distribution networks (CDNs) (e.g., [1]). Such networks involve the deployment of managed workstations all over the Internet, thereby providing a nice platform for payment related functionalities.

The Wuala storage system ensures fair exchange through a system of quota that directly depends on the measure of the uptime of a peer. Fair exchange in this system is ensured by a central authority that keeps track of exchanges between peers. In contrast, P2P storage systems may have no dedicated authority tracking all exchanges. In that case, ensuring the scalability of the system makes it necessary to resort to a type of fair exchange protocol called optimistic [68] in which the TTP does not necessarily take part in peer interactions, but may be contacted to arbitrate litigations. In the cooperative backup system of [55], a central server considered as a TTP tracks the partners of each peer participating in the backup system. Each peer takes note of its direct experience with a partner, and if this partner does not cooperate voluntarily or not beyond some threshold, the peer may decide to establish a backup contract with a different partner that is obtained through the central server.

Smart cards have been used in the P2P storage system PAST [81] to ensure the fairness of peer contributions. Smart cards issued by a third party are held by each PAST peer to support a quota system that balances supply and demand of storage space in the system. Peers cannot use more remote storage than they are providing locally. With fixed quotas and expiration dates, peers are only allowed to use as much storage as they contribute.

If data storage should be achieved in a large-scale and open P2P system, deploying designs based on trusted environments may be infeasible. In that case, implementing the optimistic fair exchange protocol would have to be done by relying solely on peers. [69] describes design rules for such cryptographic protocols making it possible to implement appropriate fair-exchange protocols. For instance, the distribution of the banking function to multiple peers may make the realization of a scalable system easier. In the KARMA framework [95], the exchange of some payment against some resource is supported by multiple peers that collaborate to provide a fair exchange. A fair exchange system for P2P storage system might be implemented using that framework in which the bank (trusted authority) is replaced by a set of peers, termed the bank-set, randomly assigned for each peer. The karma values, which is the name of the currency, are maintained for each peer by its bank-set who is collectively responsible for continuously updating the karma value as the peer contributes and consumes resources from the P2P system. The bank-sets independently track the credits belonging to their assigned peers, and periodically agree on a given balance of credits with a majority rule. Even if there were inconsistencies in peers' balances, transactions among peers correspond to tiny micropayments and thus do not produce considerable gains or losses to peers. The fair exchange protocol in KARMA is similar to an online TTP-based exchange but with additional features for guaranteeing the consistence and synchronization of balances.

Payments by Installment

A payment scheme for a file sharing application as described in [95] cannot be assimilated to P2P storage since in the former case payments are immediately charged after the exchange of the file, whereas in the latter case payments for storage are by installment i.e., they are billed at a due date that corresponds to the confirmation (after a verification) of the cooperative behavior of the holder. A payment scheme should thus be supplemented by an escrowing mechanism to guarantee the effective payment of credits promised by the peers towards a cooperative holder. Before interacting with others, a peer must escrow, i.e., set aside and store in a trusted repository, the amount of credits it agrees to pay at the end of the interaction upon defined conditions. The escrowing is an additional mechanism required for implementing fair-exchange in P2P storage systems since the misbehavior of a peer and a related compensation may not be determined immediately, but only at a later time when the peer in question might have left the network or would not respond. Escrowed credits thus form a commitment for future payments. Here again, trusted environments like TPMs or smartcards may prove helpful to implement the escrowing feature. Otherwise, third parties have to be used in every protocol that might imply some form of monetary compensation.

Preventing Starvation

Payment-based schemes generally suffer from starvation, e.g., see [9]. In a P2P storage system, starvation means the inability of a peer to store data in the system because it cannot commit money for potential compensation. Auctions provide a solution for mitigating that starvation phenomenon. Since auctioning reveals the real preferences of bidders, a solution is to make it necessary for peers left with a small number of credits to contribute more to the system. These peers would offer lower prices for storing the same amount of data in order to attract data owners in priority. First-price or second-price auctions (Vickrey auction) are equally possible.

V. Validation Based on Game Theory

Cooperation incentives prevent selfish behaviors whereby peers free-ride the storage system, that is, they store data onto other peers without contributing to the storage infrastructure. Remote data verification protocols are required to implement the auditing mechanism needed by any efficient cooperation incentive mechanism. In general, a cooperation incentive mechanism is proven to be effective if it is demonstrated that any rational peer will always choose to cooperate whenever it interacts with another cooperative peer. One-stage games or repeated games have been mostly used to validate cooperation incentives that describe individual strategies; in addition, the use of evolutionary dynamics can help describe the evolution of strategies within large populations.

A. Definitions

Game theory is a branch of applied mathematics that models interactions among individuals making decisions. It attempts to mathematically capture individual rational behavior in strategic situations where individuals' decisions are based on their preferences and also depend on the other individuals' choices. It then provides a language to describe, analyze, and understand strategic scenarios [91].

1. Game

A game consists of:

- A set of *players* $\{p_1, ..., p_n\}$ which are the individuals who make decisions
- A set of *strategies* i.e., moves for each player S_i, $i=1, ..., n$
- A specification of each player's *payoffs* which are the numeric values assigned to the outcomes produced by the various combinations of strategies. Payoffs represent the preference ordering of players over the outcomes. Payoffs are expressed using player's *utility function U_i*:

$$U_i: S_1 \times S_2 \times ... \times S_n \to \Re$$

The game assumes that all players are *rational*; this means that they will always choose the strategy that maximizes their payoffs. Players are then participants in the game with the goal of choosing the actions that produce their most preferred outcomes.

2. Game Types

A game can be one of two types: *non-cooperative* or *cooperative*. In the first type, players are selfish and are only concerned with maximizing their own benefit. In the second type, some players cooperate and form a coalition in order to achieve a common goal, and then the coalition and the rest of players play non-cooperatively the game.

A game can be a *repeated game* that consists in a finite or infinite number of iterations of some one-stage game. In such one-stage game, players' choices are referred to as actions rather than strategies (a term reserved to the repeated game) and these actions take into account their impact on the future actions of other players.

Evolutionary game theory also provides a dynamic framework for analyzing repeated interactions. In such games, randomly chosen players interact with each other, then the player with the lower payoff switches to the strategy of the player with the higher payoff i.e., players reproduce proportionally to their payoffs. Hence, strategies with poor payoffs eventually die off, while well-performing strategies thrive.

3. Game Equilibria

Finding a solution to a game equates to finding equilibria in the game. At the equilibrium, each player of the game has adopted a strategy that they are unlikely to change. Many equilibrium related concepts have been developed in an attempt to capture this idea. The most famous is the *Nash equilibrium*. A Nash Equilibrium is the set of players' strategy choices such that no player can benefit by changing its strategy while the other players keep their strategies unchanged. So, it is a set of strategies $\{\sigma_1 \in S_1, ..., \sigma_n \in S_n\}$, such that:

$$U_i(\sigma_1, ..., \sigma_i, ..., \sigma_n) \geq U_i(\sigma_1, ..., \sigma'_i, ..., \sigma_n), \ \forall \ i \in \{1, ..., n\} \text{ and } \sigma'_i \in S_i$$

An *Evolutionary stable strategy* (ESS) defines strategies conducting to a Nash equilibrium and such that, if adopted by a population of players, cannot be invaded by any alternative strategy that is initially rare. For a two-player game with a strategy space S, a strategy σ^* is an ESS if and only if for any $\sigma' \neq \sigma^*$, either one of the following two conditions holds:

a) $U(\sigma^*, \sigma^*) > U(\sigma', \sigma^*)$
b) $U(\sigma^*, \sigma^*) = U(\sigma', \sigma^*)$ and $U(\sigma^*, \sigma') > U(\sigma', \sigma')$

Here, $U(.,.)$ is the payoff function of the associated two-player game.

To achieve a socially optimal equilibrium for a self-organizing system with autonomous peers, different incentive mechanisms have been proposed in the literature. These incentives include providing virtual or real payment incentives or establishing and maintaining a reputation index for every peer in the network.

B. Reputation Incentive Modeling

The cooperation enforcement property of reputation schemes can be proven with game theoretical tools. The modeling may operate with static games that consider interaction between peers that have persistent strategies. On the other hand, dynamic games involve peers that constantly change their strategy. The following reviews static and dynamic game models that describe several features of reputation approaches.

1. Static Games

Reputation schemes have received a great deal of attention for enforcing node cooperation in mobile ad hoc networks. Notably, [85] proposed CORE as a collaborative reputation mechanism motivating nodes to forward packets, and used a game theoretical approach to assess the features and validate the mechanism. This work relies on a cooperative game that uses a two-period structure: players first decide whether or not to join a coalition, and then both the coalition and the remaining players choose their behavior non-cooperatively. Additionally, the model employs a preferential structure as suggested by the ERC-theory [30]. A player i's utility is based on the absolute payoff y_i and on the relative payoff:

$$\sigma_i = \frac{y_i}{\sum_j y_j}$$

The ERC utility function is derived then as:

$$U_i = \alpha_i u(y_i) + \beta_i r(\sigma_i)$$

where α_i and β_i are parameters describing the preferences of the nodes.

The study of the model demonstrates that there is a Nash equilibrium where at least half of the total number of nodes cooperate. Nodes may also have a continuous strategy space where they may choose their cooperation levels instead of discretely choosing just between cooperation and defection. The study reveals that for identical ERC preferences and for a sufficiently small ratio α/β (i.e., nodes are interested enough in being close to the equal share), then the grand coalition is stable, i.e., no player has an incentive to leave the coalition. Still, the assumption that the nodes will be much interested in their relative payoff (small α/β) may not be met in practice.

2. Dynamic Games

In contrast to [85] that addresses a specific mechanism, [16] introduces a general game theoretical framework to model and analyze cooperation incentive policies, and to more specifically focus on their dynamics. In the proposed model, peer strategies are expressed using an $n \times n$ generosity matrix G with G_{ij} being the probability that a peer of strategy s_i will provide service for peer of strategy s_j. The expected payoff of a peer of strategy s_i at time t is derived as:

$$\bar{P}_i(t) = \sum_{j=1}^{n} x_j(t) \times (\alpha G_{ji} - G_{ij})$$

where $x_j(t)$ denotes the fraction of peers with strategy s_j in the peer population at time t, $\alpha > 0$ is the gain of a peer receiving a service from another peer, while it loses β (normalized payoff with $\beta = 1$) when it provides a service to another peer. Thus, the total expected performance of the system is:

$$\bar{P}(t) = x^T G x$$

with the vector $x = (x_1, x_2, \ldots, x_n)$.

Instead of game equilibria, the model studies the game dynamics where strategies change according to two learning models: the current-best (CBLM) and the opportunistic (OLM) learning models. In CBLM, each peer may switch to another strategy with probability γ_a (adapting rate). The peer chooses the strategy s_h that has the highest payoff. The peer of strategy s_i will switch to strategy s_h with probability $\gamma_s(\bar{P}_h(t) - \bar{P}_i(t))$, where γ_s represents the sensitivity rate to the performance gap. System dynamics are then expressed by the following equations:

$$\dot{x}_i = -\gamma x_i (\bar{P}_h(t) - \bar{P}_i(t)); \ \forall i \neq h$$

$$\dot{x}_h = \gamma (\bar{P}_h(t) - \bar{P}(t)); \ \gamma = \gamma_a \gamma_s \text{(learning rate)}$$

In the second learning model OLM, each peer randomly chooses another peer as its *teacher* with probability γ_a. If the teacher has a better payoff than the peer, the latter adapts to the teacher's strategy with sensitivity γ_s to their performance gap. OLM is similar to evolutionary game concepts where the so-called teacher is the co-player of the peer. For this reason, the evolution of the system with OLM follows the replicator dynamics (the payoff is in number of offsprings):

$$\dot{x}_i = \gamma x_i \left(\bar{P}_i(t) - \bar{P}(t) \right)$$

The main parameter of comparison between these learning models is robustness: a system is robust if it stays at a high contribution level despite perturbations such as peer arrivals or departures from the network. The mathematical analysis demonstrates that a system with CBLM is less robust than with OLM, the latter being akin to a typical evolutionary game model. Moreover, the analysis allows comparing two incentive policies. The first considered policy is the mirror incentive policy under which a peer provides service with the same probability as the requester serves other peers in the system. On the other hand, in a second policy named the proportional incentive policy, the peer serves the requester with a probability equal to the requester's contribution to consumption ratio. The study shows that the mirror incentive policy may lead to a complete system collapse, while the proportional incentive policy can lead to a robust system. This result is quite interesting because it demonstrates that a policy motivating fairness in terms of contributions and consumptions of resources achieves better stability than participatory incentives.

Another reputation technique to support cooperative behavior in a P2P system, named reciprocative strategy, is proposed in [61]. In this strategy, a peer j cooperates with another peer i depending on its normalized generosity value:

$$g_j(i) = \frac{g(i)}{g(j)}$$

where peer i's generosity $g(i) = p_i/c_i$, and p_i and c_i are respectively the services the peer i has provided and consumed. The reputation technique resembles the proportional incentive policy of [16], though the normalization overcomes the system bootstrapping problem.

To validate the reputation technique while taking into account several challenging issues of P2P systems such as their large populations, high turnover, asymmetry of interest of peers, and zero-cost identities, the authors propose a dynamic and asymmetric game model based on the generalized Prisoner's Dilemma (GPD). The dynamic model is composed of multiple rounds. In each round, every player plays a client role in one game, then a server role in another game. Every such player may subsequently either mutate by switching to a randomly picked strategy, or learn by switching to a strategy with a higher score determined by reputation, or turnover by leaving the system, or finally stay with the same strategy.

[48] also opted for an evolutionary study of applications in P2P systems. The authors proposed a model that they call a generalized form of the Evolutionary Prisoner's Dilemma (EPD). Though the model is very similar to the traditional EPD, they argue that the new model permits asymmetric transactions between a client peer and a server peer. The proposed model consists of several generations of rounds. At the end of a generation, the history of other players' actions is cleared and players evolve according to $r_i^{t+1} = r_i^t \times s_i^t$, where r_i^{t+1} is the frequency of peers playing strategy i at the $(t+1)^{\text{th}}$ generation, and r_i^t at the tth generation. s_i^t is their average score obtained after the tth generation. Peers decide whether to cooperate based on a reciprocative decision function that sets the probability to cooperate with a given peer X to the ratio (rounded to a value in [0, 1]):

$$\frac{cooperation\ X\ gave}{cooperation\ X\ received}$$

Such a function is comparable to the proportional incentive policy of [16] in which EPD is simulated under various situations. This work shows that techniques relying only on private history, where solely peer experiences are taken into account, fail in stimulating cooperation among peers as the population size increases. However, techniques based on a shared history scale better to large populations.

The evolutionary game proposed in [74] attempts to validate a large scale P2P storage system that is based on private history to estimate reputation. The reputation scheme relies on a verification routine to detect selfish behavior. Thus, peers may play several roles throughout the game: owner, holder, or verifier. In the proposed game inspired from the donor-recipient model of [38], the owner is considered a recipient, the r holders and m verifiers are donors. The owner gains b if at least one holder donates at a cost $-c$; however if no holder donates then the owner gains βb if at least one verifier donates at a cost $-\alpha c$ ($\alpha \leq 1$) for each verifier. The latter case corresponds to the situation where the cooperative verifier informs the owner of the data destruction, and then the owner may replicate its data elsewhere in the network thus maintaining the security properties of the stored data (e.g., the replication rate of the data).

Holders and verifiers have the choice between cooperating and defecting. The following peer strategies are specifically studied: altruistic peers that always donate, defectors that never donate and discriminators that donate under conditions. If the discriminator does not know its co-player, it will always donate; however, if it had previously played with its co-player, it will only donate if its co-player donates in the previous game. This strategy resembles Tit-For-Tat but differs from it in that both the owner (the donor) and its verifiers may decide to stop cooperating with the holder in the future.

The evolution of these strategies is analyzed using the replicator dynamics. The basic concept of replicator dynamics is that the growth rate of peers taking a strategy is proportional to the fitness acquired by the strategy. Thus, the strategy that yields more fitness than average for the whole system increases, and vice versa.

The study of the convergence of the system to equilibrium proves that there exist parameter values for which discriminators may win against free-riding defectors. Discriminators are not hopeless when confronting defectors, even if the latter may dominate altruists. At the equilibrium of the game, both discriminators and defectors may coexist if there is some churn in the system, otherwise discriminators will dominate. The number of verifiers increases the frequency of discriminators at the equilibrium whereas a costly storage or an increase of the replication rate reduce this frequency.

3. Whitewashing Problem

An inherent problem to a cooperation incentive mechanism implemented in a dynamic system where peers may join or leave at any time is the whitewashing problem. Whitewashers are peers that repeatedly misbehave then leave the storage system and come back with new identities thus escaping the punishment imposed by the incentive mechanism. The whitewashing problem is essentially due to the presence of free or cheap pseudonyms for peers. Therefore, countering the whitewashing attacks demands either the use of irreplaceable pseudonyms, e.g., through the assignment of strong identities by a central trusted authority, or requires imposing a penalty on all newcomers. The first solution reduces the decentralized nature of P2P systems and introduces a single point of failure. The second option requires defining the right penalty parameter for the system. The penalty corresponds to the best tradeoff for restricting whitewashers while encouraging newcomers to participate.

The simulation results of [48] demonstrate that cooperation with strangers fails to encourage cooperation in the presence of whitewashers. The authors thus propose an adaptive policy in which the probability of cooperation with strangers becomes equal to $p_C^{t+1} = (1-\mu) \times p_C^t + \mu \times C_t$ at time $t+1$, where $C_t=1$ if the last stranger cooperated and equal to 0 otherwise. Simulations validate the adaptive policy by demonstrating that incentives based on such a policy make the system converge to higher levels of cooperation.

[60] studies in more detail the whitewashing problem in P2P systems using a game theoretical model that particularly takes into account the heterogeneity of user behaviors. Indeed, each user is characterized by a type that reflects its willingness to contribute resources (its generosity level): users of type t_i will contribute if and only if $t_i > 1/x$ where x is the fraction of contributing users. The fraction of contributors is then determined by the solution to:

$$x = Probability(t_i > 1/x)$$

In order to sustain the system when the societal generosity is low (low x), punishment mechanisms against free-riding users are required. The proposed punishment mechanism consists in imposing a penalty on free-riding behavior with probability $(1-p)$. The optimal value for the probability p is defined by the maximum performance obtained from the system. The authors express such a performance as:

$$W_{system} = (\alpha x^\beta - 1)\ (x + (1-x)(1-p));\ \alpha > 0 \text{ and } 0 < \beta \leq 1$$

where $Q = \alpha x^\beta$ is the maximum benefit received by each user, an increasing function of the number of contributors with diminishing returns. The performance of the system is maximized with $p = p^* \geq 1/\alpha$. Still, such a mechanism can be undermined by the availability of cheap pseudonyms through which a free-rider may choose to whitewash. To measure the effect of a whitewashing behavior, the authors compute the system performance at $p = p^*$ considering the cases of permanent identities and free identities, in addition to different turnover rates that represent user arrival and departure rates (arrivals and departures are assumed to be *type-neutral*, i.e., they do not alter the type distribution). This study demonstrates that the penalty mechanism is effective when both the societal generosity and the turnover rate are low; otherwise a notable societal cost due to whitewashing is experienced.

[73] studies the penalty mechanism described in [60] with the evolutionary game model of [74] by changing the strategy of discriminators such that the latter only cooperate probabilistically with strangers and also introducing whitewashers into the game. The study of the game equilibrium convergence demonstrates that discriminators are not hopeless in front of whitewashers and that they may even win over them provided system parameters are chosen sensibly. The fraction of discriminators in the system should in particular not be null initially, and the replication rate and the churn sensed in the system should not be too high.

The simulation results also show that there is an optimal probability p for the penalty mechanism that achieves a high social welfare for the whole P2P storage system. However, a non-zero welfare is only obtained if the whitewashing phenomena is restricted to a given fraction of defectors. For instance, if all defectors are whitewashing, discriminators are entirely eliminated and the system collapses. This result motivates the requirement to supplement the proposed penalty mechanism with other means that prevent or at least limit the whitewashing behavior such as controlling the peers that join the system using a cryptographic puzzle [95] or the payment of a membership fee. Another solution is to force or motivate peers to stay online a minimum amount of time in the system like in Wuala [97] ($1/w$ is then increased) because peer connection time must be taken into consideration.

The penalty mechanism adopted with strangers can be adaptive. The probability that a peer cooperates with a stranger is defined in [61] as p_s/c_s where p_s and c_s are respectively the number of services that strangers have provided and consumed. The results of the simulation of the dynamic game model show that a system with this strategy can ensure the cooperation of peers with a sufficiently low turnover.

C. Payment Incentive Modeling

One of the first studies that considered payment schemes in P2P systems is [83], which uses a game theoretical model to study the potential benefits of introducing micro-payment methods into centralized P2P file-sharing systems such as Napster. In such systems, the strategies have two independent actions in order to catch the asymmetric aspect of interactions between peers, which are also called agents: sharing, i.e., providing the service, and downloading, i.e., acquiring the service. Agent actions and other several considerations are put together into one utility function that is defined for each agent a_i as:

$$U_i = (f_i^{AD}(AD) + f_i^{NV}(NV) + f_i^{AL}(AL)) - (f_i^{DS}(DS) + f_i^{BW}(BW)) - FT$$

where variables AD, NV, AL, DS, BW, and FT respectively denote the amount of files the agent desires to download, the number of options from where the agent may download, the altruism derived from contributing to the system, the disk space used, the bandwidth used, and the financial transfer for using the system. Concerning functions f, they are arbitrary functions: each of them maps a variable to its financial value conferred by the agent. Relying on this theoretical model, the authors have analyzed the equilibrium solution for multiple situations. Without considering any incentives ($FT=0$) as it is the case with Napster and disregarding the altruism variable of agents' utility functions ($f_i^{AL}(AL)=0$), the outcome of the equilibrium analysis results in an unique equilibrium where nothing is shared and nothing can be downloaded. With some level of altruism in the system, all agents, both altruistic and free-rider, are unrestrained from downloading, the whole cost then weighing over the small number of altruistic agents. Therefore, the authors propose alternatives based on payment to overcome the free-riding problem. The first proposed payment scheme consists in charging agents for every download, and rewarding them for every upload. The result of the equilibrium analysis of the model with the payment scheme shows that there is one unique and strict equilibrium where agents are extensively sharing and downloading files. This result validates the payment scheme; still, the analysis does not take into account the fact that agents share diverse files and some of them may store files that are sufficiently rare thus unfairly receiving a large fraction of all the download requests for these files. For that reason, the authors propose a second payment-based alternative that continues to penalize downloads, but rewards agents in proportion to the amount of material they share rather than the number of uploads they provide. The equilibrium analysis of the model shows that two strict equilibria may be reached through either full file sharing or no sharing at all; in contrast, simulation experiments of the model demonstrate that the system converges to an equilibrium where all agents cooperate by sharing files.

[51] takes a different direction for defining peer utility function that relies on payment more than the model of [83] does. The authors of [51] model a P2P backup service as a non-cooperative game using an economic model that relies on the following user utility:

$$U_i(C_i^s, C_i^o, \epsilon_i) = V_i(C_i^s) - P_i(C_i^o) - \epsilon_i$$

where C_i^s is the capacity of data to be stored in the system and C_i^o is the capacity of the offered disk space. V_i gives the price the user is willing to pay and P_i gives the price it is willing to be paid for. The monetary compensation is denoted ϵ_i:

$$\epsilon_i = p^s C_i^s - p^o C_i^o$$

where p^s and p^o are unit prices. The authors define demand and supply functions, d_i and s_i, as:

$$d_i(p) = (V_i')^{-1}(p) \text{ and } s_i(p) = (P_i')^{-1}(p)$$

These functions follow a chosen common form:

$$d_i(p) = a_i \times p \text{ and } s_i(p) = b_i \times p$$

The parameters, a_i and b_i, associated with the demand and supply functions and characterizing the profile of each user, turn out to be playing a crucial role on justifying the use of a pricing scheme or imposed symmetry with respect to the optimal situation of the service that is maximizing the social welfare defined as:

$$W := \sum_i V_i(C_i^s) - P_i(C_i^o)$$

Indeed, the theoretical study of the economic model shows that if users are homogeneous in terms of a_i and b_i, then it is better to opt for imposed symmetric user contributions rather than a pricing scheme. However, for a heterogeneous user population, which is the general case in P2P networks, the use of a pricing scheme by which a monopoly is introduced to fix unit prices for buying and selling storage resources is validated. Still the involvement of the operator in fixing prices for a P2P backup reduces the social welfare of the system by ¼ times its maximum.

A P2P storage system purely self-organized that uses a probabilistic verification routine to detect selfish holders and that relies on a payment scheme to punish these holders is modeled as a Bayesian game in [79]. In this game, the information about the characteristics of other players is incomplete because the verification protocol allows only probabilistic detection; thus, nature is introduced as a player for modeling uncertainty. The owner is not informed about the holder's type, which may be either cooperative or selfish. Such situations that cannot be discriminated belong to the same so-called "set of information". The owner still can probabilistically determine the holder's type based on its prior beliefs: with every verification operation performed, it updates its beliefs according to Bayes' formula.

The one-stage game produces a Nash equilibrium in which the owner and the holder are not cooperative. However, the perfect Bayesian equilibrium results in the cooperation of both players for some defined conditions. The study of the repeated Bayesian game proves that the iteration of the game favors the cooperativeness of the holder as well as that of the owner. The study also identifies which actions the owner must follow for a given initial belief about the cooperativeness of the holder. Finally, the study reveals the expressions that parameters of the payment scheme (e.g., reward, punishment) should verify. [79] approaches the definition of payment parameters from a design theory point of view rather than a game theory approach in that it endeavors to design a game in which the behavior of strategic players results in the socially desired outcome.

VI. Conclusion

Peer-to-Peer (P2P) systems have emerged as an important paradigm for distributed storage in that they aim at efficiently exploiting untapped storage resources available in a wide base of peers. Data are outsourced to several heterogonous storage sites in the network, the major expected outcome being an increased data availability and reliability, while also achieving reduced storage maintenance costs, and high scalability. Addressing security issues in such P2P storage applications represents an indispensable part of the solution satisfying these requirements. Security relies on low level cryptographic primitives, remote data possession verification protocols, for observing malicious and selfish behaviors. Such an assessment of peer behavior is crucial to the more complex enforcement of cooperation, which is necessary due to the self-organized nature of P2P networks. It is also crucial to address open issues, such as how to mitigate denial of service attempts to the long-term storage as well as to the security and storage maintenance functions.

References

[1]   Akamai technologies, inc. http://www.akamai.com/

[2]   Alfred J. Menezes, Paul C. van Oorschot, and Scott A. Vanstone. *Handbook of Applied Cryptography*. CRC Press, 1996.

[3]   AllMyData Tahoe. http://allmydata.org/

[4]   Amazon. http://www.amazon.com/

[5]   Andrew C. Huang, Benjamin C. Ling, Shankar Ponnekanti, and Armando Fox. Pervasive computing: What is it good for?. In *Proceedings of the ACM International*

Workshop on Data Engineering for Wireless and Mobile Access, pages 84-91, Seattle, WA, August 1999. ACM Press.

[6]   Anind K. Dey and Gregory D. Abowd. CybreMinder: A context-aware system for supporting reminders. In Proceedings of Second International Symposium on Handheld and Ubiquitous Computing, HUC 2000, pages 172-186, Bristol, UK, September 2000. Springer Verlag.

[7]   Antony Rowstron and Peter Druschel. Pastry: Scalable, distributed object location and routing for large-scale peer-to-peer systems. In *Proceeding of the IFIP/ACMInternational Conference on Distributed Systems Platforms*, Heidelberg, Germany, November 2001.

[8]   Ari Juels and Burton S. Kaliski PORs: *Proofs of retrievability for large files. Cryptology ePrint archive,* June 2007. Report 2007/243.

[9]   Attila Weyland, Thomas Staub and Torsten Braun. Comparison of Incentive-based Cooperation Strategies for Hybrid Networks. *3rd International Conference on Wired/Wireless Internet Communications* (WWIC 2005), pp 169-180, ISBN: 3-540-25899-X, Xanthi, Greece, May 11-13, 2005.

[10] Audun Jøsang and Roslan Ismail. The Beta Reputation System. In *Proceedings of the 15th, Bled Electronic Commerce Conference*, Bled, Slovenia, June 2002.

[11] Audun Jøsang, Roslan Ismail, and Colin Boyd. A Survey of Trust and Reputation Systems for Online Service Provision. In *Proceedings of Decision Support Systems,* 2005.

[12] Ben Y. Zhao, John Kubiatowicz, and Anthony D. Joseph. Tapestry: An infrastructure for fault-tolerant wide-area location and routing. *Technical Report* UCB//CSD-01-1141, University of California, Berkeley, April 2000.

[13] BitTorrent. http://www.bittorrent.com/

[14] Bogdan C. Popescu, Bruno Crispo and Andrew S. Tanenbaum. Safe and Private Data Sharing with Turtle: Friends Team-Up and Beat the System. In *12th International Workshop on Security Protocols,* Cambridge, UK, April 2004.

[15] Brian Neil Levine, Clay Shields, and N. Boris Margolin. A Survey of Solutions to the Sybil Attack. *Technical Report* 2006-052, University of Massachusetts Amherst, Amherst, MA, October 2006.

[16] Bridge Q. Zhao, John C. S. Lui, Dah-Ming Chiu. *Analysis of Adaptive Protocols for P2P Networks.* In IEEE INFOCOM 2009.

[17] Daniel Stutzbach and Reza Rejaie. Towards a Better Understanding of Churn in Peer-to-Peer Networks. *Technical Report CIS-TR-04-06*, University of Oregon, November 2004.

[18] David Goldschlag, Michael Reed, and Paul Syverson. Onion Routing for Anonymous and Private Internet Connections. *Communications of the ACM,* vol. 42, num. 2, February 1999.

[19] Décio Luiz Gazzoni Filho and Paulo Sérgio Licciardi Messeder Barreto. Demonstrating data possession and uncheatable data transfer. In *IACR Cryptology ePrint Archive,* 2006.

[20] Douglas Samuel Jones and B. D. Sleeman. *Differential Equations and Mathematical Biology.* London: Allen & Unwin, 1983.

[21] eBay. http://ebay.com

[22] Ee-Chien Chang and Jia Xu. *Remote Integrity Check with Dishonest Storage Server.* ESORICS 2008: 223-237.

[23] Emil Sit and Robert Morris. *Security Considerations for P2P Distributed Hash Tables.* IPTPS 2002.

[24] Emmanuelle Anceaume and Aina Ravoaja. Incentive-Based Robust Reputation Mechanism for P2P Services. *Research Report* PI 1816 (2006), IRISA, http://hal.inria.fr/inria-00121609/fr/

[25] Francesc Sebe, Josep Domingo-Ferrer, Antoni Martínez-Ballesté, Yves Deswarte, and Jean-Jacques Quisquater. Efficient Remote Data Possession Checking in Critical Information Infrastructures. IEEE Transactions on Knowledge and Data Engineering, 06 Aug 2007. IEEE Computer Society Digital Library. *IEEE Computer Society,* 6 December 2007 http://doi.ieeecomputersociety.org/10.1109/TKDE.2007.190647

[26] François Lesueur, Ludovic Mé, and Valérie Viet Triem Tong. A Sybilproof Distributed Identity Management for P2P Networks In *Proceedings of the 13th IEEE Symposium on Computers and Communications (ISCC) 2008*, IEEE Computer Society, Marrakech, Morocco.

[27] François Lesueur, Ludovic Mé, Valérie Viet Triem Tong. Contrôle d'accès distribué à un réseau Pair-à-Pair. *SAR-SSI 2007*, Annecy, France.

[28] Frazer Bennett, Tristan Richardson, and Andy Harter. Teleporting - making applications mobile. In *Proceedings of IEEE Workshop on Mobile Computing Systems and Applications,* pages 82-84, Santa Cruz, California, December 1994. IEEE Computer Society Press.

[29] Garrett Hardin. *The Tragedy of the Commons. Science,* Vol. 162, No. 3859 (December 13, 1968), pp. 1243-1248.

[30] Gary E Bolton and Axel Ockenfels. ERC: a theory of equity, reciprocity, and competition. *American Economic Review* 90(1): 166-193, 2000.

[31] Gayatri Swamynathan, Ben Y. Zhao, Kevin C. Almeroth, S. Rao Jammalamadaka. Towards Reliable Reputations for Dynamic Networked Systems. In *IEEE Proceedings on Symposium on Reliable Distributed Systems* (SRDS'08), October 2008.

[32] Germano Caronni and Marcel Waldvogel. Establishing Trust in Distributed Storage Providers. In *Proceeding of the Third IEEE P2P Conference*, Linkoping 03, 2003.

[33] Giuseppe Ateniese and Randal Burns and Reza Curtmola and Joseph Herring and Lea Kissner and Zachary Peterson and Dawn Song. Provable data possession at untrusted stores. In *Proceedings of the 14th ACM conference on Computer and communications security*, ACM, 2007, 598-609.

[34] Gnutella. http://www.gnutella.com/

[35] Google. http://www.google.com/

[36] Grokster. http://www.grokster.com/

[37] Haifeng Yu, Michael Kaminsky, Phillip B. Gibbons, and Abraham Flaxman. *SybilGuard: defending against sybil attacks via social networks.* SIGCOMM 2006: 267-278.

[38] Hannelore Brandt and Karl Sigmund. The good, the bad and the discriminator--errors in direct and indirect reciprocity. *Journal of Theoretical Biology,* Volume 239, Issue 2, 21 March 2006, Pages 183-194.

[39] Hovav Shacham and Brent Waters. *Compact Proofs of Retrievability.* ASIACRYPT 2008: 90-107.

[40] iMesh. http://imesh.com

[41] Ion Stoica, Robert Morris, David Karger, M. Frans Kaashoek and Hari Balakrishnan. Chord: A scalable peer-to-peer lookup service for internet applications. In *Proceedings of SIGCOMM,* San Diego, CA, Aug. 27–31, 2001.

[42] Jian Liang, Rakesh Kumar, and Keith W. Ross. The FastTrack overlay: A measurement study. *Computer Networks,* 50, 842-858, 2006.

[43] Jinyang Li and Frank Dabek. F2F: reliable storage in open networks. In *Proceedings of the 5th International Workshop on Peer-to-Peer Systems (IPTPS)*, February 2006.

[44] John Kubiatowicz, Davic Bindel, Yan Chen, Steven Czerwinski, Patrick Eaton, Dennis Geels, Ramakrishna Gummadi, Sean Rhea, Hakim Weatherspoon, Westley Weimer, Chris Wells, Ben Zhao. OceanStore: An architecture for global-scale persistent storage. In *Proceedings of the Ninth international Conference on Architectural Support for Programming Languages and Operating Systems* (ASPLOS 2000), Nov. 2000.

[45] John R. Douceur. The Sybil attack. In Proceedings of the 1st International Workshop on Peer-to-Peer Systems (IPTPS'02). *MIT Faculty Club,* Cambridge, MA, 2002.

[46] KaZaA. http://www.kazaa.com/

[47] Kenji Koyama, Ueli Maurer, Tatsuaki Okamoto, and Scott Vanstone. New Public-Key Schemes Based on Elliptic Curves over the Ring Zn. Advances in Cryptology - CRYPTO '91, *Lecture Notes in Computer Science,* Springer-Verlag, vol. 576, pp. 252-266, Aug 1991.

[48] Kevin Lai, Michal Feldman, Ion Stoica, and John Chuang. Incentives for Cooperation in Peer-to-Peer Networks. In *Proceedings of the 1st Workshop on Economics of Peer-to-Peer Systems,* UC Berkeley, Berkeley, California, USA, June 2003.

[49] Landon P. Cox and Brian D. Noble. Pastiche: making backup cheap and easy. in *Proceedings of the Fifth USENIX Symposium on Operating Systems Design and Implementation,* Boston, MA, December 2002.

[50] Larry Page, Sergey Brin, R. Motwani, and T. Winograd. The PageRank Citation Ranking: Bringing Order to the Web. *Technical report, Stanford Digital Library Technologies Project,* 1998.

[51] Laszlo Toka and Patrick Maillé. Managing a peer-to-peer backup system: does imposed fairness socially outperform a revenue-driven monopoly?. *4th International Workshop on Grid Economics and Business Models* (GECON 2007), August 28, 2007, Rennes, France, pp 150-163.

[52] Levente Buttyan and Jean-Pierre Hubaux. Stimulating Cooperation in Self-Organizing Mobile Ad Hoc Networks. *ACM/Kluwer Mobile Networks and Applications,* 8(5), October 2003.

[53] Lik Mui, Mojdeh Mohtashemi, Cheewee Ang, Peter Szolovits, and Ari Halberstadt. Ratings in Distributed Systems: A Bayesian Approach. In *Proceedings of the Workshop on Information Technologies and Systems* (WITS), 2001.

[54] Manuel Blum, William S. Evans, Peter Gemmell, Sampath Kannan, and Moni Naor. *Checking the Correctness of Memories. Algorithmica* 12(2/3): 225-244 (1994).

[55] Mark Lillibridge, Sameh Elnikety, Andrew Birrell, Mike Burrows, and Michael Isard. A Cooperative Internet Backup Scheme. In *Proceedings of the 2003 Usenix Annual Technical Conference* (General Track), pp. 29-41, San Antonio, Texas, June 2003.

[56] Markus Jakobsson, Jean-Pierre Hubaux, and Levente Buttyan. A Micro-Payment Scheme Encouraging Collaboration in Multi-Hop Cellular Networks. In *Proceedings of Financial Crypto,* La Guadeloupe, Jan. 2003.

[57] Michael Beigl. MemoClip: A location-based remembrance appliance. *Personal Technologies,* 4(4):230-233, September 2000.

[58] Michael Piatek, Tomas Isdal, Thomas Anderson, and Arvind Krishnamurthy. Do incentives build robustness in BitTorrent?. In *Proceedings of the ACM/USENIX Fourth Symposium on Networked Systems Design and Implementation* (NSDI 2007), 2007.

[59] Michal Feldman and John Chuang. *The Evolution of Cooperation under Cheap Pseudonyms.* CEC 2005: 284-291.

[60] Michal Feldman, Christos Papadimitriou, John Chuang and Ion Stoica. Free-Riding and Whitewashing in Peer-to-Peer Systems. Selected Areas in Communications, *IEEE Journal* on, Vol. 24, No. 5. (2006), pp. 1010-1019.

[61] Michal Feldman, Kevin Lai, Ion Stoica, and John Chuang. Robust Incentive Techniques for Peer-to-Peer Networks. *Proceedings of ACM E-Commerce Conference* (EC'04), May 2004.

[62] Miguel Castro, Peter Druschel, Ayalvadi Ganesh, Antony Rowstron and Dan S. Wallach. Secure routing for structured peer-to-peer overlay networks. *Symposium on Operating Systems and Implementation,* OSDI'02, Boston, MA, December 2002.

[63] Mihir Bellare, Oded Goldreich and Shafi Goldwasser. *Incremental Cryptography and Application to Virus Protection.* STOC 1995: 45-56.

[64] Ming Zhong, Kai Shen, Joel I. Seiferas. The Convergence-Guaranteed Random Walk and Its Applications in Peer-to-Peer Networks. *IEEE Trans. Computers* 57(5): 619-633 (2008).

[65] Moni Naor and Guy N. Rothblum. *The Complexity of Online Memory Checking.* FOCS 2005: 573-584.

[66] Morpheus. http://www.morpheus.com/

[67] Mudhakar Srivatsa and Ling Liu. Countering Targeted File Attacks using LocationGuard. In *Proceedings of the 14th USENIX Security Symposium,* to appear August 2005.

[68] N. Asokan, Matthias Schunter, and Michael Waidner. Optimistic Protocols for Fair Exchange. In *Proceedings of the 4th ACM Conference on Computer and Communications Security,* Zurich, April 1997.

[69] N. Asokan, Victor Shoup, and Michael Waidner. Asynchronous protocols for optimistic fair exchange. In *Proceeding of the IEEE Symposium on Security and Privacy,* 1998, 3-6 May, p. 86-99, Oakland, CA, USA.

[70] Napster. http://www.napster.com/

[71] Natalia Marmasse and Chris Schmandt. Location-aware information delivery with ComMotion. In *Proceedings of Second International Symposium on Handheld and Ubiquitous Computing,* HUC 2000, pages 157-171, Bristol, UK, September 2000. Springer Verlag.

[72] Neal Koblitz. *Elliptic curve cryptosystems. Mathematics of Computation,* 48 (1987), 203-209.

[73] Nouha Oualha and Yves Roudier. A Game Theoretical Approach in Securing P2P Storage against Whitewashers. In *the 5th International Workshop on Collaborative Peer-to-Peer Systems* (COPS'09), June 29 - July 1, 2009, Groningen, Netherlands.

[74] Nouha Oualha and Yves Roudier. Evolutionary game for peer-to-peer storage audits. In *the 3rd International Workshop on Self-Organizing Systems* (IWSOS'08), December 10-12, Vienna, Austria.

[75] Nouha Oualha and Yves Roudier. Reputation and Audits for Self-Organizing Storage. In *the 1st Workshop on Security in Opportunistic and SOCial Networks* (SOSOC 2008), Istanbul, Turkey, September 2008.

[76] Nouha Oualha and Yves Roudier. Reputation and Audits for Self-Organizing Storage. In *the 1st Workshop on Security in Opportunistic and SOCial Networks* (SOSOC 2008), Istanbul, Turkey, September 2008.

[77] Nouha Oualha and Yves Roudier. Securing ad hoc storage through probabilistic cooperation assessment. 3rd Workshop on Cryptography for Ad hoc Networks, July 8th, 2007, Wroclaw, Poland. *Electronic Notes in theoretical computer science,* Volume 192, N°2, May 26, 2008, pp 17-29.

[78] Nouha Oualha, Melek Önen, and Yves Roudier. A Security Protocol for Self-Organizing Data Storage. *23rd International Information Security Conference* (SEC 2008), Milan, Italy, September 2008.

[79] Nouha Oualha, Pietro Michiardi, and Yves Roudier. A game theoretic model of a protocol for data possession verification. TSPUC 2007, *IEEE International Workshop on Trust, Security, and Privacy for Ubiquitous Computing,* June 18, 2007, Helsinki, Finland.

[80] Patrick P. C. Lee, John C. S. Lui and David K. Y. Yau. *Distributed collaborative key agreement and authentication protocols for dynamic peer group.* IEEE/ACM Transactions on Networking, 2006.

[81] Peter Druschel and Antony Rowstron. PAST: A large-scale, persistent peer-to-peer storage utility. In *Proceedings of HotOS VIII*, May 2001.

[82] Philipp Obreiter and Jens Nimis. *A Taxonomy of Incentive Patterns - the Design Space of Incentives for Cooperation.* Technical Report, Universität Karlsruhe, Faculty of Informatics, 2003.

[83] Philippe Golle, Kevin Leyton-Brown, Ilya Mironov. Incentives for Sharing in Peer-to-Peer Networks. In *Proceedings of the 3rd ACM conference on Electronic Commerce,* October 2001.

[84] Philippe Golle, Stanislaw Jarecki, Ilya Mironov. Cryptographic Primitives Enforcing Communication and Storage Complexity. In *Proceeding of Financial Crypto 2002.*

[85] Pietro Michiardi. Cooperation enforcement and network security mechanisms for mobile ad hoc networks. *PhD Thesis,* December 14th, 2004.

[86] Roger R. Dingledine. The Free Haven project: Design and deployment of an anonymous secure data haven. *Master's thesis,* MIT, June 2000.

[87] Sepandar D. Kamvar, Mario T. Schlosser, and Hector Garcia-Molina. The EigenTrust Algorithm for Reputation Management in P2P Networks. In *Proceedings of the Twelfth International World Wide Web Conference*, Budapest, May 2003.

[88] Shane Balfe, Amit D. Lakhani and Kenneth G. Paterson. Trusted Computing: Providing security for Peer-to-Peer Networks. In *Proceedings of the 5th International Conference on Peer-to-Peer Computing* (P2P), 2005.

[89] Sylvia Ratnasamy, Paul Francis, Mark Handley, Richard Karp, and Scott Shenker. A scalable content-addressable network. In *Proceedings of SIGCOMM,* San Diego, CA, Aug. 27–31, 2001.

[90] Thai-Lai Pham, Georg Schneider, and Stuart Goose. Exploiting location-based composite devices to support and facilitate situated ubiquitous computing. In

Proceedings of Second International Symposium on Handheld and Ubiquitous Computing, HUC 2000, pages 143-156, Bristol, UK, September 2000. Springer Verlag.

[91] Theodore L. Turocy and Bernhard von Stengel. Game theory. Cdam Research report lse-cdam-2001-09, *London School of Economics,* October 2001.

[92] Thomas Schwarz, and Ethan L. Miller. Store, forget, and check: Using algebraic signatures to check remotely administered storage. In *Proceedings of the IEEE Int'l Conference on Distributed Computing Systems* (ICDCS '06), July 2006.

[93] UbiStorage. http://www.ubistorage.com/

[94] Victor Miller. Uses of elliptic curves in cryptography Advances in Cryptology, Proceedings of Crypto'85, *Lecture Notes in Computer Science,* 218 (1986), Springer-Verlag, 417-426.

[95] Vivek Vishnumurthy, Sangeeth Chandrakumar and Emin Gun Sirer. KARMA: A Secure Economic Framework for P2P Resource Sharing. In *Proceedings of the Workshop on the Economics of Peer-to-Peer Systems*, Berkeley, California, June 2003.

[96] Wenrui Zhao, Yang Chen, Mostafa Ammar, Mark Corner, Brian Levine, and Ellen Zegura. Capacity Enhancement using Throwboxes in DTNs. *IEEE International Conference on Mobile Ad hoc and Sensor Systems (MASS),* Vancouver, Canada, October 2006.

[97] Wuala. http://wua.la/en/home.html

[98] Yves Deswarte, Jean-Jacques Quisquater, and Ayda Saïdane. Remote Integrity Checking. In *Proceedings of Sixth Working Conference on Integrity and Internal Control in Information Systems* (IICIS), 2004.

In: Peer-to-Peer Networks and Internet Policies
Editors: Diego Vegros and Jaime Sáenz, pp. 41-75

ISBN: 978-1-60876-287-3
© 2010 Nova Science Publishers, Inc.

Chapter 2

COMPUTER LAW OF COLOMBIA AND PERU: A COMPARISON WITH THE U.S. UNIFORM ELECTRONIC TRANSACTIONS ACT

Stephen E. Blythe[*]

New York Institute of Technology, New York, USA

Abstract

The computer laws of Colombia and Peru take a similar hybrid perspective in terms of technological neutrality. They recognize the legal validity of all types of electronic signatures, but show a preference for the digital signature by including detailed rules regarding Certification Authorities ("CA") and Public Key Infrastructure ("PKI"), two concepts only associated with the digital signature. In contrast, the U.S. approach is that of technological permissiveness—a legal recognition of all types of electronic signatures with no preference shown toward any of them. Accordingly, the U.S. law does not mention CA's or PKI because that would have been indicative of favoritism toward the digital signature. That is the essential difference between U.S. law and that of Colombia and Peru—the latter's statutes contain extensive coverage of CA's and PKI.

Colombia's statute covers both E-commerce contracts and electronic signatures, but Peru has enacted two separate statutes pertinent to those topics. Colombian law allows an electronic document to comply with a statutory requirement for production of an original paper document or a requirement for storage of a document, but Peru's statute does not mention those statutory requirements. Colombia covers carriage contracts, but Peru does not. Peru creates Registration Agents ("RA"), essentially clerks of CA's who are authorized to perform ministerial duties, but may not issue certificates or maintain a repository of them; Colombia

---

[*] Professor of Law, New York Institute of Technology, CERT Technology Park, Abu Dhabi, United Arab Emirates. Ph.D. (Info. Tech. Law), The University of Hong Kong, 2010; LL.M. (Info. Tech. Law) *with distinction*, University of Strathclyde (Scotland, U.K.), 2005; LL.M. (Int'l Bus. Law), University of Houston, 1992; J.D. *cum laude*, Texas Southern University, 1986; Ph.D. (Business Administration), University of Arkansas, 1979; M.B.A., Arkansas State University, 1975; B.S.P.A., University of Arkansas, 1970; Attorney at Law, Texas and Oklahoma; C.P.A., Texas. He practiced solo (employment-discrimination litigation) in Houston, Texas, was *of counsel* with the Cheek Law Firm (insurance-defense litigation) in Oklahoma City, and has been a management consultant for the city government of Haikou, China. Additionally, he has taught law, accounting, management, economics and international business at fourteen universities located in the United States, Africa and the Middle East. Comments are welcomed at: itlawforever@aol.com.

does not mention RA's. The Colombian statute and the U.S. model law contain a list of exclusions from coverage, but the Peruvian statute does not. The author recommends that: Colombia should enact a comprehensive computer crimes law; Peru should eliminate the position of RA and use CA's alone; the U.S. should eliminate its wills exclusion and join Colombia and Peru in granting the digital signature most-favored status among electronic signatures; Colombia and Peru should enact E-government statutes and should explicitly claim long-arm jurisdiction in their E-commerce statutes; and all three nations should enact more stringent consumer protections for E-commerce buyers and should establish Information Technology Courts.

Objectives of the Article

The objectives of this article are to: (1) introduce the reader to Colombia and Peru; (2) concisely describe the basic aspects of electronic signatures and public-key-infrastructure technology; (3) analyze and compare the computer laws of Colombia and Peru with their U.S. counterpart; and (4) make recommendations for improvement of those statutes.

An Introduction to Colombia and Peru

Colombia

The country known as Colombia today was once part of "Gran Colombia" consisting of the areas that comprise present-day Colombia, Ecuador and Venezuela. In 1830, however, Gran Colombia separated into the three nations currently in existence. For the past forty years, there has been an ongoing struggle between the Colombian government and anti-government insurgents and paramilitary forces. The latter two receive a great deal of financial support from the drug producers. In the 1990s, this struggle escalated but the anti-government forces were unable to muster sufficient popular support to be successful, and violence has been diminishing since 2002. Nevertheless, the insurgents and paramilitary groups continue to remain in control of many rural areas.[1]

Colombia's population is the third largest in Latin America, after Brazil and Mexico.[2] For the past ten years, the country has been changing to a free market economy from one that was once highly regulated.[3] The Colombian economy has been experiencing steady growth during the past five years. Its coffee industry is prospering again due to the recent increase in coffee prices and the capture of an increased share of the U.S. coffee market. The government's policies of budgetary cuts, reduction of public debt and growth of exports have been yielding dividends.[4] In 2007, the annual rate of the economy's gross domestic product ("GDP") is estimated to have been a respectable 7.7 %.[5] The government's efforts to get its economic house in order have resulted in praise from several international financial organizations. President Uribe is still faced with a need to reduce unemployment, undertake oil exploration

---

[1] U.S. Central Intelligence Agency ("CIA"), THE WORLD FACTBOOK, "Colombia," 4 December 2008, p. 1; http://www.cia.gov/cia/library/publications/the-world-factbook/print/co.html .

[2] U.S. Department of State, Bureau of Western Hemisphere Affairs, BACKGROUND NOTE: COLOMBIA, November, 2008, p.1; http://www.state.gov/r/pa/ei/bgn/35754.htm .

[3] Id. at 3.

[4] Note 2 supra at 6.

to offset declining production, and confront the challenge of pension reform.[6] Colombia is the world's largest cocaine producer and supplies most of the U. S. purchases of cocaine. Large amounts of opium and heroin are also produced in Colombia. However, to its credit, the government seems to be attempting to control drug production and is cooperating with the United States in that regard.[7] In a country with a population of 45 million, 12 million are internet users; the proportion of Colombians using the internet has grown remarkably during the past several years. Colombia has eighteen internet service providers and more than 1.5 million internet hosts; the latter statistic has also seen a recent surge in growth.[8]

The foundation of Colombia's legal system is its Constitution which became effective in 1991. The Constitution is based upon the law of Spain and allows for judicial review of legislative and executive acts. Notwithstanding its Spanish legal heritage, a new criminal code was drafted in 2004 using U.S. criminal law as a model and was fully implemented in January, 2008. However, Colombia does not recognize compulsory jurisdiction of the International Court of Justice.[9]

Peru

The history of civilization in Peru includes the period of the domination of the Incas, who were conquered by Spanish invaders in 1533. Peru declared her independence from Spain in 1821 and was victorious over the Spanish military forces in 1824. After years of military rule, Peru adopted a democratic political system in 1980. However, like Colombia, the country has had to endure the continuing presence of insurgent forces due to unrest caused by the economic underdevelopment. During the 1990s, President Fujimoro was able to achieve substantial progress on the economic front and the influence of the guerrilla forces waned. Nevertheless, he fell into political disfavor because of his authoritarianism and an economic recession in the latter years of the decade. Although reelected to a third term in 2000, the Peruvian Congress forced him to resign due to alleged corruption; in 2001, he was succeeded by President Toledo. President Garcia took office in 2006 after making campaign promises to attain fiscal reform and to improve social conditions.[10]

Population-wise, Peru ranks fifth in Latin America behind Brazil, Mexico, Colombia and Argentina.[11] Since the last decade, Peru has had one of the strongest economies in Latin America because of a substantial increase in exports and in mining and construction activity. The Garcia Administration has done a good job of managing the economy; Peru's annual rate of GDP growth was an impressive 9.0 % in 2007.[12] In spite of the strong macroeconomic performance, however, unemployment and poverty have remained high.[13] In a population of 29 million, only 7 million persons currently use the internet; however, the growth rate of

---

[5] Note 3 supra.

[6] Note 2 supra at 6.

[7] Note 2 supra at 11.

[8] Note 2 supra at 3, 10.

[9] Note 2 supra at 4-5.

[10] U.S. Central Intelligence Agency ("CIA"), THE WORLD FACTBOOK, "Peru," 4 December 2008, p. 1; http://www.cia.gov/library/publications/the-world-factbook/print/pe.html .

[11] U.S. Department of State, Bureau of Western Hemisphere Affairs, BACKGROUND NOTE: PERU, October, 2008, p. 1; http://www.state.gov./r/pa/ei/bgn/35762.htm .

[12] Id. at 1, 3.

[13] Note 11 supra at 6.

internet usage is remarkably high. Peru has ten internet service providers and more than 271,000 internet hosts.[14]

Like Colombia, Peru also has a Spanish legal foundation, a legacy of Spanish colonization of the country. Thus, both nations have civil law systems. Unlike Colombia, however, Peru does recognize the compulsory jurisdiction of the International Court of Justice, albeit with some reservations.[15]

Electronic Signatures

Contract law worldwide has traditionally required the parties to affix their signatures to a document.[16] With the onset of the electronic age, the electronic signature made its appearance. It has been defined as "any letters, characters, or symbols manifested by electronic or similar means and executed or adopted by a party with the intent to authenticate a writing,"[17] or as "data in electronic form which are attached to or logically associated with other electronic data and which serve as a method of authentication."[18] An electronic signature may take a number of forms: a digital signature, a digitized fingerprint, a retinal scan, a pin number, a digitized image of a handwritten signature that is attached to an electronic message, or merely a name typed at the end of an e-mail message.[19]

A well-known U.S. consumer group has stated, "Given the current state of authentication technology, it's much easier to forge or steal an e-signature than a written one."[20] This statement seems to assume that all E-signatures offer an equal degree of security. However, such an assumption would be erroneous; some electronic signatures offer more security than others. It is prudent for E-Commerce participants to use the more secure types of electronic signatures, notwithstanding their greater degree of complexity and expense.

Online Contracts: Four Levels of Security

When entering into a contract online, four degrees of security are possible.

---

[14] Note 11 supra at 3, 10.

[15] Id. at 4, 5.

[16] See, e.g., U.C.C. Sect. 2-201, 2-209 (1998).

[17] Thomas J. Smedinghoff, "Electronic Contracts: An Overview of Law and Legislation," 564 PLI/P at 125, 162 (1999).

[18] EUROPEAN UNION DIRECTIVE 1999/93/EC OF THE EUROPEAN PARLIAMENT AND OF THE COUNCIL OF 13 DECEMBER 1999 ON A COMMUNITY FRAMEWORK FOR ELECTRONIC SIGNATURES, (1999/93/EC)—19 January 2000, OJ L OJ No L 13 p.12. Peruvian law defines an electronic signature as "any symbol in electronic media, used or adopted by a party with the specific intention of being linked to or authenticating a document, fulfilling all or some of the characteristic functions of a handwritten signature." DSL, Note 139 infra, art. 1.

[19] David K.Y. Tang, "Electronic Commerce: American and International Proposals for Legal Structures," in REGULATION AND DEREGULATION: POLICY AND PRACTICE IN THE UTILITIES AND FINANCIAL SERVICES INDUSTRIES 333 (Chrisopher McCrudden ed., 1999).

[20] Michael Dessent, "Browse-Wraps, Click-Wraps and Cyberlaw: Our Shrinking (Wrap) World," 25 T. JEFFERSON L. REV. 1, 4 (2002).

1. The first level would exist if a party accepted an offer by merely clicking an "I Agree" button on a computer screen.[21]
2. The second level of security would be incurred if secrets were shared between the two contracting parties. This would be exemplified by the use of a password or a credit card number to verify a customer's intention that goods or services were to be purchased.[22]
3. The third level is achieved with biometrics. Biometric methods involve a unique physical attribute of the contracting party, and these are inherently extremely difficult to replicate by a would-be cyber-thief. Examples include: a voice pattern, face recognition, a scan of the retina or the iris within one's eyeball, a digital reproduction of a fingerprint,[23] or a digitized image of a handwritten signature that is attached to an electronic message. In all of these examples, a sample would be taken from the person in advance and stored for later comparison with a person purporting to have the same identity.[24] For example, if a person's handwriting was being used as the biometric identifer, the "shape, speed, stroke order, off-tablet motion, pen pressure and timing information" during signing would be recorded, and this information is almost impossible to duplicate by an imposter.[25]

Biometrics, despite its potential utility as a form of electronic signature, has at least two drawbacks in comparison with the digital signature: (1) The attachment of a person's biological traits to a document does not ensure that the document has not been altered, i.e., it "does not freeze the contents of the document;"[26] and (2) The recipient of the document must have a database of biological traits of all signatories dealt with in order to verify that a particular person sent the document.[27] The digital signature does not have these two weaknesses and most seem to view the digital signature as preferable to biometric identifiers.[28] Many also recommend the use of both methods; this was the course taken by the Hong Kong government in designing its identity card.[29]

---

[21] Jonathan E. Stern, Note, "Federal Legislation: The Electronic Signatures in Global and National Commerce Act," 16 BERKELEY TECH. L.J. 391, 395 (2001).

[22] Id.

[23] In the highly successful Hong Kong Identity Card, the two thumb prints are used as a biometric identifier. See, Rina C.Y. Chung, "Hong Kong's 'Smart' Identity Card: Data Privacy Issues and Implications for a Post-September 11th America," 4 ASIAN-PACIFIC L. & POL'Y J. 442 (2003).

[24] Note 22 supra at 395-96; and "The Legality of Electronic Signatures Using Cyber-Sign is Well Established," CYBER-SIGN, at http://www.cybersign.com/news news.htm

[25] Id.

[26] K.H. Pun, Lucas Hui, K.P. Chow, W.W. Tsang, C.F. Chong & H.W. Chan, "Review of the Electronic Transactions Ordinance: Can the Personal Identification Number Replace the Digital Signature?," 32 HONG KONG L.J. 241, 256 (2002).

[27] Id. at 257.

[28] Id. However, one of the experts in computer law and technology—Benjamin Wright—is a notable exception. Wright contends that biometrics is a more preferable authentication method in the case of the general public, although he concedes that digital signatures using PKI are preferable for complex financial deals carried out by sophisticated persons. In PKI, control of the person's "private key" becomes all-important. The person must protect the private key; all of the "eggs" are placed in that one basket, and the person carries a great deal of responsibility and risk. With biometric methods, the member of the general public would be sharing the risk with other parties involved in the transaction, and the need to protect the "private key" is not so compelling. See, Benjamin Wright, "Symposium: Cyber Rights, Protection, and Markets: Article, 'Eggs in Baskets: Distributing the Risks of Electronic Signatures,'" 32 WEST L.A. L. REV. 215, 225-26 (2001).

[29] Note 24 supra.

4.   The digital signature is considered the fourth level because it is more complex than biometrics. Many laypersons erroneously assume that the digital signature is merely a digitized version of a handwritten signature. This is not the case, however; the digital signature refers to the entire document.[30] It is "the sequence of bits that is created by running an electronic message through a one-way hash function and then encrypting the resulting message digest with the sender's private key."[31] A digital signature has two major advantages over other forms of electronic signatures: (1) it verifies authenticity that the communication came from a designated sender; and (2) it verifies the integrity of the content of the message, giving the recipient assurance that the message was not altered.[32]

Digital Signature Technology: Public Key Infrastructure

The technology used with digital signatures is known as Public Key Infrastructure, or "PKI."[33] PKI consists of four steps:

1.   The first step in utilizing this technology is to create a public-private key pair; the private key will be kept in confidence by the sender, but the public key will be available online.
2.   The second step is for the sender to digitally "sign" the message by creating a unique digest of the message and encrypting it. A "hash value" is created by applying a "hash function"—a standard mathematical function—to the contents of the electronic document. The hash value, ordinarily consisting of a sequence of 160 bits, is a digest of the document's contents. Whereupon, the hash function is encrypted, or scrambled, by the signatory using his private key. The encrypted hash function is the "digital signature" for the document.[34]
3.   The third step is to attach the digital signature to the message and to send both to the recipient.

---

[30] The Hong Kong E-commerce law typically defines a digital signature as follows: "an electronic signature of the signer generated by the transformation of the electronic record using an asymmetric cryptosystem and a hash function such that a person having the initial untransformed electronic record and the signer's public key can determine: (a) whether the transformation was generated using the private key that corresponds to the signer's public key; and (b) whether the initial electronic record has been altered since the transformation was generated." Hong Kong Special Autonomous Region, ELECTRONIC TRANSACTIONS ORDINANCE, Ord. No. 1 of 2000, s 2.

[31] Note 18 supra at 146. Colombian law defines a digital signature as "a numerical value adhered or attached to a data message and which, using a known mathematical procedure, linked to initiator password and to message text allows to determine that such value has been exclusively obtained through initiator password and the initial message has not been amended after effecting the respective transformation." ETL, Note 84 infra, art. 2. Peruvian law defines a digital signature as "that electronic signature which utilizes a symmetrical cryptography technique based on the use of a unique pair of codes, associated with a private code and a public code, mathematically related to each other in such a way that persons who have knowledge of the public code cannot derive the private code from it." DSL, Note 139 infra, art. 3.

[32] Christopher T. Poggi, "Electronic Commerce Legislation: An Analysis of European and American Approaches to Contract Formation," 41 VA. J. INT'L L. 224, 250-51 (2000).

[33] Susanna Frederick Fischer, "California Saving Rosencrantz and Guildenstern in a Virtual World? A Comparative Look at Recent Global Electronic Signature Legislation," Association of American Law Schools 2001 Annual Meeting, Section on Law and Computers, 7 B.U. J. SCI. & TECH. L. 229, 233 (2001).

[34] Note 27 supra at 249.

4. The fourth step is for the recipient to decrypt the digital signature by using the sender's public key. If decryption is possible the recipient knows the message is authentic, i.e., that it came from the purported sender. Finally, the recipient will create a second message digest of the communication and compare it to the decrypted message digest. If they match, the recipient knows the message has not been altered.[35]

Advantages of the Digital Signature

Unlike biometric and other forms of electronic signatures, the digital signature will "freeze" the contents of the document at the time of its creation. Any alterations to the document's contents will result in a different hash value. Furthermore, the encryption of the hash value with the signatory's private key "links uniquely the digital signature to the signatory, i.e., the owner of the private key."[36] Although a handwritten signature is only "signatory-specific," the digital signature is both "signatory-specific" and "document-specific."[37]

The digital signature is the only form of electronic signature which satisfies all three of the UNCITRAL evaluation factors, i.e., that an electronic signature should: (1) authorize; (2) approve; and (3) protect against fraud.[38] Authorization is achieved because the digital signature will accompany the document, which allows for confirmation of the identity of the signatory. Approval is attained via computation of the hash value of the electronic document, which freezes the contents of the document at the time of its creation, and allows for detection of any subsequent alterations. Finally, there is protection against fraud because it is extremely unlikely—virtually impossible—for anyone to determine a signatory's private key with only the public key as a starting point.[39]

Disadvantages of the Digital Signature

The digital signature has at least two drawbacks. Firstly, since the private key of each person is rather difficult to memorize, they are most often stored in computers. If the computer is not kept in a secure location, the contents of the private key may be vulnerable. This heightens the necessity of maintaining the security of the private key and protecting it from intruders. However, it should be noted that this weakness of the digital signature is also common to most other forms of electronic signatures. The password or the PIN face similar security problems. Therefore, with good security policies and procedures, this disadvantage can be minimized.[40]

The other disadvantage of the digital signature pertains to the digital certificate, which must be issued by a Certification Authority ("CA"). Obtaining the certificate and having to

---

[35] Jochen Zaremba, "International Electronic Transaction Contracts Between U.S. and E.U. Companies and Customers," 18 CONN. J. INT'L L. 479, 512 (2003).
[36] Note 27 supra at 250.
[37] Id.
[38] Note 27 supra at 243.
[39] Note 27 supra at 252.
[40] Note 27 supra at 253.

interact with the CA is somewhat inconvenient and costly for the user, but over time this disadvantage should be alleviated as digital signatures become more popular, easier to use, and cheaper.[41] Because the CA plays such a vital role in the viability of the digital signature, it is essential for the user to understand exactly what the CA does.

The Critical Role of the Certification Authority

In order for PKI to realize its potential, it is crucial that the user be able to ensure the authenticity of the public key (available online) used to verify the digital signature. If Smith and Jones are attempting to consummate an online transaction, Smith needs an independent confirmation that Jones' message is actually from Jones before Smith can have faith that Jones' public key actually belongs to Jones. It is possible that an imposter could have sent Jones his public key, contending that it belongs to Smith. Accordingly, a reliable third party—the Certification Authority[42]—must be available to register the public keys of the parties and to guarantee the accuracy of the identification of the parties.[43]

The most important job of the CA is to issue certificates which confirm basic facts about the subscriber, the subject of the digital certificate. Of course, the certificate is a digitized, computer-held record containing the most pertinent information about a transaction between two transacting parties. Typical information contained in a certificate includes the following: the name and address of the CA that issued the certificate; the name, address and other attributes of the subscriber; the subscriber's public key; and the digital signature of the CA.[44] Sufficient information will be contained in the certificate to connect a public key to the particular subscriber.[45]

In making an application to a CA for a certificate, the prospective subscriber must provide some sort of photo I.D., e.g., a passport or a driver's license. If the application is approved and the certificate is issued, the CA will issue a private key to its new subscriber which corresponds to the public key. This is done, however, without disclosing the specifics of the private key.[46] The steps in this application procedure vary somewhat from CA to CA, according to the type of certificate being offered by the CA. Ordinarily, however, once the

---

[41] Id.

[42] Certification Authority ("CA") is the term used in this article because it seems to be the most commonly used designation around the world. Colombian law refers to a CA as a "Certifying Entity" and defines it as "the person who authorized in accordance with this Law is empowered to issue certificates related to digital signatures of persons, offer or facilitate recording and chronological stamping services for the transmission and reception of data messages, as well as to perform some other duties related to communications based on digital signatures." ETL, Note 84 infra. art. 2. Peruvian law refers to a CA as a "Certification Agency" and states that it "performs the function of issuing or cancelling digital certificates, as well as providing other services inherent to the certificate itself or to those that provide security to the certificate system in particular or the system of electronic commerce in general." DSL, Note 139 infra, art. 12.

[43] Tara C. Hogan, Notes and Comments—Technology, "Now That the Floodgates Have Been Opened, Why Haven't Banks Rushed Into the Certification Authority Business?," 4 N.C. BANKING INST. 417, 424-25 (2000).

[44] A. Michael Froomkin, "The Essential Role of Trusted Third Parties in Electronic Commerce," 75 OR. L. REV. 49, 58 (1996).

[45] Note 44 supra at 425-426.

[46] Note supra at 149.

CA has verified the genuine connection between the subscriber and the public key, the certificate will be issued.[47]

In order to indicate the authenticity of the digital certificate, the CA will sign it with her digital signature. Ordinarily, the public key corresponding to the subscriber's private key will be filed in the CA's online repository which is accessible to the general public and to third parties who have need of communication with the subscriber. Additionally, the online repository contains information pertaining to digital certificates which have been revoked or suspended by the CA due to lost or expired private keys. This is an important positive aspect of PKI technology: the general public has access to the status of digital signatures, and relying third parties are kept informed, allowing them to judge whether they should place reliance on communications signed with a certain private key.[48]

One of the recurring problems for digital signature lawmakers is in trying to fairly apportion the liability for risk of computer fraud between the CA and the subscriber. Nations around the world, and the states within the U.S., have arrived at different conclusions regarding this apportionment. The problem is compounded if each CA is required to modify its practices every time it issues a certificate pertaining to a transaction affecting another jurisdiction which happens to have dissimilar digital signature laws.[49]

A digital certificate is only as reputable as the CA who issued it. If the CA is unreliable and untrustworthy, the digital certificate is also unreliable and untrustworthy. In the final analysis, a party contracting with an unknown stranger must rely upon the CA's registration expertise and its judgment that the subscriber's identification is accurate.[50]

Three Generations of Electronic Signature Law

The First Wave: Technological Exclusivity

In 1995, the U.S. State of Utah became the first jurisdiction in the world to enact an electronic signature law.[51] In the Utah statute, digital signatures were given legal recognition, but other types of electronic signatures were not.[52] The authors of the Utah statute believed, with some justification, that digital signatures provide the greatest degree of security for electronic transactions. Utah was not alone in this attitude; other jurisdictions granting exclusive recognition to the digital signature include Bangladesh, India[53], Malaysia, Nepal[54] and Russia.[55]

---

[47] Note 18 supra at 150. Peruvian law uses the phrase "digital certificate" and defines it as "the electronic document generated and signed digitally by a Certification Agency, which links a pair of codes to particular person, confirming his identity." DSL, Note 139 infra, art. 6.

[48] Note 44 supra at 426-27.

[49] Andrew B. Berman, Note, "International Divergence: The 'Keys' To Signing on the Digital Line—The Cross-Border Recognition of Electronic Contracts and Digital Signatures," 28 SYRACUSE J. INT'L L. & COM. 125, 143-44 (2001).

[50] David Hallerman, "Will Banks Become E-commerce Authorities?," 12 BANK TECH. NEWS, June 1, 1999.

[51] UTAH CODE ANNOTATED 46-3-101 *et seq.* (1999).

[52] Id.

[53] Stephen E. Blythe, "A Critique of India's Information Technology Act and Recommendations for Improvement," 34 SYRACUSE JOURNAL OF INTERNATIONAL LAW AND COMMERCE 1 (2006), a publication of the College of Law, Syracuse University, Syracuse, New York USA. Available at Lexis-Nexis: http://www.lexisnexis.com.eproxy3.lib.hku.hk/us/lnacademic/results/docview/docview.do?risb=21_T3229558

Unfortunately, these jurisdictions' decision to allow the utilization of only one form of technology is burdensome and overly-restrictive. Forcing users to employ digital signatures gives them more security, but this benefit may be outweighed by the digital signature's disadvantages: more expense, lesser convenience, more complication and less adaptability to technologies used in other nations, or even by other persons within the same country.[56]

The Second Wave: Technological Neutrality

Jurisdictions in the Second Wave overcompensated. They did the complete reversal of the First Wave and did not include any technological restrictions whatsoever in their statutes. They did not insist upon the utilization of digital signatures, or any other form of technology, to the exclusion of other types of electronic signatures. These jurisdictions have been called "permissive" because they take a completely open-minded, liberal perspective on electronic signatures and do not contend that any one of them is necessarily better than the others. In other words, they are "technologically neutral." Permissive jurisdictions provide legal recognition of many types of electronic signatures and do not grant a monopoly to any one of them. Examples of permissive jurisdictions include the majority of states in the United States,[57] the United Kingdom,[58] Australia and New Zealand.[59]

The disadvantage of the permissive perspective is that it does not take into account that, in fact, some types of electronic signatures *are* better than others. A PIN number and a person's name typed at the end of an E-mail message are both forms of electronic signatures, but neither is able to even approach the degree of security that is provided by the digital signature.

The Third Wave: A Hybrid

Singapore was in the vanguard of the Third Wave. In 1998, this country adopted a compromise, middle-of-the-road position with respect to the various types of electronic signatures. Singapore's lawmakers were influenced by the UNCITRAL Model Law on

---

475&format=GNBFI&sort=RELEVANCE&startDocNo=1&resultsUrlKey=29_T3229558480&cisb=22_T322 9558479&treeMax=true&treeWidth=0&csi=140728&docNo=3 .

[54] Stephen E. Blythe, "On Top of the World, and Wired: A Critique of Nepal's E-Commerce Law," 8:1 JOURNAL OF HIGH TECHNOLOGY LAW ___ (2008), a publication of Suffolk University School of Law, Boston, Massachusetts   USA; http://findarticles.com/p/articles/mi_m5GES/is_1_8/ai_n25431661/pg_1?tag=artBody;col1 .

[55] Note 34 supra at 234-37.

[56] It is debatable as to whether technological-neutrality or technological-specificity is the correct road to take. See, Sarah E. Roland, Note, "The Uniform Electronic Signatures in Global and National Commerce Act: Removing Barriers to E-Commerce or Just Replacing Them with Privacy and Security Issues?" 35 SUFFOLK U. L. REV. 625, 638-45 (2001).

[57] For concise coverage of American and British law, see Stephen E. Blythe, "Digital Signature Law of the United Nations, European Union, United Kingdom and United States: Promotion of Growth in E-Commerce With Enhanced Security," 11: 2 RICHMOND JOURNAL OF LAW AND TECHNOLOGY 6 (2005). For more comprehensive coverage of American law, see "E-Commerce and E-Signature Law of the United States of America," THE UKRAINIAN JOURNAL OF BUSINESS LAW, pp. ___, November, 2008. This journal is published monthly in Kiev, Ukraine. Abstract: http://www.ujbl.info/. Full article: ftp://mail.yurpractika.com .

[58] Id.

[59] Note 34 supra at 234-37.

Electronic Commerce.[60] In terms of relative degree of technological neutrality, Singapore adopted a "hybrid" model—a preference for the digital signature in terms of greater legal presumption of reliability and security, but not to the exclusion of other forms of electronic signatures. Singapore did not want to become "hamstrung" by tying itself to one form of technology. The Singapore legislators realized that technology is continually evolving and that it would be unwise to require one form of technology to the exclusion of others. The digital signature is given more respect under the Singapore statute, but it is not granted a monopoly as in Utah. Singapore allows other types of electronic signatures to be employed. This technological open-mindedness is commensurate with a global perspective and allows parties to more easily consummate electronic transactions with parties from other nations.[61]

The drafters of the Colombian and Peruvian computer laws joined the Third Wave. Those two nations recognize the security advantages afforded by the digital signature and indicate a preference for the digital signature over other forms of electronic signatures. This preference is exhibited in several ways: (1) utilization of a digital signature using a PKI system is explicitly required for authentication of an electronic record; (2) utilization of a digital signature with PKI seems to be necessary in order for an electronic record to comply with any statutory requirement that a record be in paper form; and (3) in order for a signature in electronic form to comply with a statutory requirement that a pen-and-paper signature be affixed, it must be a digital signature created with PKI. Nevertheless, the Colombian and Peruvian laws do not appear to be as technologically-restrictive as some other jurisdictions. For example, they do not compel the E-commerce participant to use only the digital signature, *in lieu* of other forms of electronic signatures, as the State of Utah did in its original statute of 1995.

The moderate position adopted by Singapore, Colombia and Peru has now become the progressive trend in international electronic signature law. The hybrid approach is the one taken by the European Union's E-Signatures Directive,[62] Armenia,[63] Azerbaijan[64] Barbados,[65]

---

[60] United Nations Commission on International Trade Law ("UNCITRAL"), MODEL LAW ON ELECTRONIC COMMERCE WITH GUIDE TO ENACTMENT (hereinafter "MLEC"), G.A. Res. 51/162, U.N. GAOR, 51st Sess., Supp. No. 49, at 336, U.N. Doc. A/51/49 (1996); http://www.uncitral.org/english/texts/electcom/ml-ecomm.htm . See Stephen E. Blythe, Note 58 supra.

[61] Republic of Singapore, ELECTRONIC TRANSACTIONS ACT (Cap. 88) ("ETA"), 10 July 1998; http://agcvldb4.agc.gov.sg/ (Accessed 15 February 2006). Although granting legal recognition to most types of electronic signatures, the Singapore statute implicitly makes a strong suggestion to users—in two ways—that they should use the digital signature because it is more reliable and more secure than the other types of electronic signatures: (1) digital signatures are given more respect under rules of evidence in a court of law than other forms of electronic signatures, and electronic documents signed with them carry a legal presumption of reliability and security—these presumptions are not given to other forms of electronic signatures; and (2) although all forms of electronic signatures are allowed to be used in Singapore, its electronic signature law established comprehensive rules for the licensing and regulation of Certification Authorities, whose critical role is to verify the of authenticity and integrity of electronic messages affixed to electronic signatures. Id. See Stephen E. Blythe, "Singapore Computer Law: An International Trend-Setter with a Moderate Degree of Technological Neutrality," 33 OHIO NORTHERN UNIVERSITY LAW REVIEW ___ (2006).

[62] Note 19 supra; see Stephen E. Blythe, Note 58 supra. For concise coverage of European Union law, see Stephen E. Blythe, "E-Signature Law and E-Commerce Law of the European Union and its Member States," THE UKRAINIAN JOURNAL OF BUSINESS LAW, pp. 22-26, May, 2008. This journal is published monthly in Kiev, Ukraine. An abstract of the article is available at http://www.ujbl.info/ .

[63] Stephen E. Blythe, "Armenia's Electronic Document and Electronic Signature Law: Promotion of Growth in E-Commerce via Greater Cyber-Security," ARMENIAN LAW REVIEW, May, 2008, a publication of the Department of Law, American University of Armenia, Yerevan, Republic of Armenia; http://www.aua.am/aua/masters/law/pdf/esignaturelaw.pdf.

Bermuda,[66] Bulgaria,[67] China[68] Croatia,[69] Dubai,[70] Finland,[71] Hong Kong,[72] Hungary,[73] Iran,[74] Japan,[75] Lithuania,[76] Pakistan,[77] Slovenia,[78] South Korea,[79] Taiwan,[80] Tunisia,[81] Vanuatu[82] and many other nations.

---

[64] Stephen E. Blythe, "Azerbaijan's E-Commerce Statutes: Contributing to Economic Growth and Globalization in the Caucasus Region," 1:1 COLUMBIA JOURNAL OF EAST EUROPEAN LAW 44-75 (2007).

[65] Stephen E. Blythe, "The Barbados Electronic Transactions Act: A Comparison with the U.S. Model Statute," 16 CARIBBEAN LAW REVIEW 1 (2006).

[66] Note 34 supra at 234-37.

[67] Stephen E. Blythe, "Bulgaria's Electronic Document and Electronic Signature Law: Enhancing E-Commerce With Secure Cyber-Transactions," 17:2 TRANSNATIONAL LAW AND CONTEMPORARY PROBLEMS 361 (2008), a publication of the University of Iowa College of Law, Iowa City, Iowa USA.

[68] Stephen E. Blythe, "China's New Electronic Signature Law and Certification Authority Regulations: A Catalyst for Dramatic Future Growth of E-Commerce," 7 CHICAGO-KENT JOURNAL OF INTELLECTUAL PROPERTY 1 (2007), a publication of Chicago-Kent College of Law, Illinois Institute of Technology, Chicago, Illinois USA. Available at http://jip.kentlaw.edu/art/volume%207/7%20Chi-Kent%20J%20Intell%20Prop%201.pdf and at Lexis-Nexis: http://www.lexisnexis.com.eproxy3.lib.hku.hk/us/lnacademic/results/docview/docview.do?risb=21_T3229558475&format=GNBFI&sort=RELEVANCE&startDocNo=1&resultsUrlKey=29_T3229558480&cisb=22_T3229558479&treeMax=true&treeWidth=0&csi=221052&docNo=2 .

[69] Stephen E. Blythe, "Croatia's Computer Laws: Promotion of Growth in E-Commerce Via Greater Cyber-Security," 26: 1 EUROPEAN JOURNAL OF LAW AND ECONOMICS 75-103 (August, 2008), a publication of Springer Netherlands Ltd., Amsterdam ; abstract (*gratis*) and article (by subscription) at http://www.springerlink.com/content/p64m283715154146/ .

[70] Stephen E. Blythe, "The Dubai Electronic Transactions Statute: A Prototype for E-Commerce Law in the United Arab Emirates and the G.C.C. Countries," 22:1 JOURNAL OF ECONOMICS AND ADMINISTRATIVE SCIENCES 103 (2007).

[71] Stephen E. Blythe, "Finland's Electronic Signature Act and E-Government Act: Facilitating Security in E-Commerce and Online Public Services," 31:2 HAMLINE LAW REVIEW 445-469 (2008), a publication of Hamline University School of Law, St. Paul, Minnesota USA. This article will become available at Lexis-Nexis.

[72] Before amending its original digital signature law, Hong Kong only recognized digital signatures and was therefore a member of the First Wave. After amendments were made, Hong Kong joined the Third Wave. *See* Stephen E. Blythe, "Electronic Signature Law and Certification Authority Regulations of Hong Kong: Promoting E-Commerce in the World's 'Most Wired' City," 7 NORTH CAROLINA JOURNAL OF LAW AND TECHNOLOGY 1 (2005); Available at http://www.ncjolt.org/content/view/87/75/ and at Lexis-Nexis: http://www.lexisnexis.com.eproxy3.lib.hku.hk/us/lnacademic/results/docview/docview.do?risb=21_T3229558475&format=GNBFI&sort=RELEVANCE&startDocNo=1&resultsUrlKey=29_T3229558480&cisb=22_T3229558479&treeMax=true&treeWidth=0&csi=241400&docNo=5 .

[73] Stephen E. Blythe, "Hungary's Electronic Signature Act: Enhancing Economic Development With Secure E-Commerce Transactions," 16:1 INFORMATION AND COMMUNICATIONS TECHNOLOGY LAW 47-71 (2007), a publication of Routledge Publishing Co., a member of the Taylor & Francis Group. Executive Editor: Prof. Indira Carr, Centre for Legal Research, Middlesex University, London, U.K.; http://www.tandf.co.uk/journals/journal.asp?issn=1360-0834&linktype=5 .

[74] Stephen E. Blythe, "Tehran Begins to Digitize: Iran's E-Commerce Law as a Hopeful Bridge to the World," 18 SRI LANKA JOURNAL OF INTERNATIONAL LAW ___ (2006).

[75] Stephen E. Blythe, "Cyber-Law of Japan: Promoting E-Commerce Security, Increasing Personal Information Confidentiality and Controlling Computer Access," 10 JOURNAL OF INTERNET LAW 20 (2006); http://www.accessmylibrary.com/coms2/summary_0286-17306641_ITM.

[76] Stephen E. Blythe, "Lithuania's Electronic Signature Law: Providing More Security in E-Commerce Transactions," 8 BARRY LAW REVIEW 23 (2007); Available at Lexis-Nexis: http://www.lexisnexis.com.eproxy3.lib.hku.hk/us/lnacademic/results/docview/docview.do?risb=21_T3229558475&format=GNBFI&sort=RELEVANCE&startDocNo=1&resultsUrlKey=29_T3229558480&cisb=22_T3229558479&treeMax=true&treeWidth=0&csi=254558&docNo=6 .

[77] Stephen E. Blythe, "Pakistan Goes Digital: the Electronic Transactions Ordinance as a Facilitator of Growth for E-commerce," 2:2 JOURNAL OF ISLAMIC STATE PRACTICES IN INTERNATIONAL LAW 5 (2006); Available at: http://electronicpublications.org/catalogue.php?id=46 .

[78] Stephen E. Blythe, "Slovenia's Electronic Commerce and Electronic Signature Act: Enhancing Economic Growth With Secure Cyber-Transactions," 6: 4 THE I.C.F.A.I. JOURNAL OF CYBER LAW 8-33 (2007), a publication of ICFAI University Press, Institute of Chartered Financial Analysts of India, Hyderabad, India; http://www.iupindia.org/ijcl.asp .

Colombian Computer Law

Colombia enacted its computer law (hereinafter Electronic Trade Law, or "ETL")[83] in 1999[84] and it went into effect immediately.[85] The ETL is applicable to all data messages,[86] with these exceptions: (1) international treaties and covenants between Colombia and other nations; and (2) product warnings which are statutorily required to be printed in writing on the product's label due to risk incurred as a result of the product's "marketing, use or consumption."[87]

These are factors to be considered in the interpretation of the ETL: (1) the international influences on the development of the ETL[88] (2) a desire for uniformity and consistency in the ETL's implementation; and (3) a need for the ETL to observe standards of good faith.[89] Furthermore, related legal issues not explicitly covered in the ETL should be decided based upon the general principles established by the ETL.[90]

Legal Recognition of the Digital Form

Recognition of Data Messages

The ETL provides that the legal validity, enforceability and admissibility of data messages shall not be denied based on the mere fact of their digital form.[91]

---

[79] Stephen E. Blythe, "The Tiger on the Peninsula is Digitized: Korean E-Commerce Law as a Driving Force in the World's Most Computer-Savvy Nation," 28: 3 HOUSTON JOURNAL OF INTERNATIONAL LAW 573-661 (2006); Available at: http://goliath.ecnext.com/coms2/gi_0199-5799352/The-tiger-on-the-Peninsula.html; and at https://www.entrepreneur.com/tradejournals/article/147302385_1.html .

[80] Stephen E. Blythe, "Taiwan's Electronic Signature Act: Facilitating the E-Commerce Boom With Enhanced Security," a paper presented and published in the PROCEEDINGS OF THE SIXTH ANNUAL HAWAII INTERNATIONAL CONFERENCE ON BUSINESS, Honolulu, Hawaii U.S.A., May 25-28, 2006; the entire Proceedings is available at: http://www.hicbusiness.org/Proceedings_Bus.htm .

[81] Stephen E. Blythe, "Computer Law of Tunisia: Promoting Secure E-Commerce Transactions With Electronic Signatures," 20 ARAB LAW QUARTERLY 317-344 (2006); http://www.ingentaconnect.com/content/brill/alq .

[82] Stephen E. Blythe, "South Pacific Computer Law: Promoting E-Commerce in Vanuatu and Fighting Cyber-Crime in Tonga," 10: 1 JOURNAL OF SOUTH PACIFIC LAW (2006); http://www.paclii.org/journals/fJSPL/vol10/

[83] Republic of Colombia, LAW REGULATING DATA MESSAGES, ELECTRONIC TRADE, DIGITAL SIGNATURES AND CERTIFICATION ENTITIES (hereinafter Electronic Trade Law or "ETL"), 13 January 1999, Official Translation No. 7 by Maria del Pilar Mejia de Restrepo; http://www.qmw.ac.uk/~t16345/colombia_en_final.htm .

[84] Id. (ETL) at Preamble.

[85] ETL, art. 47. The Superintendent of Industry and Trade was given twelve months to assign responsibility for regulation of Certification Authorities to one of its subordinate departments. ETL, art. 45.

[86] A data message is defined as "information generated sent, received, stored or communicated by electronic, optical or similar means, as they could be, among others, Data Electronic Exchange (DEE), Internet, electronic mail, telegram, telex or telefacsimile." ETL, art. 2. This broadly-worded definition is evidence of an open-minded perspective toward a number of technological forms and shows that Colombia is not "hamstrung" by insistence on only one particular type of technology. DEE is defined as "data electronic transmission from a computer to another one, structured under technical regulations agreed for such purpose." Id.

[87] ETL, art. 1.

[88] United Nations law has had an especially profound impact on the evolution of E-commerce law around the world. For concise coverage of U.N. law relating to digital signatures, *see* Stephen E. Blythe, Note 58 supra.

[89] Note 84 supra (ETL), art. 3.

[90] Id.

[91] ETL, art. 5.

Compliance with Writing Requirement

If another statute mandates that a document must be in written form on paper to be enforceable, the mandate will be complied with if the document is in the form of a digital message, provided it is readily accessible. This provision applies in cases where a party is either legally obliged to have a written document, or if a legal detriment will be incurred in the absence of a written document.[92]

Compliance with Signature Requirement

Whenever a statute mandates that a signature in ink must have been executed on a paper document in order to be enforceable, that mandate is met if an electronic signature has been attached to a digital message. However, these provisions must be met: (1) the identity of the sender must be expressed; (2) the sender must have approved the content of the digital message; and (3) the method used to confirm the identity of the sender and the content of the message must be reliable, taking into account the purpose of the message. This applies both in cases where the presence of a signature is legally required, and also where certain consequences will occur if the signature is absent.[93]

Compliance with Original Requirement

Whenever a statute mandates that a document must be produced in its original form, that requirement may be met by production of the information in the form of a data message, provided: (1) there is a reliable means of ensuring that the content of the information has not changed from the time it was created until the time it is retrieved; and (2) if information must be presented to another person, that it must be capable of being presented. This rule applies irrespective of whether there is a legal requirement for production of the original, or adverse consequences will ensue if the original is not produced.[94] The data message must be kept unmodified, except for changes inherent to an endorsement or "a communication, file or presentation process." The degree of reliability of the security procedures will be evaluated in view of the purpose of the generation of the information and all other factors in the situation.[95]

Admissibility in Court

Data messages are admissible evidence in court. Their admissibility into evidence cannot be challenged based on the mere fact that they are in digital form.[96]

---

[92] ETL, art. 6.

[93] ETL, art. 7.

[94] ETL, art. 8.

[95] ETL, art. 9.

[96] ETL, art. 10. The "probative force" of a data message is determined by Chapter VIII, Title XIII, Third Section, Second Book of the Colombian Code of Civil Procedure. Id. In determination of the probative force of a data message, the following factors should be considered: reliability of the generation, transmission and storage methods; reliability of the digital form pertinent to maintenance of information integrity; the method of identification of the sender of the data message; and other factors. ETL, art. 11.

Compliance with Retention Requirement

If a statute mandates that documents are to be retained for a given length of time, then this requirement is deemed met if the document is stored as a data message, provided: (1) the data message is readily accessible; (2) the data message is kept in the same format as the paper document, or its digital format indicates that the data message contains the same information as the paper document; (3) the data message contains the points of transmission and reception and the date and hour it was transmitted (or produced) and received; (4) it is not necessary to store information whose only purpose is to facilitate the transmission of the data message; and (5) the records of traders must be maintained using technology which ensures they can be retrieved in their exact form.[97]

Rules Pertaining to E-Commerce Contracts

The ETL has adopted a number of specific rules relating to contracts which are established online. These rules may be varied by agreement of the contracting parties.[98]

Legal Recognition of Digital Contracts

Contracts partially or fully negotiated in digital form are legally recognized. They cannot be challenged based on the mere fact of their digital form.[99] Furthermore, another party involved in the negotiation of a contract cannot deny the receipt of the first party's data message based on the mere fact of its digital form.[100]

Attribution Rules

An electronic message is legally presumed to have been delivered by a specific sender if it is delivered by: (1) the sender herself; (2) the sender's agent; or (3) a computer information system which automatically generated the message after being programmed by the sender.[101]

A data message is legally presumed to have been sent by a specific sender whenever:

(1) a previously-agreed-to procedure has been applied by the receiver and it indicates the sender in question is the transmitter; or (2) the message is received because of the acts of a person that has a relationship with the sender (or the sender's attorney), and that person has been entrusted with the sender's secret method of identification that the message is that of the sender.[102]

---

[97] ETL, art. 12. A person's agent may also retain documents in digital form, provided the agent complies with these provisions. ETL, art. 13.

[98] ETL, art. 4. Of course, if another applicable statute proscribes modification of the rules by agreement of the parties, then they will not be allowed to do that. Id.

[99] ETL, art. 14.

[100] ETL, art. 15. This is different from many other jurisdictions of the world which refuse to require a party to accept a digital message when the party has voiced a preference for another medium of communication. This is progressive on the part of Colombia and will promote the utilization of the electronic form of contracting.

[101] ETL, art. 16 An information system is defined as "every system used to generate, send, receive, file or process data messages in any way." ETL, art. 2.

[102] ETL, art. 17.

Whenever a data message is received from a sender or is so understood, or whenever the receiver has a right to act pursuant to such an understanding, then the receiver may assume that the data message received is the one that the sender intended to send, and may act accordingly. However, the receiver may not assume this if she could have discovered with due diligence that an error had been made, or would have discovered an error if a previously-agreed-to procedure had been applied.[103]

The receiver may generally assume that each data message received is new and independent. However, if a duplicate data message is received, it may not considered to be new and independent if either: (1) due diligence on her part would have indicated that it was a duplicate; or (2) an agreed-to procedure would have so indicated.[104]

Acknowledgement of Receipt

If the parties have agreed for the receiver to acknowledge receipt of a message, but no specific means of acknowledgement has been agreed to, then the confirmation may be achieved by: (1) any type of communication from the receiver to the sender, either automated or non-automated; or (2) any act of the receiver which would indicate a receipt of the message.[105]

If the sender has conditioned her performance on the receipt of acknowledgement, then the sender does not have to perform until the acknowledgement is received, and until it is, may act as if the data message was never delivered.[106]

If the sender receives an acknowledgement, there is a legal presumption that the receiver has received the data message. However, this does necessary imply that the delivered message was accurate. But, if the acknowledgement states that the technical requirements of any regulation have been complied with, then this will create a legal presumption of that fact.[107]

Time of Sending and Receiving

A data message shall be deemed to have been transmitted when it enters a computer information system not under the control of the sender (or a sender's agent acting on behalf of the sender).[108]

If the receiver has specified a computer information system as a target for the sender, the data message shall be deemed to have been received when: (1) it enters that specific computer information system; or (2) if sent to a different computer information system under the receiver's control, then the time is when the receiver retrieves the message.[109]

---

[103] ETL, art. 18.
[104] ETL, art. 19.
[105] ETL, art. 20.
[106] Id.
[107] ETL, art. 21. Articles 20 and 21 are legally controlling only with respect to acknowledgement of receipt. They do not control the legal ramifications of the content of the data message. ETL, art. 22.
[108] ETL, art. 23.
[109] ETL, art. 24.

On the other hand, if the receiver has not designated a specific computer information system as a target for the data message, then the data message is deemed delivered when it enters any computer information system under the control of the receiver.[110]

Place of Sending and Receiving

The general rule regarding location is that data messages are assumed to have been sent from the sender's place of business, and received at the receiver's place of business. If one of those parties has more than one place of business, then the applicable location will be the one having the "closest relation with its underlying operation." But, if there is no underlying operation, then the principal place of business will be the applicable one. If either party has no place of business, then the party's residence will be the applicable location.[111]

Attachments to a Data Message

If attachments are made to a data message which are easily accessible, and contain additional information pertinent to an agreement, that information should be considered to have been incorporated by reference in the contract and is just as much a part of the contract as if it was a part of the data message itself.[112]

E-Contracts Pertaining to Carriage of Goods

The ETL has adopted rules governing electronic contracts pertinent to the delivery of goods. The specific parts of a carriage contract controlled by these rules include, but are not limited to, the following: (1) detailed description of the goods; (2) issuance of receipt; (3) confirmation of shipment; (4) notification of terms of the contract; (5) instructions to be conveyed to the transporter; (6) request of delivery of the goods; (7) authorization to deliver the goods; (7) buyer's notification of loss or damage of goods during transit; (8) seller's promise to deliver the goods to buyer or her agent; and (9) acquisition, waiver or transfer of rights in the agreement.[113]

Data messages may be used in the creation or implementation of carriage contracts, notwithstanding the fact that another statute may mandate the utilization of paper documents. This applies regardless of whether the statute creates a legal requirement, or provides for detrimental consequences if paper documents are not used. However, in order for data messages to be used in the transfer of a right or obligation under a carriage contract, a "reliable method" [114] must be employed to ensure the security and integrity of the message. Once data messages have begun to be used, paper documents are no longer valid. A party cannot revert to the use of paper documents until the other party has been informed that, henceforth, paper documents are to be used instead of data messages. Reversion to paper

---

[110] Id. The rules in Article 24 apply even if the receiver's computer information system is located in a place that is different from the assumed place of reception according to Article 25. ETL, art. 24.

[111] ETL, art. 25.

[112] ETL, art. 44.

[113] ETL, art. 26.

[114] The degree of necessary reliability depends on the circumstances of each case and the reason why the right or obligation has been transferred. ETL, art. 27.

documents will not affect the rights of the parties which were created with data messages. If a legal regulation exists in reference to paper documents relating to a carriage contract, that regulation will also be applied to a digital message used in lieu of paper documents.[115]

Digital Signatures

Presumption of Agreement with Message

If a digital signature is attached to a data message, there is a legal presumption that the creator of the digital signature—the signatory—intended to subscribe the data message and approves of the data message's contents.[116]

Same Legal Impact as Handwritten Signature

A digital signature will be treated in the eyes of the law the same as a handwritten signature if it: (1) uniquely identifies the signatory; (2) is capable of being confirmed; (3) is under the control of the signatory, and only the signatory; (4) is connected to the data message in a manner so that, if the message is altered, the digital signature becomes invalid; and (5) complies with regulations of the Colombian government.[117]

Regulation of Certification Authorities

The Superintendent of Industry and Trade licenses Colombian Certification Authorities ("CA")[118] and is responsible for the regulation of their business operations.[119]

Licensing Qualifications

The following are required qualifications to become a CA:

(1)   either be a public/private, foreign/domestic corporation, or a chamber of commerce which has been authorized by the Superintendent of Industry and Trade;
(2)   possess sufficient financial resources to engage in a certification business;
(3)   possess technical knowledge and expertise sufficient to create and issue digital signatures, to issue related certificates, and to store the certificates; and
(4)   the entity's representative or administrator must not have a history of criminal convictions resulting in imprisonment (other than for political crimes or for criminal negligence).[120]

---

[115] ETL, art. 27.
[116] ETL, art. 28.
[117] Id.
[118] Colombian law refers to a Certification Authority as a "Certification Entity." However, Certification Authority ("CA") is a more popular term internationally and is used in this article.
[119] ETL, art. 30 and 41.
[120] ETL, art. 29.

Authorized Acts of a Licensed CA

Licensed CA's are legally empowered to engage in the following activities: (1) issue certificates in verification of: digital signatures of individuals or corporations, alterations of a data message, or related to certain rights of parties in carriage contracts; (2) generate a certified digital signature, or advertise such services; (3) provide "registration or stamping services" relating to data messages; and (4) provide filing and retention services pertaining to data messages.[121] CA's themselves determine the fees they will charge their clients.[122]

Legal Obligations of CA's

CA's are legally mandated to do the following: (1) issue certificates pursuant to the agreement it has with its subscribers; (2) utilize secure computer information systems; (3) ensure the confidentiality of the subscribers' private information in its possession; (4) plan to provide ongoing certification service to its clients; (5) promptly respond to requests of subscribers and attempt to comply with legal requests; (6) make public notices as required by the ETA and other laws; (7) cooperate with the courts in making available digital signatures and data messages under its control; (8) cooperate with the government of Colombia when audits are made of its activities; (9) prepare a publicly-available registry[123] of certificates that have been issued; and (10) draft and publish a list of standard operating procedures[124] to be employed in the conduct of its everyday business, and adhere to those procedures.[125]

Termination of CA's Obligations

A CA may discontinue its service to a subscriber if it provides the subscriber with at least ninety days' notice. On the date of termination of service, the certificates should be revoked.[126] A CA may go out of business altogether if it has received the permission of the Superintendent of Industry and Trade.[127]

A subscriber may discontinue its relationship with a CA if it gives the CA at least thirty days' notice.[128]

Certificates

A certificate issued[129] by a CA is mandated to contain the following: (1) the digital signature of the CA; (2) the name and address of the subscriber; (3) the subscriber's identity

---

[121] ETL, art. 30.

[122] ETL, art. 31.

[123] The length of time the registry must be maintained depends upon the law which controls a particular business or legal act. ETL, art. 38.

[124] The idea of a CA drafting a list of its standard operating procedures originated in the United States. In the U.S., this document is referred to as the "Certification Practice Statement," or "CPS." *See* ABA DIGITAL SIGNATURE GUIDELINES, Note 162 infra. Hong Kong is an example of a jurisdiction with detailed CPS requirements. *See* Stephen E. Blythe, Note 73 supra.

[125] ETL, art. 32.

[126] ETL, art. 33.

[127] ETL, art. 34.

[128] ETL, art. 33.

[129] Issuance of a certificate will also be assumed to have occurred if the CA maintains it in its repository. ETL, art. 36.

number; (4) the name and business address of the CA; (5) the "public password"[130] to be used by relying third parties, and the confirmation method required to be used; (6) the serial number of the certificate; and (7) the period of validity of the certificate.[131]

Subscribers may request their certificate to be revoked at any time. A subscriber must request the CA to revoke her certificate whenever her password has been lost or its security has been compromised. Regardless of whether the subscriber requests revocation, the subscriber is responsible for damages incurred by innocent third parties due to the loss or compromise of the security of the password. A CA is mandated to revoke a certificate whenever: (1) a subscriber or her agent so requests; (2) the subscriber dies; (3) a corporate subscriber is liquidated; (4) it learns that any statement contained in the certificate is false; (5) the CA's private password or the security of its computer information system has been placed in jeopardy; (6) the CA ceases its business activities, either temporarily or permanently; or (7) in response to a legal order of a court or regulatory authority.[132]

Subscribers holding a certificate have the following legal obligations: (1) to accept a digital signature from the CA or to create it using the means supplied by the CA; (2) convey necessary and accurate information to the CA; (3) ensure that the digital signature's security is maintained; and (4) promptly request the CA to revoke the certificate whenever her password has been lost or its security has been compromised.[133]

Subscribers not fulfilling these obligations will be held legally accountable.[134]

The Regulatory Agency

The Superintendent of Industry and Trade is assigned the following duties: (1) license, oversee and periodically audit CA's; (2) revoke or suspend CA's licenses and impose other sanctions against them if necessary;[135] (3) request information relating to the execution of its responsibilities; (4) revoke certificates if the CA did not apply the legal requirements; (5) if a statute mandates it to do so, appoint repositories and CA's to carry out specific functions; (6) issue certificates in support of CA's digital signatures; (7) ensure that CA's adhere to consumer protections,[136] commercial laws and are competent; and (8) issue directives relating to regulatory responsibilities of CA's.[137]

---

[130] This is often referred to as the "public key."

[131] ETL, art. 35. Certificates issued by foreign CA's may also be recognized in Colombia if a domestic CA is willing to guarantee the validity of the foreign certificate and that it is in compliance with all of the requirements for issuance of certificates under Colombian law. ETL, art. 43.

[132] ETL, art. 37.

[133] ETL, art. 39.

[134] ETL, art. 40.

[135] The Superintendent of Industry and Trade may impose penalties upon CA's and its employees that have violated the ETL, its implementation regulations or other pertinent laws, as follows: suspend or revoke the CA's license, and prohibit it from engaging in CA work (either directly or indirectly) for a period of five years; impose a fine against the CA organization in the amount of up to 2,000 times the amount of a monthly minimum legal wage currently in effect; and impose a fine against offending employees of CA's in the amount of up to 300 times the amount of a monthly minimum legal wage currently in effect. ETL, art. 42.

[136] Consumer protection laws in effect at the time of enactment of the ETL continued in effect thereafter. ETL, art. 46.

[137] ETL, art. 41.

Peruvian Computer Law

The Digital Signature Law

Peru's Law Regulating Digital Signatures and Certificates (hereinafter Digital Signature Law, or "DSL")[138] was enacted on 28 May 2000[139] in order to facilitate the use of electronic signatures.[140] The DSL provides that electronic signatures are just as valid and enforceable as ink-on-paper signatures so long as they are a "manifestation of will" of the signatory.[141] Furthermore, to achieve legal recognition under the DSL, an electronic signature must comply with high security standards by: (1) having a logical association with the data message it is attached to, (2) providing a connection with, and identifying, the signatory; and (3) ensuring the authenticity and integrity of the electronic documents it is attached to.[142]

The Role of the Digital Certificate

The Subscriber

Peru takes an open-minded perspective toward all types of electronic signatures, but shows favoritism toward the digital signature because it is best able to achieve the high security standards set by the DSL. A digital signature's "owner"[143] or subscriber is the person to whom the signature is attributed, the person whose name is on the certificate that has been issued by the CA, and the person that is associated with the attached data message.[144]

Duty of Subscriber

To Give Accurate Information

Certificates are used to verify the identity of the owner to relying third parties and to confirm that the digital signature belongs to her. In order to get a certificate, a person should apply to a CA for one to be issued in the applicant's name. In the application, the person is required to provide complete and accurate information. If the certificate is issued to the applicant, at that point she becomes the owner. Thereafter, the owner must continue to keep the CA informed of relevant information so that the certificate's contents can be kept up-to-

---

[138] Republic of Peru, LAW REGULATING DIGITAL SIGNATURES AND CERTIFICATES (hereinafter "Digital Signature Law" or "DSL"), 28 May 2000, translated by National Law Center for Inter-American Free Trade; http://natlaw.com/interam/ar/ec/tn/tnarecl.htm .

[139] DSL, Preamble. The DSL went into effect sixty (60) days after its enactment. DSL, art. 16.

[140] DSL, art. 1.

[141] Id.

[142] DSL, art. 2. The DSL assumes that the only type of electronic signature which complies with these high standards is the digital signature. On the record, however, Peru remains "technologically neutral" and open-minded toward the recognition of other types of electronic signatures utilizing different technologies. So long as the security requirements of the DSL are complied with, the DSL authorizes the Peruvian regulatory body to consider approval of other types of electronic signatures utilizing different technologies. If such approval occurs, the regulatory body would create regulations applicable to the implementation of those other electronic signatures and related technologies. DSL, Third Supplemental, Transitory and Final Provisions.

[143] Many other jurisdictions, including the U.S., refer to the owner as the "subscriber."

[144] DSL, art. 4. Peru uses the designation "Certification Agency" instead of Certification Authority ("CA"). However, CA is more popular internationally and is used in this article.

date. Furthermore, the owner has a duty to convey accurate information to third parties who are relying upon the information contained in the certificate.[145]

Contents of a Certificate

A certificate is required to include the following information: (1) information which will conclusively identify the signatory; (2) the name of the CA; (3) the public code;[146] (4) a description of the method used to confirm the signatory's identity—"a digital signature attached to a data message;" (5) the certificate's serial number; (6) the date of issuance and expiration; and (7) the CA's digital signature.[147]

Confidentiality

A Registration Agency, covered infra, has a legal duty to maintain confidentiality of information that it receives from the subscriber. The information must be gathered directly from the subscriber and not from third parties. Private codes and data relating to the digital signature which are not used in the certification process have a special need for confidentiality. These codes and data should never be released without the specific consent of the subscriber or the issuance of a court order mandating the release.[148]

Grounds for Permissive

Cancellation of a Certificate

A certificate and its related digital signature may be cancelled whenever: (1) the subscriber so requests; (2) the CA has revoked them; or (3) the period of validity of the certificate has expired.[149]

Grounds for Mandatory

Revocation of a Certificate

A certificate and its related digital signature must be revoked by the CA whenever: (1) the information in the certificate contains inaccuracies or has been changed without authorization; (2) the subscriber dies; or (3) the subscriber has breached its contract with the CA.[150]

Recognition of Foreign Certificates

The legal validity of a certificate issued in another country by a foreign CA will be recognized in Peru if the certificate is guaranteed by a Peruvian CA. The domestic CA must

---

[145] DSL, art. 5.
[146] This is what is ordinarily referred to as the "public key."
[147] DSL, art. 7.
[148] DSL, art. 8.
[149] DSL, art. 9.
[150] DSL, art 10.

be willing to attest to the certificates validity, that it was issued under procedures comparable to those of Peru, and that its period of validation has not expired.[151]

The Role of CA's and RA's

CA's

They are responsible for: (1) issuance and cancellation of certificates; (2) performing other services pertinent to certificates; and (3) attainment of security in relation to certificates and to E-commerce.[152] Additionally, the CA may carry out the functions of a Registration (Verification) Agency ("RA").[153]

RA's

They are more ministerial in nature than CA's. An RA could be described as a "CA's clerk." They perform the relatively more mundane tasks of : (1) taking applications for certificates and confirming the information that has been received pertinent to those applications; (2) confirming the identity of the subscriber to relying third parties for authentication; (3) taking requests for issuance of digital signatures, considering those requests, and authorizing requests that have merit; and (4) taking requests for cancellation of digital signatures, considering those requests, and carrying out those requests if the situation so dictates.[154]

The CA's

Repository Responsibilities

A CA is required to maintain a publicly-accessible repository of information pertaining to certificates it has issued: (1) the public code (public key); and (2) whether the certificate is currently valid (with the period of validity indicated), or has been cancelled or revoked (with the date and hour of cancellation or revocation). This repository is kept in paper copy at the office of the CA. However, as a convenience to relying third parties, the CA is also required to maintain this repository in digital form at its website as well. It is critical that all information contained in the repository pertinent to the outstanding certificates is accurate. After all, relying third parties are depending upon the contents of the certificate. The repository cannot be used for any function other than the functions stated in the DSL.[155]

Governmental Registry

The executive branch of the Government of Peru is responsible for the assignment of the responsibility of regulation of CA's and RA's to an administrative body, which will maintain

---

[151] DSL, art. 11.

[152] DSL, art. 12.

[153] Id.

[154] DSL, art. 13. Peru is the first nation the author has encountered which creates the post of Registration (Verification) Agency. In other countries, the CA alone performs all of the tasks which are carried out by the CA's and RA's in Peru.

[155] DSL, art. 14.

a registry of these two groups. Furthermore, that regulatory body will be charged with the licensing of these two groups and ensuring they are in compliance with "international technical standards."[156]

E-commerce Contract Law

Peru's E-Commerce Contract Law[157] provides for: (1) the legal validity of E-documents; (2) the acceptability of expressing one's intent to enter into a contract using digital means, such as when one clicks on an "I Agree/I Accept button;" (3) the legal recognition of contracts that are negotiated and consummated in digital form; (4) a ban on discrimination against either the electronic form or the paper form in contracts; (5) a divergence from the U.S. "mailbox" rule by recognizing that acceptance of a contract occurs not when the offeree sends the acceptance (as in the U.S.), but when the offeree receives acknowledgement of receipt from the offeror; and (6) the admissibility of electronic records as evidence in a court of law.[158]

Computer Crimes Law

Peru's Computer Crimes Law[159] adds two new articles to the Criminal Code: (1) Article 207A prohibits wrongfully gaining access to a computer information system in order to commit fraud, with a punishment of up to two years' imprisonment or 52-104 days of community service; and (2) Article 207B prohibits acts of destruction of computer software or the data contained in a computer information system, with a punishment of up to two years' imprisonment.[160]

---

[156] DSL, art. 15. CA's and RA's coming into existence before the creation of the government registry were required to complete their registration with forty-five (45) days after the creation of the registry. DSL, First Supplemental, Transitory and Final Provisions. In order to implement the DSL, the regulatory body has adopted a glossary of pertinent terms which are consistent with the definitions employed by international organizations that Peru is a member of. DSL, Second Supplemental, Transitory and Final Provisions.

[157] Republic of Peru, LAW PERMITTING ELECTRONIC CONTRACTS (LAW 27291), 24 June 2000; http://www.munizlaw.pe/Productos/Revista-Legal/2002/JUNIO.PDF#search=peru%20law%20electronic%20contracts%202027291 .

[158] Hugo Gallegos C., General Manager, Peruvian Institute for Electronic Commerce, PERU'S LEGAL FRAMEWORK FOR ELECTRONIC COMMERCE AND SOME IMPLICATIONS FOR CONSUMER PROTECTION, 14 February 2002; http://www.ftaa-alca.org/spcomm/derdoc/eci124e.ppt . *See also* Eduardo Barboza, "Electronic Contracts Under Peruvian Law," ESTUDIO LUIS ECHECOPAR GARCIA—PERU NEWSLETTER; http://www.bomchilgroup.org/permay01.html .

[159] Republic of Peru, LAW ON COMPUTER-RELATED CRIMES (LAW 27309), 17 July 2000, cited in Hugo Gallegos C. and Eduardo Barboza, Id.

[160] Id.

Computer Law of the United States

The ABA Digital Signature Guidelines

The American Bar Association ("ABA") was the first organization in the United States to address issues pertaining to regulation of digital signatures.[161] The ABA's Information Security Committee completed its final version of the Digital Signature Guidelines in 1996.[162] The preliminary draft of these Guidelines was closely followed by the State Legislature of Utah when it enacted its digital signature statute in 1995, the first state in the U.S. to do so.[163] One objective of the Guidelines was to create a legal structure that would limit the risk of legal liability to developers of digital signatures. Another objective was the establishment of a legal foundation for CA's so that they could function a trustworthy and objective third parties.[164]

In the early 1990's, the ABA took the lead in the development of its Guidelines because no U.S. legal precedents were available to deal with digital signature issues. The Guidelines established legal duties for CA's,[165] subscribers using the services of CA's,[166] and for other persons relying on digital signature certificates.[167] The Guidelines were drafted by those with expertise in PKI technology who realized that it would not be used in E-Commerce until a legal structure had been created and implemented. Thus, the Guidelines are decidedly biased in favor of PKI and do not consider other forms of electronic signatures.[168] The Guidelines pro-PKI stance undoubtedly influenced Utah as it prepared the first state digital signature statute.[169] However, only a few states were to take a prescriptive, pro-PKI attitude with abandonment of technological neutrality.[170] Most states, to greater or lesser degrees, have been more tolerant of other forms of electronic signatures.[171]

The Guidelines include general statements of principle pertaining to PKI technology. CA's must disclose digital certificates and inform relying third parties of any revocation of them.[172] The CA must confirm the identity of the applicant before issuance.[173] The Guidelines include factors to be considered by the CA in making the issuance decision in order to attain some degree of uniformity.[174] A CA's system of checking out the applicants must be

---

[161] American Bar Association ("ABA"), Section of Science & Technology, Information Security Committee, Electronic Commerce & Information Technology Division, DIGITAL SIGNATURE GUIDELINES: LEGAL INFRASTRUCTURE FOR CERTIFICATION AUTHORITIES AND SECURE ELECTRONIC COMMERCE (ABA Net, 1995 and 1996) p. 9; http://www.abanet.org/ftp/pub/scitech/ds-ms.doc .

[162] Jane Kaufman Winn, "Open Systems, Free Markets, and Regulation of Internet Commerce," 72 TUL. L. REV. 1177, 1240 (1998).

[163] Brian W. Smith & Timothy E. Keehan, "Digital Signatures: The State of the Art and the Law," 114 BANKING L.J. 506, 509-10 (1997).

[164] Note 163 supra at 1241-1242.

[165] Note 162 supra at Sec. 3.2 and Sec. 3.7.

[166] Note 162 supra at Sec. 4.3.

[167] Note 162 supra at Sec. 3.11.

[168] Note 162 supra at p. 19-20.

[169] Note 164 supra at 509-510.

[170] "Survey of State Electronic & Digital Signature Legislative Initiatives," INTERNET LAW & POLICY FORUM; http://www.ilpf.org/groups/update.htm .

[171] Thomas J. Smedinghoff & Ruth Hill Bro, Baker & McKenzie, "Electronic Signature Legislation," FINDLAW PROFESSIONALS (1999); http://profs.lp.findlaw.com/signatures/signature_6.html .

[172] Note 162 supra at Sec. 3.12.

[173] Note 162 supra at Sec. 3.7.

[174] Note 162 supra at Sec. 3.2.

trustworthy and the CA's employees must also support the system's integrity and maintenance.[175] The subscriber is definitely responsible for ensuring security and protection of his/her private key that corresponds to the public key in the certificate.[176]

Critics of the Guidelines have noted that they do not contain explicit, understandable definitions.[177] Also, the issue of legal capacity to enter an E-commerce contract is not addressed.[178] Additionally, the absence of legal precedent at the time the Guidelines were written resulted in ambiguous rules for CA's to follow in carrying out their duties.[179] For example, the Guidelines assume that the CA will not have an intimate knowledge of the applicant's business situation and will not disclose to the applicant the types of security procedures to be used in E-commerce.[180]

U.S. Model State Law: Uniform Electronic Transactions Act

After E-Commerce began to develop in the 1990s, several U.S. states enacted laws to regulate it. However, a hodgepodge of dissimilar laws began to develop, a potential obstacle in the development of U.S. interstate commerce. In an effort to move toward greater consistency and uniformity in E-Commerce law among the states, the U.S. National Conference of Commissioners on Uniform State Laws (NCCUSL) drafted the Uniform Electronic Transactions Act (UETA).[181] Since its release in 1999, UETA has been adopted in almost all of the U.S. jurisdictions, either in its original form or with amendments.[182]

Purpose

The purpose of UETA is to facilitate E-Commerce by giving electronic records and agreements the same legal status as "hard" copy records and agreements. UETA is procedural and does not affect the substantive law of contracts.[183]

Broad Definitions of Electronic Record and Signature

Several of the definitions in UETA are noteworthy. "Transaction" is broadly defined to encompass any action pertaining to business or governmental affairs which occurs between individuals, business entities, or governmental agencies.[184] "Electronic" is defined as "relating to technology having electrical, digital, magnetic, wireless, optical, electromagnetic, or similar capabilities.[185] An "electronic record" is any record "created, generated, sent,

---

[175] Note 162 supra at Sec. 3.4.
[176] Note 162 supra at Sec. 4.3.
[177] Note 163 supra at 1243.
[178] Id. at 1244.
[179] Id. at 1242.
[180] Id. at 1242.
[181] U.S. National Conference of Commissioners on Uniform State Laws, UNIFORM ELECTRONIC TRANSACTIONS ACT ("UETA"), 7A U.L.A. 20 (Supp. 2000).
[182] Christopher W. Pappas, "Comparative U.S. & E.U. Approaches to E-Commerce Regulation: Jurisdiction, Electronic Contracts, Electronic Signatures and Taxation," 31 DENV. J. INT'L L. & POL'Y 325, 341 (2002).
[183] Id.
[184] Note 182 supra at sect. 2(16).
[185] Id. at sect. 2(5).

communicated, received or stored by electronic means."[186] Finally, an "electronic signature" is considered to be an "electronic sound, symbol or process attached to or logically associated with a record and executed or adopted by a person with the intent to sign the record."[187] These are open-minded, inclusive definitions for a very good reason: UETA is "technologically neutral" and does not give any preference to more sophisticated or more secure technologies, such as PKI.[188]

Use of Electronic Agents

Under UETA, it is perfectly acceptable for a contract to be entered into through the use of an electronic agent. This is allowed even though no person was aware of the electronic agent's action or the resulting contract.[189]

Exclusions

UETA provides for several "safe havens" which escape its coverage. This model law does not apply to: (1) wills and trusts;[190] (2) transactions that are covered by the Uniform Commercial Code (UCC), other than documents invoking Section 1-107 and 1-206, Article 2 and Article 2A;[191] (3) the Uniform Computer Information Transactions Act;[192] and (4) other laws to be identified by the states.[193]

Section 7: The Centerpiece

The heart of UETA is found in Section 7, which states:

1. A record or signature may not be denied legal effect or enforceability solely because it is in electronic form.
2. A contract may not be denied legal effect or enforceability solely because an electronic record was used in its formation.
3. If a law requires a record to be in writing, an electronic record satisfies the law.
4. If a law requires a signature, an electronic signature satisfies the law.[194]

Admissibility of Electronic Records and Signatures

In any legal proceeding, "evidence of a record or signature may not be excluded solely because it is in electronic form."[195]

---

[186] Id. at sect. 2(7).
[187] Id. at sect. 2(8).
[188] Ian A. Rambarran, "I Accept, But Do They?: The Need for Electronic Signature Legislation on Mainland China," 15 TRANSNAT'L LAW 405, 419-20 (2002). However, some of the state laws passed prior to UETA give preference at trial to electronic records or signatures using PKI; the state of Illinois is an example. 5 ILL. COMP. STAT. 175/1-101 TO 175/99-1 (West 2001).
[189] Note 182 supra at sect. 14(1).
[190] Id. at sect. 3(b)(1).
[191] Id. at sect. 3(b)(2).
[192] Id. at sect. 3(b)(3).
[193] Id. at sect. 3(b)(4).
[194] Id. at sect. 7.

Sworn Statement Requirement

UETA disposes of the notarization requirement with dispatch by simply stating that an electronic record satisfies that requirement if it is attached or logically associated with the electronic signature of the person authorized to sign the record.[196]

Retention Requirement

Whenever the law requires persons to store certain records, UETA provides that such records may be retained in electronic form.[197]

E-commerce Contract Rules

Attribution

The most basic of these rules relate to attribution—whether there is a sufficient legal linkage between the message that was received and the person who purportedly sent the message. UETA provides that it is sufficient attribution if one can prove that the electronic message was transmitted as a result of that party's actions.[198]

Electronic "Mailbox" Rule

In traditional, paper-document contract law, one of the more complex issues pertains to when a contract comes into existence whenever the parties are in different locations. The "Mailbox" rule developed to cover situations in which a signed contract is mailed by the offeree to the offeror. A contract is deemed to come into existence at the moment the signed contract is posted. In the case of electronic contracts, comparable rules had to be developed; UETA supplies them. An electronic message will be considered "sent" when it is properly addressed or directed through an information processing system pursuant to the instructions of the recipient.[199] An electronic message will be considered "received" when it enters a previously designated information processing system and is capable of being retrieved by the recipient.[200] For example, if a business agreement was being made by E-mail, a contract will come into existence at the moment the offeree sends a message of acceptance to the offeror at the E-mail address provided to the offeree by the offeror. The contract will exist as soon as the acceptance could have been retrieved by the offeror, notwithstanding that the offeror has not yet read the message of acceptance. This is similar to the impact of the traditional "mailbox" rule.

Location of Sending and Receiving

UETA also contains rules governing the location that an electronic message is legally deemed to have been sent and received. Because the offeror and the offeree may reside in

---

[195] Id. at sect. 13.
[196] Id. at sect. 11.
[197] Id. at sect. 12.
[198] Id. at sect. 9.
[199] Id. at sect. 15(a)(1).
[200] Id. at sect. 15(b).

different jurisdictions, their locations are significant in determination of which jurisdiction's law will be controlling in case of a dispute. Ordinarily, a message is considered to have been sent from the sender's place of business and received at the recipient's place of business.[201]

Transferable Records

UETA effectively supplements the U.S. Uniform Commercial Code. Negotiable instruments (promissory notes under Article 3, and other documents under Article 7) are considered to be "transferable records" when in electronic form.[202] This status means that only one authoritative copy of the record is in existence and is unalterable in the "control" of a person.[203] The person in control of the negotiable instrument is the holder for purposes of transferring or negotiating that record under the Uniform Commercial Code.[204]

Summary and Conclusions

Colombian Law

Colombia's Electronic Trade Law ("ETL") covers both electronic contracts and electronic signatures. The ETL recognizes the legal validity of a data message and states that its enforceability cannot be denied merely because of its electronic form. Data messages in digital form are in compliance with a statutory requirement for a document to be written on paper. Electronic data messages with a digital signature attached to them are sufficient to comply with a statutory mandate for an ink signature to be executed on a paper document. Presentation of a digital data message is sufficient to comply with a statutory requirement for an original document to be presented. Electronic data messages are sufficient to comply with a statutory requirement for a document to be kept in storage for a given amount of time.

The ETL recognizes the legal validity of E-commerce contracts negotiated and consummated entirely with electronic data messages. Attribution rules have been adopted in reference to whether a particular electronic message that has been received can legally be considered to have originated from a particular person. Rules for acknowledgement of receipt have been formulated in order to deal with the issue of whether the receiver of an electronic message should acknowledge a data message, how it should be acknowledged, the effect upon the transmitter's performance, and the means of acknowledgement. Rules have been established pertaining to the assumed time and place that an electronic message has been sent and received. Finally, a rule deals with the issue of incorporation by reference to an attached data message.

Special rules have been developed for electronic contracts relating to transportation and delivery of goods. Electronic data messages may be used to make communiqués relating to all aspects of carriage contracts, including these: description of the goods that were shipped, instructions to be given to the carrier; authorization to deliver the goods; buyer's notification of loss or damage during shipment; and transfer of rights in the agreement.

---

[201] Id. at sect. 15(d).
[202] Id. at sect. 16.
[203] Id. at sect. 16.
[204] Id. at sect. 16 (citing U.C.C. sect. 1-201(20)).

Detailed rules have been adopted regarding digital signatures. This is an indication that, although all types of electronic signatures may be recognized, the digital signature is preferred. The attachment of a digital signature to a data message gives rise to a legal presumption that the signatory agrees with and approves the contents of the message. If the requirements are met, a digital signature has the same legal effect of an ink signature on paper.

The Superintendent of Industry and Trade licenses and regulates the activities of Certification Authorities ("CA"). To become a licensed CA, an entity must meet the qualifications, including the possession of sufficient financial resources and technical expertise. The most important acts of a CA are to issue certificates and to verify the fact that a subscriber is in possession of a private key which has been issued by the CA. CA's are allowed to go out of business only after giving sufficient notice to the regulatory authority.

The certificates issued by CA's must contain a number of items of information, including the name and address of the subscriber and the CA, and the public key to be used by relying third parties to decrypt an encrypted electronic message which has been sent by the subscriber. When the certificate is issued, the CA will also issue the private key to the subscriber which can be used to create the subscriber's digital signature. The subscriber has a legal obligation to maintain the security of the private key, and the CA must be promptly informed whenever the private key's security has been compromised. Whereupon, the CA will quickly give notice to all relying third parties of the insecure situation so that they may be on guard against possible defrauders.

Peruvian Law

Digital Signature Law

Peru's Digital Signature Law ("DSL") focuses on digital signatures and the regulation of Certification Authorities ("CA"). The DSL recognizes the legal validity of electronic signatures and declares they may be just as enforceable as an ink-and-paper signature provided: (1) they are a manifestation of the will of the signatory; and (2) they are created using high security standards which consist of a logical association between the signature and the attached document, identification of the signatory, and authenticity and integrity of the electronic documents.

The DSL is open-minded toward all digital signatures, but favors the digital signature. The subscriber is the person who applies to a CA for issuance of a certificate attesting to the fact that the subscriber has been issued a private key used to create the signatory's unique digital signature. When applying for a certificate, the subscriber is mandated to provide full and accurate information to the CA. If the application is approved, a certificate will be issued and it must contains the name and address of the subscriber, the name and address of the CA, a serial number, and the CA's digital signature.

Besides processing applications for certificates and issuing certificates, the CA performs other services relating to certificates, maintains a public repository of information pertaining to outstanding certificates and their public keys, and is responsible for attainment of a high degree of security regarding its certificates, private keys, digital signatures and E-commerce. Unlike Colombian law, Peruvian law also provides for Registration Agents ("RA") in addition to CA's. The scope of authority of the RA is more narrow than that of the CA. The RA is only authorized to perform the following ministerial duties: accept applications for certificates; confirm the information received from applicants; confirm the identity of the subscriber to relying third parties for authentication purposes; issue digital signatures to meritorious applicants; and accept and process requests for cancellation of digital signatures. A CA is also authorized to perform the functions of an RA. The RA may work for the CA either as an employee or an independent contractor. Unlike the CA, the RA does not issue certificates and does not maintain a public repository of certificates. Both CA's and RA's have a legal duty to maintain confidentiality of information they receive pertaining to subscribers. The government of Peru maintains a registry of qualified CA's and RA's.

A CA may cancel an outstanding certificate if the subscriber so requests, if a CA has revoked them, or if the period of validity has elapsed. However, an RA must revoke a certificate if it discovers that any information in it is inaccurate, upon the death of the subscriber, or there has been a breach of contract between the subscriber and the CA.

Certificates issued in foreign nations by foreign CA's may be legally recognized in Peru if a Peruvian CA is willing to attest to the certificate's validity, that it was issued under laws and regulations comparable to those of Peru, and its period of validity has not expired.

E-commerce Contract Law

The E-commerce Contract Law amended Peru's Civil Code to provide for: (1) the legal validity of E-documents; (2) the acceptability of expressing one's intent to enter into a contract using digital means; (3) the legal recognition of contracts that are negotiated and consummated in digital form; (4) a ban on discrimination against either the electronic form or the paper form in contracts; (5) the admissibility of E-contracts in a court of law; and (6) a requirement for the party electronically accepting a contractual offer to receive acknowledgement of receipt from the other party before a contract is consummated.

Computer Crimes Law

This law proscribes: (1) unlawfully accessing a computer information system in order to commit fraud; and (2) destroying another's computer software or data.

Law of the United States

The American Bar Association's Digital Signature Guidelines, released in 1995, were rather closed-minded insofar as they failed to consider all types of electronic signatures—they provided guidelines for digital signatures only. Perhaps this was the reason the first states to enact digital signature laws in the U.S. allowed only digital signatures to be used, and no other forms of electronic signatures. In other words, Utah and the other early states were technologically-specific, recognizing the legal validity of one form of technology (the digital signature) and no other. However, this viewpoint changed significantly by the time of the drafting of the U.S. Uniform Electronic Transactions Act ("UETA") in 1999. The UETA was the brainchild of the National Conference of Commissioners on Uniform State Laws, and pure or modified forms of that model law have since been adopted in a majority of the fifty U.S. states.

Instead of being technologically specific, the UETA went entirely in the opposite direction and took a technologically-neutral stance. In other words, UETA recognizes the legal validity of many types of electronic signatures, and does not favor one form of technology over the other. This is evident in UETA's open-minded, inclusive definitions of "electronic," "electronic record" and "electronic signature." Furthermore, UETA does not contain specific rules governing digital signatures: certification authority regulations, issuance and revocation of certificates; and legal liabilities of CA's. Being technologically neutral, it is natural that UETA would not contain such provisions because that would be a not-so-implicit signal of favoritism toward the digital signature (and a signal that other types of electronic signatures were in disfavor)—and UETA goes out of its way to ensure that no favoritism toward any one type of technology is shown.

At the time of its drafting, it was generally accepted that electronic documents should not be used in every conceivable type of legal situation. The fact that UETA contains a list of exclusions, therefore, should not be surprising. The exclusions include wills, trusts, some of the transactions covered by the Uniform Commercial Code, and situations in which the Uniform Computer Information Transactions Act is applicable. UETA also recognized that the state legislatures might want to add additional exclusions to this list.

The centerpiece of UETA is its recognition of electronic records and electronic signatures. The mere fact of their form is an insufficient ground on which to challenge their legal impact or enforceability. Similarly, a contract consummated wholly or in part using an electronic record cannot be contested based on that mere fact. Furthermore, an electronic record meets a statutory requirement for a record to be in writing on paper. Additionally, if a statute mandates that a signature must have been executed on a paper document in order to incur an enforceable legal right, an electronic signature affixed to an electronic record will comply with that requirement.

UETA also deftly dealt with prior statutes mandating a notarization requirement for paper documents, or requiring paper documents to be kept in storage. An electronic record "signed" by the attachment of an electronic signature is deemed to be in compliance with a notarization requirement. Furthermore, if a statute requires paper documents to be retained in storage for a given length of time, that mandate is deemed met if the records are in electronic form.

UETA includes rules pertaining to E-commerce transactions. A good example is the set of attribution rules—those rules which determine whether there is a legal presumption that a received electronic message should be assumed to have emanated from a particular transmitter. Furthermore, UETA contains the electronic equivalent of the "mailbox" rule: an acceptance is legally considered to be effective at the time it is sent by the transmitter, notwithstanding the fact that the other party may not read the message until some time later. Additionally, there are rules regarding the time and place that an electronic message can be assumed to have been sent and received. Ordinarily, it is assumed that the parties' place of business was the place of transmission or receipt of electronic messages.

A Comparison of Colombian, Peruvian and U.S. Computer Laws

Overall, the statutes of Colombia and Peru are more similar than different because they both employ a hybrid perspective in terms of technological neutrality. In other words, Colombia and Peru recognize the legal validity of all types of electronic signature, but show a preference for the digital signature by including detailed rules in reference to CA's and PKI, two concepts only associated with the digital signature. In contrast, the U.S. approach is that of technological permissiveness. In other words, the American perspective on technology not only recognizes all types of electronic signatures, but also "bends over backwards" to be totally neutral. The U.S. law does not contain any references to CA's or PKI because that would be evidence of favoritism toward the digital signature. That is the critical difference between U.S. law and that of Colombia and Peru—the latter's statutes contain extensive coverage of CA's and PKI.

Colombia's statute covers both E-commerce contracts and electronic signatures, but Peru has enacted two separate statutes pertinent to those topics. Colombian law allows electronic documents to comply with an original requirement and a retention requirement, but Peru does not. Colombia covers carriage contracts, but Peru does not. Peru provides for RA's, essentially helpers of CA's who are authorized to perform ministerial duties, but may not issue certificates or maintain a repository of them; Colombia (nor any other country that the author is aware of) does not mention RA's. Peru does not have a list of exclusions from coverage in its statute, but the American model law and the Colombian statute do contain a list of exclusions.

Recommendations for Improvement

Colombia

The author did not encounter a computer crimes statute in his research of Colombian law. If it has not enacted one, it should consider inclusion of the following computer crimes in its new statute: (a) Unauthorized Access to Computer Material; (b) Unauthorized Tampering with Computer Information; (c) Unauthorized Use of a Computer Service; (d) Unauthorized Interference in the Operation of a Computer; and (e) Unauthorized Dissemination of Computer Access Codes or Passwords. For a basic computer crimes law, the Peruvian statute (covered supra) can be used as a model. For a more comprehensive statute, the Singapore Computer Misuse Act can be used.[205]

Peru

The post of the Registration Agency ("RA")—the Certification Authority's ("CA") clerk—should be eliminated. The author has not encountered any other nation which employs such a post. Having both CA's and RA's is, in all likelihood, confusing to the general public. It also creates a situation where an RA could easily pose as a CA and issue certificates without the authority to do so.

---

[205] Republic of Singapore, COMPUTER MISUSE ACT (Cap. 50A), 30 August 1993; http://agcvldb4.agc.gov.sg/non_version/cgi-bin/cgi_gettopo.pl?actno=1998-REVED-50A .

United States

Give the Digital Signature Most-Favored Status

Presently, the United States is technologically neutral, recognizing all forms of electronic signatures with no preference exhibited for any one of them. The U.S. should change to the position taken by Colombia and Peru in terms of technological neutrality. Those two countries are essentially technologically-neutral—they recognize the validity of all types of electronic signatures—but a preference is shown for the digital signature by granting it most-favored-status. That favoritism is exhibited with a legal assumption that the digital signature provides more authenticity and integrity than other types of electronic signatures. Colombia and Peru are in the group of nations with the most progressive E-commerce laws, and the United States should join them. Accordingly, the U.S. model law should be changed to include rules relating to CA's and to PKI.

Eliminate the Exclusion for Wills

The U.S. model law excludes wills from its coverage. The result is that the model law effectively requires a will to be in paper form and for a signature to have been affixed to the paper in order for a will to be enforceable. This exclusion should be eliminated.[206]

Recommendations for Colombia and Peru

Mandatory E-Government

In order to reduce cost and to make governmental functions more convenient for citizens, E-government needs to be emphasized and mandated. E-government statutes are becoming more and more prevalent around the world.[207] Colombia and Peru should enact such statutes in order to establish deadlines for implementation of online government services in those departments which are most amenable to them. In Hong Kong, for example, a substantial number of government services may now be accessed online, e.g., the scheduling of an interview for a visa or the scheduling of a wedding before a public official.[208]

Assert Long-Arm Jurisdiction

Against Foreign Parties

Because so many of the E-commerce transactions incurred by Colombians and Peruvians will be with foreign parties, it would be prudent for these two nations to explicitly state their claim of "long arm" jurisdiction against any party who is a resident or citizen of a foreign

---

[206] There is evidence that the aversion to electronic wills is beginning to dissipate. In 2005, the U.S. State of Tennessee became the first American jurisdiction to recognize the legal validity of a will that is executed with an electronic signature. *See* Chad Michael Ross, Comment, "Probate—Taylor v. Holt—The Tennessee Court of Appeals Allows a Computer Generated Signature to Validate a Testamentary Will," 35 U. MEM. L. REV. 603 (2005).

[207] For an example, see Republic of Finland, Ministry of Justice, ACT ON ELECTRONIC SERVICES AND COMMUNICATION IN THE PUBLIC SECTOR, 1 February 2003; http://www.finlex.fi.

[208] *See* Stephen E. Blythe, Note 73 supra.

country, so long as that party has established "minimum contacts" with Colombia or Peru.[209] Minimum contacts will exist, for example, if a cyber-seller outside of either country makes a sale to a party living within one of those nations. In that situation, the computer laws of Colombia or Peru should be applicable to the foreign party because that party has had an effect upon the respective country through the transmission of an electronic message that was received in Colombia or Peru. The foreign party should not be allowed to evade the jurisdiction of the Colombian or Peruvian courts merely because she is not physically present in the country. After all, E-commerce is an inherently international phenomenon.

Recommendations for all Three Nations

More Stringent Consumer Protections

All three nations are deficient in consumer protections for E-commerce buyers. The Republic of Tunisia can be used as a model for good consumer protections. The Tunisian E-commerce statute gives consumers: (1) a "last chance" to review the order before it is entered into; (2) a 10-day window of opportunity to withdraw from the agreement after it has been made; (3) a right to a refund if the goods are late or if they do not conform to the specifications; and (4) no risk during the 10-day trial period after the goods have been received. Tunisian E-consumers enjoy some of the best protections in the world.[210]

Information Technology Courts

Because of the specialized knowledge often required in the adjudication of E-commerce disputes, Information Technology Courts should be established as a court-of- first-instance for them. The I.T. Courts would be tribunals consisting of three experts. The chairperson would be an attorney versed in E-commerce law, and the other two persons would be an I.T. expert and a business management expert. The attorney would be required to hold a law degree and be a member of the bar with relevant legal experience; the I.T. person would be required to hold a graduate degree in an I.T.-related field and have experience in that field; and the business management expert would be required to hold a graduate degree in business administration and have managerial experience. The E-commerce law of Nepal can be used as a model.[211]

---

[209] The Republic of Tonga is an example of a nation that has claimed long-arm jurisdiction over E-commerce parties, and its statute may be used as a model. *See* Stephen E. Blythe, Note 83 supra.

[210] Republic of Tunisia, ELECTRONIC EXCHANGES AND ELECTRONIC COMMERCE LAW, 2000, art. 25-37; http://www.bakernet.com.org. See Stephen E. Blythe, Note 82 supra. One of the few nations that may offer better consumer protections is Korea. That country has enacted a separate statute specifically for E-commerce consumer protections—the E-Commerce Transactions Consumer Protection Act. *See* Korean Legislation Research Institute, Act on the Consumer Protection in the Electronic Commerce Transactions (hereinafter "CPA"), STATUTES OF THE REPUBLIC OF KOREA, Vol. 13, pp. 481 to 485-30. Originally enacted by Law No. 6687 (30 March 2002), and amended by Act Nos. 7315, 7344 and 7487 (all of which became effective by 1 April 2006). For an analysis of the CPA, *see* Stephen E. Blythe, Note 80 supra. Iran also provides good consumer protections, including a window of opportunity to withdraw from an E-transaction previously entered into; however, the window in Iran is only seven days, as opposed to Tunisia's ten days. *See* Stephen E. Blythe, Note 78 supra.

[211] Nepal, ELECTRONIC TRANSACTIONS ORDINANCE NO. 32 OF THE YEAR 2061 B.S. (2005 A.D.), s 60-71. The original version, in Nepalese Language, is available at the website of the Nepal Telecommunications Authority; http://www.nta.gov.np/cyber_law.html. An official English version was released by the Nepal Ministry of Law, Justice and Parliamentary Affairs and was published in the *Nepal Gazette* on 18 March 2005; http://www.hlcit.gov.np/pdf/englishcyberlaw.pdf. See Stephen E. Blythe, Note 55 supra.

In: Peer-to-Peer Networks and Internet Policies
Editors: Diego Vegros and Jaime Sáenz, pp. 77-107

ISBN: 978-1-60876-287-3
© 2010 Nova Science Publishers, Inc.

Chapter 3

A FRAMEWORK TO INTEGRATE THE GULF OF MEXICO DATA SOURCES[*]

Longzhuang Li[†]

Department of Computing Sciences, Texas A&M University-Corpus Christi,
Corpus Christi, TX, USA

Yonghuai Liu[‡]

Department of Computer Science, Aberystwyth University, Ceredigion, UK

Abstract

The integration of a variety of environmental, hydrographic, meteorological, and oceanographic data collected from the Gulf of Mexico (GOM) will become a valuable resource for the public, local government officials, scientists, natural resource managers, and educators. Due to the nature of the schematic heterogeneity, domain diversification, and unstable availability of the Internet-based data, a new framework is proposed and being developed to integrate and retrieve results from the underlying data sources to answer user queries.

The framework is a peer-to-peer based system, called GDS (the Gulf of Mexico Dataspace), which exploits a hybrid method to handle a user's query. To be more specific, the current data is searched and retrieved on demand in real time from the Internet while the historical data is returned from the data archives created by employing a client-server grid architecture, integrated rule-oriented data system (iRODS). In the framework, a peer represents the data sources from an application domain, and peers share information with each other through the attribute mapping and JXTA communication technique. In addition, spatial features, such as partonomic, distance, topological relations, and directional relations between data sources, are utilized and developed to facilitate the data retrieval and integration of spatial-related data from the GOM.

---

[*] Research is supported in part by the National Science Foundation under grant CNS-0708596 and CNS-0708573.
[†] E-mail address: Longzhuang.Li@tamucc.edu
[‡] E-mail address: yyl@aber.ac.uk

1. Introduction

Historically, environmental, hydrographic, eteorological, and oceanographic data have been collected by numerous local, state, and federal agencies as well as by universities around the Gulf of Mexico (GOM). Currently, users have to manually interact with these large collections of Internet data sources, determine which ones to access and how to access, and manually merge results from different sources. Without an adequate system and personnel for managing data, the magnitude of the effort needed to deal with such large and complex data sets can be a substantial barrier to the GOM research community.

The common problem faced by organizations today is to query multiple, disparate information sources and repositories, including databases, object stores, knowledge bases, file systems, digital libraries, and information retrieval systems, etc. Sometimes observers or decision makers may need information from heterogeneous sources, but they are unable to get and fuse the required information in a timely fashion because of difficulty in accessing the data source systems and also the information gathered may be inconsistent and at times contradictory.

On December 17, 2004, the US Ocean Commission created IOOS, the Integrated Ocean Observing System [31]. The IOOS calls for the creation of regional associations of ocean observing systems. To that end, the GOM Coastal Ocean Observing System (GCOOS) (see Figure 1) was created as a grassroots effort to foster cooperation among the Gulf states to augment and integrate a sustained observing system for the GOM as part of the IOOS. Unfortunately, neither IOOS nor GCOOS is funded by the Federal government at levels that will promote systems development or implementation at the state or local levels. The need to move forward with the implementation of a regional system falls on the local and state governments as well as universities and other research groups. As a result, GCOOS does not yet exist as an implementation. In addition, GCOOS lacks the highly desired biological and ecological components.

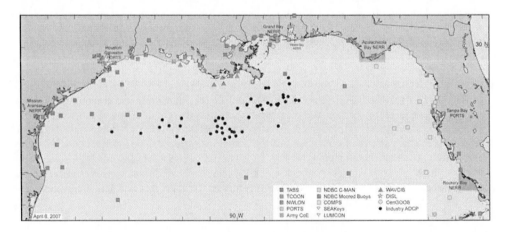

Figure 1. GOM ocean observing systems (GCOOS)[1].

This paper is to propose and develop a data integration framework, called GDS (the Gulf of Mexico Dataspace), which enables researchers to store, manage, analyze, query, visualize,

---

[1] http://gcoos.tamu.edu/old-site/System/gom.htm

and disseminate multi-dimensional data sets in a variety of related research domains. The proposed GDS framework exploits a hybrid method to handle a user's information needs (see Figure 2). To be more specific, the current data is searched and retrieved on demand in real time from the Internet while the historical data is returned from the data archives created by employing an existing grid architecture, integrated rule-oriented data system (iRODS) [50]. In the infrastructure, a peer represents the data sources from an application domain, and peers share information with each other through the attribute mapping and JXTA communication technique [34]. In addition, spatial features, such as partonomic, distance, topological relations, and directional relations [43,65] between data sources, are utilized and developed to facilitate the data retrieval and integration of spatial-related data from the GOM.

2. The GOM Data Sources

The data incorporated into the system is derived from a variety of sources and formats, which will include both real time and historical data containing spatial as well as temporal components. By referring to the Gulf of Alaska Ecosystem Monitoring and Research Program [22], we have identified sources of the GOM data sources as follows:

Observational Data. Observational data are collected by human observation, laboratory results, and manual data entry. These data includes species counts and locations and can include a large number of ad hoc observations of conditions or unrelated sightings, which are unrepeatable. This kind of data is generally less consistent, low volume, and error prone because they are manually recorded to capture a person's observations or calculations. Te metadata describing collection and or processing location and sometimes the conditions is not standardized and interoperable.

An example of this type of data is the fish databases, such as FishBase and FishNet, which can be integrated by Darwin Core [9]. The *Darwin Core* is a developing standard schema expressed in XML to facilitate the exchange of information about the geographic occurrence of species and the existence of specimens in collections.

Measured Data. These data are mostly measurements of physical variables such as water level, air temperature or salinity, but they may also include biological variables as in the case of the acoustic measurements of the biomass of nekton or zooplankton. These data are collected automatically and usually stored in files/databases with formats that are consistent with the collection instrument. The size of the files and the number of the files can be large, but still lack of interoperability with other systems. The metadata include instrument details and conditions, and the data formats are standard enough to allow customized processing during retrieval.

An example of the observational data sources is the GCOOS in situ observations (see Figure 1), which providing continuing measurements of physical and ecosystem data on the GOM. Among all the GCOOS in situ observational systems, (1) TCOON, TABS, and NWLON, etc. measure the physical aspects, such as water level and wind speed; (2) NERR, WAVCIS, and LUMCON cover the ecosystem aspects, such as DissolvedInOrgranicNitrogen and OxygenSaturation.

Geographic Data. These data are the data collected by GIS and include base layers such as elevation (bathymetry) and shorelines, but can also include soil types or habitat characterization. These data are usually interoperable across different systems and may be stored at several different locations. The metadata are focused on the spatial definition and may include information about the resolution or precision of the data.

There are a number of world databases that provide coral reef data in the GOM, such as OBIS (Ocean Biogeographic Information System), WoRMS (World Register of Marine Species), EOL (Encyclopedia of Life). Especially, NOAA (National Oceanic and Atmospheric Administration) website is the best place to look for coral reef databases and programs from using satellite imagery to predict coral bleaching to coral MPA networks. Also, the National Oceanic Data Center and National Coral Reef Institute include all data collected in the Gulf (and elsewhere).

Remotely Sensed Data. Remotely sensed data can come from satellite or aerial platforms. These are generally large files and may be used on a regular basis by the analysis being conducted by the researchers. These data will require a large amount of storage and are quite interoperable with GIS and image-analysis tools. The metadata describe the instrument and platform and often include details of the image quality and the spatial reference system.

A number of satellite image sources on meteorology and environment, such as *Texas Meteorological Satellite Images* and *Satellite Wind Products*, are available over the GOM. Those satellite images are taken periodically in order to observe the weather changes. Some of the observation systems have been operating for years and their database schemas are quite stable and similar, including attributes *satellite*, *region*, *date*, and *product*, etc. Even new sources are added later, the database schemas of new sources will not differ much from the existing ones.

Modeled Data. Data of this type is generated in a high volume by utilizing numeric models, and to some degree statistical models. As an example, the harmonic analysis can provide a prediction of water level along the coast of the GOM at real time. However, unlike most other data sets, these data can be recreated. These data are consistent across the data set and are not generally interoperable. The metadata need to describe the classification and version of the model and may need to include relevant input parameters. In this framework, we are not going to integrate this type of data.

3. Framework

Designing and implementing this framework is a challenge in itself, given highly distributed and heterogeneous data resources of a variety of domains as well as a lack of interchange standards (formal metadata content specifications and domain ontologies) and information about the relationships among various programs and projects.

We design a flexible GDS system, which is a peer-to-peer system and consists of multiple peers such that data from different domains could be easily incorporated and shared. Each peer should be allowed to join or leave the system without disturbing the regular operation. From a user's perspective, she should be able to ask queries that span multiple data sources without requiring the data to be standardized or requiring her to query each single database in isolation, and should be able to receive the query results in a certain time limit. In addition, the system should be easily maintained and allow for the future augment and expansion.

As a result, the proposed GDS system will exploit a hybrid method to store, manage, and handle the data and a user's information need. On the one hand, the historical data is returned from the data archives created by employing an existing grid architecture, integrated rule-oriented data system (iRODS), which will store as much as necessary a replication of data from various GOM in situ observing databases and the biological and ecological databases as well as some satellite imagery. The archives can guarantee that the important historical data will be available during the natural disaster, such as in the hurricane season. On the other hand, the current/new data is searched and retrieved on demand in real time from the Internet because it is impractical/unaffordable to save all the data in the archives out of the consideration of storage cost and update effort needed. In addition, we will adhere to standards wherever possible and use open source wherever possible. For example, the EML (Ecological Markup Language) and Darwin Core will be used integrate the ecological data.

In this paper, a peer represents a set of mediated data sources from the same application domain, and peers share information with each other through the attribute mappings and JXTA communication technique. In addition, spatial features, such as partonomic, distance, topological relations, and directional relations [StH04] between data sources, are utilized and developed to facilitate the data retrieval and integration of spatial-related data from the GOM.

3.1. System Architecture

The GDS framework has two types of integration, the virtual as well as the materialized data integration [18,19,26,32,35]. The virtual data integration employs a peer-to-peer database network to incorporate data sources in different domains, with each peer making use of a mediator to integrate the data from the databases of the same domain. The materialized data integration is fulfilled via the mirror and duplicate the historical data in the iRODS archives [49,64,70].

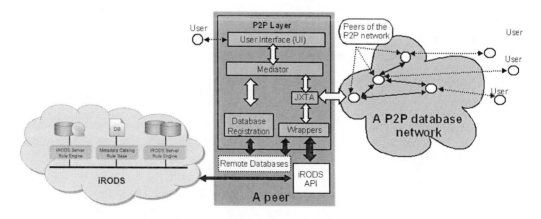

Figure 2. The architecture of the proposed community infrastructure.

The system architecture, inspired by [4,16,50], is presented in Figure 2. A peer consists of P2P Layer, remote databases, and iRODS API. P2P Layer consists of User Interface (UI), Mediator, JXTA, Database Registration, and Wrappers. Peers connect to a P2P database network by means of connecting to other peer(s) (see Figure 2).

By means of the UI users can carry out network queries and iRODS API operations, browse streaming results, start peer discovery procedures, and so on. Among other things, the UI allows to control other modules of P2P Layer. For instance, user can modify the set of coordination rules defined in the JXTA w.r.t. other peers, define connection details for Wrapper, etc. Mediator processes both user queries and queries coming from the network. JXTA is responsible for all peer's activities on the network, such as discovering of previously unknown peers, creating pipes with other nodes, sending messages containing queries, or query results, etc. Wrappers manage connections to remote databases and execute data format conversion. This is a module which is adjusted depending on the underlying databases. For instance, when a remote database does not support disjunctive queries, then this is the responsibility of Wrapper to provide this support. Database registration service is utilized to specify a new remote data source in order to make the mediator aware of the new data source available.

The remote databases rectangle has dashed border to mean that the current/recent data is retrieved on demand in real time from the remote sites which we have no control, while the solid border of iRODS API rectangle represents that the historical data will be returned via iRODS archives. The data sources can be relational databases, XML repositories, plain text, images, or excel files, etc. When a user requests data from iRODS servers, the metadata catalog will provide the lookup information on which iRODS server contains the asked data. iRODS itself is a grid-based distributed system operating continuously, in parallel, and in multiple locations. These parallel systems would provide redundancy and backup that would allow continuous data and information availability to the outside user in the event of a localized or coast wide event.

3.2. Virtual Data Integration

Next, the virtual data integration components of the GDS framework are presented. Especially, the current data integration approaches and our design for data sources in different domains as well as in the same domain are discussed.

3.2.1. Virtual Peer-to-peer Data Integration for Sources in Different Domains

Many P2P-based integration approaches have been developed and proposed since the year 2001. Those approaches can be roughly classified into two categories: fully decentralized P2P systems [16,52,61,62,63] and mediator-based P2P systems [1, 28,52]. In the fully decentralized P2P systems, no global schema is assumed and coordination rules allow data retrieval and updates from one peer to another. Mappings are defined in each peer by a data curator. The problems with the type of approaches are: (1) The complex schema mapping rules have to be defined. (2) Users can easily flood the network with queries. (3) It is difficult to identify redundant data and enforce integrity constraints. (4) Sometimes it is a long path to reach other nodes. (5) Query answering is undecidable in general. In the mediator-based P2P systems (see Figure 3), each peer consists of a mediator and a set of relevant data sources. The mediator, where the domain schema is defined, is utilized to facilitate the schema mapping between peers as well as provide an easy communication tool between the mediator and the underlying data sources (See Figure 3). One of the difficulties with this type of approaches is how to create mediators that incorporate various query capabilities of the underlying data sources [11]. In the GDS framework, the mediator-based P2P approach is followed to access the underlying distributed and heterogeneous sources of variant domains and answer complex queries.

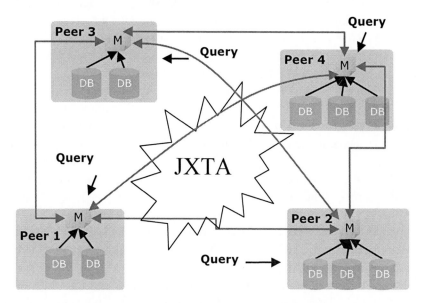

Figure 3. Mediator-based peer-to-peer data integration system.

There are two ways to map from one peer to another peer, peer schema mapping and attribute value mapping. The peer schema mapping approaches employ the coordination rules to connect two peers [1,15,16,27,28,29,53,54,55,61,63], while the attribute value mapping approaches build the relationships by relating the attribute values from different peers [2,36,37]. For the data sources around the GOM, the peer schema mapping approach is a more appropriate choice, where the databases of different domains and with heterogeneous schemas are connected by coordination rules. Each peer can not only be queried in its domain schema for data, but also fetch data from its neighbors if the coordination rules are present. The semantic relationships between peers of different domains are created using location and/or time. For example, the meteorological information can be obtained according to where and when the fish was found.

Each peer in the system utilizes JXTA technology to communicate with others. The open source, JXTA, is a set of XML based protocols to cover typical P2P functionality. It provides a Java binding offering a layered approach for creating P2P applications (core, services, applications). In addition to remote service access (such as offered by SOAP), JXTA provides additional P2P protocols and services, including peer discovery, peer groups, peer pipes, and peer monitors.

3.2.2. Mediator-based Data Integration for Sources in the Same Domain

In the mediator-based integration for source in the same domain (see Figure 4, which integrates five GOM ocean observational data sources, TCOON, TABS, NWLON, NDBC, and COMPS.), a uniform query interface in each peer is provided to take a user's query over a mediated schema in the first place, then the global query is broken down to sub-queries over local data sources and the local data is retrieved and renamed/reformatted in accordance with the mediated schema by utilizing wrappers. There are two major techniques, the *Global as View* (GAV) [5,6,21,24,46,57,59] and *Local as View* (LAV) [14,25,38,39,40,47], to describe the mapping between the mediated schema and the underlying local schemas. In the *GAV*, the mediated schema is designed to be a view over the sources. The *GAV* is very easy conceptually and is used due to the simplicity involved in answering queries issued over the mediated schema. The drawback of the *GAV* is the need to rewrite the view for the mediated schema whenever a new source is to be integrated and/or an existing source changes its schema [30]. On the other hand, In the *LAV* each data source is expressed as a view over the mediated schema. The *LAV* is very flexible and employs the power of the entire query language to define the contents of local sources [25,47]. A change to a data source can be handled locally by modifying only view descriptions concerning this source. Hence, the *LAV* can easily distinguish between contents of closely related sources, and is the primary choice to integrate data sources of the same domain. But we still allow some domain to be integrated based on the *GAV* approach if this domain is well established and very stable.

Registration of new data source is based on property statements and schema information, basically telling the network, which kind of schema the data source uses, with some possible value constraints.

For each peer, the mediator should be developed in a unified format compatible with the developing national standards, also called ontologies [8,12,69]. This would make it easy to incorporate the heterogeneous data sources as well as ensure that the data collected and provided would be as widely utilized as possible. For example, the mediator of the fish data sources will follow the Darwin Core.

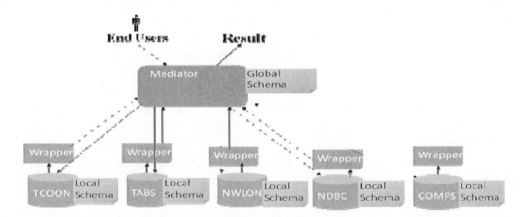

Figure 4. Mediator architecture for data sources of the same domain.

In mediator systems, the data sources to be integrated generally have different limitations and ways that users have to follow to query on their Web interface. For example, to retrieve data from TCOON[2] and TABS[3], TCOON requires at least one station from a station list and at least one field from a list of series identifiers, while TABS mandates only one station ID. Next, we present how to incorporate the query capabilities of multiple underlying data sources in the mediator design [LFG08].

3.3. iRODS Data Archives

The iRODS system is based on expertise gained through nearly a decade of applying the Storage Resource Brokage (SRB) technology [48] in support of Data Grids, Digital Libraries, Persistent Archives, and Real-time Data Systems [50]. With too many functions and hard-coded operations, SRB is quite complex and any extension or modification is not an easy task. As a result, iRODS system was developed to provide flexible collection management by using the rule-based architecture. In particular, micro services can be defined and triggered by the rules ustomly defined at user/collection level.

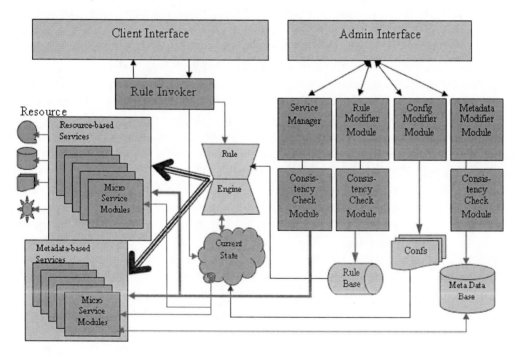

Figure 5. Architecture of iRODS data archive system [58].

The architecture of the iRODS system is shown in Figure 5 [58]. The architecture consists of two components, the administrative commands needed to manage the rules via the administration interface, and the rules that invoke data management modules by the client interface [58]. When a user invokes a service, it fires a rule that uses the information from the rule base, status, and metadata catalog to invoke micro-services. The micro-services either change the metadata catalog or change the resource (read/write/create/etc).

---

[2] http://lighthouse.tamucc.edu/pq/
[3] http://tabs.gerg.tamu.edu/Tglo/

Before a data source can be archived in the iRODS, it is required to be registered into the metadata catalog. Descriptive metadata can be based on some standard schema or ontology, e.g., Dublin Core for provenance information the Federal Geographic Data Committee standard to describe geo-spatial data.

4. Query Capabilities and Interface Design

On the Web, data sources typically publish their query processing capabilities through query forms or base-view templates, which are filled out by users and submitted to the data sources as queries. Each data source may have more than one base view. We allow users to select single or multiple values for an attribute, and allow the answers to come from a subset of the data sources for the union operator. In this paper we use *data source* and *base view* interchangeably.

All the current methods [56,66,71] demand that the mediator queries satisfy the query conditions of all the underlying data sources for the union operator. This requirement is impractical in our data integration on the GOM. Unlike the simple bookstore database examples in [56,66,71], each GOM database measures and collects various environmental, biological, or ecological information at different locations with different sample rates. Although some attributes are measured by multiple GOM databases, no two GOM databases contain the same values for these attributes because they are measured at different locations and different times. In addition, the data collected from the GOM is usually limited and incomplete. As a consequence, even partial results are highly desirable for the GOM research, if not all the databases satisfy the query conditions for the union operator. For example, to retrieve data from TCOON and TABS, we must select at least one TCOON station and only one TABS station, but each station is exclusive, belonging to TCOON or TABS but not both.

In [41], we extended the method in [YLG99] in several aspects. First, it allows users to select single or multiple values for an attribute. For example, the method in [71] only permits the single value selection for an attribute, which can not emulate multiple value selections for TCOON's station ID or series identifier attribute. Second, it allows the partial answer from a subset of data sources, if not all data sources satisfy the query conditions for the union operator. Correspondingly, we develop the preprocessing technique to handle the partial answer. And finally, we employ the new attribute adornments for the design of a mediator's user interface.

4.1. Attribute Adornments

We use attribute adornments to specify how the attributes participate in supported queries. In [41], we adapted and extended the five attribute adornments (f, u, b, c, o) developed in [71] to the following eleven adornments:

- f: the attribute value is optional in the query;
- u: the attribute value can not be specified in the query;
- b: one attribute value must be specified in the query;
- $sc[l]$: one attribute value must be chosen from the list l;

- $mc[l]$: one or more attribute values must be chosen from the list l;
- $so[l]$: the attribute is optional in the query, and if specified, one attribute value must be chosen from the list l;
- $mo[l]$: the attribute is optional in the query, and if specified, one or more attribute values must be chosen from the list l.
- $bsc[l]$: one attribute value must be specified or chosen from the list l, which is equivalent to b or $sc[l]$;
- $bmc[l]$: one attribute value must be specified in the query, or one or more attribute values must be chosen from the list l, which is same as b or $mc[l]$,
- $fso[l]$: the attribute is optional in the query, and if specified, it may be a user specified value or be chosen from the list l, which is equivalent to f or $so[l]$;
- $fmo[l]$: the attribute is optional in the query. it may be a user specified value or multiple values are chosen from the list l, which is same as f or $mo[l]$.

The first seven adornments are used to model both the data source and mediator's query capabilities, while the last four adornments are employed mostly for the capability interface design of the mediators. In particular, $bsc[l]$ and $bmc[l]$ can be simplified to b, and $fso[l]$ and $fmo[l]$ to f, respectively, if the list $l \subset b$ or $l \subset f$. But we choose to keep the last four adornments for two reasons: (1) we intend to emulate the underlying data sources' user interface as much as possible; (2) the users do not have to remember the mandatory/optional list of values in the underlying data sources. On the other hand, if the list l contains all the eligible values for the attribute, such that $l \equiv b$ or $l \equiv f$, $bsc[l]$ and $bmc[l]$ can be simplified to $sc[l]$ and $mc[l]$, and $fso[l]$ and $fmo[l]$ to $so[l]$ and $mo[l]$, respectively. But in the following sections, we assume that $l \subset b$ or $l \subset f$.

Next, we focus on computing mediator view templates for base views. Both mediator views and base views as well as the associated adornments are represented using the notation $R(ATTR_1 \ (adorn_1), ATTR_2 \ (adorn_2), ..., ATTR_n \ (adorn_n))$. For example, a data source view $D(X \ (b), Y \ (f), Z \ (u))$ means that the data source D has three attributes X, Y, and Z, and the associated adornments are b, f, and u, respectively. An instance of the source is $D(x_i, y_i, z_i)$.

4.2. Query Processing

In this section, we present three mediator query processing techniques, *preprocessing*, *post-filtering*, and *pass binding*. By combining the above three techniques, we can answer more user queries as well as obtain more comprehensive query results.

Because a mediator query does not have to satisfy the query requirements of all the underlying data sources for the union operator, preprocessing means we break down the query into sub-queries and submit them to the appropriate data sources. The same sub-query may be submitted more than once because we allow the users to choose multiple values for an attribute. Post-filtering means that the returned results from a base view can be filtered according to the pre-specified attribute values. Pass binding is a technique that passes values from one base view to another base view for the common attributes in both base views. Since the attribute values returned from one base view query can be passed to the next base view query to satisfy the join requirements, the order to execute the sub-queries is important. Next, two examples demonstrate the usage and effectiveness of the above three techniques for union and join operators, respectively. For more detail, please refer to [41].

4.2.1. Union Views

The symmetric Table 1 presents the union-view attribute adornment template computed from the two base-view attribute adornments. For example, the combination of f and b is f because even if the data source with the b adornment can not execute without specifying a value, the second data source with f adornment can still return some partial results. When only one attribute adornment contains a list of single or multiple choices, users are able to specify a value or choose value(s) from the list. For instance, the combination of f and $sc[l5]$ is $fso[l5]$, which means for the attribute users have three options: either specify a value not in the list $l5$, leave it blank, or choose a value from the list $l5$. For the first two options, the query is submitted only to the data source with the f adornment, while for the third option, the query is submitted to the both data sources.

When the attribute adornment of a data source is u, the mediator can start a query on the data source without specifying a value for this attribute and then filter out the results that are not supported by a value optionally specified by the mediator query for this attribute in the post-processing step. As a result, the u adornment is treated the same way as the f adornment. For example, the combination of u and $sc[l_7]$ is $fso[l_7]$. For this case, no matter what value is specified or chosen and whether or not the value is in l_7, the results from the data source with the u adornment can be filtered in the post-processing step using the given value. Similarly, the union-view combination of so or mo adornments with other adornments can be computed.

Table 1. Union-view template using both preprocessing and post-filtering techniques

	f	**u**	**b**	**sc[l5]**	**mc[l6]**	**so[l7]**	**mo[l8]**
f	f	f	f	$fso[l_5]$	$fmo[l_6]$	$fso[l_7]$	$fmo[l_8]$
u	f	f	f	$fso[l_5]$	$fmo[l_6]$	$fso[l_7]$	$fmo[l_8]$
b	f	f	b	$bsc[l_5]$	$bmc[l_6]$	$fso[l_7]$	$fmo[l_8]$
sc[l1]	$fso[l_1]$	$fso[l_1]$	$bsc[l_1]$	$sc[l_1 \cup l_5]$	$mc[l_1 \cup l_6]$	$fso[l_1 \cup l_7]$	$fmo[l_1 \cup l_8]$
mc[l2]	$fmo[l_2]$	$fmo[l_2]$	$bmc[l_2]$	$mc[l_2 \cup l_5]$	$mc[l_2 \cup l_6]$	$fmo[l_2 \cup l_7]$	$fmo[l_2 \cup l_8]$
so[l3]	$fso[l_3]$	$fso[l_3]$	$fso[l_3]$	$fso[l_3 \cup l_5]$	$fmo[l_3 \cup l_6]$	$fso[l_3 \cup l_7]$	$fmo[l_3 \cup l_8]$
mo[l4]	$fmo[l_4]$	$fmo[l_4]$	$fmo[l_4]$	$fmo[l_4 \cup l_5]$	$fmo[l_4 \cup l_6]$	$fmo[l_4 \cup l_7]$	$fmo[l_4 \cup l_8]$

Example 1

Given two data sources $D_1(X\ (b),\ Y\ (f),\ Z\ (sc[l_1]))$ and $D_2(X\ (b),\ Y\ (u),\ Z\ (u))$, the union-view mediator M of D_1 and D_2 is defined as $M(X\ (b),\ Y\ (f),\ Z\ (fso[l_1]))$. With the preprocessing and post-filtering techniques, the query $M(x_1, y_1, Z)$ can only retrieve partial result from D_2 because the query condition for D_1 is not satisfied. With the pass binding, results can be obtained from both D_1 and D_2. To retrieve the answer for query $M(x_1, y_1, Z)$, the mediator first invokes the feasible subquery $D_2(x_1, Y, Z)$, then applies the condition $(Y = y_1)$ on the result of $D_2(x_1, Y, Z)$ to get $D_2(x_1, y_1, Z)$. Furthermore, the mediator can pass the attribute Z values from D_2 to D_1. In particular, for each value z_i of Z from the results of $D_2(x_1, y_1, Z)$, the mediator invokes the sub-query $D_1(x_1, y_1, z_i)$ if $z_i \in l5$. The union of the results from D_1 subqueries and D_2 sub-query provides the answer to the query $M(x_1, y_1, Z)$.

The query in Example 1 is not answerable by the existing methods [56,66,71] because the existing methods require the mediator queries to satisfy the query conditions of all the underlying data sources, but can be answered by the combination of preprocessing technique and partial results from the underlying data sources.

4.2.2. Join Views

A mediator with the preprocessing technique treats a query on a join view as follows. First, the mediator query is broken down to the sub-queries and passed to the each corresponding joining base view, then the results from each base view are joined. For the mediator on a join view, the join attributes need to appear in every joining base views and the non-join attributes appears in only one of the base views. In addition, answers are required from both joining base views, which is different from the union-view templates in Table 1 because a union-view template allows the partial answer from only one base view. As a result, the computation of attribute adornments in a join-view template is different from that in a union-view template.

To join two base views, the adornments of all the non-join attributes are simply copied over from the base view templates. The adornment computation of the join attributes in two base view templates is shown in Table 2. In Table 2, when both base-view attribute adornments must choose from their given lists, the two lists are intersected. On the other hand, when both base-view adornments offer the optional choices from the given lists, the two lists are unioned together. For example, the combination of $sc[l_1]$ and $mc[l_6]$ is $mc[l_1 \cap l_6]$ because the multiple chosen values from $l_1 \cap l_6$ can be sent one by one to the base-view with the adornment $sc[l_1]$, then results are joined with those from the base-view with the adornment $mc[l_6]$. Another example is that the base-view adornments $so[l_3]$ and $so[l_7]$ generates the join-view adornment as $fso[l_3 \cup l_7]$ because if when both base view adornments are so or mo, the mediator can start a query on base views without specifying a value for this attribute and then filter out the results using the optional specified attribute value in the post-filtering step. The treatment of u with so or mo is similarly defined.

When combining f with $so[l_7]$ and $mo[l_8]$, the resulting join-view adornments are $fso[l_7]$ and $fmo[l_8]$, respectively. Because if a specified value is not in l_7 or l_8, then the base view with the adornment $so[l_7]$ or $mo[l_8]$ is treated with no value specified for the attribute. Similarly, the computation for the combination of b with $so[l_7]$ and $mo[l_8]$ are $fso[l_7]$ and $fmo[l_8]$, respectively, and the combination for the combination of u with $so[l_7]$ and $mo[l_8]$ are $fso[l_7]$ and $fmo[l_8]$, respectively.

Table 2. Join-view template using preprocessing, post-filtering, and pass binding

	f	u	b	sc[l₅]	mc[l₆]	so[l₇]	mo[l₈]
f	f	f	f	$so[l_5]$	$mo[l_6]$	$fso[l_7]$	$fmo[l_8]$
u	f	f	f	$so[l_5]$	$mo[l_6]$	$fso[l_7]$	$fmo[l_8]$
b	f	f	b	$sc[l_5]$	$mc[l_6]$	$fso[l_7]$	$fmo[l_8]$
$sc[l_1]$	$so[l_1]$	$so[l_1]$	$sc[l_1]$	$sc[l_1 \cap l_5]$	$mc[l_1 \cap l_6]$	$so[l_1]$	$so[l_1]$
$mc[l_2]$	$mo[l_2]$	$mo[l_2]$	$mc[l_2]$	$mc[l_2 \cap l_5]$	$mc[l_2 \cap l_6]$	$mo[l_2]$	$mo[l_2]$
$so[l_3]$	$fso[l_3]$	$fso[l_3]$	$fso[l_3]$	$so[l_5]$	$mo[l_6]$	$fso[l_3 \cup l_7]$	$fmo[l_3 \cup l_8]$
$mo[l_4]$	$fmo[l_4]$	$fmo[l_4]$	$fmo[l_4]$	$so[l_5]$	$mo[l_6]$	$fmo[l_4 \cup l_7]$	$fmo[l_4 \cup l_8]$

When one base-view adornment has the mandatory sc or mc and the second base-view adornment has the optional adornment so or mo, the combined adornment ends up with some optional adornment. For example, the merge of $sc[l_1]$ and $so[l_7]$ is $so[l_1]$ because no matter a value is chosen from l_1 or not, we can always conduct the sub-query on the base view with the attribute adornment $so[l_7]$, then pass binding with the base view with $sc[l_1]$ by removing attribute values not in l_1.

Example 2

Given two data sources $D_1(X\ (b),\ Y\ (f),\ Z\ (b))$ and $D_2(Z\ (so[l_7]),\ O\ (u),\ P\ (b))$, the join-view mediator M of D_1 and D_2 is defined as $M(X\ (b),\ Y\ (f),\ Z\ (fso[l_7]),\ O\ (u),\ P\ (b))$. For the attribute Z in the above join-view mediator M, the user may choose a value $z_i \in l_7$, specify a value $z_i \notin l_7$, or specify no value. For the first option, the answer for the mediator query $M(x_1, Y, z_1, O, p_1)$, $z_1 \in l_7$ can be obtained by joining results from two sub-queries $D_1(x_1, Y, z_1)$ and $D_2(z_1, O, p_1)$. In the second option, to answer the query $M(x_1, Y, z_1, O, p_1)$, $z_1 \notin l_7$, the query result from $D_2(Z, O, p_1)$ should be filtered by removing tuples with different Z values before D_2 results joins D_1 results. For the third option, the query $M(x_1, Y, Z, O, p_1)$ is answered in the following three steps: (1) The mediator first runs the sub-query $D_2(Z, O, p_1)$; (2) then another sub-query $D_1(x_1, Y, Z)$ can be executed multiple times by bind passing each value z_i of Z from the result of $D_2(Z, O, p_1)$; (3) join and combine the results from $D_2(Z, O, p_1)$ in step 1and each running of $D_1(x_1, Y, z_i)$ in step 2.

4.3. Projection and Selection Views

Unlike the union or join attributes which occur in both the underlying data sources, the projected attributes only appear in one of the two underlying data sources. When receiving a query on a projection view, the mediator passes the derived sub-queries down to the corresponding base views without specifying values for the hidden base attributes, which only appear in the base views. So during the projection, we do not produce a projection-view template if any of the hidden attributes has a b, sc, and mc adornment in a base-view template. The attribute adornments u, so, and mo are projected to f, fso, and fmo adornments, respectively by using the post-filtering technique.

Similar to the projection view, the selection view attributes only appear in one of the two base views. A selection-view query is processed by passing it down to the underlying base view and applied the selection predicate on the results of the base view. Therefore, a selection-view is generated by copying the corresponding base-view template. But the selected attribute adornments u, so, and mo are changed to f, fso, and fmo adornments, respectively based on the post-filtering technique.

4.4. A Case Study

In this mini-case study, we combine two existing coastal wide data collection platform (DCP) networks: The Texas Coastal Ocean Observation Network (TCOON) and The Texas Automated Buoy System (TABS).

4.4.1. Mediator Schema for TCOON and TABS

There is only one table in the TCOON database, *Tcoon(sid, date, time, ser, smv)*, where *sid* is the station identification, *date* and *time* are the month/date/year and hour: minute of the measurement, *ser* is the series identifier, and *smv* is the value of a series identifier. The *ser* attribute takes one of the 12 values, *pwl* (primary water level), *sig* (water level standard deviation), *out* (water level outlier), *atp* (air temperature), *wtp* (water temperature), *wsd* (wind speed), *wgt* (wind gust), *wdr* (wind direction), *bpr* (barometric pressure), *bat* (battery voltage), *cla* (calibration temperature A), *clb* (calibration temperature B).

The TABS database contains three tables, velocity, meteorology, and buoy system. The three tables are defined as: *Velocity(sid, date, time, wtd, wdr, wtp)*, *Meteorology(sid, date, time, wsd, atp, bpr, wgt, compass, tx, ty, par, relhum)*, *Buoy(sid, date, time, bat, sigstr, compass, nping, tx, ty, adcpv, adcpcur, vbatt2)*.

From the above four tables from two databases, it is easy to identify that both databases share the following ten attributes/values: *sid, date, time, atp, bat, bpr, wdr, wgt, wsd, wtp*. Especially, *atp, bat, bpr, wdr, wgt, wsd*, and *wtp* are attributes in TABS database but are a subset of a list of values that *ser* may take in TCOON database.

The mediator schema of TCOON and TABS consists of two virtual tables *Observation* and *Facility* based on the *GAV* approach. The first table contains the oceanic observational data and the second table the hardware device information. The *Observation* is obtained by union of *Velocity* and *Meteorology* tables with *Tcoon* table, and the *Facility* by union of *System* table with *Tcoon* table. *Velocity* and *Meteorology* tables are inner joined together.

    Observation(sid, date, time, ser, smv, wtd, par, relhum) :-
        (*Velocity(sid, date, time, wtd, wdr, wtp)* JOIN
        Meteorology(sid, date, time, wsd, atp, bpr, wgt, compass, tx, ty, par, relhum))
    UNION
        (*Tcoon(sid, date, time, ser, smv)* AND (*ser* in ('pwl', 'sig', 'out', 'atp', 'wtp', 'wsd', 'wgt', 'wdr', 'bpr')))

    Facility(sid, date, time, ser, smv, sigstr, compass, nping, tx, ty, adcpv, adcpcur, vbatt2) :-
        System(sid, date, time, bat, sigstr, compass, nping, tx, ty, adcpv, adcpcur, vbatt2)
    UNION
        (*Tcoon(sid, date, time, ser, smv)* AND (*ser* in ('bat', 'cla', 'clb')))

4.4.2. Query Capabilities of the Mediator for TCOON and TABS

To retrieve data from TCOON, users must choose at least one station from a station list l_1 and at least one field from a list of series identifiers $l_2 \cup l_3$, respectively. l_2 is {'pwl', 'sig', 'out', 'atp', 'wtp', 'wsd', 'wgt', 'wdr', 'bpr'} and l_3 is {'bat', 'cla', 'clb'}. In addition, the *date* attribute is optional, and the attribute *time* and *smv* can not be specified. As a result, the query capability of the base-view TCOON is expressed as *Tcoon (sid (mc[l_1]), date (f), time (u), ser (mc[$l_2 \cup l_3$]), smv (u))*.

The TABS website provides a query form that allows users to extract data by specifying one station ID from the station list l_4. The attribute *date* is optional and all the other attributes can not be specified. So the query capabilities of base-view TABS are: *Velocity(sid (sc[l_4]),* *date* (*f*), *time* (*u*), *wtd* (*u*), *wdr* (*u*), *wtp* (*u*)), *Meteorology*(*sid* (*sc*[l_4]), *date* (*f*), *time* (*u*), *wsd* (*u*), *atp* (*u*), *bpr* (*u*), *wgt* (*u*), *compass* (*u*), *tx* (*u*), *ty* (*u*), *par* (*u*), *relhum* (*u*)), and *System*(*sid* (*sc*[l_4]), *date* (*f*), *time* (*u*), *bat* (*u*), *sigstr* (*u*), *compass* (*u*), *nping* (*u*), *tx* (*u*), *ty* (*u*), *adcpv* (*u*), *adcpcur* (*u*), *vbatt2* (*u*)).

To compute the query capabilities of the mediator, we apply the union-view template (see Table 1) to the attributes occurring in both databases (such as *sid*) and the projection-view template (see Section 4.3) to the attributes appearing in only one of the two databases (such as *par*). The computed results are as follows: *Observation*(*sid* (*mc*[$l_1 \cup l_4$]), *date* (*f*), *time* (*f*), *ser* (*fmo*[l_2]), *smv* (*f*), *wtd* (*f*), *par* (*f*), *relhum* (*f*)), *Facility*(*sid* (*mc*[$l_1 \cup l_4$]), *date* (*f*), *time* (*f*), *ser* (*fmo*[l_3]), *smv* (*f*), *sigstr* (*f*), *compass* (*f*), *nping* (*f*), *tx* (*f*), *ty* (*f*), *adcpv* (*f*), *adcpcur* (*f*), *vbatt2* (*f*)).

5. Qualitative Spatial Representation and Reasoning

The integration system should be able to not only answer the traditional keyword-based queries, but also take the consideration of the spatial terms/concepts in the search. The examples of the spatial-aware queries are (see Figure 6):

- The water level in *Houston* coastal area.
- The wind speed in the area close to *TABS* station *F*.
- The water temperature to the south of *TCOON* station 068.

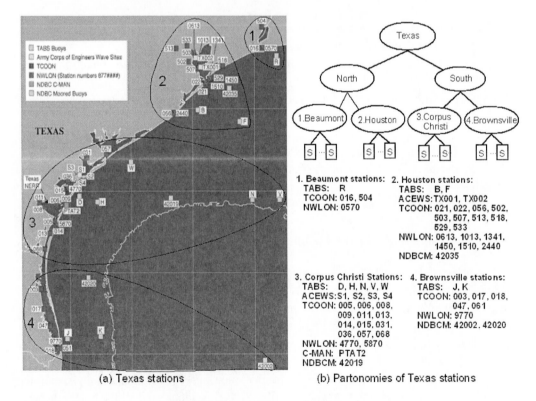

(a) Texas stations   (b) Partonomies of Texas stations

Figure 6. Texas stations and partonomies.

Most ocean observational station contains geospatial information including addresses and geographic references ((x, y)-coordinates). This information can be exploited and used to provide spatial awareness to integration systems. Yet most people use place names to refer to geographical locations, and will usually be entirely ignorant of the corresponding coordinates. As a result, we employ a qualitative notion instead of a quantitative notion of spatial information because the chosen representation does not need to worry about the real data and measurements. Verbal descriptions are typically not metrically precise, but sufficient for the task intended. Imprecise descriptions are necessary in query languages where one specifies some spatial properties such as the wind temperature not far away from *Corpus Christi* coast.

Techniques for representing and reasoning about qualitative spatial information have been extensively studied in *Artificial Intelligences* (AI). The efficient spatial problem solving in this line of research depends on the abstraction of spatial details. Three levels of spatial abstraction have been identified in terms of topology, ordinal and metrics [65], which correspond to the topological, directional and distance relations defined in Section 1, respectively.

The spatial abstraction and reasoning approaches developed in AI research are inadequate for the field of information retrieval and data integration because we have to explicitly represent and reason spatial relevance as well as retrieve conceptually relevant data. Although it is possible to use OWL (Web Ontology Language) to describe as well as reason about spatial properties, OWL has very limited build-in inference capabilities, and an extension of the formal semantics to integrate spatial relations into OWL turns out to be undecidable [23]. A better solution is to evaluate the queries with conceptual and spatial criteria separately. As a result, *Stuckenschmidt* et al. [65] proposed to represent the spatial information in four relations: partonomic, topological, directional, and distance relations. But the four relations have never been applied to a real system and the scenarios handled are relative simple in [65] with the four relations considered separately, while the proposed probability-based heuristic method takes into the consideration the combination of distance and directional relations. BUSTER system [60,65,68] is the only implemented system that supports the partonomic and neighborhood relations, which are derived from the geographic tessellation of homogeneous decomposition. Spatial relevance is determined by the weighted sum of the partonomic and neighborhood relations. In addition, a system of eight calculus RCC-8 is widely used in GIS applications to describe the region connection relations [7,13,45]. Next, we use Texas area as an example to present four spatial relations and the same idea can be applied to other GOM US states, such as Florida. The major idea of this section come from [43].

5.1. Partonomic Relation

We consider areas $A_1,...,A_n$ as a partition of a larger area A if (1) $A_1 \cup ... \cup A_n = A$ and (2) $A_i \cap A_j = 0$ for all $i \neq j$ from $(1,....,n)$ [65]. Partonomies are created by recursively applying the above partition method to divide an area, such as A_1, to multiple smaller areas $A_{11},...,A_{1m}$. Figure 6(a) represents station partonomies in Texas area from north to south: 1. *Beaumont*, 2. *Houston*, 3. *Corpus Christi*, and 4. *Brownsville*, and Figure 6(b) shows the corresponding decomposition tree, where S represents a station or a buoy. Each partonomy contains several different types of stations, and one type of station can appear in more than one partonomy. For example, *TABS*, *TCOON*, and *NWLON* stations can be found in all four partonomies, and the partonomy *Corpus Christi* includes *TABS*, *Army Corps of Engineers Wave Sites* (*ACEWS*), *TCOON*, *NWLON*, and *NDBC Moored* (*NDBCM*) buoys.

This partition is sort of coarse and other finer partitions may be created based on the application needs. The simple queries can be answered by partonomic information including the water level in the *Houston* area or in the south Texas, etc.

5.2. Distance Relation

The Texas observational systems can be classified to three categories: coast, offshore, and ocean based upon their distance from the land. The coastal stations are the ones that are installed on the shore and are just a little bit stick out to the water from the land. Figure 7 shows that there are four kinds of costal stations: *ACEWS*, *TCOON*, *NWLON*, and *NDBC C-MAN*. The offshore stations usually are the buoy systems that are not close to the land but within the continental shelf. All of the *TABS* and part of *NDBCM* buoys fall in this category (see Figure 6). The ocean stations are those far away from the land and are outside of the continental shelf. The only station in Figure 7 that can be put in this category is *NDBCM Buoy 42002* in the partonomy *Brownsville*.

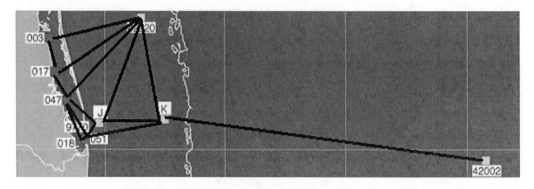

Figure 7. Station neighborhood graph in *Brownville, Texas* area.

Correspondingly, we adopt from [Fra06] the five-step distance with five symbols: *very close* (*VC*), *close* (*C*), *medium* (*M*), *far* (*F*), and *very far* (*VF*). The concept of distance in [17] is defined as the straight line length between two point objects. The distance between two nearest coastal stations, between one costal station and one offshore station, and between one offshore station and one ocean station in one area are usually defined as *very close* or *close*, *medium*, and *far*, respectively. For example, in Figure 7 the distance is *very close* from *TCOON* 051 to *TCOON* 018, *close* from *TCOON* 017 to *TCOON* 047, *medium* from *TCOON* 051 to *TABS K*, and *far* from *TABS K* to *NDBC 42002*. The last symbol *very far* is used to describe the distance that is farther than *far*, for example, between a Texas coastal station and a Florida coastal station (not shown in Figure 7).

Based upon the above distance concept, the distance addition operation is defined as $X + Y = succ(X, Y)$ if $X=Y$, otherwise $X + Y = max(X, Y)$. For instance, $VC + VC = C$, $C + C = M$, $C + M = M$, and $C + F = F$, *etc*. The operations obey the associative law. A real example for $C + C = M$ is that in Figure 5 *TCOON* 003 indirectly links to 047 through 017, so the distance between 003 and 047 is *M*. The neighborhood graph is introduced in Section 5.3.

The simple queries can be answered by combining partonomic and distance relations including the water level *close* to *TABS* Station J, and the salinity not far away (*medium*) from *TCOON* Station 047, etc.

5.3. Topological Relation

Topology is useful in information integration and retrieval because many spatial modeling operations require only topological information instead of coordinates (latitude and longitude). In GIS, the mostly considered topological relationships are neighborhood (what is next to what), containment (what is enclosed by what), and proximity (how close something is to something else). Because there is no containment relationship between any observational sites, we only consider the neighborhood and proximity relationships in the paper. To be more specific, proximity graphs are exploited to represent the neighborhood of a set of points in the Euclidean plane. The neighborhood graph of the ocean observational stations is a graph $G = (N, E)$, where N represent stations and E the imaginary edges between two neighboring stations.

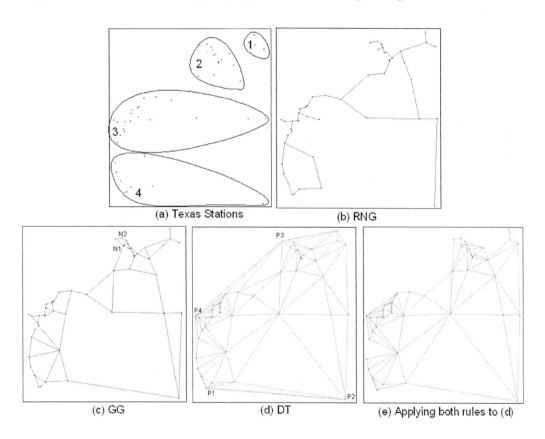

Figure 8. Neighborhood graphs of Texas stations.

We now look at four types of neighborhood relations, minimum spanning tree (MST), relative neighborhood graph (RNG) [67], Gabriel graph (GG) [20], and Delaunay triangulation (DT) [3]. A point in MST has the least number of neighbors while a node in DT has the most neighbors. In other words, for a given set of points N, each neighborhood graph (the graph giving for each point its set of neighbors) in the following list is a subgraph of the subsequent one: MST $\subseteq$ RNG $\subseteq$ GG $\subseteq$ DT. Stronger requirement of neighborhood makes it relatively difficult for two points to be neighbors. In the paper, we do not consider MST neighborhood relation because each point has the least neighbors in the above four neighborhood relations.

The Texas stations and the corresponding neighborhood graphs of RNG, GG, and DT are shown in Figure 8(a), 8(b), 8(c), and 8(d), respectively. It is easy to tell from Figure 8(b) that the RNG graph is not a good candidate for our application because most nodes only have two direct neighbors. Too few direct neighbors complicate the queries in which the user is requesting the information around a station. Although more edges have been added in Figure 8(c), the GG graph still has the similar not-enough-direct-neighbor problem. In the same area we expect that the closely neighboring nodes are connected. For example, both coast stations N_1 and N_2 are located in *Houston* area but N_1 is not directly linked to N_2. On the other hand, the DT graph Figure 8(d) generates some extra unnecessary neighbors. The problems in Figure 8(d) are two folds: (1) a coastal station should not connect to an ocean station because the environmental and weather situation in one area is quite different from that of another remote area. For example the coastal station P_1 should not be the direct neighbor of the ocean station P_2. (2) A coastal station in one region should not link to the coastal station in another region. The reason is that the coastal stations are usually classified as C (*close*) in terms of distance and the correlation between two coastal stations in different regions is low. For example, P_3 in *Houston* should not link to P_4 in *Corpus Christi*.

As a result, an intermediate neighborhood graph between GG and DT will suit our application needs. There are two ways to achieve this goal: one way is to add more edges to produce an enhanced GG graph and another way is to delete unnecessary connections from DT to create a reduced DT graph. We have chosen the latter one because it is relatively easy and straightforward to implement. We have designed two rules to eliminate extra edges: (1) coastal stations in one area do not connect to coastal stations in another area; (2) a coastal station does not link to an ocean station. The first rule is proposed to add the partonomic factor to the neighborhood graph, and the second rule is exploited to handle the connection of far away stations. The results of applying both rules are shown in Figure 8(e), respectively.

5.4. Directional Relation

Qualitative direction is a function between two points in the plane that maps onto a symbolic direction. The n different symbols available for describing the directions are given as a set C_n. The value of n depends on the specific system of direction used, e.g., C_4={*North, East, South, West*} or more extensively C_8={*North, Northeast, East, Southeast, South, Southwest, West, Northwest*} (see Figure 9(a)). In the paper, we employ the cone-shaped direction system C_8. For instance, the direction *Northeast* refers to a cone-shaped section with the angular degree [22.5°, 67.5°]. This type of direction system results in the feature that the allowance area for any given direction increase with distance [17].

In the qualitative directional reasoning, we should be able to reason directional information of indirectly connected points, or the composition of two directional relations to derive a new directional relation. A typical composition is like: given B is east of A and C north of B, what is the directional relationship between A and C (see Figures 9(b), 9(c), and 9(d))? The composition table of the eight cone-shaped cardinal direction relation is shown in Table 3 [17,44]. For 64 compositions in Table 3, only 8 can be inferred exactly with one answer, 8 (represented by *) may be any of the eight directions, and the remaining 48 generate two possible answers, three possible answers, or four possible answers. The reason is that the mere directional relationships do not provide enough information to infer the result of a composition. For example, C may be east (see Figure 9(b)), northeast (see Figure 9(c)), or north (see Figure 9(d)) of A depending on directions and distances between A and B and between B and C. In our application domain, we need to provide a unique and precise answer for each user's spatial query instead of two, three, or four possible answers. Next, we first present a probabilistic solution [10] to reason a unique composition answer for the scenarios, such as Figure 9(c), where the two distances, A to B and B to C, are the same, e.g, *medium*. Then we propose the heuristics to improve the above probabilistic method for the cases where two composition distances vary. For example, AB is *medium*, and BC is *close* and *far* in Figures 9(b) and 9(d), respectively.

Dehak et. al. [10] proposed a probabilistic method to uniquely determine the angular relationship γ between two points, A and C, giving the angular value α from A to B and the angular value β from B to C. Under the assumption of uniform distribution for all points in a circular region and no knowledge of the point coordination information (longitude and latitude), γ is calculated as:

$$
r = \begin{cases}
\dfrac{\alpha + \beta}{2} & \text{if } |\beta - \alpha| \in \left[2k\pi, 2k\pi + \dfrac{\pi}{2} \right] \\[2ex]
\pi + \dfrac{\alpha + \beta}{2} & \text{if } |\beta - \alpha| \in \left[2k\pi + \dfrac{3\pi}{2}, (2k+2)\pi \right] \\[2ex]
\dfrac{\varphi(\alpha, \beta)}{\sigma(\alpha, \beta)} & \text{if } |\beta - \alpha| \in \left(2k\pi + \dfrac{\pi}{2}, 2k\pi + \dfrac{3\pi}{2} \right), \quad \alpha < \beta, \quad |\beta - \alpha| \neq \pi \\[2ex]
\pi + \dfrac{\varphi(\alpha, \beta)}{\sigma(\alpha, \beta)} & \text{if } |\beta - \alpha| \in \left(2k\pi + \dfrac{\pi}{2}, 2k\pi + \dfrac{3\pi}{2} \right), \quad \alpha > \beta, \quad |\beta - \alpha| \neq \pi \\[2ex]
\alpha + \dfrac{6\pi}{7} & \text{if } \beta = \alpha + \pi, \quad \text{or} \qquad \alpha - \dfrac{6\pi}{7} \text{ if } \alpha = \beta + \pi
\end{cases}
\tag{1}
$$

with

$$
\begin{aligned}
\varphi(\alpha, \beta) = &-4((2\beta - \alpha - \pi)^2 - \beta^2 + 1)\cos(\alpha - \beta) + 5\cos(3\alpha - 3\beta) - \cos(5\alpha - 5\beta) \\
&- (12\alpha - 20\beta + 8\pi)\sin(\alpha - \beta) + (8\alpha - 10\beta + 5\pi)\sin(3\alpha - 3\beta) \\
&- (2\beta - \pi)\sin(5\alpha - 5\beta),
\end{aligned}
$$

and

$$
\sigma(\alpha, \beta) = 8(\alpha - \beta + \pi)\cos(\alpha - \beta) + 8\sin(\alpha - \beta) - 2\sin(3\alpha - 3\beta) - 2\sin(5\alpha - \beta)
$$

Equation (1) works well if two distances (AB and BC) are similar.

In the GDS framework, we have the knowledge of cardinal directions, such as north or southwest, between two points, but the real angular information between two points is unknown. So we have to employ the average angular degree of a cone-shaped section to represent the angle of a direction. For example, the direction northeast is between $\pi/8$ and $3\pi/8$ and is represented by the average angle $\pi/4$. In this case, the values of α and β can only be 0, $\pi/4$, $\pi/2$, $3\pi/4$, π, $5\pi/4$, $3\pi/2$, or $7\pi/4$ for eight directions, respectively. As a result, Equation (1) only returns two types of γ values when $|\beta - \alpha|$ is in the first or fourth quadrant: γ is right on the delimiter of two cone-shaped sectors when $|\beta - \alpha| = \pi/4 \, or \, 7\pi/4$, or γ is the average angle of a cone-shaped sector when $|\beta - \alpha| = 0, \pi/2, or \, 3\pi/2$. For instance, $\alpha = 0$, $\beta = \pi/4$, then $\gamma = (\alpha + \beta)/2 = \pi/8$, which is the degree that separates east and northeast. In the above example, to determine a direction for AC, we may use some heuristics or randomly pick one if the two distances, AB and BC, are the same.

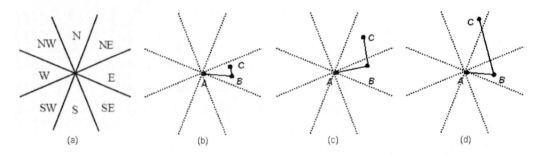

(a)   (b)   (c)   (d)

Figure 9. The eight direction system and a composition example when $|\beta - \alpha| = \pi/2$.

Table 3. The composition results for eight cone-shaped cardinal direction relations

	N	S	E	W	NE	NW	SE	SW
N	N	*	N,NE, E	N,NW, W	N,NE	N,NW	N,NE, E,SE	N,NW, W,SW
S	*	S	S,SE, E	S,SW, W	S,SE, E,NE	S,SW, W,NW	S,SE	S,SW
E	E,NE, N	E,SE, S	E	*	E,NE	E,NE, N,NW	E,SE	E,SE, S,SW
W	W,NW, N	W,SW, S	*	W	W,NW, N,NE	W,NW	W,SW, S,SE	W,SW
NE	NE,N	NE,E, SE,S	NE,E	NE,N, NW,W	NE	NE,N, NW	NE,E, SE	*
NW	NW,N	NW,W, SW,S	NW,N, NE,E	NW,W	NW,N, NE	NW	*	NW,W, SW
SE	SE,E, NE,N	SE,S	SE,E	SE,S, SW,W	SE,E, NE	*	SE	SE,S, SW
SW	SW,W, NW,N	SW,S	SW,S, SE,E	SW,W	*	SW,W, NW	SW,S, SE	SW

On the other hand, the two distances can vary widely, for example, *AB* is *medium* and *BC* is *far* in Figure 9(d). If we do not take the distance into consideration, the result of Equation (1) may drift away from the real angle between *A* and *C*. To handle the above disparate distance problem, we propose heuristics to improve the performance of Equation (1) according to the $|\beta - \alpha|$ value and length of *AB* and *BC*. Next, we discuss the heuristics proposed for various scenarios.

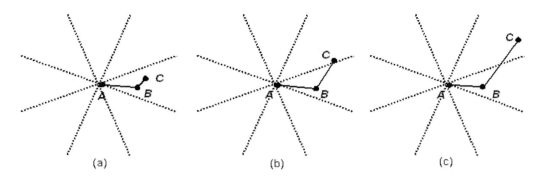

(a)   (b)   (c)

Figure 10. Composition results when $|\beta - \alpha| = \pi / 4$.

Heuristics 1: When $|\beta - \alpha| = \pi/2$ or $3\pi/2$, *AC* is in the same direction with the longer one of *AB* and *BC*, or *AC* is in the same direction with the middle section between *AB* direction and *BC* direction if *AB* and *BC* are of same length. For example, in Figure 9, $\alpha = 0$, $\beta = \pi/2$, and $\gamma = \pi/4$ according to Equation (1). Suppose the distance of *AB* is *medium*, *C* is east of *A* if *BC* is *short* (see Figure 9(b)), *C* is northeast of *A* if *BC* is *medium* (see Figure 9(c)), or C is north of A if BC is *far* (see Figure 9(d)).

Heuristics 2: When $|\beta - \alpha| = \pi/4$ or $7\pi/4$, *AC* is in the same direction with the longer one of *AB* and *BC*, or *AC* is in the same direction with *BC* if *AB* and *BC* are of same distance. For example, *B* is east of *A* and *C* is northeast of *B*, then $\alpha = 0$, $\beta = \pi/4$, and $\gamma = \pi/8$ according to Equation (1). Suppose the distance of *AB* is *medium*, *C* is east of *A* if *BC* is *short* (see Figure 10(a)), or *C* is northeast of *A* if *BC* is *medium* or *far* (see Figure 10(b) and 10(c)).

Heuristics 3: When $|\beta - \alpha| = 3\pi/4$ or $5\pi/4$, the direction of *AC* is determined by the result of Equation (1) if *AB* and *BC* are of same length. Otherwise, γ is increased/decreased by $\pi/8$ if *AB* is shorter than *BC*, or γ is increased/decreased by $\pi/2$ if *AB* is longer than *BC*. The reason we do this is because usually the value γ falls in the third or fourth direction from *AB* direction. For example, in Figure 11, *B* is east of *A* and *C* is northwest of *B*, then $\alpha = 0$, $\beta = 3\pi/4$, and $\gamma \approx 1.95$, which is about $112°$ and north of *A* according to Equation (1). Suppose the distance of *AB* is *medium*, in Figure 11(a) *C* is east of *A* because BC is *short* and γ is decreased by $\pi/2$ to 0.38 (about 22°), while in Figure 11(d) *C* is northwest of *A* since *BC* is *far* and γ is increased by $\pi/8$ to 2.34 (about 134°). Figures 11(b) and 11(c) show two possible locations of C when AB and BC are of same length.

Another heuristics we utilize is when one of AB and BC is *very close* and the length of AB and BC varies, the direction of AC is inferred the same as the longer one of AB and BC. For example, in Figure 7, the distance between *TCOON* 051 and *TABS J* is *close* and the distance from *TCOON* 051 to *TCOON* 018 is *very close*, then the direction from *TABS J* to *TCOON* 018 is the same as that from *TABS J* to *TCOON* 051, which is southwest.

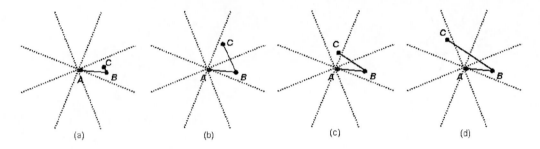

Figure 11. Composition results when $|\beta - \alpha| = 3\pi/4$.

6. Preliminary Results

We have not fully implemented the proposed framework. We are investigating the integration of GCOOS in situ observational data sources [51] and the integration of GCOOS satellite observations [42] by using mediator-based approach (see Section 3.2.2). In addition, we have also studied the integration of GCOOS in situ observations with two fish databases, FishNet and FishBase, by using the P2P technique (see Section 3.2.1) [33].

In [51], we integrated five GCOOS in situ data sources, TCOON, TABS, NWLON, NDBC, and COMPS. The above data sources are mediated via the GAV technique. The mediator interface, developed to query different web data sources, is as shown in Figure 12. In Figure 12, the list of stations and all the observatory elements (both water level observations and meteorological observations) are shown. In Figure 12(a), the user can select multiple stations simultaneously with one or more ocean observatory series selected. In addition, the user has the option of choosing the specific date to query the different web data/information sources. When a user submits a query, the mediator sends different sub queries in the form of http requests to different data sources. Once the http response is received, internally it shall be processed to avoid unnecessary data apart from the requested data by the user. The result of the selected query can also be seen is Figure 12(b).

In [42], the prototype system has been implemented to integrate images from four GOM satellite observational sources, *APL*, *CIMSS*, *COAPS*, and *TSMI*, and can be easily extended to include other sources using the *LAV* technique. The system takes as input satellite, region, and product, etc., and extracts, merges, and displays the images from multiple data sources. User interface (UI) of the developed prototype system is shown in Figure 13. In the UI a user may select multiple values for an attribute, such as *Satellites*, *Region*, and *Product*. The UI ignores the values of un-selected attributes. For example, the system will return results for any region in the GOM if the user does not specify a region.

In [33], a P2P prototype system is developed to retrieve fish data, such FishBase and FishNet, and meteorological data, such as TCOON and TABS, from the GOM. By using P2P technology, we do not need to develop a global schema. Instead we build a XML file defining P2P mapping rules. When this file is known by all the peers on the P2P network, the system is initialized and then we can do the query on every peer based on the rules.

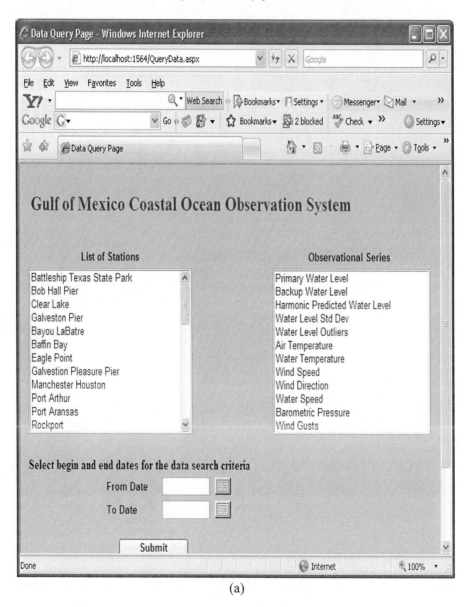

(a)

Figure 12. Continued on next page.

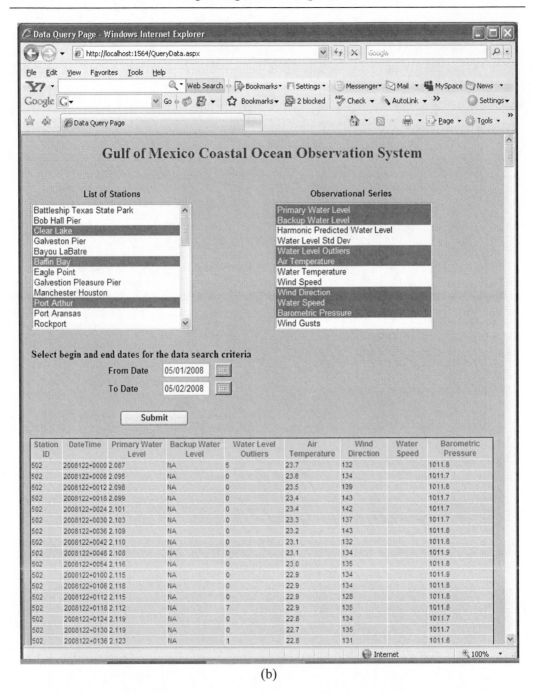

(b)

Figure 12. The integration user interface for GCOOS in situ observations.

A data source can easily be removed from and joined to the existing P2P system without disturbing the normal system functioning. Each peer can not only be queried in its schema for data, but also fetch data from its neighbors if the coordination rule is present. The system prototype is shown in Figure 14.

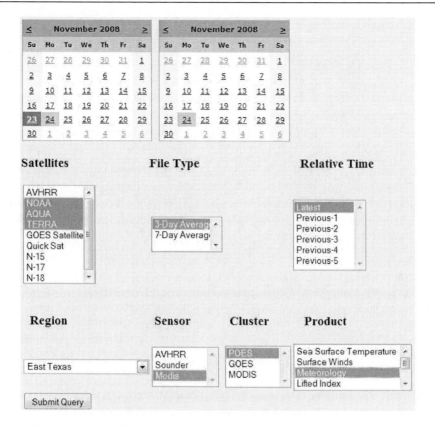

Figure 13. The integration user interface for GCOOS satellite observations.

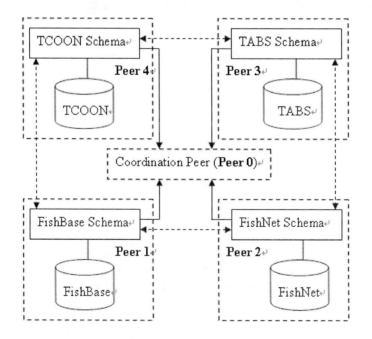

Figure 14. Architecture of the P2P prototype system.

7. Conclusion

In this paper, we developed a P2P framework, called GDS (the Gulf of Mexico Dataspace), which exploits a hybrid method to satisfy the GOM researchers' information need by retrieve and merge both the current data and the historical data. The current data is searched and retrieved on demand in real time from the Internet while the historical data is returned from the data archives created by employing a client-server grid architecture, integrated rule-oriented data system (iRODS). In addition, spatial features, such as partonomic, distance, topological relations, and directional relations between data sources, are utilized and developed to facilitate the data retrieval and integration of spatial-related data from the GOM. One important use of the data collected by the framework would be for import into various models and forecast programs. The programs will produce models and forecasts of parameters such as water level, wind, and waves. During the hurricane season, models will provide a wealth of information on storm surge, wave parameters, and their effects on evacuation routes. The lack of this type of information is evident after the passage of hurricanes Katrina and Rita. Had officials known in advance the level of water moving toward the Gulf Coast many more lives would have been saved.

References

[1]   D. Alvarez, A. Smukler, and A. Vaisman. Peer-To-Peer Databases for e- Science: A Biodiversity Case Study. In *Brazilian Symposium in Databases*, 2005.

[2]   Arenas M., Kantere V., Kementsietsidis A., Kiringa I., Miller R., and Mylopoulos J.. The hyperion project: From data integration to data coordination. *SIGMOD Record*, 32(3), 2003.

[3]   M. de Berg, M. van Kreveld, M. Overmars, and O. Schwarzkoph. *Computational Geometry: Algorithms and Applications*. Springer 2000.

[4]   P. Bernstein, F. Giunchiglia, A. Kementsietsidis, J. Mylopoulos, L. Serafini, and I. Zaihrayeu. Data Management for Peer-To-Peer Computing: A Vision. In *ACM SIGMOD WebDB Workshop*, 2002.

[5]   S. Chawathe et al. The TSIMMIS project: Integration of Heterogeneous Information Sources. In *Proc. 10th Meeting of the Information Processing Society of Japan*, 1994.

[6]   S. Cluet, C. Delobel, J. Simeon, and K. Smaga. Your Mediators Need Data Conversion. In *SIGMOD Conf. on Management of Data*, 1998.

[7]   A. Cohn and J. Renz. Qualitative spatial representation and reasoning. In *Handbook of Knowledge Representation*. Elsevier, 2008.

[8]   Cruz and H. Xiao. The Role of Ontologies in Data Integration. *Journal of Engineering Intelligent Systems*, Vol. 13, pp. 245-252, 2005.

[9]   DarwinCore, http://www.tdwg.org/activities/darwincore/.

[10] S. Dehak, I. Bloch, and H. Maitre. Spatial reasoning with incomplete information on relative positioning. *IEEE Trans. on Pattern Analysis and Machine Intelligence*, 27(9), pp.1473-1484, 2005.

[11] Deutsch, A., B. Ludäscher, and A. Nash. 2005. Rewriting Queries Using Views with Access Patterns Under Integrity Constraints. Intl. Conference on Database Theory (ICDT'05), Edinburgh, Scotland, January 2005.

[12] D. Dou and P. LePendu. Ontology-based Integration for Relational Databases. In *Proc. of the ACM Symposium on Applied Computing*, 2006.

[13] M. Duckham, J. Lingham, K. Mason, and M. Worboys. Qualitative reasoning about consistency in geographic information. *Information Sciences*, 176(6), pp.601-627, 2006.

[14] M. Duschka and M. R. Genesereth, Infomaster - An Information Integration Tool, in *proceedings of the International Workshop "Intelligent Information Integration"* during the 21st German Annual Conference on Artificial Intelligence, 1997.

[15] Franconi E., Kuper G., Lopatenko A., Serafini L. A Robust Logical and Computational Characterization of Peer-to-Peer Database Systems. *International Workshop On Databases, Information Systems and Peer-to-Peer Computing*, 2003.

[16] E. Franconi, G. Kuper, A. Lopatenko, I. Zaihrayeu. The coDB Robust Peer to Peer Database System, *The Second Workshop on Semantics in Peer-to-Peer and Grid Computing*, 2004.

[17] A. Frank. Qualitative Spatial Reasoning: Cardinal Directions as an Example. *Twenty Years of the Intel. Journal of Geographical Information Science and Systems*. CRC Press, 2006.

[18] M. Franklin, A. Halevy, and D. Maier. From Databases to Dataspaces: A New Abstraction for Information Management. *ACM SIGMOD Record*, 34(4), p. 27-33, 2005.

[19] M. Franklin, A. Halevy, and D. Maier. A first tutorial on dataspaces. *Proceedings of the VLDB Endowment*, August, 1(2), p. 1516-1517, 2008.

[20] R. Gabriel and R. R. Sokal. A new statistical approach to geographic variation analysis. *Systematic Zoology,* vol. 18, pp. 259–270, 1969.

[21] H. Garcia-Molina, Y. Papakonstantinou, D. Quass, A. Rajaraman, Y. Sagiv, J. Ullman, V. Vassalos, and J.Widom. The TSIMMIS approach to mediation: Data models and Languages. *Journal of Information Systems*, 1997.

[22] Gulf of Alaska Ecosystem Monitoring and Research Program (GEM), *The GEM Program Document*, July 9, 2002.

[23] V. Haarslev, C. Lutz, and R. Moeller. Foundations of spatioterminological reasoning with description logics. In *Principles of Knowledge Representation and Reasoning*, 1998.

[24] Haas, D. Kossman, E. L. Wimmers, and J. Yang. Optimizing Queries across Diverse Data Sources. *VLDB* 1997.

[25] A. Halevy, Answering queries using views: A survey, *VLDB Journal*, Vol. 10(4), pp.270-294, 2001.

[26] Halevy, M. Franklin, and D. Maier. Principles of Dataspace Systems. PODS '06: Proceedings of the 25th ACM SIGMOD-SIGACT-SIGART symposium on principles of database systems, June 26-28, 2006.

[27] Halevy, Z. Ives, P. Mork, I. Tatarinov., Piazza: Data Management Infrastructure for Semantic Web Applications. *World Wide Web Conference*, 2003.

[28] Halevy, Z. Ives, M. Rodrig, and D. Suciu. Schema mediation in peer data management systems. In *ICDE Conference*, 2003.

[29] Halevy, Z. Ives, D. Suciu, I. Tatarinov., Schema mediation for large-scale semantic data sharing, *VLDB Journal*, Vol. 14, 2005.

[30] Halevy, A. Rajaraman, and J. Ordille., Data integration: The teenage years, in *the Proc. of the 32nd Intl. Conf. on VLDB*, 2006.

[31] An Integrated and Sustained Ocean Observing System (IOOS) for the United States: Design and Implementation. *Ocean.US*, Arlington, VA, 2002

[32] S. Jeffery, M. Franklin, A. Halevy: Pay-as-you-go user feedback for dataspace systems. *SIGMOD Conference*, 2008.

[33] Jin, L.Li, A. Nalluri, and H. Guo, Peer to peer data integration system for the Gulf of Mexico, to appear in *the workshop on Data Integration and Management on the Gulf of Mexico*, Corpus Christi, May 15-16, 2009.

[34] JXTA programming guide. Home Page. Available from www.jxta.org/.

[35] Kanaracus (2008). Could Google's 'dataspaces' reshape search? InfoWorld, May 19, 2008.

[36] A. Kementsietsidis and M. Arenas. Data sharing through query translation in autonomous sources. In International Conference on Very Large Data Bases, 2004.

[37] Kementsietsidis, M. Arenas, and R. J. Miller. Mapping data in peer-to peer systems: Semantics and algorithmic issues. In *ACM SIGMOD*, 2003.

[38] T. Kwok, D. S Weld. Planning to Gather Information. In *Proc. AAAI 13th National Conference on Artificial Intelligence*, 1996.

[39] Y. Levy, A. Rajaraman, and J. J. Ordille. Querying Heterogeneous Information Sources Using Source Descriptions. *VLDB 1996*.

[40] Y. Levy, A. Rajaraman, and J. J. Ordille. Query Answering Algorithms for Information Agents. In *Proc. of AAAI*, 1996.

[41] Li, J. Fernandez, and H. Guo. A framework for query capabilities and interface design of mediators on the Gulf of Mexico data sources. To appear in *Asia-Pacific Web Conference*, 2008.

[42] Li, Y.Liu, S. Kothapally, C. Jin, and A. Nalluri. Data Integration for the Gulf of Mexico Satellite Observations. in *the Fourth International Conference on Internet and Web Applications and Services (ICIW)*, Venice, Italy, May 24-28, 2009.

[43] L.Li, Y. Liu, A. Nalluri, and C. Jin. Qualitative Spatial Representation and Reasoning for Data Integration of Ocean Observational Systems. in *The Joint International Conferences on Asia-Pacific Web Conference (APWeb) and Web-Age Information Management (WAIM)*, 2009.

[44] G. Ligozat. Reasoning about cardinal directions. *Journal of Visual Languages and Computing*, vol. 9, pp.23-44, 1998.

[45] Y. Liu, Y. Zhang, and Y. Gao. GNet: a generalized network model and its applications in qualitative spatial reasoning. *Information Sciences*, 178(9), pp.2163-2175, 2008.

[46] S. Madria, K. Passi, and S. Bhowmick. An XML schema integration and query mechanism system. In *Data Knowl. Eng.* 65(2), 2008.

[47] Manolescu, D. Florescu, and D. Kossmann. Answering XML Queries on Heterogeneous Data Sources. *VLDB 2001*.

[48] R. Moore. Digital Libraries and Data Intensive Computing. In *China Digital Library Conference* , Beijing, China, September 2004.

[49] R. Moore. Building Preservation Environments with Data Grid Technology, *Society of American Archivists*, 2006.

[50] R. Moore and A. Rajasekar, Building Data Grids with iRODS, *NeSC*, May 2008.

[51] A. Nalluri, L.Li, C. Jin, and J. Fernandez, "Mediator-based data integration system for the in situ ocean observations in the Gulf of Mexico", to appear in *the workshop on Data Integration and Management on the Gulf of Mexico*, Corpus Christi, May 15-16, 2009.

[52] W. Ng, B. Ooi, K. Tan, and A. Zhou. Peerdb: A p2p-based system for distributed data sharing. In *ICDE Conference*, 2003.

[53] W. Nejdl, W. Siberski, and M. Sintek. EDUTELLA: A P2P Networking Infrastructure Based on RDF, in *WWW* 2002.

[54] W. Nejdl, W. Siberski, and M. Sintek. Design Issues and Challenges for RDF- and Schema-Based Peer-To-Peer Systems. *SIGMOD Record* 32(3): 41-46, September 2003.

[55] W. Nejdl, B. Wolf, S. Staab, and J. Tane. EDUTELLA: Searching and Annotating Resources within an RDF-based P2P Network. In *Semantic Web Workshop*, 2002.

[56] A. Pan, P. Montoto, and A. Molano. A Model for Advanced Query Capability Description in Mediator Systems. In *Int'l Conf. on Enterprise Information Systems*. 2002.

[57] Y. Papakonstantinou, V. R. Borkar, etc. XML Queries and Algebra in the Enosys Integration Platform. In *Data Knowl. Eng.* 44(3), 2003.

[58] A. Rajasekar, M. Wan, r. Moore, and W. Schroeder. A prototype Rule-based Distributed Data Management System. In *HPDC workshop on "Next Generation Distributed Data Management"*, May 2006, Paris, France.

[59] Roth and P. Schwarz. Don't Scrap it, Wrap it! A Wrapper Architecture for Legacy Data Sources. In *VLDB* 1997.

[60] A. Schlieder, T. Vogele, and U. Visser. Qualitative spatial representation for information retrieval by gazetteers. In *Conference of Spatial Information Theory* (COSIT), 2001.

[61] L. Serafini, F. Giunchiglia, J. Mylopoulos, and P. Bernstein. The logical relational model: Model and proof theory. In *Technical Report 0112-23*, *ITC-IRST*, 2001.

[62] W. Siong Ng, B. Chin Ooi, K. L. Tan, and A. Ying Zhou. Bestpeer: A selfconfigurable peer-to-peer system. In *International Conference on Data Engineering (ICDE)*, 2002.

[63] W. Siong, B. Chin, K. Tan, and Y. Zhou. PeerDB: A p2p based system for distributed data sharing. *International Conference on Data Engineering (ICDE)*, 2003.

[64] M. Smith, R. Moore. Digital Archive Policies and Trusted Digital Repositories. *Digital Curation & Trusted Repositories: Seeking Success"*, *Digital Curation Centre Conference*, Glasgow, November 2006.

[65] H. Stuckenschmidt and F. V. Harmelen. *Information Sharing on the Semantic Web*. Springer 2004.

[66] Tang, W. Zhang, and W. Xiao, An Algebra for Capability Object Interoperability of Heterogeneous Data Integration Systems. In *Asia-Pacific Web Conference*, 2005.

[67] G. T. Toussaint. The relative neighborhood graph of a finite planar set. *Pattern Recognition*, vol. 12, pp. 261-268, 1980.

[68] U. Visser. *Intelligent Information Integration for the Semantic Web*. Springer, 2004.

[69] H. Wache, T. Voegele, U. Visser, H. Stuckenschmidt, G. Schuster, H. Neumann, and S.Huebner. Ontology-based integration of information - a survey of existing approaches. In *Ontologies and Information Sharing*, number 47, pp. 108–117, 2001.

[70] A. Weise, M. Wan, W. Schroeder, and A. Hasan. Managing Groups of Files in a Rule Oriented Data Management System (iRODS). *The 8th International Conference on Computational Science*, 2008.

[71] R. Yerneni, C. Li, H. Garcia-Molina, and J. D. Ullman. Computing Capabilities of Mediators. In *SIGMOD Conference*, 1999.

In: Peer-to-Peer Networks and Internet Policies   ISBN: 978-1-60876-287-3
Editors: Diego Vegros and Jaime Sáenz, pp. 109-134   © 2010 Nova Science Publishers, Inc.

Chapter 4

AN INTRUSION DETECTION MODEL USING BAYESIAN GAME IN AD HOC NETWORKS

Nikos Komninos[*] *and George Christakis*

Algorithms & Security Group, Athens Information Technology
Peania, GR-19002, Greece

Abstract

This chapter presents a Bayesian game to detect intruders in ad hoc networks. We use game theory techniques to model the interactions among nodes of an ad hoc network where each node plays a game among other neighboring nodes in the network and identifies potential attackers in peer-to-peer approach.

Key words: Bayesian game, intrusion detection, ad hoc networks, multiple games support

1. Introduction

A computer system should provide confidentiality, integrity and assurance against denial of service. However, due to increased connectivity (especially on the Internet), and the vast spectrum of financial possibilities that are opening up, more and more systems are subject to attack by intruders. These subversion attempts try to exploit flaws in the operating system as well as in application programs and have resulted in spectacular incidents.

There are two ways to handle subversion attempts. One way is to prevent subversion itself by building a completely secure system. We could, for example, require all users to identify and authenticate themselves; we could protect data by various cryptographic methods and very tight access control mechanisms. However this is not really feasible because:

1. In practice, designing and implementing a totally secure system is an extremely difficult task.

---
[*] E-mail address: nkom@ait.edu.gr

2. The vast installed base of systems worldwide guarantees that any transition to a secure system, (if it is ever developed) will be long in coming.

3. Cryptographic methods have their own problems. Passwords can be cracked, users can lose their passwords, and entire crypto-systems can be broken.

4. Even a truly secure system is vulnerable to abuse by insiders who abuse their privileges.

5. It has been seen that that the relationship between the level of access control and user efficiency is an inverse one, which means that the stricter the mechanisms, the lower the efficiency becomes.

A wireless ad hoc network is a decentralized wireless network. The network is ad hoc because each node is willing to forward data for other nodes, and so the determination of which nodes forward data is made dynamically based on the network connectivity. This is in contrast to wired networks in which routers perform the task of routing. It is also in contrast to managed (infrastructure) wireless networks, in which a special node known as an access point manages communication among other nodes.

Game theory is a branch of applied mathematics that attempts to mathematically capture behavior in strategic situations, in which an individual's success in making choices depends on the choices of others. While initially developed to analyze competitions in which one individual does better at another's expense, it has been expanded to treat a wide class of interactions, which are classified according to several criteria. Today, game theory is a sort of umbrella or 'unified field' theory for the rational side of sciences, and includes human as well as non-human players.

In this work, we use dynamic Bayesian game to model the interactions between attacker and defender in ad hoc networks. This allows the two players to choose their optimal strategies according to the action history profile and their beliefs about the types of their opponents, and hence help to overcome the limitations of one-stage static game.

Following this introduction, sections are organized as follows. Section 2 presents related works of intrusion detection systems with the use of game theory. Section 3 describes intrusion detection systems in ad hoc networks and their usage. Section 4 introduces game theory and how it is used in ad hoc networks. Section 5 presents experimental results and section 6 concludes the chapter.

2. Related Work

A game theoretic framework is suitable for modeling security issues such as intrusion prevention and intrusion detection. In the context of intrusion detection, several game theoretic approaches have been proposed to wired networks, WLANs, sensor networks, and ad hoc networks.

Kodialam and Lakshman [1] have proposed a game the theoretic framework to model the intrusion detection game between two players: the service provider and the intruder. A successful intrusion is when a malicious packet reaches the desired target. In the game, the objective of intruder is to choose a particular path between the source node and the target node, and the objective of the service provider is to determine a set of links on which sampling has to be done in order to detect the intrusion. Essentially, the game is formulated as a two-person zero-sum game, in which the service provider tries to maximize his pay-off, which is defined by the probability of detection, and on the other hand, the intruder tries to minimize the probability of being detected.

Alpcan and Basar [2] presented a game theoretic approach to intrusion detection in distributed virtual sensor networks, where each agent in the network has imperfect detection capabilities. They model the interaction between the attacker(s) and the IDS as a non cooperative non-zero-sum game with two versions: finite and continuous-kernel versions.

A two-player non cooperative, non-zero-sum game has also been studied by Agah et al. [3] and Alpcan and Basar [4] to address attack-defense problems in sensor networks. Similar to one-stage attacker/defender game, in their model, each player's optimal strategy depends only on the pay-off function of the opponent, and the game is assumed to have complete information. However, this assumption has limitations in a real network. Most game-theoretic solutions previously proposed for ad hoc networks focus on modeling cooperation and selfishness of the network. In these games, each node choose whether to forward or not forward a packet based on the concern about his cost, his benefit, and the collaboration offered to the network by the neighbors. Each of these works try to show that by enforcing cooperation mechanisms, a selfish node not abiding the rules will have low throughput in return from the network.

In this work, we use dynamic Bayesian game to model the interactions between attacker and defender in ad hoc networks. This allows two players to choose their optimal strategies according to the action history profile and their beliefs about the types of their opponents, and hence help to overcome the limitations of one-stage static game.

3. Intrusion Detection Systems in Ad-Hoc Networks

An Intrusion detection system (IDS) is software and/or hardware designed to detect unwanted attempts at accessing, manipulating, and/or disabling of computer systems, mainly through a network, such as the Internet. These attempts may take the form of attacks. An IDS cannot directly detect attacks within properly encrypted traffic. An intrusion detection system is used to detect several types of malicious behaviors that can compromise the security and trust of a computer system. This includes network attacks against vulnerable services, data driven attacks on applications, host based attacks such as privilege escalation, unauthorized logins and access to sensitive files, and malware (viruses, trojan horses and worms).

An IDS can be composed of several components: Sensors which generate security events, a Console to monitor events and alerts and control the sensors, and a central Engine that records events logged by the sensors in a database and uses a system of rules to generate alerts from security events received. There are several ways to categorize an IDS depending on the type and location of the sensors and the methodology used by the engine to generate alerts. In many simple IDS implementations all three components are combined in a single device or appliance.

To deal with all intrusions in general, many intrusion detection systems have been formalized. It is worthwhile to explore some of these systems in further detail.

3.1. Classification of Intrusion Detection Systems

Intrusions can be divided into 6 main types:

1. Attempted break-ins, which are detected by atypical behavior profiles or violations of security constraints.
2. Masquerade attacks, which are detected by atypical behavior profiles or violations of security constraints.
3. Penetration of the security control system, which are detected by monitoring for specific patterns of activity.
4. Leakage, which is detected by atypical use of system resources.
5. Denial of service, which is detected by atypical use of system resources.
6. Malicious use, which is detected by atypical behavior profiles, violations of security constraints, or use of special privileges.

Generally, the primitive intrusion detection systems simply detect all traffic and discern malicious traffic from legitimate use. Modern and more evolved intrusion detection systems now have the ability to take responsive or pre-emptive actions. However, some intrusion detection systems can be classified as passive and reactionary to others that are aggressive and thus we can divide the techniques of intrusion detection into two main types. The most famous and widely deployed network intrusion detection systems are misuse detection and anomaly detection.

3.2. Anomaly Detection Systems

Anomaly detection techniques assume that all intrusive activities are necessarily anomalous. This means that if we could establish a "normal activity profile" for a system, we could, in theory, flag all system states varying from the established profile by statistically significant amounts as intrusion attempts. However, if we consider that the set of intrusive activities only intersects the set of anomalous activities instead of being exactly the same, we find a couple of interesting possibilities: (a) Anomalous activities that are not intrusive are flagged as intrusive. (b) Intrusive activities that are not anomalous result in false negatives (events are not flagged intrusive, though they actually are).

The main issues in anomaly detection systems thus become the selection of threshold levels so that neither of the above two problems is unreasonably magnified, and the selection of features to monitor. Anomaly detection systems are also computationally expensive because of the overhead of keeping track of, and possibly updating several system profile metrics.

Statistical, predictive pattern generation and neural networks are some major approaches to anomaly intrusion detection systems.

3.2.1. Statistical Approaches

In this method, initially, behavior profiles for subjects are generated. As the system continues running, the anomaly detector constantly generates the variance of the present profile from the original one. We note that, in this case, there may be several measures that affect the behavior profile, like activity measures, CPU time used, number of network connections in a time period, etc. In some systems, the current profile and the previous profile are merged at intervals, but in some other systems profile generation is a one time activity.

The main advantage to statistical systems is that they adaptively learn the behavior of users, they are thus potentially more sensitive than human experts. However there are a few problems with statistical approaches: they can gradually be trained by intruders so that eventually, intrusive events are considered normal, false positives and false negatives are generated depending on whether the threshold is set too low or too high, and relationships between events are missed because of the insensitivity of statistical measures to the order of events.

An open issue with statistical approaches, in particular, and anomaly detection systems in general, is the selection of measures to monitor. It is not known exactly what the subset of all possible measures that accurately predicts intrusive activities is. Static methods of determining these measures are sometimes misleading because of the unique features of a particular system. Thus, it seems that a combination of static and dynamic determination of the set of measures should be done. Some problems associated with this technique have been remedied by other methods, such as the predictive pattern generation, which takes past events into account when analyzing the data.

3.2.2. Predictive Pattern Generation

This method of intrusion detection tries to predict future events based on the events that have already occurred [25]. This method of intrusion detection uses a rule base of user profiles defined as statistically weighted event sequences. This system develops sequential rules of the form

$$E1 - E2 - E3 \rightarrow (E4 = 94\%, E5 = 6\%) \tag{1}$$

where the various E's are events derived from the security audit trail, and the percentage on the right-hand side of the rule represent the probability of occurrence of each of the consequent events given the occurrence of the antecedent sequence. This would mean that for the sequence of observed events $E1$ followed by $E2$ followed by $E3$, the probability of event $E4$ occurring is 94% and that of $E5$ is 6%.

The rules are generated inductively with an information theoretic algorithm that measures the applicability of rules in terms of coverage and predictive power. An intrusion is detected if the observed sequence of events matches the left-hand side of the rule but the following events significantly deviate from the right-hand side of the rule.

There are several advantages to this approach. The main advantage of this approach is its ability to detect and respond quickly to anomalous behavior. That is because rule based sequential patterns can detect anomalous activities that were difficult with traditional methods. Also, systems built using this model are highly adaptive to changes. This is because low quality patterns are continuously eliminated, leaving the higher quality patterns behind. Nevertheless, it is easier to detect users who try to train the system during its learning period. And of course, anomalous activities can be detected and reported within seconds of receiving audit events.

The main problem with the system is its inability to detect some intrusions if that particular sequence of events have not been recognized and created into the rules. Another approach for anomaly detection systems is the use of neural networks.

3.2.3. Neural Networks

The idea here is to train the neural network to predict a user's next action or command, given the window of *n* previous actions or commands. The network is trained on a set of representative user commands. After the training period, the network tries to match actual commands with the actual user profile already present in the net. Any incorrectly predicted events (events and commands are used interchangeably in this discussion) actually measure the deviation of the user from the established profile.

Some advantages of using neural networks follow [19]: they cope well with noisy data, their success does not depend on any statistical assumption about the nature of the underlying data, and they are easier to modify for new user communities. However, they have some problems. First, a small window will result in false positives while a large window will result in irrelevant data as well as increase the chance of false negatives. Second, the net topology is only determined after considerable trial and error. And third, the intruder can train the net during its learning phase.

3.3. Misuse Detection Systems

The concept behind misuse detection schemes is that there are ways to represent attacks in the form of a pattern or signature recognition so that even variations of the same attack can be detected. This means that these systems are not unlike virus detection systems; they can detect many or all *known* attack patterns, but they are of little use for as yet unknown attack methods. An interesting point to note is that anomaly detection systems try to detect the complement of "bad" behavior. Misuse detection systems try to recognize known "bad" behavior. The main issues in misuse detection systems are how to write a signature that encompasses all possible variations of the pertinent attack, and how to write signatures that do not also match non-intrusive activity. Several methods of misuse detection, including a new pattern matching model are discussed later.

Expert systems are modeled in such a way as to separate the rule matching phase from the action phase. The matching is done according to audit trail events. The Next Generation Intrusion Detection Expert System (NIDES) is an interesting case study for the expert system approach. NIDES follow a hybrid intrusion detection technique consisting of a misuse detection component as well as an anomaly detection component. The anomaly detector is based on the statistical approach, and it flags events as intrusive if they are largely deviant from the expected behavior. To do this, it builds user profiles based on many different criteria (more than 30 criteria, including CPU and I/O usage, commands used, local network activity, system errors etc.) [19]. These profiles are updated at periodic intervals. The expert system misuse detection component encodes known intrusion scenarios and attack patterns (bugs in old versions of send mail could be one vulnerability). The rule database can be changed for different systems. One advantage of the NIDES approach is that it has a statistical component as well as an expert system component. This means that the chances of one system catching intrusions missed by the other increase. Another advantage is the problem's control reasoning is cleanly separated from the formulation of the solution.

There are some draw backs to the expert system approach. For example, the expert system has to be formulated by a security professional and thus the system is only as strong as the security personnel who program it [18]. This means that there is a real chance that expert systems can fail to flag intrusions. It is for this reason that NIDES has an anomaly as well as a misuse detection component. These two components are loosely coupled in the sense that they perform their operations independently for the most part. The NIDES system runs on a machine different from the machine(s) to be monitored, which could be unreasonable overhead. Furthermore, additions and deletions of rules from the rule-base must take into account the inter-dependencies between different rules in the rule-base. And there is no recognition of the sequential ordering of data, because the various conditions that make up a rule are not recognized to be ordered.

3.3.1. Keystroke Monitoring

Keystroke monitoring is a very simple technique that monitors keystrokes for attack patterns. The main approach is to pattern match the sequence of keystrokes to some predefined sequences to detect the intrusion. Unfortunately the system has several defects in which user definable aliases are present. The main problem with this approach is a lack of support from the operating system to capture the keystroke sequences. The method does not analyze the running of a program, only the keystrokes. However, there are many ways of expressing the sequence of keystrokes for the same attack. Some shell programs like bash, ksh have the user definable aliases utility. These aliases make it difficult to detect the intrusion attempts using this technique unless some semantic analysis of the commands is used. Automated attacks by malicious executables cannot be detected by this technique as they only analyze keystrokes. This means that a malicious program cannot be flagged for intrusive activities.

Since operating systems do not offer much support for keystroke capturing, the keystroke monitor should have a hook that analyses keystrokes before sending them on to their intended receiver. An improvement to this would be to monitor system calls by application programs as well, so that an analysis of the program's execution is possible.

3.3.2. Model Based Intrusion Detection

Keystroke monitoring states that certain scenarios are inferred by certain other observable activities. If these activities are monitored, it is possible to find intrusion attempts by looking at activities that infer a certain intrusion scenario.

The model based scheme consists of three important modules [15]. The *anticipator* uses the active models and the scenario models to try to predict the next step in the scenario that is expected to occur. A scenario model is a knowledge base with specifications of intrusion scenarios. The *planner* then translates this hypothesis into a format that shows the behavior as it would occur in the audit trail. It uses the predicted information to plan what to search for next. The *interpreter* then searches for this data in the audit trail. The system proceeds this way, accumulating more and more evidence for an intrusion attempt until a threshold is crossed. At this point, it signals an intrusion attempt.

This is a very clean approach. Because the planner and the interpreter know what they are searching for at each step, the large amounts of noise present in audit data can be filtered, leading to excellent performance improvements. In addition, the system can predict the attacker's next move based on the intrusion model. These predictions can be used to verify an intrusion hypothesis, to take preventive measures, or to determine what data to look for next. However, there are some critical issues related to this system. First, patterns for intrusion scenarios must be easily recognized. Second, patterns must always occur in the behavior being looked for. And finally, patterns must be distinguishing. They must *not* be associated with any other normal behavior.

Although the vulnerabilities of the past eighteen years may persist, model-based anomaly detection provides a mechanism to prevent attackers exploiting vulnerability from accessing or damaging the system. Intrusion detection systems (IDS) fill the gap between attack prevention and attack mitigation. An IDS attempts to identify attacks as they occur, and then prevents the attacks from completing successfully. A model-based anomaly detector is a type of IDS that has a pre computed model of acceptable execution behavior for each monitored process. The model describes actions that a process is allowed to execute. The anomaly detector interposes a monitor between a process and the operating system.

The monitor compares a stream of events, often system calls, flowing from the process to the operating system against the model and flags deviations as intrusion attempts. To be useful, anomaly detection systems should be both practical and effective. Practical detectors operate without human interaction and impose only small performance degradation upon process execution. Effective detectors precisely characterize the process expected behavior and detect attacks without producing false alarms.

Research in model-based anomaly detection falls into three categories: *model construction, model design, and model evaluation.*

- *Construction.* Development of a model-based anomaly detection system that automatically constructs program models via static analysis of the program's binary code. This analysis operates over legacy programs, requires no human interaction, and builds models that generate no false alarms.
- *Design.* A statically-constructed program model that characterizes precisely function call and return behavior and can be efficiently enforced by an execution monitor. Further models design that are customized to the execution environment every time the model is loaded for enforcement.
- *Evaluation.* Evaluation techniques to determine a model's ability to detect attacks. Even when those attacks come from knowledgeable, motivated attackers.

The advantage of model based intrusion detection is its basis in a mathematically sound theory of reasoning in the presence of uncertainty. The structuring of the planner provides independence of representation of the underlying audit trail syntax. Furthermore, this approach has the potential of reducing substantial amounts of processing per audit record. It would do this by monitoring for coarser-grained events in the passive mode and then actively monitoring ner-grained events when those events are detected.

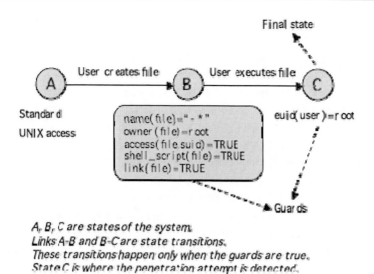

Figure 1. A State Transition Diagram for an example penetration in UNIX.

The disadvantage of model based intrusion detection is that it places additional burden on the person creating the intrusion detection models to assign meaningful and accurate evidence numbers to various parts of the graph representing the intrusion model. It is also not clear from the model how behaviors can be compiled efficiently in the planner and the effect this will have on the run time efficiency of the detector. This, however, is not a weakness of the model, but a consideration for successful implementation.

3.3.3. The State Transition Analysis

The State transition analysis approach uses the state transitions of the system to identify intrusions. This method constructs the state transition diagram, which is the graphical representation of intrusion behavior as a series of state changes that lead from an initial secure state to a target compromised state. State transition diagrams list only the critical events that must occur for the successful completion of the intrusion. Using the audit trail as input, an analysis tool can be developed to compare the state changes produced by the user to state transition diagrams of known penetrations. A transition takes place on some Boolean condition being true (for example, the user opening a file). State transition diagrams are written to correspond to the states of an actual computer system, and these diagrams form the basis of a rule-based expert system for detecting penetrations, called the state transition analysis tool (STAT). The STAT prototype is implemented in unix state transition analysis tool (USTAT) on UNIX-based systems. The approach followed in USTAT [17] is to have state transitions from safe to unsafe states based on known attack patterns.

The point of this attack is that whenever a hard link to a file is created, a new node with the target's original permissions is created. Since invoking a script invokes a sub shell, and further, if the name of the sub shell begins with a dash an interactive shell is created, we see that the attacker has obtained an interactive shell with root privileges. The state diagram for this is shown in Figure 1. We see that for the final compromised state to be reached, some conditions have to be fulfilled. If these guard conditions are true, then there is almost certainly an intrusion attempt going on. However, if any of these conditions do not hold, the probability of an intrusive action is considerably decreased. We see that the guard conditions exist to filter the intrusive activities from the non-intrusive ones. Hence, this can serve as a data pruning mechanism as observed in the model based scheme above.

The main advantage of the method is that it detects intrusions independent of the audit trial record. It is also able to detect cooperative attacks, variations to known attacks and attacks spanned across multiple user sessions and it can foresee impending compromise situations based on the present system state and take pre-emptive measures. This system has to be used along with some anomaly detector, because USTAT can detect only misuse intrusions.

However there are also a few problems with state transition systems. It can only construct patterns from sequences of events but not from more complex forms and therefore some attacks cannot be detected, as they cannot be modeled with state transitions. There are no general purpose methods to prune the search except through the assertion primitives described above. And finally, they cannot detect denial of service attacks, failed logins, variations from normal usage, and passive listening. This is because these items are either not recorded by the audit trail mechanism, or they cannot be represented by state transition diagrams.

A small point to be noted is that USTAT was never meant to be a stand-alone intrusion detection system, as discussed above, it is meant to be used with an anomaly detector so that more intrusion attempts may be detected by their combination. Some of the weaknesses of state transition systems are remedied by the Pattern Matching Model, discussed next.

3.3.4. Pattern Matching

Kumar [18] proposed a new misuse detection system based on Pattern Matching. This model encodes known intrusion signatures as patterns that are then matched against the audit data. Like the state transition analysis model, this model attempts to match incoming events to the patterns representing intrusion scenarios. Intrusions signatures are classified using structural inter relationships among the elements of the signatures. These structural interrelationships are defined over high level events or activities, which are themselves, defined in terms of low-level audit trail events. This categorization of intrusion signatures is independent of any underlying computational framework of matching. The patterned signatures are matched against the audit trails and any matched pattern can be detected as intrusion. Intrusions can be understood and characterized in terms of the structure of events needed to detect them. Model of pattern matching is implemented using colored pertinent in IDIOT (Intrusion Detection In Our Time).

The implementation makes transitions on certain events, called *labels*, and Boolean variables called *guards* can be placed at each transition. The difference between this and the state transition model is that the state transition model associates these guards with states, rather than transitions. The system can be clearly separated into three parts, intrusion signatures as patterns, the audit trails as an abstracted event stream and the detector as a pattern matcher. This makes different solutions to be substituted for each component without changing the overall structure of the system. Pattern specifications are declarative, which means pattern representation of intrusion signatures can be specified by defining what needs to be matched than how it is matched. Declarative specification of patterns enables them to be exchanged across different operating systems with different audit trails. Intrusion signatures can be moved across sites without rewriting them as the representation of patterns is standardized.

The important advantages of this model are:

1. Declarative Specification: It only needs to be specified what patterns need to be matched, not how to match them.
2. Multiple event streams can be used together to match against patterns for each stream without the need to combine streams. This means that streams can be processed independently, and their results can be analyzed together to give evidence of intrusive activity.
3. Portability: Since intrusion signatures are written in a system independent script, they need not be rewritten for different audit trails. The patterns' declarative specifications enable them to be exchanged across different Operating Systems and different audit trails.
4. It has excellent real-time capabilities. Kumar reports a CPU overhead of 5-6% when scanning for 100 different patterns, which is excellent.
5. It can detect some attack signatures like the failed logins signature that the state transition model cannot do.

However, there are few problems in this approach. Constructing patterns from attack scenarios is a difficult problem and needs human expertise. This model can only detect attacks based on known vulnerabilities (a problem with misuse detection systems in general) In addition, pattern matching is not very useful for representing ill-defined patterns and it is not an easy task to translate known attack scenarios into patterns that can be used by the model. Also, it cannot detect attacks involving passive methods of attack like wire-tapping intrusions, or spoofing attacks where a machine pretends to be another machine by using its IP address.

3.4. Other Models and Directions in Research

3.4.1. Generic Intrusion Detection Model

Dorothy Denning [14] introduced a Generic Intrusion Detection Model that was independent of any particular system, application environment, system vulnerability, or type of intrusion. The basic idea of the model is to maintain a set of profiles for *subjects* (usually, but not necessarily users of a system). When an audit record is generated, the model matches it with the appropriate profile and then makes decisions on updating the profile, checking for abnormal behavior and reporting anomalies detected. To do this, it monitors system services such as file accesses, executable programs, and logins. It has no specific knowledge of the target system's vulnerabilities, although this knowledge would be extremely useful in making the model more valuable. In fact, the Intrusion Detection Expert System (IDES) developed at SRI was based on this model. The basic ideas in this model appear with little modification in many systems built. However, there are some systems that do not fit easily into this model.

3.4.2. Network Security Monitor

NSM (Network Security Monitor) is an intrusion detection system developed at the University of California-Davis. NSM is a network-based IDS that differs from all of the IDS discussed earlier because it does not use or analyze the host machine(s) audit trails. Rather, it monitors network traffic in order to detect [20]. Since network based attacks are expected to be prevalent in the future due to the mushrooming of the Internet, NSM could prove to be a valuable tool to detect intrusive activity.

NSM has several perceived advantages. First, the IDS gets instantaneous access to network data. Second, the IDS is hidden from the intruder because it is passively listening to network traffic. Therefore, it cannot be shut off or its data compromised. Finally, the IDS can be used with any system, because it is monitoring network traffic, protocols for which (TCP, UDP etc.) are standardized. There is no problem with different audit files, for example. Researchers at Purdue University are working on several issues in intrusion detection.

3.4.3. Autonomous Agents

Crosbie and Spafford [14] propose to build an IDS using *Autonomous Agents*. Instead of a single large IDS defending the system, they propose an approach where several independent, small processes operate while co-operating in maintaining the system. The advantages claimed for this approach are efficiency, fault tolerance, resilience to degradation, extensibility and scalability. The foreseen drawbacks include the overhead of so many processes, long training times, and the fact that if the system is subverted, it becomes a security liability. An interesting possibility they open up is that of an active defense, that can respond to intrusions actively instead of passively reporting them (it could kill suspicious connections, for example).

4. Game Theory in Ad-Hoc Networks

Game theory is the study of the ways in which *strategic interactions* among *rational players* produce *outcomes* with respect to the *preferences* (or *utilities*) of those players, none of which might have been intended by any of them. The mathematical theory of games was invented by John von Neumann and Oskar Morgenstern (1944). For reasons to be discussed later, limitations in their mathematical framework initially made the theory applicable only under special and limited conditions. This situation has gradually changed, in ways we will examine as we go along, over the past six decades, as the framework was deepened and generalized. Despite the fact that game theory has been rendered mathematically and logically systematic only recently, however, game-theoretic insights can be found among philosophers and political commentators, going back to ancient times [4].

4.1. Basic Elements and Assumptions of Game Theory

An agent is, by definition, an entity with *preferences*. Game theorists, like economists and philosophers studying rational decision making, describe these by means of an abstract concept called *utility*. This refers to the amount of 'welfare' an agent derives from an object or an event. By 'welfare' we refer to some normative index of relative well-being, justified by reference to some background framework. For example, we might evaluate the relative welfare of countries (which we might model as agents for some purposes) by reference to their per capita incomes, and we might evaluate the relative welfare of an animal, in the context of predicting and explaining its behavioral dispositions, by reference to its expected fitness. In the case of people, it is most typical in economics and applications of game theory to evaluate their relative welfare by reference to their own implicit or explicit judgments of it. Thus a person who, say, adores the taste of pickles but dislikes onions would be said to associate higher utility with states of the world in which, all else being equal, she consumes more pickles and fewer onions than with states in which she consumes more onions and fewer pickles.

Some other theorists understand the point of game theory differently. They view game theory as providing an explanatory account of strategic reasoning. For this idea to be applicable, we must suppose that agents at least sometimes do what they do in non-parametric settings *because* game-theoretic logic recommends certain actions as the rational ones. Still other theorists interpret game theory *normatively*, as advising agents on what to do in strategic contexts in order to maximize their utility. Fortunately for our purposes, all of these ways of thinking about the possible uses of game theory are compatible with the tautological interpretation of utility maximization.

A crucial aspect of the specification of a game involves the information that players have when they choose strategies. The simplest games, such as chess, are an instance of such a game. Since game theory is about rational action given the strategically significant actions of others, it should not surprise you to be told that what agents in games know, or fail to know, about each others' actions makes a considerable difference to the logic of our analyses, as we will see. The difference between games of perfect and of imperfect information is closely related to (though certainly not identical with) a distinction between *ways of representing* games that is based on *order of play*.

4.2. Decision Theory

Decision theory [26] is a mean of analyzing which of a series of options should be taken when it is uncertain exactly what the result of taking the option will be. Decision theory concentrates on identifying the "best" decision option, where the notion of "best" is allowed to have a number of different meanings, of which the most common is that which maximizes the expected benefit to the decision maker. Since self-interested entities are assumed to be acting best when maximizing expected benefits, decision theory is often claimed to be able to make the most rational choice.

Game theory is close related to decision theory. In the same way that decision theory can be claimed to provide a means of making rational decisions under uncertainty, so game theory can be claimed to provide a rational means of analyzing interactions. Decision theory can be considered to be the study of games against nature, where nature is an opponent that does not seek to gain the best payout, but rather acts randomly. Although the area grew up long before the concept of an intelligent agent was conceived, such agents are canonical examples of the decision makers which can usefully employ classical decision theory.

4.3. Probability Theory

An agent operating in a complex environment is inherently uncertain about that environment. It simply does not have enough information about the environment to know neither the precise current state of its environments, nor how that environment will evolve. Indeed there is no universal agreement on what probabilities mean. Of the various conflicting schools of thought [27] there are two main positions. The first, historically, interprets a probability as a frequency of occurrence. The second, Bayesian, position suggests that a probability is related to the odds that a rational person will bet on the event in question.

For instance, the agent may be interested in choosing an action that will allow it to achieve a goal, and might therefore be interested in choosing that action which has the greatest chance of succeeding in achieving that goal. When the agent has many goals it could achieve, this strategy could be extended to make the agent choose to achieve the goal which has the greatest chance of being achieved, and to do this by applying the action which gives this greatest chance. To take account of this problem, decision theory makes use of the idea of *utility*.

4.4. Utility Theory

Let's start from the assumption that each agent (or decision maker) has its own preferences and desires about how the world is. Next, we assume that there is a set $\Omega = \{\omega 1, \omega 2, \ldots\}$ of "outcomes" or "states" that the agents have preferences over. Then let's capture the preferences that an agent has by means of a utility function, which assigns to every outcome a real number, indicating how "good" the outcome is. The larger the number, the better, from the point of view of the agent with the utility function. Thus:

$$U_i : \Omega \rightarrow R \tag{2}$$

It is not difficult to see that this leads to a preference ordering over outcomes. For example if ω and ω are both possible outcomes in Ω and $U_i(\omega) \geq U_i(\omega')$ then outcome ω is preferred by agent i at least as much as ω.

We can see that the above relation is a (partial) ordering, in that it has the following properties:

Reflexivity: For all $\omega \in \Omega$, we have that $\omega \geq \omega$.
Transitivity: If $\omega \geq \omega'$ and $\omega' \geq \omega''$, then $\omega \geq \omega''$.
Comparability: For all $\omega \in \Omega$ and $\omega' \in \Omega$ we have that either $\omega \geq \omega'$ *or* $\omega' \geq \omega$.

4.5. Bayesian Game

IDSs are important means to detect malicious node behavior. In ad hoc networks, most IDSs are proposed to individual nodes (e.g. [1, 2, 3, 4]) due to the lack of centralized management. To better defend a network, every defending node is suggested to be equipped with an IDS, and each IDS is assumed to be always on. That is to say, each defending node has to be in promiscuous mode. From a system usage perspective, always-on is not an efficient option because mobile nodes are often resource-constrained. To improve defender's monitoring efficiency, a game-theoretic approach is suggested to model the interactions between attacking node (attacker) and defending node (defender).

We formulate the attacker/defender game model in both static and dynamic Bayesian game contexts, and investigate the equilibrium strategies of the two players. The motivation behind our Bayesian game formulation is that generally an attacker/defender game is an incomplete information game [28] where the defender is uncertain about the type of his opponent (regular or malicious). A Bayesian game formulation provides a framework for the defender to select his strategies based on his belief on the type of his opponent.

The difference between a static and a dynamic Bayesian game is that the former does not take into account the game evolution, and the defender has fixed prior beliefs about the types of his opponent. In contrast, the latter is a more realistic game model because the defender can dynamically update his beliefs based on new observations of the opponent's actions and the game history, and then can adjust his monitoring strategy accordingly.

In the dynamic game model, a new Bayesian hybrid detection approach is suggested for the defender, with one being used as a lightweight monitoring system to estimate his opponent's action in each stage game, and the other being used as a heavyweight monitoring system, which functions as a last resort of defense. The heavyweight monitoring system is assumed to have more detection power than the lightweight monitoring system, e.g., can resolve attack sources or has higher detection rate. We show that the dynamic game produces energy-efficient monitoring strategies for the defender, while improving the overall hybrid detection power.

4.6. Static Bayesian Game

Consider a flat ad hoc network with a fixed number of N nodes in the network. It is assumed that any defending node is equipped with an IDS. Depending on the capability of the IDS, the defending node can detect an attacking node in the neighborhood or any node in the network. We consider a two-player static Bayesian game. One player is a potential attacking node, denoted by i. The other player is a defending node, denoted by j. Player i has private information about his type, which is either regular, denoted by $\mu_i = 0$, or malicious, denoted by $\mu_i = 1$. In other words, the maliciousness of player i is unknown to defender j. Defender j is of regular type denoted by $\mu_j = 0$. The type of defender j is common knowledge to the two players. The malicious type of player i has two pure strategies: Attack and Not attack. The regular type of player i has one pure strategy: Not attack. Defender j has two pure strategies: *Monitor* and *Not monitor*. The two players choose their strategies simultaneously at the beginning of the game, assuming common knowledge about the game (costs and beliefs).

Assume defender j's security value is worth of w, where $w > 0$. In practice, w represents a loss of security whose value is equivalent to a degree of damage such as loss of reputation, loss of data integrity, cost of damage control, etc. Therefore w is subject to different security policies. We also assume that there is an equal gain/loss w for both the defender and the attacker. This is reasonable when dealing with malicious nodes.

Table 1. Payoff matrix of Static Bayesian Game

(a)

	Monitor	Not monitor
Attack	$(1 - 2\alpha)w - c_a, (2\alpha - 1)w - c_m$	$w - c_a, -w$
Not *attack*	$0, -\beta w - c_m$	$0, 0$

(b)

	Monitor	Not monitor
Not *attack*	$0, -\beta w - c_m$	$0, 0$

(a) Player i is malicious. (b) Player i is regular.

Table 1 illustrates the payoff matrix of the game in strategic form.

In the matrix, α represents the detection rate of the IDS, β represents the false alarm rate of the IDS, and $\alpha, \beta \in [0, 1]$. w is defender j's security value. Costs of attacking and monitoring are denoted by c_a and c_m respectively, where $c_a, c_m > 0$. It is reasonable to assume that $w > c_a, c_m$, since otherwise the attacker does not have incentive to attack and the defender does not have incentive to monitor. In a resource-constrained network, cost of monitoring (c_m) can be defined as a function of energy consumption with respect to the monitoring activities. Cost of attacking (c_a) can be defined as a function of energy consumption with respect to the attack activities.

In Table 1(a), for the strategy combination (*Attack, Not monitor*), defender j's payoff is $-w$, and the malicious type of player i's payoff is his gain of success minus the attacking cost, i.e. $w - c_a$. For the strategy combination (Attack, Monitor), defender j's payoff is the expected gain of detecting the attack minus the monitoring cost c_m. The expected gain of detecting the attack depends on the value of α, which is:

$$\alpha w - (1 - \alpha)w = (2\alpha - 1)w \tag{3}$$

Note that $1 - \alpha$ is the false negative rate. In contrast, the malicious type of player i's gain is the loss of defender j, which is $(1 - 2\alpha)w$. Thus the payoff of player i is his gain minus the attacking cost. In both cases, defender j's payoff is 0 if he decides not to monitor, and he has a monitoring cost cm and an expected loss $-\beta w$ due to false alarms if he monitors.

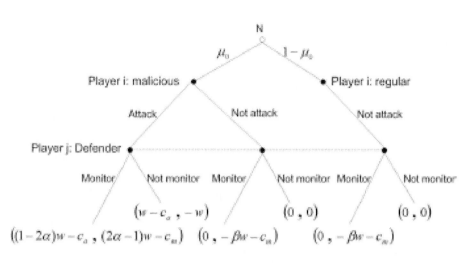

Figure 2. A Static Bayesian game.

In *Table 1(b)*, the payoff of the regular type of player i is always 0. The payoff of defender j is 0 if he decides not to monitor, and has a monitoring cost c_m and an expected loss due to the false alarm $-\beta w$, if he monitors.

4.7. Equilibrium Analysis

Suppose defender j assigns a prior probability μ_0 to player i being malicious. Figure 2 illustrates the extensive form of the static Bayesian game. In the figure, node N represents a "nature" node, who determines the type of player i. The objective of both players is to maximize their expected payoffs. This implies that we assume that both players are rational. The attacker would like to play a Bayesian strategy to minimize his chances of being detected, and the defender would also want to play a Bayesian strategy in order to maximize his chance of detecting attacks without overspending his energy on monitoring. In the following, we analyze the bayesian nash equilibrium (BNE) based on the assumption that μ_0 is a common prior, i.e. player i knows defender j's belief of μ_0.

If player i plays his pure strategy pair (*Attack* if malicious, *Not attack* if regular), then the expected payoff of defender j playing his pure strategy *Monitor* is:

$$Eu_j(Monitor) = \mu_0((2\alpha - 1)w - c_m) - (1 - \mu_0)(\beta w + c_m) \qquad (4)$$

And his expected payoff of playing his pure strategy *Not monitor* is

$$Eu_j(Notmonitor) = -\mu_0 w \qquad (5)$$

So if:

$$Eu_j(Monitor) > Eu_j(Notmonitor) \qquad (6)$$

or if:

$$\mu_0 > \frac{(1 + \beta)w + c_m}{(2\alpha + \beta - 1)w} \tag{7}$$

Then the best response of player j is to play *Monitor*. However, if defender j plays *Monitor*, *Attack* will not be the best response for the malicious type of player i, and he will move on to play *Not attack* instead. Hence, ((*Attack* if malicious, *Not attack* if regular), *Monitor*, μ_0) is not a BNE. However, if:

$$\mu_0 < \frac{(1 + \beta)w + c_m}{(2\alpha + \beta - 1)w} \tag{8}$$

the best response for defender j is *Not monitor* and thus ((*Attack* if malicious, *Not attack* if regular), *Not monitor*, μ_0) is a pure-strategy BNE.

If the malicious type of player i plays his pure strategy *Not attack*, defender j's dominant strategy is to play *Not monitor*, regardless of μ_0. However, if defender j plays Not monitor, the best response for the malicious type of player i is to play *Attack*, which reduces to the previous case. So strategy ((*Not attack* if malicious, *Not attack* if regular), *Not monitor*) is not a BNE.

We previously showed that no pure-strategy BNE exists for the game when

$$\mu_0 > \frac{(1 + \beta)w + c_m}{(2\alpha + \beta - 1)w} \tag{9}$$

A mixed strategy BNE is derived as follows. Let p be the probability with which player i plays *Attack*, and q be the probability with which defender j plays *Monitor*. The expected payoff of defender j playing *Monitor* is:

$$Eu_j(Monitor) = p\mu_0((2\alpha - 1)w - c_m) - (1 - p)\mu_0(\beta w + c_m) - (1 - \mu_0)(\beta w + c_m) \tag{10}$$

and the expected payoff of defender j playing *Not monitor* is:

$$Eu_j(Notmonitor) = -p\mu_0 w \tag{11}$$

By imposing $Eu_j(Monitor) = Eu_j(Notmonitor)$, we get that the malicious type of player i's equilibrium strategy is to play *Attack* with probability:

$$p^* = \frac{\beta w + c_m}{(2\alpha + \beta)w\mu_0} \tag{12}$$

Similarly, by imposing $Eu_i(Attack) = Eu_i(Notattack)$, we get that defender j's equilibrium strategy is to play *Monitor* with probability:

$$q^* = \frac{w - c_a}{2\alpha w} \tag{13}$$

Thus, strategy pair $((p^*$ if malicious, *Not attack* if regular), q^*, μ_0) is a mixed-strategy BNE. [7]

4.8. Dynamic Bayesian Game

The aforesaid static Bayesian game is a one-stage game, for which the defender maximizes his payoff based on a fixed prior belief about the maliciousness of his opponent. Due to the difficulty of assigning accurate prior probabilities for player i's types, we extend the static Bayesian game to a multistage dynamic Bayesian game, where the defender updates his beliefs according to the game evolution. We assume that the static Bayesian game is repeatedly played in each time period *tk*, where $k = 0, 1, \cdots$. An interval of T seconds may be selected for each stage game. We consider that the game has an infinite horizon because in general any node will not have the information about when his neighboring node leaves the network. The payoffs of the players in each stage game are the same as in the preceding static game, and we assume that there is no discount factor with respect to the payoffs of the players. That is to say that the payoffs remain the same in every stage game.

4.9. Rule of Beliefs

Since the lightweight monitoring system may inevitably produce false positives and false negatives, the "observed" actions may not always accurately reflect the reality. In order to avoid the effect of false alarm and misdetection errors for the lightweight IDS, the beliefs are updated by appropriately determining the conditional probabilities $P(a_i(t_k) \mid \theta_i, h_i^j(t_k))$. In more detail, by denoting with α_p and β_p the detection rate and false positive rate of the lightweight monitoring system, respectively, the above conditional probabilities can be updated as follows:

$$P(a_i(t_k) = \text{Attack} \mid \theta_i = 1, h_i^j(t_k)) = \alpha_p p + \beta_p(1 - p) \tag{14}$$

$$P(a_i(t_k) = \text{Notattack} \mid \theta_i = 1, h_i^j(t_k)) = (1 - \alpha_p)p + (1 - \beta_p)(1 - p) \tag{15}$$

$$P(a_i(t_k) = \text{Attack} \mid \theta_i = 0, h_i^j(t_k)) = \beta_p \tag{16}$$

$$P(a_i(t_k) = \text{Notattack} \mid \theta_i = 0, h_i^j(t_k)) = 1 - \beta_p \tag{17}$$

Note that $1 - \alpha_p$ represents the false negative rate, and $1 - \beta_p$ represents the true negative rate.

A Dynamic Bayesian game is a multi-stage game with observed actions and incomplete information. In a sequential game, the player's best responses are often guided by the threats about certain reactions for other players. In what follows, it is shown that the proposed multi-stage attacker/defender game has a perfect Bayesian equilibrium. At stage game tk, if defender j observes that the action of his opponent i was *Attack*, then his expected payoff for playing Monitor is:

$$Eu_j(a_j(t_k) = \text{Monitor} \mid a_i(t_k) = \text{Attack}) =$$

$$(((2\alpha - 1)w - c_m)p + (-\beta w - c_m)(1 - p))\mu_j(\theta_i = 1 \mid \cdot) + (-\beta w - c_m)\mu_j(\theta_i = 0 \mid \cdot) \tag{18}$$

and his expected payoff for playing *Not monitor* conditional on his observation is:

$$Eu_j(a_j(t_k) = \text{Notmonitor} \mid a_i(t_k) = \text{Attack}) = -wp\mu_j(\theta_i = 1 \mid \cdot) \tag{19}$$

So, player i chooses p^* (the probability with which player i plays *Attack*) to keep defender j indifferent between *Monitor* and *Not monitor*. That is, p^* is derived by setting the above equations equal. Consequently, we have:

$$p^* = \frac{\beta w + c_m}{(2\alpha + \beta)w\mu_j(\theta_i = 1 \mid \cdot)} \tag{20}$$

On the other hand, q^* (the probability with which defender j plays *Monitor*) is selected to keep the malicious type of player i indifferent between his strategies *Attack* and *Not attack*. The indifference condition is given as:

$$(((1 - 2\alpha)w - c_a)q + (w - c_a)(1 - q)) = 0 \tag{21}$$

and thus defender j's equilibrium strategy is to choose q^* as

$$q^* = \frac{w - c_a}{2\alpha w} \tag{22}$$

The PBE for the game is given as p^*, q^*, μ with p^*, q^*, μ given by the above equations, and to see why there is no pure strategy equilibrium for this game, we determine the best response strategy (BR) for both players to be:

$$BR_j = \text{Monitor if } p > \frac{\beta w + c_m}{(2\alpha + \beta)w\mu_j(\theta_i = 1 \mid \cdot)}$$

$$BR_j = \text{Attack if } q < \frac{w - c_a}{2\alpha w} \tag{23}$$

Using the above argument, we see that there is no pure strategy equilibrium for the analyzed dynamic Bayesian game.

4.10. Advantage of Dynamic and Multiplayer Consideration

The advantage of implementing the IDS system as a Bayesian hybrid IDS is that it allows to save significant energy (potentially spent on continuously monitoring the network), while minimizing the potential damage inflicted by an undetected attacker. This comes as a result of an interesting property of the equilibrium solution: the monitoring probability does not depend on the current belief of the defender on his opponent's maliciousness, but rather influences the attacker behavior. A high belief for the defender on his opponent being malicious results in the attacker drastically reducing his attacks. This is a result of the fact that both the attacker and the defender are rational players, and the costs and beliefs are common knowledge for both players. In practice, the attacker may estimate defender's beliefs according to his observations on defender's actions. Our simulation results show that by adding the very simple coarse-grained node-to-node analysis system in front of the association-rule analysis system will reduce the probability of false alarm for the overall equivalent IDS.

Both the static and dynamic Bayesian games proposed so far are two-player games. As we have already mentioned for the cross-feature analysis IDS, the two-player game can also be set up as the defender, against his entire neighborhood. This relaxes the assumption of pair wise interactions in the attacker/defender game. For our proposed hybrid IDS systems, the defender has also the option to evaluate each of his neighboring nodes individually using the coarse-grained node-to-node analysis system. In general, a maximum degree of uncertainty on the neighboring nodes' types can be reflected by selecting equal prior probabilities for the types of each node. As the game evolves, the defender learns about his neighbors through their past actions, and updates his beliefs accordingly. At each stage of the game, the defender can then determine his equilibrium monitoring strategy based on his highest posteriori belief on maliciousness among his active neighbors. Here, "active" means the nodes that have interactions with the defender.

5. Experimental Results and Simulation

For our experimental results we used a dynamic group of nodes (i.e. nodes can be added and removed from this group at any time) where they can be either malicious or regular (i.e. it might or might not attack other nodes) and have defending strategy from any malicious node that might attempt to attack them.

The nodes in the set play a *dynamic bayesian game*. In every round of this game, each node selects another one to play the game with. The former plays the role of the *potential attacker*, whereas the latter plays the role of the *defender*. It is assumed that all necessary parameters μ_0, w, c_a, c_m, α, β (described in subsection 5.6) are common knowledge between all nodes of the set.

After a specific node has found another node to play the game with, each node in this pair decides how it should move: the potential attacker decides whether it should *Attack* or *Not attack* and the defender whether it should *Monitor* or *Not monitor*. These *attack* and *monitor* decisions are made based on the value of the equations presented in 5.9.

5.1. Belief Update

The beliefs of each node for some or all other nodes in the set are updated after the completion of each round of the game. In particular, every defender updates its belief about the corresponding potential attacker and every node updates its belief about each neighboring node which is based on other nodes' beliefs at the end of each round of the game.

Initially, $\theta_{ij} = 0.5$ for all i, j which means that all nodes are initially believed to be neutral (neither regular nor malicious). Let us assume that in one of the rounds of the game node i selects node j to play the game with. Let θ_{ji} be the belief of defender j about potential attacker i before the beginning of the round and let θ_{ji}' be the belief of j about i after the completion of this specific round. Then:

$$\theta_{ji}' = \frac{\theta_{ji} + \text{update}}{2} \tag{24}$$

where update is equal to 0, if i did not attack j, or is equal to 1, if i decided to play *Attack* against j in this round. Based on the above equation, every defender is able to adjust its belief about any potential attacker, with which it has interacted, based on the move of the latter.

If interacting with a node was the only way for another node to know whether the former is regular or malicious, then every node would believe that any node, with which it had not interacted yet, is neutral, although it might have already attacked every other node in the set.

The proposed scheme allows the nodes of the set to exchange their opinions about each other. Essentially, after every game round, each node that has somehow updated its belief about some node (i.e. every node that played the defender's role in the specific round), send to every node in the set its beliefs about all nodes in the set. Once a node i receives the beliefs of another node j about the nodes of the set, it has two options: either to discard these beliefs, if they come from a node that it does not trust in the first place ($\theta_{ij} \leq 0.5$), or to take them into account and use them to update its own beliefs, if i has some evidence that j is not malicious.

Let θ_{ik} be the belief of node i about a node k, before node i receives the beliefs of node j. If θ_{ik}' is the new belief of i about k, after i has received j's beliefs, then:

$$\theta_{ik}' = w_{ij}\theta_{jk} + (1 - w_{ij})\theta_{ik} \tag{25}$$

where $w_{ij} = 0.5 - \theta_{ij}$. The above equation denotes that in every node i will value the opinion of any node j about a third node k *only as much as it values its own opinion about* k.

The advantage of the proposed scheme is that, by allowing every node to publish its beliefs about all other nodes in the set, it makes it possible for nodes to defend themselves against nodes with which they have not previously interacted (Figure 3).

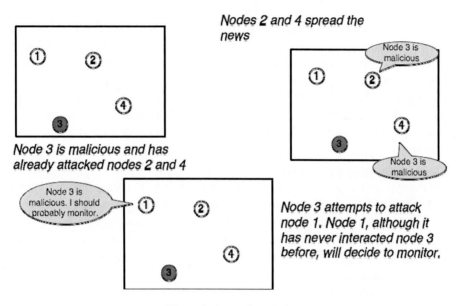

Figure 3. A good scenario.

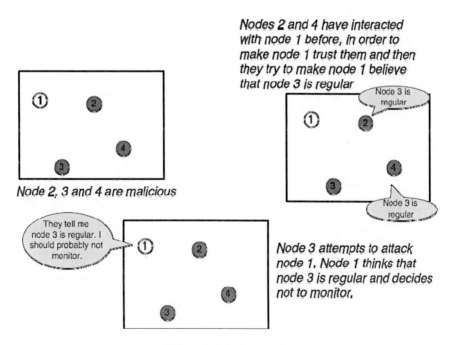

Figure 4. A bad scenario.

The proposed scheme suffers from the disadvantages that all approaches that are based on the cooperation between entities suffer: if the "bad guys" are more than the "good ones", then the "bad guys" will win (Figure 4).

6. Concluding Remarks

In this chapter, a Bayesian game formulation for IDS implementation in ad hoc networks is proposed. In these games, each player tries to maximize its payoff: the attacker seeks to inflict the most damage in the network without being detected, while the defender tries to maximize his defending capabilities with a constraint on its energy expenditure for heavy traffic monitoring using IDS, and without complete information on the type of his opponent. The dynamic game, allows the defender to update his belief about his opponent's type based on new observed actions and the game history. It is also shown that the dynamic game has a mixed-strategy.

A model of Bayesian hybrid detection approach, which uses the dynamic game model to derive equilibrium strategies for both players, is proposed. The equilibrium strategies can preserve energy expenditure, and improve the performance of the hybrid detection approach. It is shown that, while the equilibrium depends on the malicious node's knowledge on the defender's utility for different actions, and depends on what he thinks about the defender's updated belief, it is fairly robust to the malicious node's imperfect knowledge on the performance of the defender's lightweight monitoring system.

Finally, the most important aspect is that this Bayesian model works with nodes that act as a team with regard to how monitoring or attacking is performed.

References

[1]   M. Kodialam and T.V. Lakshman. Detecting network intrusions via sampling: A game theoretic approach. In *Proc. IEEE INFOCOM 2003*, volume 3, pages 1880-1889, March-April 2003.

[2]   T. Alpcan and T. Basar. A game theoretic analysis of intrusion detection in access control systems. In *Proceeding of the 43rd IEEE Conference on Decision and Control (CDC)*, December 2004.

[3]   A. Agah, S.K. Das, K. Basu, and M. Asadi. Intrusion detection in sensor networks: A non-cooperative game approach. In *Proceedings of the Third IEEE International Symposium on Network Computing and Applications (NCA'04)*, pages 343{346, August-September 2004.

[4]   T. Alpcan and T. Basar. A game theoretic approach to decision and analysis in network intrusion detection. In *Proceeding of the 42nd IEEE Conference on Decision and Control (CDC)*, December 2003.

[5]   Y. Zhang and W. Lee, "Intrusion Detection in Wireless Ad Hoc Networks", *The 6th Annual International on Mobile Computing and Networking*, Boston, April, 2000.

[6]   Farooq Anjum, Dhanant Subhadrabandhu , Saswati Sarkar "Signature based Intrusion Detection for Wireless Ad-Hoc Networks: A Comparative study of various routing protocols", *IEEE Vehicular Technology Conference*, October, 2003.

[7] Yu Liu, Cristina Comaniciu, Hong Man, "A Bayesian Game Approach for Intrusion Detection in Wireless Ad Hoc Networks", *ACM International Workshop on Game theory for communications and networks*, Italy, 2006.

[8] Simon Parsons, Michael Wooldridge, An introduction to game theory and decision making theory, Department of Computer Science, University of Liverpool, United Kingdom, Chapter 1, 2002.

[9] Anis Alazzawe, Asad Nawaz, Murad Mehmet Bayraktar, "Game theory and intrusion detection systems, secure e-commerce", *Secure e-Commerce*, Spring 2006.

[10] Marco Domenico Aime, Giorgio Calandriello, Antonio Lioy, "A wireless distributed system and a new attack model", *11th IEEE Symposium on Computers and Communications*, 2006.

[11] Christopher Kruegel, Darren Mutz, William Robertson, Fredrik Valeur, "Bayesian event classification for intrusion detection", *Annual Computer Security Applications Conference, Las Vegas*, 2003.

[12] J.P Anderson, *Computer Security Threat Monitoring and Surveillance*, Technical report, James P Anderson Co., Fort Washington, Pennsylvania, April 1980.

[13] Mark Crosbie and Eugene Spafford, *Defending a Computer System Using Autonomous Agents*, Technical Report CSD-TR-95-022, Department of Computer Sciences, Purdue University, 1995.

[14] Dorothy E Denning, "An Intrusion Detection Model", *In IEEE Transactions on Software Engineering*, Number 2, page 222, February 1987.

[15] T D Garvey and Teresa F Lunt, "Model based intrusion detection", *In Proceedings of the 14th National Computer Security Conference*, pages 372-385, October 1991.

[16] Koral Ilgun, "USTAT - A Real-time Intrusion Detection System for UNIX", *Master's Thesis*, University of California at Santa Barbara, November 1992.

[17] Sandeep Kumar, "Classification and Detection of Computer Intrusions", *Ph.D. Dissertation*, August 1995.

[18] Teresa F Lunt, "Detecting Intruders in Computer Systems", *FTA/MTC Conference on Auditing and Computer Technology*, 1993.

[19] Teresa F Lunt, "A survey of intrusion detection techniques", *In Computers and Security*, 12(1993), pages 405-418.

[20] Biswanath Mukherjee, L Todd Heberlein and Karl N Levitt, "Network Intrusion Detection", *IEEE Network*, May/June 1994, pages 26-41.

[21] Barton P Miller, David Koski, Cjin Pheow Lee, Vivekananda Maganty, Ravi Murthy, Ajitkumar Natarajan, Jeff Steidl, "Fuzz Revisited: A Re-examination of the Reliability of UNIX Utilities and Services". *Computer Sciences Department*, University of Wisconsin, 1995.

[22] Steven E Smaha, "Haystack: An Intrusion Detection System". *In Fourth Aerospace Computer Security Applications Conference*, pages 37-44, Tracor Applied Science Inc., Austin, Texas, December 1988.

[23] Eugene H Spafford, "The Internet Worm Program: An Analysis", *In ACM Computer Communication Review*, 19(1), pages 17-57, Jan 1989.

[24] Eugene H Spafford, *Security Seminar*, Department of Computer Sciences, Purdue University, Jan 1996.

[25] Henry S Teng, Kaihu Chen and Stephen C Lu., "Security Audit Trail Analysis Using Inductively Generated Predictive Rules", *In Proceedings of the 11th IEEE National*

Conference on Artificial Intelligence Applications, pages 24-29, Piscataway, NJ, March 1990.

[26] Raiffa, H. (1968), *Decision Analysis: Introductory Lectures on Choices Under Uncertainty*, Addison-Wesley, Reading, MA.

[27] Pratt, J. W., Raiffa, H. and Schaifer, R. (1995). *Introduction to Statistical Decision Theory*. MIT Press, Cambridge, MA.

[28] D. Fudenberg and J. Tirole. *Game Theory*. The MIT Press, Cambridge, Massachusetts, 1991.

In: Peer-to-Peer Networks and Internet Policies   ISBN: 978-1-60876-287-3
Editors: Diego Vegros and Jaime Sáenz, pp. 135-158   © 2010 Nova Science Publishers, Inc.

Chapter 5

COURSE DESIGN AND TEACHING MATERIALS FOR NETWORK LITERACY

Taeko Ariga

Department of Information and Media, Doshisha Women's College, Kyoto, Japan

Tomoko Yoshida

Department of Cross-Cultural Studies, Kyoto Norte Dame University, Kyoto, Japan

Abstract

This chapter deals with a teaching course for network literacy. We define network literacy as the ability to access, evaluate, and use digital information on the Internet, as well as to create digital information for dissemination on the Internet. It includes necessary skills for people to live in a networked information society.

In higher education all students, regardless of their major, need to learn how to use information on the Internet for solving their problems. Since students have been exposed to various kinds of information on the Internet before reaching college or university, they appear to have enough network literacy skills. In fact, many of them have adequate skills in the functional dimension, but not in the problem-solving dimension. They lack attitudes and skills that are necessary to evaluate information quality and to communicate effectively.

We designed a course for network literacy and developed teaching materials to cultivate skills and utilize the Internet effectively for solving problems. The course is composed of four units: (1) understanding what we can do with the Internet and basic technical knowledge about computer networks; (2) communication via e-mail; (3) critical evaluation of Web pages, including Web logs (blogs); (4) creation and evaluation of Web pages. In this chapter we provide checklists that were developed as teaching materials for the following purposes: to send e-mail for successful communication, to read Web pages critically, and to plan and evaluate original Web pages. These checklists guide students to effective learning.

The style and functions of information on the Internet have evolved with amazing speed. We can access new tools and contents on new Internet services, such as blog systems and social network systems. However, the appearance of new tools and services has not changed the core literacy skills that should be learned: how to evaluate information from the Internet and how to communicate over the Internet. In order to solve problems encountered at school, at work, and at home, it is essential for students to learn these skills in courses on network literacy. This course was originally designed for students of college or university; however, it can be applied in all disciplines and professions for people who did not study it in school.

1. Introduction

The development of computer networks, especially the development of the Internet, has brought big changes in information gathering, information exchange, and forms of media and means of transmission. As a result, in higher education all students, regardless of their major, need to study how to use information on the Internet for solving their problems.

Computer literacy education of the past emphasized basic knowledge of computer science and how to operate basic software. Arden introduces a syllabus for a first course in computing (Arden, 1964). "Curriculum 68" is an important document in the history of computer science education (Atchison,et al, 1968). It is quite detailed, and it shows how much things have changed since 1968.

The idea of information literacy grew from the late 1980s. A common definition of the term at that time states that "Information literacy is a set of abilities requiring individuals to recognize when information is needed and have the ability to locate, evaluate, and use effectively the needed information" (Hubbard, 1987). By integrating concepts of both library skills and computer literacy, information literacy has developed. In 1987 Eli Cohen argued that we should replace computer literacy with information literacy in general education (Cohen, 1987).

A lot of work was done in the 1990s, and then "Information Literacy Competency Standards for Higher Education" by the Association of College and Research Libraries (ACRL) was published in 2000 (ACRL, 2000). It is intended to ensure that post-secondary students have a firm grasp of how to access, evaluate, and use information in all forms appropriately.

On the other hand, in the late 1990s, the time when the Internet spread to general society, the usage of software related to the network began to be added to computer literacy education. Some new education courses on the Internet are reported, including the thesis of Gurwits (1997). However, the course only introduced training and the experience of the skill improvement. Revisions of the syllabus and the educational goals were not clear. In order to solve those kinds of problems, we treated network literacy education as a separate subject, independent from computer literacy education. We defined it as "network literacy," which is to study how to use information on the Internet for solving their problems. Furthermore, we designed a course for network literacy and developed teaching materials to cultivate skills and utilize the Internet effectively. We first announced it 1998 (Yoshida & Ariga, 1998) and another paper (Ariga & Yoshida, 1998) with teaching materials for it.

The concept of the course is an even broader principle of network computer literacy. Since 1998, we have promoted our network literacy course as members of the Information Processing Society of Japan (IPSJ). As a part of the activity, we published a book (Ariga & Yoshida, 1999) and a paper (Ariga & Yoshida, 2003). We received an "IPSJ Excellent Teaching Tool Developer Award" for the literacy course and the teaching materials in 2003.

Our course shares some features with "cyber-literacy," a term that appeared after 2000. For example, Stiller, et al, write about cyber-literacy, which seems related to our course (Stiller, et al, 2006). Although new terms have appeared, our course is still useful.

2. The Course for Network Literacy

2.1. Goal of the Course

The goal of our course is to offer detailed teaching materials for effective education. Because this network literacy cannot be acquired only by the experience of using computers, it needs a structured educational curriculum. It is the same thing that we can draw more accurately after the art class to learn perspective or an effective way to apply shadows. A class, even for a short time, helps us more than just drawing for an excessive amount of time.

One is likely to find some necessary information by chance, after clicking buttons for a certain period. The information might make you impressed. Generally speaking, to get the necessary information by using the Internet or to communicate by e-mail is a good experience. However, experience is no substitute for education in network literacy because it does not cultivate attitudes and skills to evaluate information quality and to communicate effectively.

2.2. Basic Principle of the Course

Let us think about the basic principle of the course next. It is to come to evaluate the actions of others and ourselves in critical ways and, based on that, to know what to do for solving problems that require new knowledge. For instance, it is ability that we can choose the Internet as an effective means to solve the problem, and can use it effectively. Even if the Internet is very convenient, it is not always the best source to use, and there are other ways to choose. The ACRL Information Literacy Competency Standards mention this in Standard Two as "student selects the most appropriate investigative methods or information retrieval systems for accessing the needed information."

Furthermore, we cultivate the ability to deal with a large amount of information, including that of poor quality. The ACRL Information Literacy Competency Standards mention this in Standard Three as "student evaluates information and its sources critically and incorporates selected information into his or her knowledge base and value system."

For all these abilities, we think the network literacy course should include not only operations but also basic technical knowledge about computer networks. Students have already had many kinds of courses, for example, a driving school course. It includes not only driving skills but also lectures concerning traffic rules. We believe both are necessary for driving without doubt. Similarly the network literacy course needs both.

2.3. Target Audience for the Course

This course was originally designed for students of college or university; it was developed for a class that meets once a week for 90 minutes over 14 weeks of one semester. We have applied the course to undergraduates since 1998. The number of students each year was from 150 to 200. Besides weekly classes, from 1998 to 2002 we conducted face-to-face intensive university courses with five 90-minute sessions each day for three days. The course has been offered as a subject for mainly first-year students in universities and colleges.

However, we don't focus on only undergraduates, but also on all persons within any discipline or profession who don't learn about network literacy in their school days. Our book (Ariga & Yoshida, 1999) was written to fit their independent study.

Finally, the course we designed and teaching materials we developed chiefly assume the use for three kinds of learners.

(a) For self-study by members of society and students who want to acquire network literacy.
(b) As a course text by students of university, vocational school, and high school.
(c) As teaching materials by teachers of university, vocational school, junior and senior high school, and elementary school courses.

For any kinds of learners, teaching materials such as worksheets and checklists are useful. We make some of them open to the public on the Internet.

2.4. The Structure of the Course

There are four units in detail for network literacy education. Table 1 shows the contents and skills. The content of each component is described in more detail.

Table 1. Outline of the network literacy course

Concepts	Contents	Tools and Technology
(1) Basic technical knowledge about computer networks	Structure of the Internet Comparison of communication	IP address, Domain names, TCP/IP, DNS, Encoding of English (ASCII Code) and Japanese characters, etc.
(2) Communication by e-mail	Characteristics of e-mail Manner of e-mail Evaluating one's own e-mail	Mailer, Mailing list, Mail system, Attached file, etc.
(3) Critical evaluation of Web pages	Characteristics of Web pages Evaluating Web pages	Web browser, Directory system, Search engine, etc.
(4) Creation and evaluation of one's own Web pages	Project, design and creation of one's own Web pages Evaluating one's own Web pages	HTML, Text editor, CSS, RGB color system, etc.

(1) Basic Technical Knowledge about Computer Networks

This unit leads to understand what we can do with the Internet and basic technical knowledge about computer networks. To learn the structure of the Internet is useful for understanding the characteristic of it. For example, the brief history, IP(Internet Protocol) address and domain names, the protocol used by the Internet, TCP/IP, DNS(Domain Name System), the encoding of English and Japanese characters.

Additionally, students can understand that there are services on the Internet other than e-mail and the Web, as well as other technologies. For example, they come to be able to think by comparing mail and past means of information exchange, such as telephone and postal mail. Besides, there are FTP (File Transfer Protocol), video conference, and using computers by remote login.

(2) Communication by E-mail

The ability of writing sentences by using e-mail is a significant combination of skills to express accurately what you want to communicate. In addition, smooth communication by e-mail needs understanding of the characteristics of e-mail and techniques to deal with e-mail effectively.

(3) Critical Evaluation of Web Pages

This unit is concerned with search strategies and how the Web is different from other sources, such as encyclopedia, books and newspapers. First of all, we teach the differences of search engines of the directory type and the full-text search type, and how to choose one of them properly. We help learners understand the range and the features of Web searching as a tool to receive intelligence and discover what possible information can be obtained from the Web through maneuvers to search out target information.

It is important to evaluate a huge amount of Web information and its sources critically for understanding the content and creating Web pages. Critical thinking about the use of Web pages is learned by using of checklists we developed.

(4) Creation and Evaluation of One's Own Web Pages

The last unit for learning Web page creation and the evaluation of one's own work emphasizes the perspective from which information is actually written. We have students create and evaluate their own Web pages, not only to study HTML tags, but also to write sentences that are appropriate for readers' levels.

In the next section, we present the contents of the course and teaching materials for units (2), (3), and (4).

3. Contents and Teaching Materials

3.1. Communication by E-mail

If you consider e-mail a traditional letter that can reach the recipient in a very short time, you may think that there is no need to learn about communication by e-mail in a network literacy course because it is the same as by post. However, the new method requires a new art of communication. The ability of writing sentences is a significant combination of skills to express accurately what you want to convey by e-mail as well as by traditional mail. In addition, smooth communication by e-mail needs understanding of the characteristics of e-mail and techniques for dealing with it effectively.

3.1.1. Understanding Characteristics of E-mail Communication

In this section of the course, at first we make students consider characteristics of e-mail from the perspectives of both senders and recipients. Understanding features of e-mail correspondence is a starting point to learn how to make good use of e-mail for communication.

The following list shows aspects from the viewpoint of a sender.

- You can write it at any time that is convenient.
- You can send it right after you finish writing it. You don't need to go to a post office.
- You can easily copy as a quotation what the other person wrote.
- You can utilize existing electronic data as part of a mail body or in attached files.
- You can send it to more than one person at a time.
- Your mail can reach its destination in a short time, wherever the physical address is.
- You don't know whether the recipient has read it or not, as well as traditional mail. In a case of telephone, you can directly convey what you want to say.
- You can never take it back after sending it. In a case of a traditional letter, you may be able to recall it before the recipient opens an envelope.
- Your original sentences in your e-mail can be easily copied as quotes, including misspelled words and mistakes. Especially in case of a mailing list, it may happen that your mistakes are spread and repeatedly copied.

For a recipient, e-mail has characteristics as follows:

- You read it on a computer monitor. You may print it and read all of it or parts of it.
- You can read it at any time that is convenient.
- You can read it at any place where you can reach the Internet wherever you are geographically.
- You can recognize the degree of urgency by the subject.
- You can categorize and save e-mail, and search e-mail by dates or keywords
- You may not be able to read e-mail because of a problem of character codes.
- You can receive attached files. These may be necessary for you or cause damage to you.

At the beginning of this unit of the network literacy course, students compare several ways for communication: e-mail, telephone, facsimile, post, and face-to-face meetings with the following viewpoints:

- response
- certainty of delivery
- degree of freedom in time for communication
- degree of freedom in place for communication
- keeping record
- confidentiality

- degree of easiness in one-many communication
- cost

This exercise makes students think choice of the best way to communicate at a certain situation as well as understand features of e-mail clearly.

There are two sides to e-mail: written documents and conversations. While e-mail is a text message, the communication by e-mail happens to be done like oral conversation, since you can respond immediately and exchange e-mail many times in a short period of time. Full usage of both good features brings a merit to e-mail communication. However, exchange of e-mail by students is inclined to conversation. The spread of mobile phones, which provide a function to correspond with short messages, exacerbates this tendency. In oral conversation, we can supplement a lack of information in real time to avoid misunderstanding. Even if e-mail is exchanged quickly and it seems like conversation with texts, additional explanations for prevention of miscommunication can't be added beforehand in response to recipients' reaction, due to a time lag. Accordingly, it is necessary to learn to write e-mail. In the next section in the course we show students a checklist of guidelines to write e-mail with careful consideration of recipients. To realize the characteristics of e-mail brings students to understand the meaning of items in the checklist.

3.1.2. Evaluating one's Own E-mail Using a Checklist

To cultivate the attitude of examining e-mail critically before sending it, we developed a checklist for e-mail before sending. When you write e-mail, it is important to check it before clicking a "send" button. We would like students to acquire the habit of reviewing written e-mail critically, based on the proper knowledge of e-mail technology and characteristics. An exercise to evaluate their own e-mail using the checklist can help to raise critical awareness.

The checklist has 36 items divided into five categories (Table 2). The four categories except the last one, "posting to a mailing list," are concerned about common checkpoints for all e-mail, and the items in the last category apply to e-mail addresses to a mailing list.

Except items (1), (2), (21), and (23), all items are yes-no questions; and each corresponds to a guideline for writing e-mail. There are two sets of choices for yes-no questions: one set has three choices: "yes/no, no/yes, need to change/check," and the other set has two choices: "yes/no, need to change/check." In case of the three choices, students answer yes or no, and then consider the necessity to change or check it. For example, if students answer no to item (19), "Do you write your full name in the body?" they are expected to state their intention of change by marking "need to change." However, it is not always inevitable. It means that they can decide not to write it if they have a reason. There is tolerance to accept a gap between actual e-mail and a guideline. The important matter is for students to recognize the lack of compliance and to be able to explain the reason for it. On the other hand, items with the two choices are much more rigid rules, and if students can't mark the first choice, they have to mark the other choice "need to change/check", and then refine their e-mail.

Table 2. Checklist for e-mail before sending

Purpose and contents	(1) Who are you sending to?	friend teacher, person in business, other ( )
	(2) What is purpose of your e-mail?	conveyance of information, greeting question, exchanging opinions, other ( )
	(3) Is it written concisely?	yes, no, need to change
	(4) Is expression of date and time proper?	yes, no, need to change
	(5) Is expression proper to a receiver's culture and language?	yes, no, need to change
	(6) Is there meaningless quotation?	no, yes, need to change
	(7) Is there flame expression?	no, yes, need to change
	(8) Is it a chain mail?	no, need to check
	(9) Do you need to ask permission to sending it?	no, need to check
Layout	(10) Is a length of a line less than 70 characters?	yes, no, need to change
	(11) Do you put a blank line between paragraphs for readability?	yes, no, need to change
	(12) Do you emphasize the important point?	yes, no, need to change
	(13) Do you put marks for quoted parts for distinction to your sentences?	yes, no, need to change
	(14) Do you put a question on a line in case of asking question?	yes, no, need to change
Elements	(15) Is subject apt for the purpose?	yes, no, need to change
	(16) Do you confirm addresses in TO and CC?	yes, no, need to change
	(17) Is sending e-mail with proper in case of using BCC?	yes, no, need to change
	(18) Is it clear from the body whom e-mail is written to?	yes, no, need to change
	(19) Do you write your full name in the body?	yes, no, need to change
	(20) Is your signature less than 3 to 5 lines?	yes, no, need to change
	(21) How many lines does your e-mail have?	about ( ) lines
	(22) Does a recipient expect and accept attached files?	yes, no, need to change
	(23) How many bytes is your attached file?	( ) bytes none
	(24) Is it proper in case of sending HTML e-mail?	yes, no, need to change
Copyright /Privacy	(25) Do you violate other's copyright?	no, need to change
	(26) Do you give the source of quotations?	yes, no, need to change
	(27) Do you invade your family or other's privacy?	no, need to change
	(28) Do you write information that should not be put in e-mail?	no, need to change
Posting to a mailing list (ML)	(29) Is the ML a proper place to post your e-mail?	yes, no, need to change
	(30) Do you get permission in case of quoting from e-mail that you received in personal?	yes, no, need to change
	(31) Do you double check addresses in TO and CC?	yes, no, need to change
	(32) Is there no expression against public order?	no, need to change
Posting to a M L	(33) Are usage of technical terms and abbreviation understandable in the ML?	yes, no, need to change
	(34) Do you obey the rules of the ML?	yes, no, need to change
	(35) Do you confirm that the ML accepts it in case of sending HTML e-mail?	yes, no, need to change
	(36) Does ML accept attached files?	yes, no, need to change
	(37) Do you know the range of the ML: who members are?	yes, need to check
	(38) Do you know whether posted e-mails will archive later on?	yes, need to check

(1) Purpose and Contents

An e-mail client program provides functions that set addresses and quote from received e-mail automatically just by clicking a button such as "reply." If students don't realize what a program does, it probably causes trouble, for example, sending e-mail to the wrong persons, or making full quotation of the original e-mail unintentionally. To avoid that, it is not enough to only know how to operate an e-mail client program; they must also understand roles of e-mail. The items of this category increase awareness of purposes and contents of e-mail. Items (1) and (2) ask about obvious matters that seem as if there is no need to answer. However, who you are writing to and what the purpose of your e-mail is determine the style of writing. To answer these questions brings out a process of reviewing the contents of one's e-mail.

Item (9) is not applicable to every e-mail. When you write e-mail on behalf of a group or an organization, the item gives you a chance to consider whether you are the right person to write it and if what you are writing is necessary.

(2) Layout

E-mail is normally read on a computer monitor, and it is harder than reading on paper. The sentences of e-mail must be brief and concise to compensate for this difficulty. Items in the second category are mainly related to layout of sentences in order to make e-mail text easier to read.

Item (10) states the length of a line. It lets students imagine a recipient's computer monitor displaying your e-mail. If a line of e-mail is longer than the length that an e-mail client program can properly handle, a line is broken at unintentional point. It makes readability decreased. Students need to direct attention to a length of a line. There is a way to begin a new line when writing a long sentence. In case that you use an e-mail client program that has a function to cut a long line short when it sends, you must check a setting of the length of a line.

Item (12) guides students to place emphasis with marks, such as a sharp or an asterisk, on important dates or keywords. The body of e-mail is plain text format; so you can't use color or special font styles for emphasis and layout like with a word processing program. Using marks properly helps for emphasis and simple visual contrast. Someone may think that we can use HTML e-mail in order to put decorations on sentences in an e-mail; however, you should not use HTML e-mail except when a recipient specially expects it.

Item (14) is for cases that your purpose of writing e-mail is to ask questions. Since you generally expect the recipient to answer your questions, it is desirable to lay out questions by thinking about the recipient's behavior. It is normally anticipated that the recipient will quote each question first and write an answer to each question. Laying out one question on a line helps the recipient write answers easily and orderly.

(3) Elements

This category gives instructions about components of e-mail: a header, a body and attached files. Items (15), (16), and (17) are related to main fields of the header that a sender sets: Subject, To, Cc, and Bcc. "Subject" gives important information for a recipient to suppose the contents of e-mail. Students tend to write greeting words for "Subject" like conversation. Since a recipient normally determines by fields "From" and "Subject" whether to read it immediately, later, or never, "Subject" should include specific keywords that reflect the contents of e-mail.

Item (16) asks students to check again recipients' addresses before clicking a "send" button in an e-mail client program. When you send e-mail to more than one person at once, you write more than one address in "To" and "Cc". That means that your e-mail announces e-mail addresses of all recipients, even if you do not intend it. Item (16) makes students consider whether it is right or not in case recipients don't know each other.

Though it is not so usual for students to send e-mail using a blind carbon copy (Bcc), they have to know its function and not to be puzzled when they receive e-mail by Bcc. Students learn about a function of Bcc and how it is shown in an e-mail program through item (17).

Students tend to think that fields "From" and "To" give enough information to identify recipients and senders. However, "From" and "To" fields don't always have real names in addition to e-mail address. Even if there is a real name in a header, the body should include the names of both the recipient and the sender to make it clear who e-mail is addressed to and from.

The body and attached files are main factors in determining the size of e-mail. The second half of items in this category is related to the size of e-mail. Your e-mail will cause less annoyance if you ask about the recipient's e-mail environment and willingness to receive large files in advance.

We already mention HTML e-mail above. Item (24) reminds students which format of e-mail they are about to send and why. If students select HTML e-mail in an e-mail client program, both plain text and HTML are sent as multipart e-mail, with the result that the length of e-mail becomes more than double. Even if recipients use an e-mail program without supporting HTML e-mail, they can read e-mail as plain text. Therefore, it may seem to be no problem if both formats of e-mail are sent. But it is a nuisance that useless double size of e-mail occupies the recipient's storage media.

(4) Copyright and Privacy

Items about copyright and privacy are matters to consider as well as for a postal corresponding. These items help students avoid violations of the law and intrusions on other persons' privacy. Even in cases of private correspondence, students have to be prudent when they include others' copyrighted works in e-mail, especially attaching documents, music, or image files. Because a digital data file can be easily copied, a file that they attach might be spread to others without realizing it.

Students' e-mails that incline to conversation are apt to include private matters of intimate people. If these matters are kept just between senders and recipients, it doesn't bring a big problem. However, a recipient may copy sensitive matters and send to other persons. Since it is easy to copy all or a part of e-mail, a situation like the gossip game, Chinese whispers, readily occurs. Item (27) directs students' attention to that situation. Item (28) makes students concerned about their own secret information like passwords. Even if e-mail is encrypted, it is possible to break the security. It is recommended not to write important information that you would not write on a postcard.

(5) Posting to a Mailing List

A mailing list is a group of members who share a common interest, and the list is used for discussion and exchanging information. When students post e-mail to a mailing list, cautions are required besides matters that are already mentioned until now. A sender must follow the rules of the mailing list: do not attach any file, and do not quote the full previous e-mail. Item (34), (35), and (36) help students raise awareness of these points.

Item (37) asks the range of members of a mailing list. A sender doesn't always know all of the recipients when sending to a mailing list. Students have to become conscious of the range of recipients. If members of a mailing list are limited to persons who have met each other in the likes of a club or class, it is easy to know the range. However in case of a big mailing list, recipients must be considered anonymous persons.

Some mailing lists keep all e-mail posted for members' convenience as archives. If you post e-mail including errors or defects, it is retained for a long time. Item (38) is for awaking awareness of this feature.

3.1.3. Exchanging E-mail with a Mobile Phone

Each country has a different situation of e-mail with mobile phones. In Japan, so-called Keitai mail prevails among users of mobile phones; Keitai means a mobile phone. Keiai mail is similar to SMS (Short Message Service) messaging, but users can exchange much longer messages and correspond with users on the Internet seamlessly. Mobile phone carriers provide e-mail addresses to users in addition to IDs for SMS. They can send e-mail to and receive from addresses on the Internet. In case of using a mobile phone, users can read and write e-mail anywhere they are. Senders expect recipients to response immediately due to this convenience. In consequence of exchanging quick responses, communication by mobile phone e-mail tends to a style of spoken conversation much more than normal e-mail on the Internet, and users come to lack basic consideration for standards designated on the checklist: for example, meaningless subjects like greetings, and no real names in the body. We put the section for communication of e-mail with a mobile phone after learning communication by e-mail.

Though everyone has a mobile phone and knows how to use it, students seldom have opportunities to be taught how to utilize them for the better communication outside of an educational framework. That is why the network literacy course also encompasses matters concerning the exchange of e-mail with mobile phones, even though the subjects to be learned in this section are basic and overlap with previous parts about e-mail.

3.2. Evaluation of Web Pages

The technology of World Wide Web was developed to share documents with people all over the world through the Internet. At first, people published Web pages on their expertise for nonprofit purposes. The style and functions of information on the Internet have changed and evolved with amazing speed from the early days of when the Internet became common. We can access new tools and contents on new Internet services, such as blog systems and social network sites. As the kinds of Web sites have been diversified, the way that people utilize Web pages has changed. Regardless of how the contents have varied, a skill of evaluating the contents is inevitable and sustainable. In a setting of solving problems encountered at school, at work, and at home, students need to judge the quality of Web information that they access, no matter what kind of Web sites they utilize. This unit in the network literacy course provides exercises to train evaluation skills.

3.2.1. Characteristics of Web Information

We start this unit of the course with understanding features of Web pages before learning the way to find information from the Internet and judge its value. Web pages have the following features:

- Hyperlinks
  Related information is provided through an anchor link. Links allow readers to navigate in a structure of information of a Web site. The order of reading is not fixed in one way.
- Diversity of media
  Web information includes not only text, but also image, sound, and movie.
- Influence of readers' environment
  Computer platforms of readers affect appearance of Web pages.
- Lack of proofreading
  No third party checks reasonableness and accuracy of Web pages for most personal Web sites. Credibility and reliability may be suspicious.
- Information retrieval
  Full-text search by automatic indexing allows readers to find information in compensation for the disorderly mass of documents on the Web.

Everyone can equally create Web sites and publish diffuse information regardless of authority, financial background, or organization. It is a great merit. On the other hand, the quality of the contents varies widely, and there is a lot of information that is incorrect and malicious. Likewise, since it is very easy to change and delete Web pages as well as to publish, we may not able to see tomorrow what we can access on the Internet today. If publishing and maintaining Web pages aren't done by sustainable organizations, they have less value as reference data.

Since no one organizes Web information space, we need a way to find information in it. It is a search engine that provides a function of full-text search. Portal service companies provide a function for searching. Such companies have original systems for automatic indexing and ranking Web pages. Students have to understand the basic mechanism of full-text search and differences between searching Web sites and consulting the index of a book.

We give students an exercise to find information from the Internet. We prepare questions for which answers exist somewhere on the Internet, for example, on a government office Web site or a researcher's Web site. This exercise trains students who are not familiar with searching to find information effectively by using a search engine. However, the main aim of the exercise is to lead students to consider the credibility of data that they find.

3.2.2. Checklist for Reading Web Sites Critically

In the process of finding information on Web pages, a problem is raised about how we can rely on them. The objective of the next section of the course is to evaluate the quality of information. There is a large literature on Web site evaluation from the information literacy perspective (see, e.g., Alexander & Tate, 1999; Cooke, 1999; Kapoun, 1998). Likewise, much has been written about the design of Web sites from the user interface, training, business, and usability perspectives. Jakob Nielsen's work is typical of this area (Nielsen, 1999; Nielsen & Tahir, 2001).

Web sites have a wide range of purposes: providing facts and data, advertising, electronic commerce, commentary, education, and so on. Cooke (2001) wrote that any assessment of quality is dependent upon the needs of the individual seeking information, as well as on the nature of the source being evaluated. Naturally, each type of Web site has specific factors for evaluation. However, a standard basis of evaluation is common for all types of Web sites in respect to conveying information. We developed an evaluation standard and checklist to read Web pages critically as teaching materials for a network literacy course (Yoshida & Ariga, 1998; Ariga & Yoshida, 2003).

Table 3 is a checklist for reading Web pages critically. It is composed of 32 items divided into five categories. It is a revised version of the checklist in our book (Ariga & Yoshida, 1999).

(1) Target / Coverage

The main subjects and purpose of a Web site should be stated at the beginning of a Web site. The first four items of this category are related to targeted readers and purposes. A Web site with clear statements about these matters enables readers to determine quickly whether it is necessary for them now. Likewise, that information provides the intention of an author or a publisher, which is one of factors in judging the credibility of a Web site. Readers can also recognize whether a Web site gives facts or opinions, original information, or reviewed information from the abstract and objectives.

(2) Source

Readers can basically decide that these are credible Web sites if they are published by companies or organizations with fixed reputations in the real world. Otherwise, readers need some information on authors' expertise or experience to judge credibility. A Web site that gives this information is more reliable.

When a Web site provides a way to make contact with an author or a publisher, it shows their attitude that they welcome feedback from readers. It is considered a positive factor in respect of creditability. Unfortunately, there are persons with malicious intention in cyberspace. If an author gives a contact e-mail address on a Web site, it might cause attacks by numerous hostile e-mails. Therefore, it is not always necessary to carry such information.

(3) Contents

Items (10) and (11) make students aware of the date of publishing and most recent update. When students read the contents of Web sites, these are understood and utilized in relation to contemporaneous knowledge and society. Therefore, the date of publishing is invaluable information as well as in books or other printed documents. In the case of the contents that should be renewed regularly, such as monthly reports, if these Web sites have been left without updating for longer than the normal period, these must be probably considered untrustworthy.

Text is the main way to carry information on Web sites. Reading texts on a computer monitor requires readers to be more patient than on paper. Readable texts enhance the quality of pages. The length of paragraphs and sentences, titles, and terms are points for scanning for readability.

Item (17) is related to accessibility. Web information comprises text, images, sounds, and movies. However, not all users can see them, depending on readers' environments. The contents should be understandable even if only text is displayed. Such Web pages meet the needs of users with disabilities and older users. In addition, such pages are appropriate for users who turn off the display of images in their browsers and those who can't see images for some reason.

Hyperlinks make the Web an effective medium, but poor hyperlinks that mislead or frustrate users diminish the value of Web sites. For example, if hyperlinked words are inappropriate, users have to look at a Web page that is totally different from what they expect. Items (18), (19), and (20) check hyperlinks. Item (18) includes broader viewpoints rather than concrete questions in item (19) and (20). It aims to lead students to ponder what appropriate hyperlinks are in terms of linked words and destinations.

(4) Composition / Design

Web users can read pages in a browser window of any size. If a Web site is developed for a fixed size of a browse window, it irritates users. Item (21) raises students' awareness of this point.

Students learn through item (17) that a Web site of high quality is understandable even if no graphical elements are displayed. Naturally, it doesn't mean to deny the role of graphics. Images, sounds, movies, and interactive elements enhance comprehensibility of the contents and users' experience. The important point is that those elements should contribute positively to the page's purpose. If such elements are not used to meet necessity for the contents, they just increase time for loading and bother users. Items (22), (23), and (24) check how such elements work.

A Web site has a non-sequential structure by hyperlinks, which help users to grasp the outline of complex contents and reach information that they seek. Items (25), (26), and (27) aim at considering effective Web navigation.

(5) Platforms

An author or a publisher can't specify users' environments to read Web pages. Regardless of which OS and browser are used, the contents of Web pages should be provided equally.

Table 3. Checklist for reading Web site critically

<table>
<tbody>
<tr><td rowspan="6">Target / Coverage</td><td>(1) Is there a clear title?</td><td>yes,   no</td></tr>
<tr><td>(2) Is there abstract of the contents at the beginning of the site?</td><td>yes,   no</td></tr>
<tr><td>(3) Who is an intended reader?</td><td>person with same interest,
student,
not specified,
other(   )</td></tr>
<tr><td>(4) What are the objectives of the site?</td><td>providing fact,
advertizing,
education,
e-commerce,
commentary,
other(   )</td></tr>
<tr><td>(5) Are the contents of the site the author's original?</td><td>yes,   no</td></tr>
<tr><td rowspan="4">Source</td><td>(6) Is this site published by an organization? Who is it?</td><td>yes,   no</td></tr>
<tr><td>(7) Is the author's background given? What is it?</td><td>yes,   no</td></tr>
<tr><td>(8) Do you think that the author has enough knowledge to provide such information? Why do you think so?</td><td>yes,   no</td></tr>
<tr><td>(9) Is there information to make contact with authors or publisher?</td><td>yes,   no</td></tr>
<tr><td rowspan="11">Contents</td><td>(10) Is the date of update given?</td><td>yes,   no</td></tr>
<tr><td>(11) Do the contents need frequent renewal?</td><td>yes,   no</td></tr>
<tr><td>(12) Are appropriate titles given for items on pages?</td><td>yes,   no</td></tr>
<tr><td>(13) Is text information properly paragraphed?</td><td>yes,   no</td></tr>
<tr><td>(14) Is length of each sentence too long?</td><td>yes,   no</td></tr>
<tr><td>(15) Are buzzwords used in the page appropriate for intended readers?</td><td>yes,   no</td></tr>
<tr><td>(16) Are there typographical errors?</td><td>yes,   no</td></tr>
<tr><td>(17) Do users understand the contents if images are not visible?</td><td>yes,   no</td></tr>
<tr><td>(18) Are links appropriate and well-structured?</td><td>yes,   no</td></tr>
<tr><td>(19) Are links to external pages clearly marked as such?</td><td>yes,   no</td></tr>
<tr><td>(20) Are any links dead?</td><td>yes,   no</td></tr>
<tr><td rowspan="7">Composition / Design</td><td>(21) Are the contents displayed properly if users change the size of a browser window?</td><td>yes,   no</td></tr>
<tr><td>(22) Do typographic style and colors contribute positively to the page's purpose?</td><td>yes,   no</td></tr>
<tr><td>(23) Are graphics necessary and effective for the page's purpose?</td><td>yes,   no,   no graphics</td></tr>
<tr><td>(24) Are interactive elements necessary and effective for the page's purpose?</td><td>yes,   no,
no such element</td></tr>
<tr><td>(25) Is the method of movement between pages (link or button) clear?</td><td>yes,   no</td></tr>
<tr><td>(26) Are navigation operations consistent through the site?</td><td>yes,   no</td></tr>
<tr><td>(27) Is a function of search inside of a site? *</td><td>yes,   no</td></tr>
<tr><td rowspan="5">Platform</td><td>(28) What OS are you using?</td><td></td></tr>
<tr><td>(29) What browser are you using?</td><td></td></tr>
<tr><td>(30) What speed of accessing to the Internet?</td><td></td></tr>
<tr><td>(31) Is speed of loading pages of the site not too slow on your environment?</td><td>yes,   no</td></tr>
<tr><td>(32) Is the site created on premise of using a specific environment? What is it?</td><td>yes,   no</td></tr>
</tbody>
</table>

* Applicable for a Web site comprised of more than several pages.

Therefore, it is not desirable that Web pages are developed on the assumption of a specific computer and browser. The items in this category first ask about students own environments of their computers and networks and then check whether a Web site takes the user's platform into consideration.

Readers have to judge the quality of information on Web sites when they seek some information and select it. Strictly speaking, the accuracy of the contents can't be checked without consulting other books, documents, or experts. However, a Web site itself gives analytic points to allow readers to consider what degree they can trust information there. The exercise of reading a Web site critically with the checklist is to lead students to a process of proofreading. We expect students to read as editors rather than as checkers who answer simply yes or no. We select a Web site that conveys information related to Internet technology for the exercise in class. At first, students read the Web site while checking with the checklist, and then we require students to comment about it as editors.

There are many personal Web sites for self-assertion or company Web sites for showing fashionable trends on the Internet. All of such sites have not been created with binding to guidelines of design and style. Therefore, in the course, we consider the evaluation of Web pages that are published for providing factual information. This exercise trains students' skill not only to find factors in determining the value of Web sites, but also to create Web sites with high quality that will learn in the fourth unit.

3.2.3. Web Blogs

Web blogs are online Web pages that are created and maintained using easy tools provided. In order to publish a Web site, an author needs some minimum knowledge of how to make a blog and access a Web server for uploading. However, in case of Web blogs, they don't need anything at all besides access to the Internet. It is one of the distinguishing characteristics from normal Web pages that anyone can easily publish his or her own personal voice on a Web blog. Therefore, many people write Web blogs of just personal experience, like diaries. On the other hand, Web blogs also have roles in business, politics, journalism, and family affairs.

Characteristics of the blog space differ among regions and countries. In North America Web blogs with social and political objectives have become very popular, and some have affected people's actions and opinions. In Japan a high percentage of Web blogs have been created for personal concerns. An organization of the Japanese government, the Institute for Information and Communications Policy (IICP) reported motivations for establishing Web blogs in 2008: 30.9% for self-expression, 25.0% for archives of personal data, 25.7% for communication of groups with common interests, 10.1% for business, and 8.4% for contribution for society. Most Web blogs that gain popularity in Japan are personal diaries established by famous athletes and entertainers. A survey by a public relations firm (Edelman & Technorati, 2006) reveals that 34% of bloggers publish Web blogs to establish authority in their fields. The respondents of this survey were from the United States (54.8%), Canada (6.58%), and Western Europe. The firm conducted a similar survey of Japanese bloggers. Only 4.7% of Japanese bloggers build their Web blogs for increasing visibility as authorities in their fields. There is a clear distinction of intentions for establishing Web blogs between Japan and the United States.

Students read Web blogs for a wide range of purposes, while differences among countries in bloggers' intentions influence students as readers. In Japan, a majority of students read Web blogs for personal amusement. In case of Web blogs for family members and intimate friends, they don't generally need to care about quality because they are using Web blogs as a tool to communicate about private matters, like letters and telephone calls. On the other hand, we have to realize that Web blogs are frequently listed in search engine results. When students read them for seeking something with durable value, critical consideration and evaluation of quality is required. Evaluation guidelines showed in Table 3 can generally apply to Web blogs. Especially information on target readers and author's biographies are important. Web blogs by anonymous authors can't be judged as valuable to read.

Moreover, there is another distinguishing feature from normal Web sites. It is that Web blogs have a framework of publishing basically in a chronological format: each article is attached to a date. Unless the main objective of a Web blog is just to show a personal diary, a calendar is not an adequate way to provide organized information. Web blog software provides a function to categorize articles besides by subjects or tags. Appropriate categories that articles are classified into make users find articles easy and increase the value of the contents for reference. Therefore, the way to find articles other than in chronological format is a key point to evaluate worthiness of reading.

3.3. Creation of Web Pages

In the final unit of the course, students learn knowledge and responsibility as information creators. A Web site with objectives related to an author's activity, job, or interest is published as a way to solve and expand various situations at school, at work, and at home. In order to simulate Web site creation in a real situation, we undertake a project in the course. What they learn through the project encompasses not only technical skill of creation, for example HTML and Cascading Style Sheets (CSS), but also planning, evaluation of their own Web sites, and maintenance as a post-production process.

3.3.1. Process of Creation

Figure 1 shows stages of the process to create a Web site:

- Planning
  Draw up a Web site plan using the planning worksheet.
- Research
  Collect data and documents related to the contents of a Web site.
- Total design
  Determine the structure of a Web site and ways of navigation.
- Page design
  Determine visual style, color, graphics, and layout
- Actual Creation
  Prepare images and text and assemble them using HTML and CSS according to the visual design to be determined in the previous process.
- Test / Evaluation

Test the whole Web site to confirm that all pages are displayed and that all implemented functions work. Additionally, evaluate whether the Web site fits the intended objectives.

- Publishing

  Upload all files that are comprised the Web site to a Web server.

- Maintenance

  Update the contents and check links to outside pages periodically in order to keep information on a Web site active and fresh.

Web site development projects must be carried out in various courses for learning Web technology. The project in class might be done like this: students learn technical matters such as HTML and editing images, and then assemble Web pages about a chosen topic. However, these just correspond to the process of actual creation in Figure 1. In our network literacy course the aim of Web site development encompasses not only the technical dimension but also the total process of creation, including planning and evaluation.

In educational goals in the total process of creation, technical knowledge such as HTML and CSS is easy to learn because these are concrete and clear. On the other hand, learning in the processes of planning, design, and evaluation is not simple conveyance of knowledge. It requires exercise in the evolution of a project from planning to evaluation. We prepare a worksheet and a checklist to enhance the effects of learning in those processes. A worksheet for planning and a checklist for evaluation are introduced in the following two sections. Worksheets for a design process are developed by Ariga and Watanabe (2008).

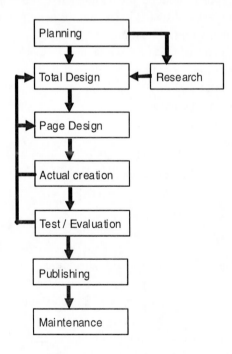

Figure 1. Process of creation.

Table 4. Planning worksheet

Theme / purpose	(1) What is theme?
	(2) What is purpose? providing fact advertizing education e-commerce commentary other
	(3) Who are intended readers? person with same interest student not specified other
	(4) What do you want to convey most?
Structure	(5) Structure of contents
Source	(6) What is the source of contents? original review archive
	(7) How do you get original information? survey interview own experience
	(8) How do you describe your background and contact address?
	(9) Do you need to ask permission to publish the contents? How, if needed?
Schedule	(10) When do you publish?
	(11) What is schedule of production
Priority	(12) Keep time of publication low 1---------- 2 ---------- 3 high (13) Provide unique information low 1---------- 2 ---------- 3 high (14) Provide elaborate structure and texts low 1---------- 2 ---------- 3 high (15) Provide excellent visual design low 1---------- 2 ---------- 3 high (16) Special point for excellence low 1---------- 2 ---------- 3 high ( )

3.3.2. Worksheet for Planning

At the beginning of a project, students are asked to determine a theme about which to create a Web site and elaborate their plan in accordance with the planning worksheet that is shown in Table 4. It has 16 items in five categories that require students to specify the theme, objective, targeted users, contents, time of publication, and production schedule. We provide the planning worksheet to students as a handout in class. The handout has more space for writing than shown in Table 4, which has been reduced to save page space.

Item (4) asks students to state what they want to express in a Web site. A theme is asked in item (1) and it might be written by a short sentence or a phrase. We require students to expand on a theme and write several sentences to describe it. In order for students to write more than two or three sentences, they need to consider how to treat their themes concretely. Consequently, the written sentences in item (4) become clearly stated objectives that help students when they have something indeterminable in the following processes, such as design or the structure of content.

Items (6) and (7) ask about sources of information on a Web site and aim to increase awareness of where students get information for their Web sites. There is a lot of useful and organized information on the Internet, such as on Wikipedia. Students easily copy data from those Web sites and paste to their Web pages. It is acceptable to quote information from the others' Web pages; however, the important thing is to develop their consciousness of sources of information.

Item (9) confirms whether permission is necessary to publish the contents that students plan for their Web sites. This is applicable when they establish a Web site on behalf of a group, or when they publish something of other persons' work or private matters.

Students are asked to set the order of priority by marking 1, 2 or 3 for the five items in the priority category. We expect students to assign high priority to item (12) because a project to create a Web site in class has a limited period of time. Besides emphasizing a deadline, this category intends to bring out each Web site's strong points by thinking which items have higher priorities. Assigning priorities is to declare their commitment to concentrate special effort on achieving their principal objectives.

3.3.3. Checklist for Evaluating one's Own Web Pages

After a process of actual creation, students proceed to a process of testing. In this process students check whether all features in a Web site are active or not. Are all pages and images displayed? Do all interactive functions behave as students intended? The result of testing is simply whether they work or not. If not, students move back to the previous process and modify errors in order to make features work correctly.

The next process after testing is to evaluate the quality of their Web pages. The process of evaluation requires students to make more intricate judgments than those in the process of testing. Therefore, we have developed checklists to lead students to evaluate their own Web pages.

Web pages are displayed on a monitor and read as having interaction with users. In this sense Web pages have user interfaces, while at the same time they have concrete contents. The process of evaluating quality is divided into two phases: one is to check the quality in terms of the interface, and the other is to reflect on the entire content. Table 5 shows the checklist for an interface, which adds a few alternations to the checklist proposed by Ariga & Yoshida (1999) and Ariga & Watanabe (2008). Table 6 shows the checklist for self-evaluation of Web contents.

Students' Web pages should comply with guidelines designated on the checklist. However, some parts of Web pages might deviate from the guidelines for the sake of expressive visual design. Therefore, it is possible for student to determine not to change elements if they answer no to the item. The important matter is for students to recognize the lack of compliance and to be able to explain the reason for it.

Items in Table 5 are divided into four categories and are in the form of yes-no questions. It is desirable to answer yes to each question. When answer is no and there is intention of changing it, students are required to check the column of "need to change." If Web pages have no elements described in an item, no mark is filled in.

Table 5. Checklist for User Interface

	Items for checking	Y	N	Need to change
Clarity	Are titles suitable for the page's contents?			
	Is important information displayed properly in terms of position and emphasis?			
	Is information on the Web site organized logically?			
	Are different kinds of information clearly separated? (e.g.,. descriptions of web pages themselves, lists, quotations, indexes)			
	Are sections aligned properly, for example indentation and structure of lists?			
	Are colors used to make contents clear?			
	Can users easily read contents on monochrome monitors or printe pages in black-and-white?			
	Are contents aligned properly using titles and paragraphs?			
	Are tables and graphics displayed clearly?			
	Are meanings of list and menu items clear?			
	Can users easily recognize the contents of pages that all links lead to?			
Consistency	Are colors and typography consistent throughout the site?			
	Are abbreviations and terminology consistent throughout the site?			
	Are icons and illustrations consistent throughout the site?			
	Is layout for instructions, menus, navigation, and titles consistent throughout the site?			
	Are the same kinds of information displayed in a consistent manner throughout the site?			
	Are navigation operations consistent throughout the site?			
Operation	Is there an easy way to the previous page in the site structure?			
	Is there a way back to the top page from wherever the user is?			
	Is there a way for users to easily find what they want?			
User's expectation	Does usage of colors follow the common practice, for example red for warning?			
	Can target users understand words, abbreviations, and units used?			
	Can target users understand the meanings of icons and illustrations used in pages?			
	Are idioms and phraseology familiar to target users?			
	Is certain information (e.g.,. date and telephone number) described in the standard notation in the target field?			
	Is information provided in consideration of diversity in users' expectations and behavior? (e.g., experts, novices, or frequent readers)			
	Can users know easily where they are in the site?			

Table 6. Checklist for Web content by self-evaluation

(1) What is the title of the site?	
(2) Do you state clearly the objectives of the site?	yes, no
(3) Do terms and expression have the proper difficulty for targeted readers?	yes, no
(4) Does the site have enough contents to convey what you intend?	yes, no
(5) Does the site have proper visual design to the theme and targeted readers?	yes, no
(6) Do images and sounds work effectively?	yes, no, not applicable
(7) Do interactive elements work effectively?	yes, no, not applicable
(8) Does the site violate someone's copyright?	yes, no
(9) Does your site include anyone's privacy?	yes, no
(10) What did you consider most about the structure of the site?	
(11) What did you contrive for visual design?	
(12) Are you satisfied with your priorities on the planning worksheet? Why?	

Four categories in Table 5 express points of enhancing usability. The items in the category Clarity require that information on Web pages to be explicit, well-classified, unambiguous, and easy to read. The category Consistency demands that ways to display information and ways to navigate to information are consistent throughout the site. The category Operation requires a flexible structure of navigation to meet users' needs. The last category designates elements in Web pages that should correspond to user's expectations.

After checking the user interface, self-evaluation of the contents is done with a checklist shown in Table 6. This process is more likely to evoke reflection rather than just checking. Items from (2) to (9) are yes-no questions. Someone might think that answers are self-evident and that there is no point in asking these questions. Since students are supposed to do their best efforts to implement their plans based on what they learned from evaluation of Web sites mentioned in section 3.2, their answers should be no to items (8) and (9) and yes to the others. Nevertheless, these items are meaningful for making students aware of points designated in each item. Items (10), (11), and (12) call for reflection on their creation process. These require students to write several sentences on what they conceive and how they make it feasible.

4. Conclusion

We have described a course for network literacy that was separated from learning of computer literacy and developed as an independent course. Checklists and a worksheet as learning materials have been introduced.

The network literacy course aims that students come to utilize a variety of information on the Internet to solve problems encountered at school, at home, and at work: to communicate over the Internet, to collect information for their interest from the Internet, and to publish results of their work on the Internet. For the sake of these aims, the course trains students to evaluate the actions of others and themselves on the Internet in critical ways rather than by merely operating software. Students need clear standards and guidelines to learn these skills;

we provide them as checklists. Four checklists are introduced for their own e-mail, reading Web sites critically, user interfaces of their own Web sites, and self-evaluation of their own Web sites. A project of Web site creation in the course starts with the elaboration of a plan with a planning worksheet and ends with self-evaluation with a checklist. If a project starts without making the target and objectives clear and ends just by browsing a Web site without reflection, it doesn't enhance skills of evaluation. We hope students will not be satisfied to merely create miniature Web sites, but to publish information for their needs in real life outside class. Learning in the total process of creation establishes the fundamental skills for this purpose.

Acknowledgment

The authors would like to express special thanks to Professor Gregory Peterson at Kyoto Notre Dame University for his kind review and helpful advice for this English manuscript.

References

Association of College and Research Libraries. (2000). Information Literacy Competency Standards for Higher Education [Online]. [Cited on April 15 2010]. Available from: http://www.ala.org/ala/mgrps/divs/acrl/standards/standards.pdf

Alexander, J.E., & Tate, M.A. (1999). Web wisdom: How to evaluate and create information quality on the web. Mahwah, NJ: Lawrence Erlbaum Associates.

Arden, B.W. (1964). On introducing digital computing. *Communications of the ACM*, **7**(4), 212-214.

Ariga, T., & Yoshida, T. (1998). Nettowa-ku riterashi-kyouiku no shirabasu to kyouiku kenkyuu [The study of the "Network Literacy" course]. *Konpyu-ta to Kyouiku,* **50**, 25-32. (SIGCE Information Processing Society of Japan 98-CE-50).

Ariga, T.,& Yoshida, T. (1999). *Internet-koza[Lecture on Internet: Learning Network Literacy]*. Kyoto: Kitaoji Publishing.

Ariga, T., & Yoshida, T. (2003). Nettowa-ku riterashi- kyouiku no jugyo sekkei to kyouzai kaihatsu [Course design and teaching materials for "Network Literacy"]. *Japan Journal of Educational Technology,* **27**, 181-190.

Ariga, T., & Watanabe, T. (2008). Teaching materials to enhance the visual expression of Web pages for students not in art or design majors. *Computers & Education.* **51**, 815–828.

Atchison, W.F., Conte, S.D., Hamblen, J.W., & et al. (1968). Curriculum 68: Recommendations for academic programs in computer science: a report of the ACM curriculum committee on computer science. *Communications of the ACM,* **11**(3),151-197.

Cohen, E. (1987). What is computer literacy: the sham, the imposter, and the misdirected. *CSC '87: Proceedings of the 15th annual conference on Computer Science*, 320-322.

Cooke, A. (2001). *A guide to finding quality information on the internet.* Library Association Publishing.

Edelman & Technorati. Public RelationSHIPS: Communications in the age of personal media [Online]. 2006[Cited 2009 2 14]. Available from: http://www.edelman.com/image/ insights/content/BloggerSurvey_FINAL_fromprinterRVSD.pdf:

Gurwits, C. (1997). The Internet as a Motivation Theme in a Math/Computer Core Course for Nonmajors. *SIGCSE BULLETIN*, **29**(1), 68-72.

Hubbard, S. (1987). Information Skills for an Information Society: A Review of Research. *ERIC Digest*, (ED327216) 4p.

Institute for Information and Communications Policy. The survey of the actual situation of weblog [Online]. 2008[Cited 2009 2 14]. Available from:

http://www.soumu.go.jp/iicp/chousakenkyu/data/research/survey/telecom/2008/2008-1-02-2.pdf:

Kapoun, J. (1998). Teaching undergrads WEB evaluation: A guide for library instruction, *College and Research Libraries News*, **59**(7), 522-525

Nielsen, J. (1999). *Designing Web usability: The practice of simplicity.* Indianapolis: New Riders Press.

Nielsen, J., & Tahir, M. (2001). *Homepage usability: 50 Websites deconstructed.* Indianapolis: New Riders Press.

Stiller, E., & LeBlanc, C. (2006). From computer literacy to cyber-literacy. *J Journal of Computing Sciences in Colleges,* **21**(6), 4-13.

Yoshida, T., & Ariga, T. (1998). *Chekkurisuto wo tsukatte Web pe-ji no hihanteki hyouka to sono kouka* [A critical evaluation checklist for Web pages and its effectiveness]. *Proceedings of the 56th conference of the Information Processing Society of Japan, 4,* 260-261.

In: Peer-to-Peer Networks and Internet Policies
Editors: Diego Vegros and Jaime Sáenz, pp. 159-178

ISBN: 978-1-60876-287-3
© 2010 Nova Science Publishers, Inc.

Chapter 6

Faculty Learning in Online Courses

Luis Miguel Villar Angulo
University of Seville, Spain
Olga María Alegre de la Rosa
University of La Laguna, Spain

Abstract

Online education is used for a variety of purposes in higher education. Two such purposes are the improving of one's performance over time and the elucidation of one's professional development for others in the context of online teaching and learning. Relying on data from some online staff development courses delivered in universities, this chapter explores online faculty learning through the lens of staff development theory. This theoretical perspective emphasizes the universities' quality assurance contexts and offers an empirical examination of the ways that faculty members learn curriculum and teaching capacities (CTC) in online staff development programs. At the core of this analysis is the contention that faculty members interprets and responds to quality teaching. Finally, this chapter highlights the points deemed important when designing, implementing and evaluating Internet training courses.

1. Introduction

In this chapter, we use six pillars as a conceptualization of quality e-development in order to gain more insight and facts regarding specific and pertinent issues, which affect faculty learning. The framework shown in Figure 1 is aligned to the management and business excellence EFQM (European Foundation for Quality Management) model.

The process flow diagram below shows the general steps involved in understanding faculty e-development program analysis.

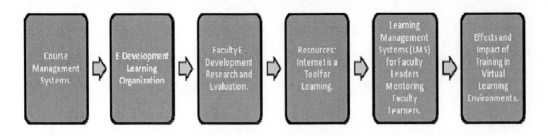

Figure 1. Staff E-Development Criteria.

2. Course Management Systems

E-development is defined as continuing professional training (CPT) that is provided for university staff 'in substantial part' using the Internet, or any other technology 'du jour'.

Online CPT for faculty learning includes courses and workshops delivered partly via the Internet for the acquisition of lower-level skills (e.g. learning to operate a projector) to higher-level competencies (e.g. faculty training in problem-based learning), while distance faculty development is training delivered through a mixture of electronic media (videotapes, interactive television, emails, Internet, and so on). Some university strategic plans and mandates to incorporate Internet technology into educational practice have proliferated in many higher education institutions. In effect, the new institutional vision for teaching and learning in higher education identifies areas of training that require urgent attention, and communication and information technological training are the most emphatically specified areas. However, there is still little formal research into various institutional and academic aspects for online CPT courses.

At the same time, universities are establishing policies to give technological support and guide hybrid-training programs in conjunction with a face-to-face course format for university teachers. Institutional support for faculty members when they design and implement e-learning courses is widespread and its value-added effect evaluated by students (Brew, 2008; Young, & Norgard, 2006). The new virtual and voluntarily teaching task is very tiring and time-consuming and believed by faculties to require more extra and unpaid work than the development of conventional face-to-face course delivery. Online CPT courses, seminars and workshops can meet the needs of both novice university personnel who attend formal multisession professional development programs and tenured professors who want to attend short, hybrid and more flexible workshops. The programs and courses are aimed at seeking academic expertise and also proficiency in interpersonal skills such as warmth, empathy, authenticity and sincere interest in the university student as a learner.

E-development may help faculty instructors to find ways to encourage reflective practice, to foster the change necessary to create an environment that promotes excellence in lifelong learning competencies, ongoing social learning, and communities of practice. Broadly speaking, faculty members are professionals engaged in self-directed CPT as adult learners. As such, university CPT units help university teachers to build knowledge on their prior experience, support learning by action, aid social participation, promote collaborative strategies to curriculum research and innovation, emphasize a respectful learning environment, and value colleague reinforcing and empowering comments from all online CPT participants (Knight, Tait, & Yorke, 2006). It is evident that the potential of online information and web interactive systems requires the fostering of a life-long learning culture by university managers and staff, which places value on professional development by staff.

For individual members of staff, various institutional support plans have been set out to facilitate their own development. For instance, postgraduate certificates in higher education have been developed in many universities as a means of supporting novice teaching staff (Hewson, & Hughes, 1999). For some universities, the provision of qualifications in higher education teaching and learning processes is related to better academic jobs, promotion, and monetary incentives. Thus, faculty participation in online innovations and courses plays a major role in the adjustment and acceptance of new technologies that will attain the university's quality mission.

2.1. Institutional Aspects of Faculty E-Development Courses

The openness, ease of use, variety and visibility of resources are essential to enable e-development processes to be used formal learning activities in higher education institutions (Malikowski, 2008). The ways, in which faculty e-development programs and concepts are organized varies, according to:

a) *Facilities* (for instance, the need to connect easily, rapidly and consistently with course websites, and the practical issue of producing study materials on DV (Digital Video).
b) *Infrastructure* (i.e., web-platform facilities, and wireless communications systems).
c) *Organization* (for example, support departments, and the activities of learning and teaching coordinators).
d) *Goals* (for example, empowerment in e-learning as the final purpose or aim in teaching).
e) *Content concepts* (e.g., knowledge society as a central policy objective).

2.2. Main Pedagogical Characteristics of the Use of E-development Systems

The use of faculty e-development is changing at least some of the ways that faculty members perceive and perform their professional duties (Galanouli, Murphy, & Gardner, 2004; Georgina, & Hosford, 2008; Georgina, & Olson, 2008). Blending e-development and traditional workshops is a valued option for faculty members on campus. Instructors see a need for blending e-development programs, or being part of the blended teaching staff, because they comprehend that e-development courses augment university teachers' meaningful interaction with their peers. Therefore, e-development systems should implement constructivist learning methodologies that will help the instructors' knowledge building through peer collaboration.

A central part of a staff e-development strategy fosters written interaction instead of oral interaction. The online CPT course dynamics change: the reading and writing pedagogical knowledge are now increased. Consequently, new faculty communication skills are demanded: instructors are to be reflective thinkers and rapid writers. Staff narratives scrutinize ideas in the mind, emotions, memory, perceptions, intentions, meaning, and other paralinguistic modes of communication.

High quality learning is characterized by being able to discover knowledge for oneself, perceive relations between old knowledge and new, and apply one's knowledge to solving problems. Online CPT programs must take the issue of time pressure for creative knowledge into account. The shift from 'fixed time' weekend workshops to e-development programs with no time boundaries creates a special set of options and difficulties for staff advisers and consultants and faculty members in order to better address curriculum and teaching conceptions and misconceptions. The amount of time needed to use many technological tools demands too much of both novice faculty teachers and course advisors. The concern that web-technology use will create a time burden for faculty is frequently expressed in metaanalysis research reports (Tallent-Runnels et al., 2006).

Below is a brief summary of the key pedagogical characteristics related to online CPT course management:

- Demand for more modes of e-development systems that can be logged into and checked for the nature, process and status of a program, seminar or workshop proposal at any point in the training process.
- Delineation of expected e-development outcomes assessment tools and quality assurance terminology.
- Meaningful social and educational identification processes for all proposed e-development courses and programs.
- Centralized contact in each department, with a knowledgeable manager who can monitor pedagogical and discipline-centered e-development proposals, as opposed to all department faculties working independently on various curriculum innovation proposals in different modes of presentation.

3. E-development Learning Organization

Universities need tools for selecting the right system for managing faculty e-development programs, because some web-based course management systems provided within CPT are not, in general, utilized to their fullest capacity. Management faculty e-development programs include planning, organizing, structuring, tracking, reporting, communicating arrangements and expectations, and many other learning activities that take time and require orderliness on the part of the manager-academics. University managers and faculty consultants want online CPT and participatory environments, not just 'CPT management' containers or training packages.

It is worth quoting Malikowski, Thompson, & Theis (2007, p. 156) at some length on this point, because it underlies the five related categories in the proposed research model that can guide the organization and the value of online CPT tools and features: "These categories are: (a) transmitting course content; (b) evaluating students; (c) evaluating courses and instructors; (d) creating class discussions; and (e) creating computer based instruction".

Effective faculty e-development platforms are tools that control and monitor individual access, involve knowledge organization, facilitate collaborative and cooperative learning, communication and problem-solving analysis, supply electronic documents, conduct thoughtful opinions, and assess electronic performance in discussions, provide feedback, and so on.

It is essential for faculty members to be given the opportunity to evaluate e-development programs, whether it is a software package (e.g., a module of a job training and counseling workshop) that can be integrated into a main program (social faculty community), or hardware like an interactive whiteboard. Bennett, & Bennett (2003) argue that faculty members need the competency to test the technology before deciding whether to adopt it. Consequently, any faculty e-development platform must meet the characteristic of trialability, or the opportunity for the faculty members to experiment with the new web course system, because the greater the trialibility of using faculty e-development platforms the more likely the intention to adopt them will be.

Also, the greater the opportunity to try a new technology, the easier it is for faculty members to adopt and evaluate it. Technological organization principles encompass key teaching concepts and learning tasks, collaborative training strategies, physical hardware and software materials and technological competencies in structuring multimedia (audio and video-enhanced learning), for faculty teachers and university advisers. More importantly, for a faculty consultant, with the new technologies such as podcasting/vodcasting, virtual labs, mobile learning, broadcasting, and videoconferencing, understanding the power of multiple methods of knowledge delivery is essential. Nowadays, faculty instructors are using different types of information delivery devices, such as "mobile telephones, Palmtops, PDAs and standard desktop PCs" (Masoodian, 2001, p. 249), but their potential benefits and constraints for classroom teaching and learning are unknown.

Finally, full-time and untenured faculty members can use e-development as an approach to personal and social critical process improvement in several ways:

a) Fulfill the dual mission of excellence in teaching as well as in research.
b) Mindful examination of action and knowledge in synchronous reflection while training or asynchronously at some point after e-development courses.
c) Small-group discussion concerning monitoring and decision making linking knowledge and action.
d) Creation, preservation and dissemination of faculty communities.

3.1. E-development Communities

Many people believe that faculty e-development will bring massive structural changes to the induction of new university staff or the proposal for continuing networked faculty development. Effective faculty e-development systems may occur in social and constructivist faculty communities. These newly envisioned faculty communities are based around a high-quality teaching profession or set of innovative and scholarly classroom teaching practice principles and behaviors. Faculty teachers from various colleges and departments usually meet via phone, videoconference, or while attending professional conferences to share systematic processes of inquiry into one's own teaching practices and students' learning, and to identify opportunities for collaborative working. Some research states that undoubtedly, the most effective faculty e-development occurs when it incorporates peer-to-peer training, manifesting in collective ideas and practices among faculty members (associate professor, assistant professor, professor emeritus, and the like).

A variety of approaches can be used to promote one's effectiveness regarding scholarly teaching and its impact on student learning and career trajectories. A source of training may include an e-development community which is considered a group of faculty members who share what they have learned from their own practices and interacts with colleagues for a scholarly action or enterprise in a web platform. A faculty community may integrate diverse faculty members by age, status, and the subject matter taught, for instance, hard and soft courses, and pure and applied disciplines.

The concept of scholarly enterprise necessarily includes pedagogical procedures that must be related to the faculty's discipline. An online CPT system should offer virtual capabilities for the faculty members that establish access above and beyond current conventional institutional associations. At the same time, faculty communities need teaching institutional repositories (TIRs) as a necessary component for classroom content, and pedagogy information to share in the scholarly world. Also, a TIR is an indispensable training factor to bring a researcher's information and scientific papers into a portal or research center web site.

A TIR can provide rich knowledge fellowship and mutual attitudinal support through the professional development of tenure-track faculty members during their first years of classroom teaching in colleges and universities. Moreover, junior faculty members need forums for the rapid exchange of professional reflections with both on-campus and external faculty communities about how to generate personal document outputs for academic promotion and tenure, annual faculty profile updates, online resumes, and curriculum vitae. A TIR mayalso include publications in peer-reviewed journals, and informal channels such as electronic listservs. The foundation of this process lies in the principles of faculty empowerment, which aims to foster teaching improvement and self-determination within higher education institutions.

Universities are changing their human resources objectives. One notable change is that faculty members are growing older and becoming tenured. Financial constraints have cast a shadow on the quality of higher-level education, and colleges and universities are less able to bring in new postdoctoral fellows and assistant professors. One possible outcome of the shortage of novice university teachers is the re-design of the aims of faculty e-development (i.e., retraining senior faculty members to teach online courses).

4. Faculty E-development Research and Evaluation

Faculty development has long been a mission of universities for self-renewal and improved vitality. A guide for online CPT should address a variety of institutional concerns. These include the provision of the following four steps:

a) Personal *vision* of instructional development, which emphasizes the development of faculty competencies involving instructional technology, media, and curriculum.
b) *Mission* statements of professional development, which enhance the growth of their faculty professional roles.

c) Career *objectives* that can be developed for implementing the mission, which require specific projects and tasks to accomplish the objectives.

d) *Organizational* development, which highlights the priorities of the faculty members in the institution (e.g., high-quality technical and social support, and good quality equipment and resources).

Faculty vitality is an intangible and positive attitude that enables purpose production. A large number of university members reports on their professional development in ways that emphasize non-formal and discontinued learning. Most self-help books, CDs, and videos provide guides for developing an inductive professional mission statement about the quality of teaching (especially the melding of self-development and shared values and experiences with the faculty community). Developing a teaching vision requires waiting. However, it portrays of what a teaching career could be like in the future. If e-development is the 'what' of a professional improvement vision, the faculty mission is the 'why'.

The advent of mass access to higher education in Western European countries, North America and the Pacific Rim is causing a new trend in the universities' instructional function. Students are now been oriented chiefly towards gaining competencies for employment, while universities are under some pressure to improve undergraduate instruction, and postgraduate programs are now being accredited to update quality standards. The personal mission statement focuses on what a faculty wants to do. It is his or her personal constitution that provides a direction for achieving a vision, e.g., virtual teaching or technology usability. These are succinct statements that clearly state the roles important to the faculty: technology use to enhance and support communication between students and faculty members.

Technology literacy training is an operational objective that benefits the needs of the faculty and the demands of accountability and high-quality performance of the institutions in our fast-paced technological and globally connected society. If universities are to survive, scholars need to develop and implement tasks and projects intended to infuse and sustain change in targeted and diverse cohorts of novice and intermediate academic instructors (i.e., from travel support, workshops, and sabbaticals, to technological tools and products). One of the greatest needs perceived by staff related to encouraging student learning in non-traditional ways is "using computer-based education methods" (Ballantyne, Borthwick, & Packer, 2000, p. 225).

This theme relates to the need for teaching and learning to be well supported by adequate equipment, computers, personnel, administrative resources, and so on. Research also states that faculty teachers need to participate in small groups with the help of a faculty consultant, because faculty members felt that they were not proficient in creating learning-based websites/pages or using online web spaces to teach. These researchers concluded that: "More research needs to be conducted about effective faculty training strategies and how they can be improved, individualized, and implemented" (Georgina, & Hosford, 2008, p. 6).

Research is not a one-way process, and the connection between applied research and development is not only indispensable but also a source of reciprocal improvement, with innovations sometimes preceding research. Diffusion of innovation theory predicts that media as well as interpersonal contacts provide information and influence opinion and judgment (Rogers, 1995).

On average, technological innovation takes many years, because most of the time the nature of university networks and the roles that attitude-tenured faculty members play in them determine the likelihood that the innovation will be integrated into classroom teaching practice. For many faculty members, web teaching is a challenge ('entry' phase). The integration of e-learning technology into teaching requires a change in the faculty's beliefs and attitudes ('adoption' phase). A tendency to incorporate word processing, databases, some graphics programs, and computer-based instruction means that an instructor is combining various media in a teaching scenario ('adaptation' phase*).* Finally, the increasing faculty proficiency in the use of e-learning materials in lectures and seminar discussions results in more innovative teaching strategies ('appropriation' phase). Generally speaking, faculties take some years to teach students to use their critical skills via the Internet. The university professorate has many cultures. When faculty members offer all students, both graduates and undergraduates, high quality teaching, they view learning as an active, creative, and socially interactive process ('invention' phase). It is in this e-development process that the support of novice faculty members has taken on particular importance.

Effectively, a mutually beneficial relationship or reflective process leads to a formalized program environment where training and coaching is made available for mentors and protégés. Therefore, trainer or mentor capacity is an academic attribute to be considered for an e-development course that emphasizes observation, recording, and evaluation practices. Along with these decisive elements in program management, faculty members should also be prepared to be 'telementors' (Villar, & Alegre, 2006). E-mentoring is a computer-mediated relationship between a faculty adviser, usually a senior professor, who is the mentor, and a lesser skilled novice faculty member, with the goal of developing the novice in a way that helps him or her be successful in transferring pedagogic ideas as well as chunks of theory (textbooks, lectures, essays, and so on), to a digital context (Bierema, & Merriam, 2002).

Many universities have experienced an exponential increase in the number of courses offered online. Faculty members are recommended to implement a systematic process by which their students can provide feedback on the courses and teaching. Among the components of the scholarship of teaching and learning – inquiry, reflection, evaluation, documentation, and communication – online assessment is a mechanism for faculty members to collect midterm (formative) feedback as well as end-of-term (summative) student ratings. Evaluation practices become 'formative', which makes it possible to provide operational help to faculty members, so that they can adapt their methods, improve their modes of teaching and, if necessary, question their beliefs and actions. Ballantyne (2003, p. 106) raises a number of issues regarding online evaluation: "response rates; anonymity, confidentiality, and authentication; differences between online and paper survey results; and comparisons of costs". As for student feedback for formative purposes, the design of effective evaluation items and the usefulness of the results from these evaluations for faculty and students are two important aspects to be considered. Along with this opinion, Hoffman (2003) found that many universities are using the Internet to report the results of student evaluations, and that online data collection and online reporting are increasing in recognition.

5. Resources: The Internet Is a Tool for Learning

Web 2.0, every so often referred to as the 'read/write Web', provides online users with interactive services where they manage and control their own data and information. Examples of Web 2.0 participatory technologies include wikis (a page or collection of Web pages designed to enable anyone who accesses it to rapidly contribute or modify its content), blogs or Internet diaries, instant messaging, Internet telephony, social bookmarking, and social networking sites. All these applications share the common feature of sustaining Internet-based interaction between and within groups. Some research results concerning Web 2.0 give support to the following assertion: "Faculty feel that integrating Web 2.0 technologies such as blogs and wikis into the classroom learning environment can be effective at increasing students' satisfaction with the course, improve their learning and their writing ability, and increase student interaction with other students and faculty" (Ajjan, & Hartshorne, 2008, p. 79).

The technology needed to support pedagogy focuses upon web-based platforms for the delivery of online teaching and learning (Blackboard Learning System, Desire2Learn, WebCT) and incorporates digital learning objects. Examples of open-source platforms are Moodle (http://moodle.org/), Ilias (http://www.ilias. de)/, Atutor (http://www.atutor.ca) and Claroline (http://www.claroline.net). A virtual learning environment typically "provides tools such as those for assessment, communication, uploading of content, return of students' work, administration of student groups, questionnaires, tracking tools, wikis, blogs, chats, forums, etc. over internet" (Martín-Blas, & Serrano-Fernández, 2009, p. 35).

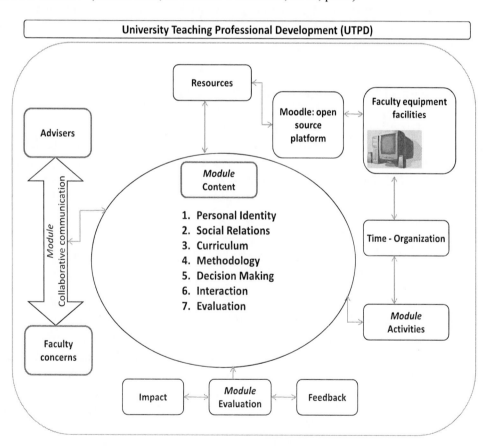

Figure 2. Moodle modules used in UTDP.

The pedagogical patterns used by other academic and enterprise platforms take a similar approach, "offering design patterns for learning categorized in terms of 'tasks' (e.g. discuss, assess), 'organizational forms' (tutorial group, project team) and 'resources' (e.g. virtual library, chat room), as a way of capturing the pedagogy" (Laurillard, 2008, p. 146). Web-based platforms utilize a variety of operating systems (Free/Open source Unix-like, Windows Server 2003, and so on) and databases (Oracle, SQL Server, Microsoft Access, MySQL, and so on), which are designed to offer an organized mechanism for storing, managing, and retrieving information; for instance, Wang, & Wu (2008, p. 1592) made use of a networked portfolio system "using Windows 2000 as its operating system and SQL Server 7.0 as its database".

It is complex to devise websites that are handy and accessible to mature people and students with disabilities, especially the comprehension of multimedia documents relying on images and sounds (e.g., websites including video clips, animated menus, and pages that are most easily reached with a mouse). Visually-impaired and hearing-impaired students required a Universal Design for Learning (UDL) environment. To meet all UDL properties, Web designers must keep in mind accessibility guidelines (e.g., the Web Content Accessibility Guidelines (WCAG) (Harper, & DeWaters, 2008). Nevertheless, certain enterprises have developed new webs for disabled people to enable visually- and mobility-impaired users to easily access, navigate, and refresh the contents (i.e., Business Objects InfoView 5.1 Universal Access or IM Speak! i).

5.1. Moodle and E-development: The UTDP Case

For almost a decade, a research team has been involved in constructing a specific version of a virtual model, called University Teaching Professional Development (UTDP), and studying its use in a variety of Spanish faculty e-development courses. UTDP is not a distinct training process. The factors (pedagogic content knowledge, faculty attitudes, online course design, communication, and interaction) that influence faculty learning in the traditional face-to-face courses, seminars and workshops are present in the blending UTDP situation. The Moodle modules most often used in the UTDP realize four typical faculty dispositions: reflection, exploration, assessment, and communication (Villar, & Alegre, 2007) (see Figure 2).

a) Promoting reflective content delivery: lessons (i.e., textual descriptions, each illustrated through exemplars from different subject areas), and learning tasks (e.g., classroom problems, practice projects, and inquiry strategies). Thinking, reasoning and analyzing are processes dealing with the mental manipulation of information storage in resources such as a virtual library (e.g., books, case studies, web links). Faculty advisers help extend faculty members' ability to analyze lesson content, because faculty mentors could easily guide university members to other information repositories to assist in their analyses.

b) Exploratory activities: inquiry and diaries in forums. Asynchronous ('anytime,' rather than same time) online interaction leads to different paradigms for training opportunities to support active, collaborative (group or team-based) learning.

c) Fostering authentic and automated assessment systems: quizzes, questionnaires, and grade delivery. Advising is an important part of the training process for meaningful feedback. UTDP monitors academic progress. One of the major advantages of using multiple-choice questions (MCQ) with online quiz systems is automated marking. Included in UTDP are two key faculty beliefs relevant for e-development competency training usage, namely perceived usefulness, and perceived ease of use, because technological perceived ease of use is a direct determinant of attitude and perceived usefulness.

d) Socializing expressive communication: online chat rooms and electronic mail. The effective role change of faculty advisers and university members in terms of nonverbal communication, intimacy, and energy/humor. Faculty consultants are proactive, although staff perceived that a faculty adviser could also be a facilitator or coach in a voluntary-based open interaction.

6. Learning Management Systems (LMS) for Faculty Leaders Mentoring Faculty Learners

A fundamental premise in Learning Management Systems (LMS) is that knowledge and understanding are promoted through dialogue, discussion and debate, either by synchronous or asynchronous modes (Barker, 2002). The LMS hypothesis is that e-development courses continually develop staff skills, knowledge and understanding, productivity and performance of learning technologies. Thus the primary faculty e-development aim is to aid staff to master capability-based technology in response to social challenges now and in the future (Phelps, Hase, & Ellis, 2005). The pillars of technology literacy for any e-development CPT university unit are as follows:

a) Connect every college and training unit to an information superhighway.
b) Supply infrastructure and modern hardware for all staff and faculty advisers.
c) Develop effective courses and accredited learning resources as an integral part of the e-development university training unit.
d) Create a culture of quality within higher education for staff training and support to help university students learn through computers and the information superhighway.

Faculty advisers and staff may select a social constructivist perspective of designing online CPT or e-learning. This constructivist idea means that learning derives from, and develops through, interaction and dialogue amongst staff and faculty advisers. For these expert instructors, staff learning and the university social and disciple context are necessarily and inevitably interwoven. Nevertheless, usually faculty e-development courses are of the adviser-centered model, which considers set sequences or fix identified topics, structured texts, and given website links for the faculty to access and download. In effect, it is assumed that online collaboration in adviser-defined tasks and questions in e-development courses is faculty-centered and flexible, because it allows decentralization of the learning process, as happens in learner-centered online learning (Gulati, 2008).

E-development courses are structured around milestone learning themes which are related to basic university pedagogic knowledge. Thus Nicol, Minty, & Sinclair (2003, p. 271) used a framework of five steps for structuring a master's course:

a) Curriculum design;
b) models of learning and of supporting learning;
c) student assessment;
d) the learning organization; and
e) evaluation.

An important issue that needs to be addressed in e-development is the nature and organization of the interactions that occur in tutorial groups. Both faculty advisors and staff are necessary to compensate for the lack of oral information. A related issue is that of advisors' conceptions of tutoring and how they approach their role in e-development courses. Consequently, there needs to be training opportunities concerning effective e-development courses and how diverse faculty advisers make sense of learning interactions. Since both members of the e-development communication dyad engaged in this association, it became conceptualized as a 'shared partnership', a training interaction in which faculty advisers and staff contribute to a collaborative learning relationship. An e-development faculty facilitator is a knowledge owner, a technology coordinator, but what is the role of a faculty advisor in an e-development environment given the structural elements of academic coursework?

The role of the e-development faculty adviser is similar to that of a coach or mentor, although the difference between coaching and mentoring is a hard one to portray. Faculty leaders mentoring faculty learners: this is a kind of peer mentoring network. Faculty mentors are used to scaffold a university learning experience and form the bridge between the virtual world of academia and practice. Central to the work within e-development coaching is the creation of an effective working relationship between the faculty coach and faculty coachee. E-development coaching focuses on the enhancement of faculty performance at work through behavioral, cognitive, and motivational interventions used by the faculty coach, which provide change in the coachee.

The core e-development coaching behaviors may include "reflecting back, being caring, and good listening" (Passmore, 2007, p. 11). These coaching behavior transitions must be made from the typical campus classrooms to the faculty development classroom in cyberspace. With these transitions in virtual space it also becomes necessary to alter faculty mentor and learner roles. Mentoring faculty leaders should create visions for e-development learning use, individualize e-development support, establishing open dialogue and collaborative relationships, and providing mutual benefits (Gabriel, & Kaufield, 2008). Besides, they need to know the basic functions of word processing and presentation software, multiple web browsers, and HTML editors.

While the altered vision of the faculty mentor in the virtual classroom may be drastic, the virtual faculty learner or coachee appears even more innovatory. In order to provide quality e-development CPT for faculty members, it must be convenient to understand their aspirations, needs, and interests, as they are key factors in the complex world of teaching and learning. Academics tend to think of issues relating to learning, teaching, and assessment in terms of their own disciplines – their own tribe and context where most of their pedagogical beliefs are nested. Therefore, we need to know a great deal more about faculty teaching beliefs and priorities. In summary, teaching beliefs are integral to pedagogical content knowledge, determining in large part what an instructor sees, absorbs, and concludes from his teaching and learning observations.

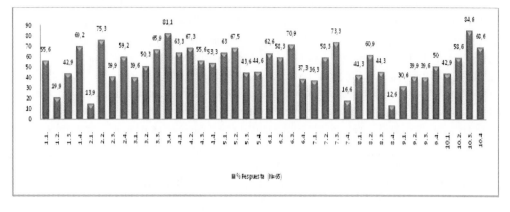

Figure 3. "Perceptions of Teaching Success Inventory (PTSI)" results.

6.1. Faculty Beliefs in the UTDP Program

In this context, it appeared sensible to show the results of a pilot and unpublished study in the UTDP program. Villar, & Alegre (n/d) asked 65 scholars participating in a faculty e-development course to describe their teaching beliefs *from their distinctive discipline angles.* In this study, the goal of the questionnaire '*Perceptions of Teaching Success Inventory (PTSI)' (see Appendix)* was to measure the frequency of beliefs in the middle of the e-development UTDP course. The *PTSI* is a blend of ten interrelated 4-item scales, and items on the scales are rated on a 5-point scale (the format of the five-level Likert scale is: Strongly disagree, Disagree, Neither agree or disagree, Agree, and Strongly Agree). (For this summary, we select the highest agreement scale score value for each item).

The results of this phase are provided for each of 40 items in Figure 3. This graph displays a representation of the resulting values regarding personal beliefs. The findings show some interesting beliefs of faculty members (i.e., the highest levels of agreement were obtained in sections three, four and ten). Staff consider that students' learning styles are mainly participatory (69.2%), and their approach to learning tasks are at depth (75.3%). I addition, academics believe that students are assessed by means of essays and/or multiple-choice tests (81.1%). Also, they judge that their students want the assessments to have a constructive tone (67.3%). Problem-based learning (PBL) was preferred as the teaching strategy by 67.5% of university teachers, and 70.9% considered new technologies a chance to empower teaching methodologies. A liberal style of thinking was reported by 73.3% of all respondents, and 60.9% considered that a critical dialogue with colleagues was a very supporting communication system. University bureaucracy caused 50% of university teachers to feel professional disappointment, and finally, 84.6% participate in activities for improving teaching. In short, our results suggest that there is much work to be done in studying staff beliefs in order to appreciate the nature of e-development substance vision and communication processes.

7. Effects and Impact of Training in Virtual Learning Environments

How do e-development practitioners make choices when they evaluate a virtual course? In other words, how is evaluation practiced? Faculty mentors use 'practical evaluation knowledge' in their virtual activity. They usually want to know results, meaning evaluation conclusions and effects. The objects to be evaluated include the level of achievement of a program's measures, ease of measuring the faculty's changes, and so on.

Methods of assessment need to be tailored to the objectives which are being pursued. The locus of control of assessment management systems is the institution and of e-portfolio is the faculty (Barrett, 2004). Therefore, we will focus on two categories of evaluation objects:

a) Program evaluation. The consideration of measuring e-development program effects or impact suggests a number of starting points that can provide information for restructuring the training process:

- Objectives. Faculty members work on a personal e-portfolio not only to show what they have achieved and learned (assessment of learning), but to reflect on their learning process (assessment of learning). Much of the work on practice-oriented evaluation models focused on whether programs are achieving their objectives.
- Faculty's training needs. Villar, & Alegre (2006, 2007, and 2008a) used a 30-item 3-point Likert-type scale to diagnose pedagogical knowledge and teaching capabilities. Evaluation of e-development courses reports a feeling for the need to improve the faculty's self-proficiency in different instructional capabilities.
- Faculty's capabilities (i.e., expert knowledge and experience; organize materials carefully; establish an appropriate classroom learning climate; use various teaching methods; develop questioning skills; improve research skills; improve presentation and platform skills; polish cooperative group skills; focus on feedback, or be an effective evaluator).
- Training design factors. A way of evaluating e-development is by conducting survey-based studies in which the associations between different aspects of the procedure are analyzed (Bliuc, Goodyear, & Ellis, 2007) (for instance, the effects of flexible scheduling).
- Delivery media (i.e., online documentation, available on disk or downloaded from the Internet, websites, Microsoft Power Point presentations, and so on).
- Other stakeholders: students. Online CPT is most effective and can impact the student classroom learning environment when it is collaborative, university-based, focused on the learning of university students, and linked to curriculum activities that are used in their classrooms (Villar, & Alegre, 2008b).

Training interventions are typically evaluated at the attitude and learning levels. Kirkpatrick (1998) created a taxonomy called a 'four-step approach' to training evaluation. E-development data may be collected at four levels:

a) 'reaction'; asking for faculty members' opinions (attitudes) about the e-development program;

b) 'learning'; asking for faculty members' capability of learning (declarative knowledge) as a result of the e-development program;

c) 'behavioral'; did the faculty members change their teaching competencies and capabilities in the classroom (procedural knowledge) as a result of the e-development program? and

d) 'results'; did the faculty members' change in competency and capability have a positive effect on the teaching organization (business results)? (Kirkpatrick, 1998).

b) Faculty capabilities are different objectives of e-portfolio assessment. E-portfolios have two major functions: a product and a process function (Lin, 2008a,b). Data structure varies with the tools used to create the portfolio (documents often converted to HTML, PDF) and data are stored in multiple options. Choices include: CD-ROM, videotape, DVD, WWW server, LAN (Barrett, 2004).

7.1. E-Portfolios: An Assessment Tool for Faculty E-development Courses

Web-based portfolio assessment is likely to archive many competencies and capabilities, such as monitoring the developing process, document self-benchmarking practices, and record production, thereby facilitating a repository of faculty development evidence. Also, e-portfolios can be an evaluation model for courses designed as small packages of learning content and other fractions of practice experience. According to Mason, Pegler, & Weller (2004, p. 726): "E-portfolios consist of discrete pieces of work and this mirrors the structure of learning objects, particularly those which are activity based".

As happens with online learning (Chang, & Tseng, 2008), explicitly which kind of faculty development result will be enhanced has not been sufficiently collected and verified. The faculty mentor's reflections on the strengths and weaknesses of e-development courses are the main motives for reconsideration. Ongoing review and improvement includes faculty learning competencies. Faculty learning competencies become more faculty-centered and more interactive as faculty members engage in self-reflection, periodically review objectives and activities, and assume responsibility for their own learning tasks.

E-portfolios allow the tracking and file documentation of episodes of tutoring and mentoring that happen in e-development. Indeed, at least five risks concerning e-development can be outlined:

- 'Unimportant evidence' – faculty document matters (words, images, web sites, and so on) that did not express reflectedness.
- 'Unsatisfactory performance' – presenting evidence in a way that does not accord with the best and truthful faculty capability.
- 'Conflict of focus and interest' – faculty self-reflection vs. summative assessment: which is the assessment focal point?
- 'Ownership' – legal issues concerning personal data protection and propriety of the information published in the website.

- 'Validation' – scoring difficulties. An e-portfolio has the disadvantage of quality assurance.

The balancing of threats and opportunities of an e-portfolio in faculty e-development courses demands wisdom. University and personal evaluation culture changes slowly. One of the most significant factors will be to keep an equal tempo between faculty e-development and the implementation of the e-portfolio as an evaluation system (for formative and/or summative purposes) on the one hand, and the change of university culture on the other. Balancing is thus more an artistic ability than a scientific discipline.

Appendix

Perceptions of Teaching Success Inventory (PTSI)

Luis M. Villar and Olga M. Alegre

Forty statements grouped into ten categories on learning styles and approaches to study, assessment and feedback, strategies, learning environments, styles of university teachers' thinking, and support and professional commitment are presented below.

INSTRUCTIONS: For each statement, select the response that best represents your Agreement or Disagreement.
Scale: *Strongly Disagree | Disagree | Neutral | Agree | Strongly Agree.*

Perceptions of Teaching Success Inventory (PTSI)	SD	D	N	A	SA
1. Students' learning styles in subject matter groups.					
1.1. In this subject matter group, students are *independent,* i.e., they like to think for themselves					
1.2. In this subject matter group, students are *collaborative*: that is, believe they can learn more by sharing their ideas and talents.					
1.3. In this subject matter group, students are *dependent,* i.e., have little intellectual curiosity and learn only what they are asked for assessment.					
1.4. In this subject matter group, students are *participatory,* i.e., they like to learn the subject matter material and attend class.					
2. Students' approaches to studying in subject matter groups.					
2.1. In this subject matter group, students learn to perform tasks in a *superficial way* (*recalling facts on which they will ask later*). Consequently, I present information that is tacitly accepted by students so as to memorize single and isolated facts.					
2.2. In this subject matter group, students learn to perform tasks *in depth* (*understanding them as a whole*). Consequently, I analyze critically new ideas, tie them to those concepts and principles previously learned and lead them to understand and retain concepts in the long term.					
2.3. In this subject matter group, students learn to perform surface tasks (they are not interested in or even have a negative attitude towards the course material). Consequently, I discretely use drawings, diagrams and charts before, during, and after oral presentation of any material.					
2.4. In this subject matter group, students learn to perform tasks *in depth* (*they have an inherent curiosity for the material of the course*). Consequently, I balance practical problem-solving methods with materials that emphasize their fundamental understanding.					

Perceptions of Teaching Success Inventory (PTSI)	SD	D	N	A	SA
3. Methods of students' assessment in class teaching.					
3.1. *Evaluation by peers*, i.e., students judge and criticize the work done by their peers.					
3.2. Self-assessment, i.e., students judge and criticize their own work, rating them.					
3.3. *Competency-based assessment*, i.e., I value empowerment and the representation of students' actions in simulated environments or in real settings.					
3.4. *Essays and / or multiple-choice tests*, i.e., I value knowledge through tests to choose the best answer or the development of written ideas.					
4. Students' perceptions of assessment and feedback in my subject matter.					
4.1. *Attitude towards assessment*. Students perceived assessment as a course obstacle to overcome and also as an indicator of learning and achievement.					
4.2. *Feedback*. Students want assessment to be clear, have a constructive tone and close to the knowledge of assessment results.					
4.3. *Requested feedback*. Students negotiate better grades and demand support in a tutoring assessment review.					
4.4. *Understanding comments*. Students strive to understand comments (feedback) based on scientific explanations I make while reviewing assessment.					
5. Teaching strategies that promote students' learning.					
5.1. *Working in cooperative groups*. In my subject matter, I perceive that cooperative groups foster students' emotional engagement and a sense of belonging.					
5.2. *Problem-based learning (PBL)*. Group tasks consist of realizing a work process for formulating a study problem and defining learning goals. Groups meet together, transfer acquired knowledge, and finally solve the problem.					
5.3. *Peer teaching*. I include models for students' peer teaching in various formats.					
5.4. *Work project*. Students prefer to invest their effort in carrying out individual work projects for learning in my subject matter.					
6. Learning environment construction.					
6.1. *Use of media and resources*. Students have the necessary media and resources to understand and realize the course tasks.					
6.2. *Hybrid teaching*. I teach subject matter contents devoting an amount of time to face-to-face and to online teaching.					
6.3. *Use of new technologies*. The use of new technologies has eased the course methodology by fostering students' autonomy and changing my role towards student-oriented learning.					
6.4. *Learning communities*. In my course, social relations are promoted through information technology (logs, weblogs) to share academic values and principles.					
7. Scholars' thinking styles about subject matter teaching.					
7.1. *Legislature*. I often assigned independent study projects for students.					
7.2. *Executive*. I think teaching guides should include strategies to implement the lessons in sequential steps.					
7.3. *Liberal*. University teachers need to set up problems, raise questions, and speak in paradoxes, dilemmas, and discrepancies that have to be solve by students.					
7.4. *Conservative*. I prefer to teach the subject matter and the same teaching cycle every year.					
8. Colleagues' workload support.					
8.1. *Mentoring*. I receive support from colleagues in the design and implementation of materials in various formats.					
8.2. *Critical dialogue*. I think about teaching in terms of planning and implementation of teaching variables (curriculum guides, competencies, evaluation, and so on) in meetings with colleagues and exchanging teaching innovations.					
8.3. *Coaching*. I'm still learning didactic instructions from reckon accredit faculty members in teaching subject matters.					
8.4. *Antistress*. The head of department advises and manages the resolution of my conflicts when an activity or teaching situation stresses me.					

Perceptions of Teaching Success Inventory (PTSI)	SD	D	N	A	SA
9. *Administrative support.* **This refers to the protection and assistance of the university management bodies.**					
9.1. University academic staff and administration and services personnel are lively, stimulating and facilitators of teaching action.					
9.2. School academic staff and administration and services personnel are lively, stimulating and facilitators of teaching action.					
9.3. Department academic staff and administration and services personnel are lively, stimulating and facilitators of teaching action.					
9.4. Administrative arbitrariness and the abuse of institutions have caused me disappointment and depression at some time in my life.					
10. *Professional commitment.* **This refers to personal obligation to teaching.**					
10.1. I am disappointed with my teaching duties due to university working conditions.					
10.2. Professional autonomy and discretion in teaching management are enough reasons to improve my professional practice.					
10.3. As part of my teaching duties, I participate in activities for improving teaching, and I engage in the annual renewal of university teaching.					
10.4. I engage in cognitive, emotional and behavioral requirements for improving university teaching.					

References

Ajjan, H. & Hartshorne, R. (2008). Investigating faculty decisions to adopt Web 2.0 technologies: Theory and empirical tests. *The Internet and Higher Education,* **11**(2), 71-80.

Ballantyne, Ch. (2003). Online Evaluations of Teaching: An Examination of Current Practice and Considerations for the Future. *New Directions For Teaching And Learning*, **96**, 103-112.

Ballantyne, R., Borthwick, J., & Packer, J. (2000). Beyond Student Evaluation of Teaching: identifying and addressing academic staff development needs. *Assessment & Evaluation in Higher Education,* **25** (3), 221-236.

Barker, P. (2002). On Being an Online Tutor. *Innovations in Education and Teaching International,* **39**(1), 3-13.

Barrett, H.C. (2004). Differentiating electronic portfolios and online assessment management systems. In Proceedings of the 2004 annual conference of the society for information technology in teacher education (SITE 2004), Atlanta, GE, March <http://electronicportfolios.org/portfolios/SITE2004paper.pdf> Retrieved December 2008.

Bennett, J., & Bennett, L. (2003). A review of factors that influence the diffusion of innovation when structuring a faculty training program. *Internet & Higher Education,* **6**(1), 53.

Bierema, L.L., & Merriam, S.B. (2002). E-mentoring: Using Computer Mediated Communication to Enhance the Mentoring Process. *Innovative Higher Education,* **26**(3), 211-227.

Bliuc, A.M., Goodyear, P., & Ellis, R.A. (2007). Research focus and methodological choices in studies into students' experiences of blended learning in higher education. *The Internet and Higher Education,* **10**(4), 231-244.

Brew, L.S. (2008). The role of student feedback in evaluating and revising a blended learning course. *The Internet and Higher Education,* **11**(2), 98-105.

Chang, C.-C. y Tseng, K.-H. (2008). Use and performances of Web-based portfolio assessment. *British Journal of Educational Technology.* Early View, Date: September 2008.

Gabriel, M.A., & Kaufield, K.J. (2008). Reciprocal mentorship: an effective support for online instructors. *Mentoring & Tutoring: Partnership in Learning,* **16** (3), 311-327.

Galanouli, D., Murphy, C., & Gardner, J. (2004). Teachers' perceptions of the effectiveness of ICT-competence training. *Computers & Education,* **43**(1-2), August-September 2004, 63-79.

Georgina, D.A., & Hosford, C.C. (2008). Higher education faculty perceptions on technology integration and training. Teaching and Teacher Education, In Press, Corrected Proof, Available online 9 December 2008.

Georgina, D.A., & Olson, M.R. (2008). Integration of technology in higher education: A review of faculty self-perceptions. *The Internet and Higher Education,* **11**(1), 1-8.

Gulati, S. (2008). Compulsory participation in online discussions: is this constructivism or normalisation of learning? *Innovations in Education and Teaching International,* **45**(2), 183-192.

Harper, K.A., & DeWaters, J. (2008). A Quest for website accessibility in higher education institutions. *The Internet and Higher Education,* **11**(3-4), 160-164.

Hewson, L., & Hughes, Ch. (1999). An Online Postgraduate Subject in Information Technology for University Teachers. *Innovations in Education and Teaching International,* **36**(2), 106-117.

Hoffman, K.M. (2003). Online Course Evaluation and Reporting in Higher Education. *New Directions for Teaching and Learning,* **96**, 25-29.

Kirkpatrick, D.L. (1998). *Evaluating training programs: the four levels.* San Francisco, Calif.: Berrett-Koehler Publishers.

Knight, P., Tait, J., & Yorke, M. (2006). The professional learning of teachers in higher education. *Studies in Higher Education,* **31**(3), 319-339.

Laurillard, D. (2008). The teacher as action researcher: using technology to capture pedagogic form, *Studies in Higher Education,* **33**(2), 139-154.

Lin, Q. (2008a). Student satisfactions in four mixed courses in elementary teacher education program. *The Internet and Higher Education,* **11**(1), 53-59.

Lin, Q. (2008b). Preservice teachers' learning experiences of constructing e-portfolios online. *The Internet and Higher Education,* **11**(3-4), 194-200.

Malikowski, S.R. (2008). Factors related to breadth of use in course management systems. *The Internet and Higher Education,* **11**(2), 81-86.

Malikowski, S. R., Thompson, M. E., & Theis, J. G. (2007). A model for research into course management systems: Bridging technology and learning theory. *Journal of Educational Computing Research,* **36**(2), 149−173.

Martín-Blas, T. & Serrano-Fernández, S. (2009).The role of new technologies in the learning process: Moodle as a teaching tool in Physics. *Computers & Education,* **52**, 35–44.

Mason, R., Pegler, Ch. y Weller, M. (2004). E-portfolios: an assessment tool for online courses. *British Journal of Educational Technology* 35(6), 717–72.

Masoodian, M. (2001). Information-Centred Design: A methodology for designing virtual meeting design environments. *Information, Communication & Society,* **4** (2), 247–260.

Nicol, D.J., Minty, I., & Sinclair, Ch. (2003). The social dimensions of online learning. *Innovations in Education and Teaching International,* **40**(3), 270-280.

Passmore, J. (2007). Coaching and mentoring - The role of experience and sector knowledge. *International Journal of Evidence Based Coaching and Mentoring Special Issue,* summer, 10-16.

Phelps, R., Hase, S., & Ellis, A. (2005). Competency, capability, complexity and computers: exploring a new model for conceptualising end-user computer education. *British Journal of Educational Technology,* **36** (1), 67-84.

Rogers, E.M. (1995). *Diffusion of innovations (4th edition).* The Free Press. New York.

Tallent-Runnels, M.K., & et al. (2006). Teaching Courses Online: A Review of the Research. *Review of Educational,* **76**(1), 93-135.

Villar, L.M., & Alegre, O.M. (2006). Online Faculty Development in the Canary Islands: A Study of E-mentoring. *Higher Education in Europe,* **31** (1), April, 65-81.*Research,* **76**(1), 93-135.

Villar, L.M., & Alegre, O.M. (2007). Faculty learns in online courses: five university cases. *International Journal of Training and Development,* **11**(3), 200-213.

Villar, L.M., & Alegre, O.M. (2008a). Measuring Faculty Learning in Curriculum and Teaching Competence (CTC) Online Courses. *Interactive Learning Environments,* **16**(2), 169-181.

Villar, L.M., & Alegre, O.M. (2008b). Supporting computer-mediated learning: a case study in online staff development and classroom learning environment assessment. *Learning Environments Research,* **11**(3), 211-226.

Villar, L.M., & Alegre, O.M. (n/d). *Faculty's beliefs about teaching.* (Unpublished research report).

Wang, S.-L., & Wu, P.-Y. (2008). The role of feedback and self-efficacy on web-based learning: The social cognitive perspective. *Computers & Education,* **51**(4), 1589-1598.

Young, A., & Norgard, C. (2006). Assessing the quality of online courses from the students' perspective. *Internet and Higher Education,* **9**(2), 107–115.

In: Peer-to-Peer Networks and Internet Policies
Editors: Diego Vegros and Jaime Sáenz, pp. 179-191

ISBN: 978-1-60876-287-3
© 2010 Nova Science Publishers, Inc.

Chapter 7

THE WORLD ACCORDING TO YOUTUBE: EXPLAINING THE RISE OF ONLINE PARTICIPATIVE VIDEO

Jacques Bughin

McKinsey, Avenue Louise, 480, 1050 Brussels, Belgium
Free University Brussels, Av. Roosevelt, B-1050 Brussels, Belgium
Department of Applied Economics, Katholieke Universiteit Leuven, Namenstraat,
B-3000 Leuven, Belgium

Abstract

The success of companies such as Myspace and YouTube have focused attention on online companies that are quickly building their business model on participative media, leveraging a set of new social-based technologies, dubbed "Web 2.0". This article describes the quickly emerging social behavior of online user-generated *video*. Five clear findings stand out:
a) Participative media is already widespread, even it is still biased socio-demographically in favor of young males; b) Participation is fostered mostly by the desire to fame, and to a lesser extent financial incentives; c) On top of those drivers, social network aspects stand as critical drivers of the growth of user-generated video; d) Online video users limit themselves to 2 to 3 sites; e) Users of online videos are keen to have a more comprehensive offering than UGC video alone- this includes conventional TV shows as well as premium content such as movies. Taking together, those findings lead to the conjecture that the market for online video will quickly evolve to a concentrated number of destination sites, aggregating all types of content.

Key words: Web 2.0, social media, user-generated content, YouTube, online video

I. Introduction

Acquisitions of such companies as social network Myspace and user-generated content YouTube by high profile media entities like Murdoch's NewsCorp and Google respectively have focused attention on companies that are quickly building their business model on the principle of participative media. Those companies leverage a new set of internet technologies, dubbed Web 2.0, that rely on inexpensive delivery and storage as well as incorporate flexible software facilitating sharing of media-rich content and services.

By harnessing the will of online users to *participate and share*, those companies have witnessed significant visitors' growth momentum, up to a point to replace "web 1.0" internet companies. Musser [19] reports on how Google maps integrated in search has taken over AOL's Mapquest. Flickr has taken leadership in photo sites by creating pictures sharing by default. Trulia is quickly growing in online classified through a mash-up of software that enhances social collaboration among real estate brokers on-line.

The development is not only US-centric. It is increasingly spreading worldwide. South Korea is a good case in point. OhMyNews.com is developing its traffic as relevant social journalism news. Naver has taken over the search market with more than 70% of the paid search, thanks to the integration of its own web search algorithm with new social data and referral input by its portal users. Europe is not in rest, with user-generated online video DailyMotion and MyVideo disputing the leadership of YouTube in the French and German markets respectively. Finally, the development of social media is moving to other platforms, notably the mobile space. In Asia, CyBird has become a lead community site where people can participate and share experience via their mobile. In Europe, SeeMeTV is a service launched on UK mobile operator "3", which similarly to YouTube on line, is devoted to share user-generated video among mobile users.

The fast growth of those sites is proving that participative media is a clear fundamental trend enhanced by the web 2.0 set of technologies. According to a study conducted in the US by the Pew Internet and American life project [13], 57 percent of the teens online have participated in some forms of social media, either through the creation of a blog, the posting of wiki-comments, stories, photos or videos online. International statistics prove the same trends in Europe and elsewhere, with between 40-50% of online broadband users claiming to have used social networks sites in Japan, UK, Germany or France [22].

However, while participation is spreading, there is not much said currently about the mechanics of social media. Questions abound like who is actually participating, under what rationales and for what kind of incentives, etc.

Regarding usage, the young and mostly male have been the early users of participative media. This has been typical of the web for any new application like P2P music Napster or for any type of software like IP-based communication Skype. The same is already quite apparent for online video sites like Revver or VideoEgg.

Regarding breadth of participation, a key driver of the perennial nature of participative online sites is the extent to which participation is sustained [1, 16 ,18] Jakob Nielsen relying on his early work [4] has coined the phrase " participation inequality" in online communities and highlighted his empirical law of "1-9-90%", that is, "90% of online do not contribute, 9% contribute a little and 1% of users account for almost all the actions". Such an empirical law appears to roughly hold: Musser [19] reports that 7% of wikipedias users are active users, while Bughin and Hagel [5] concluded that between 5-10% of social community users are active contributors. Furthermore, there is a high abandon rate in active media: in a seminal article on the depletion rate of active mailing, Butler [7] found that 50% of mailing lists had no traffic after an average of four to six months. The same phenomenon is also apparent regarding the web 2.0 phenomenon of blog creation; according to Le Figaro [9] quoting some analyses done by the Gartner Group, the life of a blog is roughly 3 months. Finally, regarding content quality, distribution is even more skewed. Kelly et al. [16] show that the 0,7% of authors of lessons among the Wholenote community members contribute 25% of the total ratings; Musser [19] claims that 0,03% of users make up 66% of Diggs' front page posts. In most cases (sites like YouTube, etc), the top 1-5% percent of entries make 70-80% of the total views [1].

The aim of this article is to provide some salient features of the nascent market of user-generated (henceforth, UGC) video online. Section 2 provides a few basic statistics of the US online video market to date. Section 3 extends the analysis to the German market (as so far, one of the most developed European markets for user generated video) to conclude that the market developments are quite similar to the US. Section 4 tests some hypotheses regarding how to foster participative media in the context of online UGC video. Section 5 concludes.

2. Describing the US UGC Video Market

While pretty much non–existent a few years ago, online video watching has spread rapidly through a series of innovations. At first, those emerged at the internet distribution level. This includes improvement in the P2P protocol (e.g., eDonkeys, BitTorrent) as well as better streaming quality (e.g., Narrowstep). Now, innovations have appeared at the navigation and usability level, with YouTube basic sharing links of videos among sites, etc. that have facilitated the viral spread of online video usage. Anecdotally, YouTube's founders have claimed themselves to be the fastest growing site on the web since its commercial creation in the early nineties.

While data are quite varied and not necessarily harmonized in trying to capture the socio-economic aspects of video online, a few stylized facts can be drawn from a variety of reports (e.g. [14, 22] and from direct usage statistics from lead companies such as Nielsen Media, Comscore or Hitwise in the US.

We have chosen to emphasize five salient features which will be later compared to our own German survey in Section 3:

1. *UGC video has become widespread across the young (mostly) male, and is moving mainstream*

    The statistics provided by Ofcom [22], through a fieldwork carried out by Synnovate in October 2006, show that more than 70% of the 18-24 year old broadband users have ever watched or downloaded videos made by other people via their pc [1]. The phenomenon is also spreading across older cohorts, with 49% and 24% reporting to have used UGC online video in the age bracket, 25-44, and 45-64 respectively in the US.

2. *UGC video audience is currently a niche of short form video, yet may evolve rapidly towards long video and television content*

    Sites like YouTube etc usually only post UGC videos of short forms, first as a policy to prevent copyright issues, second because personal videos are usually made

---

[1] InStat sample reports that 62% of surveyed households watch long and/or short form video-The survey was conducted at least 6 months earlier than the one reported in Ofcom.

of short clips. The In-Stat [14] survey confirms this in the US. 70% of UGC video users report to have watched short videos versus only 32% for long-form. Furthermore, the average monthly time of usage is quite small, roughly 100 minutes for YouTube in the US by November 2006, -to be compared with roughly 120 hours of traditional fixed TV.

However, those statistics could change rapidly. In the US, more than 50% of those not watching long video express a will to do so, mostly when bottlenecks like size screens and speed connections will be removed. Practically speaking, those constraints are being uplift quickly. The Edhstrom law means that broadband speed is doubling every 18 months, and pc-TV bridges (via simple links or complete boxes such as Akimbo) are becoming cheap and easily available.

3. *Degree of participation on UGC video is relatively skewed, and market is trying to stimulate posting activities via incentives*

We have already mentioned that the degree of active users is usually small in social communities. UGC video is no exception: for example, YouTube has recently revealed that its top 100 heaviest users spend up to 100 minutes a day on the site versus the 100 minutes per month for the average user.

There are some clear attempts (and worries) to create a much larger base of active users. For instance, a plethora of sites in the US are kick starting the provision of financial incentives (and in passing, creating large debate oas whether this will kill the open democracy of web 2.0). This includes the start by AOL revamping Netscape and providing reward the top 1% contributors to boost Nestcape traffic. This was followed by cable-based network, current TV, providing up to one thousand dollars to top ranked UGC videos, or by companies such as Revver, sharing advertising revenue 50/50 with up loaders.

4. *Market is concentrated and may concentrated further*

Taking a variety of measures (from visits to number of videos streamed, etc), the top 5 sites (YouTube, MySpace Video, Yahoo! Video, etc) account already for about 60% of the market. This will de facto concentrate as the result of YouTube being bought out by Google (and Google Video being the top 5), but also because online traffic reports either from Comscore and Nielsen suggest that visitor growth of top 5 sites has been faster than others and there is no reason to believe, *ceteris paribus*, that this will stop in the short term.

5. *Social features are getting prominent on online video sites possibly as a way to capitalize on the social networks aspects of participative media*

The fact that YouTube allows the sharing of videos on many sites is clearly a key feature that has made YouTube so successful. We are not aware of robust statistics regarding the exact use and relevance of social network aspects to stimulate the growth of UGC video.

In any case, most of the UGC video sites in the US are now incorporating a large number of social features to allow easy participation and sharing—from Revver's feature of tagging and comments reviews, to Phanfare's allowance of sharing among friends and family. A basic scan of the top 20 UGC video sites reveals in the US that the majority (65%) have included some social features in their web sites.

3. Going beyond the US: A Comparison with the German UGC Video Market

The above stylized facts from the US suggest that: a) from the user side, UGC video is being adopted quickly, moving to mainstream videos, while b) from the supply side, UGC sites are quickly incorporating a set of social features, likely with the aim to foster participative media. We now wish to check whether those dynamics are visible in other markets than the US.

To this end, we have chosen to launch a primary research survey in Germany as the reference country in our study.

Germany is a good case in point for many reasons. First, it is one of the largest online markets in Europe, and statistics as of late 2006 provided by Ofcom [22] suggest that online video usage among broadband users is more widespread than in other large European markets such as France and UK.

Second, the market for online video is quite vibrant, with YouTube leading the charge, but also with local companies vying for a share of the market, like myVideo and GoFish.

Third, the German market anticipates the likely supply dynamics in online video, that is, free-to-air broadcasters and cable are likely to enter the UGC market as a way to diversify. At current, two major German UGC video sites are either fully or partly owned by the top commercial broadcasters—myVideo is owned in part by Pro7Sat1, while Clipfish is being developed by RTL Germany. This contrasts with the US market where the networks have been late to announce their entry in the UGC video space.

The survey features are first explained before comparing Germany with the US online video market developments. The next section leverages the survey to further test hypotheses on the drivers of online video participation.

3.1. Survey Features

As primary source, we have launched an online survey comprised of 40 questions. For space reasons, the survey is not reproduced here. Questions around six key themes have been developed:

a) *Socio-demographics:* age, gender, professional and qualification background, household income range

   The first theme will allow categorizing the status of the German UGC video market against the US. It is hypothesized that the German market obeys the same feature as in the US.

b) *"Funnel" of online video:* sites brand knowledge, usage, and main usage.

   The second theme aims to understand the numbers of sites used by online video participants and how brands translate into (main) usage. The hypothesis here is one that is typical of online media, that is, - users often do not use more than three key destination sites [2].

c) *Type of online video usage:* uploading, watching, within watching, origination via top 100 lists, browsing, searching, etc.

    The third theme aims to understanding the proportion of active users, as well as the way people access video. We want to assess how loading is still a minimal activity versus watching, but may be further stimulated.

d) *Rationales for uploading:* fame, fun, sharing with friends; extra incentives like money, free mobile or broadband discount, etc

    In our fourth theme, we test the "Andy Warhol's minute of fame" to be a key motive for uploading as anecdotally mentioned in the business press. Also, we test the validity of providing money incentives to boost uploading.

e) *Social features usage:* referrals, links from friends, from blogs, groups, etc.

    Social features as core driver of UGC videos are our fifth theme. We hypothesize that they indeed play a key role in the dynamics of online videos.

f) *Extra content and features requirements:* such as premium content, long-forms videos, music and photos sharing, video searches, personal list exchanges, etc.

Our last theme concerns the evolution of UGC video. We hypothesize that UGC video users would welcome extension to a large variety of not only video, but also, other media content such as music and photos (usually already embedded with video in top sites like MySpace, Google, Yahoo! and others).

    The survey has been conducted in October for two weeks online and posted on the major portals and ISPs of the country. Because the survey was also used for a confidential client, the survey leverages the client own set of online sites (aggregate ranking in top 15 of the country). After cleaning, the sample collected involves 560 people. About 430 online users filled the survey consistently, plus 130 others who however did not have knowledge and usage of the top 10 German online video websites, and so only filled a few socio-demographic questions.

    Note that the sample is not necessarily fully representative of the online population. In fact, the sample is both biased towards youth and towards online video usage: average age of the online UGC video users is 24 years (Nielsen [4] mention 28 years), while the proportion of online video users within 18-24 is 72% versus 67% as reported by Ofcom [22]. The figures below have been reweighed to correspond to the Ofcom/Nielsen German population figures.

    The sample however captures the dynamics of the supply side, quite well. The top sites in terms of brand recognition and usage are both YouTube and MyVideo, followed by GoogleVideo and ClipFish. This matches traffic data provided by Nielsen, which shows the lead of YouTube recently being challenged by MyVideo in the late months of 2006, with GoogleVideo traffic growth slightly capping.

3.2. UGC Video: Comparing Germany with us

Based on the sample above, we now look at the confirmation of the US pattern. Broadly said, and even if the German market is pretty new, the pattern of development regarding online video usage is strikingly similar to the US. Table 1 provides background statistics for what is described below:

Table 1. Summary Survey Statistics

Which of the following video platforms...

(percent)	do you know?	do you use?	do you most use?	do you upload?
YouTube	73%	44%	55%	10%
MyVideo.de	58%	35%	37%	12%
Clipfish.de	31%	18%	5%	11%
Google Video	52%	26%	2%	9%
sevenload.de	2%	2%	0%	1%
metacafe.com	6%	4%	0%	2%
GoFish.com	6%	4%	0%	2%

Socio demographics

	Age	single	married	household annual income	household responsible
		(percent)	(percent)	(Euros)	(percent)
YouTube	27	52%	28%	23 400	49%
MyVideo.de	25	54%	27%	22 700	51%
Clipfish.de	29	49%	30%	23 500	48%
Google Video	25	50%	29%	22 450	47%
sevenload.de	26	48%	31%	24 500	47%
metacafe.com	26	48%	30%	21 700	46%
GoFish.com	28	46%	32%	24 100	46%

Rationales for usage

(percent)	watch	load		more load	
fun and laugh	73%	share with friends	41%	money	50%
keep me informed	8%	Fame	69%	free mobile	16%
friends draw attention	25%	fun and laugh	62%	free DSL	25%
heard about videos somewhere	13%	so others can benefit	31%	awards	27%
others	27%	Others	21%	others	9%

1. *UGC video has widespread across the young (mostly) male, and is moving mainstream: confirmed for Germany.*

   The statistics provided by Ofcom [22] - see above-, report that 67% of the 18-24 year old broadband users have ever watched or downloaded videos in Germany. The figure is 72% in our collected sample. This compares to the 67% and 73% reported for the US using InStat [14] and Ofcom. Ofcom also reports 37% of the 25-44 years old are online video users in Germany, versus 49% in the US. In our sample, the data show 46% of the 25-44 use UGC video.

2. *UGC video audience is currently a niche of short form video, yet may evolve rapidly towards long video and television content: confirmed for Germany.*

   Most of the videos available on the German UGC video sites are of short form. However, the sample statistics demonstrate that only 50% of users are happy with this form of video. In fact, like in the US, where more than 50% of those not watching long video express a will to do so, roughly 44% of German UGC videos users are interested in long form TV shows, 35% are interested in professional music videos and up to 49% are interested in movies on demand.

   In general also, viewers only, rather than up loaders, are interested in long form TV and video on demand (e.g., 52% of viewers only versus 39% for up loaders for TV). As expected, German up loaders are more interested in formats like reality TV and games, etc, where participatory levels are on average higher than broadcast-based formats like movies.

   Finally, we also tested for online video posters, their interest to loads other media such as photo pictures and music-- up to 35% would consider multimedia posting, providing some elements of comparative advantage for multimedia participatory sites like MySpace or Google.

3. *Degree of participation on UGC video is relatively skewed- confirmed for Germany.*

   In the US, it has been reported that 6% of people visiting Google Video has ever posted on the site. Such numbers are confirmed for Germany- as between 3-6% of people visiting one of the top 4 UGC video sites has posted videos. Our statistics go one step further and look at registered members: roughly 15% of online German UGC video visitors become registered members, and thus about 20-40% of registered members have uploaded to those sites.

   In our sample, roughly 30% of the online UGC registered users who have filled the full questionnaire claim to have ever uploaded videos online. There is some clear differences between sites, with the particularity that the proportion of loading for YouTube is lower than for top domestic sites like ClipFish and MyVideos

4. *Market is concentrated and may concentrated further-confirmed for Germany.*

   In the US, the top 3 UGC video sites make roughly 37% of the total unique visitors while the top 5 exceeds 47%. In Germany, the market is more concentrated with the top 3 making more than 75% of the unique visitors, according to Nielsen statistics. Our sample confirms such a level of concentration—albeit lower, with the top 3 sites making up 63% of total share of visitors (note: in our sample, the discrepancy is largely explained by the lower number of surveyed people reporting to use YouTube in Germany).

Further, there is a clear tendency for the market to concentrate.

On one hand, Nielsen statistics report that the top 2 sites in Germany (YouTube and MyVideo) have grown the fastest in the last months of 2006. Second, we confirm that the number of UGC video sites visited is relatively low, similar to what has been observed for portals and content sites [2, 6]. (Only) 2,7 sites are visited by each UGV video viewer, and 2,3 for video posters. Furthermore, the users of the top two sites are more "unique" to those sites, with 1,2 and 0,8 extra site visited for viewers and up loaders, implying further concentration. Finally, as discussed in the next point 5, one key driver of extra viewing and uploading is referral —the proportion of referral on top sites is slightly higher than the average of all sites, meaning again that, *everything equal*, top sites are likely to concentrate more and more viewing and uploading along the way.

5. *Social features are getting prominent on online video sites –confirmed for Germany.*

As in the US, top UGC video sites have embedded social features in Germany. This includes sharing videos with friends on MyVideo to Videobox and user-feedback on ClipFish.

Those social features are relatively important for the dynamics of the German UGC video market. 25% of UGC videos watched originates from friends' referral in our sample. For comparison, Leskovec et al [17] mention that about 25% of Amazon purchasers recommend to friends, but only a few percent of recommendations in turn leads to an extra buy.

In the same way, a non trivial amount, 41% (resp. 31%) of German video uploaders are quoting "sharing with friends" (resp., "so that others can benefit") as a key rationale to post their videos online. This compares well with the findings of clear-cut social networks embedded in Maze, a large mostly deployed in China, P2P file sharing networks, as reported by Zhao et al [21].

4. Understanding the Roots of Online UGC Video Participation

Section 3 has provided evidence that the dynamics of US UGC video sites are likely replicable in other markets. In this section, we go one step further to investigate participation motives on UGC video.

As discussed above, active contribution is usually only made by a small proportion of users. Motivating participation is thus critical and a topic of substantive analysis in social science[2]. We rely on the various theories of economic utility and social psychology (e.g., [15]) to assume that mostly the value online users will foster participative media can derive from such an activity—this value can accrue from financial incentives, but also non-monetary elements like fame.

---

[2] Economists call this the "tragedy of the commons", that is people contribute less than the optimal amount of public goods. Social psychologists call social loafing the fact that people produce less effort on a collective task than on a comparable individual task (see e.g., Harkins 1987, Beenen et al., 2004 or Rashid et al. (2006)).

The model estimated is of the form of a multinomial logit model on the total sample described above, with the dependent variable being the fact that the online UGV video users decide or not to upload videos. We are trying different models, all including as control variables, socio-demographics like C1= age (a continuous variable), C2= gender (male= 1), C3= marital status (single =1) and C4= revenue effect (eight categories, from 500 Euro per month up to more than 4500 Euros per month per household).

The first version of the model only includes binary non-monetary variables: X1= indicative of "I want to share with friends"; X2= I want the entire world to see my video"; X3= indicative of "I do it for fun"; X4= indicative of "I make my friends benefit from my videos". Based on the theory of social utility, we expect the effect of X2 and X3 to be higher than X1 and X4.

Explaining load rate among users of UGV videos

Regression results - complete model

	normalized marginal impact	normalized mean elasticity	probability of non signif.
Loading motives-non monetary			
X1 share with friends	0.17	0.20	0.08
X2 fame	0.31	0.62	0.02
X3 fun and laugh	0.18	0.33	0.06
X4 others can benefit	0.29	0.26	0.04
Loading motives-monetary			
Y1 money	0.18	0.29	0.03
Y2 Free broadband line	0.08	0.04	0.09
Y3 Free mobile minutes	0.02	0.01	0.24
Audience impact			
Z1 visitor share of main used UGC video	0.09	0.07	0.09
Z2 visitor share of all UGC video used	-0.02	-0.02	0.14
Socio-demographics			
C1 Age	-0.02	-1.63	0.06
C2 Gender (male)	0.04	0.10	0.14
C3 marital status(single)	0.65	0.87	0.02
C4 income	-0.02	-1.31	0.14

Notes:
1. Sample size restrcited to loaders.
2. Logit model based on maximum likelihood function; pseudo-R^2= 0,63.

A second version of the model includes as well monetary variables: Y1= indicative of receiving money (e.g., minimum 100 Euros for loading a video ranked in top 100 most popularly watched); Y2= indicative of having free broadband , Y3= indicative of receiving free mobile minutes. Note that free broadband and free mobile minutes mean roughly 200 Euros' on a yearly basis, but it is a one off sum of money. In contrast Y1 measures the opportunity to receive a reward for each video in the top 100, so we expect that loaders interested in financial rewards will choose Y1 over the other schemes. We are also interested in comparing the marginal impact of the Y' versus X' on the fact to post videos—this will provide an idea of the relative merits of monetary versus non-monetary values linked to the controversy of paying top 1% contributors since Nestcape [8]).

Finally, a third model includes a vector Z' of variables linked to the current audience of the online video sites: Z1= audience share of the main video site used by the loader; Z2= audience share cumulated of the total sites used by the loader (on average 2,3 sites). We hypothesize that both Z1 and Z2 are positive, i.e., loading is favored by large audience watching. Also, we want to check whether Z1>Z2, that is, the most favored site has a larger effect than the total posts.

As it turns out, the best model is the one that includes all aspects on loading including non monetary and monetary incentives, audience relevance, etc. Regression results for the third model are displayed in Table 2. Both marginal effects and standardized coefficients reflecting elasticity at the mean are displayed, with the probability of the coefficient to be non significant highlighted in last column. The complete regression exhibits a strong fit, with a (pseudo-) R2 of 63%, and the probability of a noise fit is minimal (probability is less than 0,01). The results demonstrate the following insights:

1. *Both non monetary as well as monetary incentives are clear drivers of video posting contribution.*

    All non monetary variables are statistically significant at 0.05% risk level, except sharing with friends (at 10%). Among monetary variables, Y2 and mostly Y3 are not significant at traditional risk level. While not reported, note that the inclusion of monetary variables (from model 1 to model 2) increases the fit quality by about 50%, %. In general, both marginal and elasticity impact of non-monetary variables are larger than for monetary variables- motives for posting seems thus to be more driven by others motives than money alone.

2. *Fame seems to be the largest marginal impact to contribute among all variables.*

    The mean elasticity is the highest for fame than any other variable (except for control variables linked to socio-demographics). This confirms that private utility is a higher, albeit not the only one, motivator of participation. The fact as well that fame comes as the strongest driver means that utility derived from fame is higher than the expected monetary rewards of posting in the top 100 videos- -in this case, fame elasticity is more than double the money-elasticity to post UGC videos.

    Also, benefitting others is clearly a motivating aspect of active participation in UGC video, which confirms our stylized facts that social networks effects matter for the dynamics of the market.

3. *Among monetary values, people prefer direct payment for top videos than other means.*

    The marginal impact on participation from direct payment is two times the one of a free broadband line (and five times larger in terms of normalized elasticity). This means people prefer a proportional reward to their effort rather than lump sum benefits, even as large they may be. This also corroborates the validity of the strategy followed recently by some UGC video sites like Current TV or Revvee to procure paid content.

4. *Posting is positively influenced by the audience susceptible to watch the videos.*

As one German surveyor put it in his comments, UGC is like "playing soccer—we are motivated to "play" (read: upload) as far as the stadium (read: the audience) is full". We find some, yet marginal, evidence of this externality effect. Only Z1 is positive and significant, while Z2 is not statistically significant and of the wrong sign. The normalized coefficient beta attached to Z1 is also confirmed to be higher (in absolute value) than Z2.

5. *Socio-demographics (still) matter*

Finally, socio-demographics have a clear effect on posting—age (and income, but not significant) have even a more than proportional negative effect on posting. Being young, single and male means to be more likely an active participant for UGC video content, supporting the fact that young cohorts have so far been the first movers in this market.

5. Conclusion

This article aimed at describing the dynamics of online user-generated *video*. Using both secondary data as well as a primary research survey conducted on German users, the article has illustrated the following. First, the dynamics of the market seem to be very similar across countries. Second, if contribution in participative media remains relatively small, participation can be clearly fostered, in the case of UGC video, first by the desire to fame, second (but to a lesser extent) by financial incentives. On top of those drivers, social network aspects stand as critical drivers of the growth of user-generated video.

We also have noticed that both audience and participation are linked to 2 to 3 sites maximum, while social network effects are sufficiently large to continue boost growth of the largest UGC sites. Taking together, those findings lead to the conjecture that the market for online video may quickly evolve to a concentrated number of destination sites.

References

[1]   Adar, E. & Huberman, B. A. (2000). Free riding on gnutella. *First Monday*, **5**, 10.

[2]   Agrawal, V., L. Arjona & R. Lemmens (2000), E-performance: the path towards rational exuberance, *McKinsey Quarterly*, **1**, 31-43.

[3]   Beenen, G., Ling, K., Wang, X., Chang, K., Frankowski, D., Resnick, P., et al. "Using social psychology to motivate contributions to online communities," in *CSCW '04: Proceedings of the ACM Conference On Computer Supported Cooperative Work*, 2004.

[4]   Brothers, L., Hollan, J., Nielsen, J., Stornetta, S., Abney, S., Furnas, G. & Littman, M. "Supporting informal communication via ephemeral interest groups," in *Proceedings of CSCW 92*, 1992.

[5] Bughin, J. & Hagel, J. (2001), The operational performance of virtual communities, *Electronic Markets,* **10**(4), 237-243.

[6] Bughin, J. (2003), Finding the path(s) towards profitable e-commerce, Deutsche Bank Research, *Research Notes Economics,* 7.

[7] Butler, B. (1999). *When is a group not a group: An empirical examination of metaphors for online social structure.* Pittsburgh, PA: Carnegie Mellon University.

[8] Deci, E. L., Koestner, R. & Ryan, R. M. (1999). A meta-analytic review of experiments examining the effects of extrinsic rewards on intrinsic motivation. *Psychological Bulletin,* **125** (6), 627-66.

[9] Figaro, Y. Le G. (2006), "Les français lisent de plus en plus de blogs", *Médias Publicité, December,* 24.

[10] Harkins, S. (1987). Social loafing and social facilitation. *Journal of Experimental Social Psychology,* **23** (1), 1-18.

[11] Harkins, S. G. & Petty, R. E. (1982). Effects of task difficulty and task uniqueness on social loafing. *Journal of Personality and Social Psychology,* **43**, 1214-1229.

[12] Heckman, J. (1979). Sample selection bias as a specification error. *Econometrica,* **47** (1), 153-162.

[13] Horrigan, J. (2006), *Pew Internet & American Life project:* Home Broadband Adoption.

[14] Inouye, M. & Kaufhold, G. "User Generated Content- more than just watching on YouTube and Hangin' on my space" in *Instat Report,* 2006.

[15] Karau, S. J. & Williams, K. D. (2001). Understanding individual motivation in groups: The collective effort model. In M. E. Turner (Ed.), *Groups at Work: Theory and Research* (pp. 113-141). Mahwah, NJ: Lawrence Erlbaum Associates.

[16] Kelli, S.U., Sung, Ch. & Farnham, S.H. "Designing for improved social responsibility, user participation and content in online communities," in *CHI 2002 proceedings,* 2002.

[17] Leskovek, J., Adamic, L. & Huberman, B. (2006), *The dynamics of viral marketing,* manuscript submitted to ACM.

[18] Lakhani, K. R. & Hippel, E. V. (2003). How open source software works: "Free" user to user assistance. *Research Policy* (Special issue), **32** (6), 923-943.

[19] Musser, "Web 2.0-principles and best practices," in *O'Reilly Radar Report,* 2006.

[20] Rashid, A.M., Ling, K., Tassone, R.G., Resnick, P., Kraut, R. & Riedl, J., "Motivating participation by displaying the value of contribution," in *CHI 2006 proceedings,* 2006.

[21] Zhao, Y., Hou X., Yang, M. & Dai, Y., "Measurement study and application of social network in the Maze P2P file-sharing system," in *Proceedings of the First International Conference of Scalable Information Systems,* 2006.

[22] "The international communications market 2006," in *Ofcom Research Document,* 2006.

In: Peer-to-Peer Networks and Internet Policies
Editors: Diego Vegros and Jaime Sáenz, pp. 193-204

ISBN: 978-1-60876-287-3
© 2010 Nova Science Publishers, Inc.

Chapter 8

PEER-TO-PEER CONTENT DISTRIBUTION SYSTEMS: SURVEYING THE LANDSCAPE

Dimitris Kanellopoulos[*]

Department of Mathematics, University of Patras, GR-265 00 Patras, Greece

Abstract

Peer-to-peer (P2P) systems are distributed systems consisting of interconnected nodes, able to self-organize into network topologies with the purpose of sharing resources such as content, CPU cycles, storage, and bandwidth. Content distribution systems are designed for the sharing of digital media and other data between users. P2P content distribution systems range from relatively simple direct file-sharing applications, to more complicated systems that create a distributed storage medium for securely and efficiently publishing, organizing, indexing, searching, updating, and retrieving data. P2P systems can function, scale, and self-organize in the presence of a highly transient population of nodes and network and computer failures, without the need for a central server administration. This characteristic is mainly attributed to the network organization and location and routing algorithms. In this respect, two general categories of systems can be identified: the unstructured systems and the structured (or DHT-based) systems. Both category systems are complementary and satisfactory solutions. This chapter focuses on P2P content distribution systems and infrastructures by identifying their non-functional properties, and determining the way in which these non-functional properties depend on, and are affected by various design features. The main nonfunctional characteristics include provisions for security, anonymity, fairness, increased scalability, and performance, as well as resource management, and organization capabilities. Finally, this chapter discusses open research problems, directions, and opportunities.

Key words: Peer-to-peer (P2P); P2P file sharing; P2P streaming; P2P broadcast; Overlay

1. Introduction

A great number of peer-to-peer (P2P) applications have been developed all over the world with different design philosophies and operation modes (Steinmetz and Wehrle, 2005).

---

[*] E-mail address: d_kan2006@yahoo.gr

P2P applications take advantage of the resources-storage, cycles, content, and human presence - available at the edge of the Internet. A P2P network differs from the traditional client-server paradigm in that the peers contribute the majority of the resource running the service, which includes the CPU power, the bandwidth and the storage. In a client-server application, the server is paying for the capacity. As each peer in the P2P network is a service provider, the servicing resource of the P2P network is distributed with redundancy, and this leads to a robust service. Each peer node belongs to a different owner, and pays and contributes its own resource in return of the service rendered by the P2P network. In particular, each peer is a service provider and a service consumer. It is worth noticing that a P2P application is economy to run, robust, and super-scalable. The total resource of the system increases as more and more nodes join the P2P network and demand on the system increases. According to Schollmeier (2001) a pure P2P network is a network that any single, arbitrary chosen peer can be removed from the network without having the network suffering any loss of network service. Androutsellis and Spinellis (2004, p.337) further define P2P systems as follows.

"Peer-to-peer systems are distributed systems consisting of interconnected nodes able to self organize into network topologies with the purpose of sharing resources such as content, CPU cycles, storage and bandwidth, capable of adapting to failures and accommodating transient populations of nodes while maintaining acceptable connectivity and performance, without requiring the intermediation or support of a global centralized server or authority."

Currently, there are numerous P2P systems and infrastructures. Some examples are: the late Napster (Napster, 2002), Publius (Waldman and Mazi, 2001), Gnutella (Gnutella, 2003), Kazaa (Kazaa, 2003), Freenet (Clarke et al., 2000), MojoNation (MojoNation, 2003), Oceanstore (Kubiatowicz et al., 2000), PAST (Druschel and Rowstron 2001), Chord (Stoica et al., 2001), Scan (Chen et al., 2000), FreeHaven (Dingledine et al., 2000), Groove (Groove, 2003), and Mnemosyne (Hand and Roscoe, 2002). P2P networks run on top of the Internet and can be classified based on how the content is delivered and consumed. There are three modes of content delivery: a) bulk download; b) streaming; and c) bounded broadcast.

P2P File Sharing

In the *bulk download* mode, the peer doesn't care about the source characteristics. Its operation goal is simply to retrieve the file from the P2P network as fast as possible. Usually, the file is chopped into blocks (also called packets) and these blocks are delivered in non-sequential order. Consequently, the shared file such as a shared video is not playable until the entire video is retrieved. The bulk download guarantees content quality with unbounded delivery time even on a slow connection. For example, given low connection bandwidth (e.g., 33.6 kbps modem) you may have to wait a long time, hours or days, before you can play the video file. However, video content quality is guaranteed. The most popular P2P file sharing utilities are BitTorrent, eDonkey (http://en.wikipedia.org/wiki/EDonkey2000), FastTrack and Gnutella.

P2P Streaming

The target of P2P streaming is to build a scalable P2P platform for TV/music delivery. Many companies are actively working in this area. Some example companies are PPStream (http://www.ppstream.com/), Abacast (http://www.abacast.com/), Raw-Flow (http://www.rawflow.com/), PPLive (http://www.pplive.com/), UUSee (http://www.uusee.com/), Roxbeam (http://www.roxbeam.com/), Mysee (http://www.mysee.com/), etc. In the streaming mode, the application is aware of the format, the required bandwidth, and the structure of the delivered content (video or music). During the video or music delivery, the content is played smoothly as the user favors fast response. The streaming application usually uses a playback buffer at the client. At the beginning of the streaming, the playback buffer is filled with the arriving content while the playback is suspended. The playback only starts when the playback buffer reaches a certain level. During the playback, the streaming application watchfully manages the buffer and ensures a certain buffer occupancy level, so that the playback will not be interrupted due to packet loss or jitter during the delivery, and the buffer is not excessively long which consumes unnecessary server bandwidth. The streaming application may also adapt the delivery media according to the resource available in the system and to the client. For example, for client at the end of a slow Internet link or for P2P network with deficient total network bandwidth, a low bit rate version of the video can be streamed to the client, if the video is encoded with multiple bit rate (MBR) streams or scalable stream (Kanellopoulos et al., 2009). In the streaming mode, the video may be transcoded, either through a scalable video codec or through a MBR video codec to different bit rates, e.g., 200 kbps, 100 kbps, 50 kbps and 25 kbps. For client at the end of a 33.6 kbps modem link, we can select to deliver only the 25 kbps video stream. The streaming client may also select to drop packets that have a less impact on playback quality to ensure that the video can still be smoothly played back using the available resource. Generally in streaming, the goal is to get a smooth playback experience and a bounded delivery time, which is determined by the playback buffer. Nevertheless, the content quality may be sacrificed. The delivery time delay depends on the fluctuation of the available resource to the client and in the P2P network. In practical P2P streaming implementations, such as PPLive, the delivery time delay can be 15–120s.

Bounded Broadcast

In this mode of content delivery, we have bounded delay from the creation to the consumption (the content is played back at the client). Broadcast mode applications include: audio/video conferencing, interactive gambling, Internet gaming, earning conference call, etc. Compared with the streaming application, the broadcast application not only needs to sustain playback during delivery, but also needs to put an upper bound on the maximum delay. As a result, the content delivery algorithm has to be optimized for minimizing delay, and certain tricks (e.g., the use of the playback buffer to combat packet loss and jitter) in the streaming application, cannot be used. There are many research prototypes for P2P broadcast applications, such as Microsoft ConferenceXP, NICE, Zigzag (Tran et al., 2003), ESM. However, compared with P2P file sharing and P2P streaming, the current deployment scale of P2P broadcast is much smaller in the real world.

In this chapter, we survey the state of the art of the development of efficient and robust P2P content delivery applications. The rest of the chapter is organized as follows. Section 2 examines the two important aspects to achieve the efficiency and robustness: the *P2P overlay construction* and the *P2P scheduling algorithm*. Section 3 identifies non-functional properties of content distribution systems. Finally, Section 4 concludes the chapter and presents open research problems, directions, and opportunities.

2. Achieving Efficiency and Robustness

A well-designed P2P application should have the following characteristics. It is *efficient*, meaning that it uses all resource available in the P2P network. It is *robust*, i.e., it can cope effectively with the changes and the anomaly of the peers and the network links. It *satisfies the quality of service (QoS) requirements* of the delivery mode. With streaming, this means that the playback is smooth with as high media quality as possible. With broadcast, this means that it satisfies certain delay constraint of the delivery of the media. To achieve efficient and robust P2P content delivery, we need to work on two primary modules: P2P overlay construction and P2P scheduling.

2.1. P2P Overlay

All P2P networks run on top of the Internet. Actually, a P2P network is an overlay network, with the link of the overlay being a pair of connected peers. P2P overlay construction is the first important task faced by an architect of a P2P application. Sometimes, the task is called peer matching, because it involves how a new peer finds existing peers and connects to them; and how an existing peer finds replacement peers to substitute those that leave the P2P network. Hereafter, we survey the technical approaches and issues in building the P2P overlay network. The target is to have an overlay construction strategy that may efficiently utilize the resource in the network and may effectively deal with the dynamics of the peers and the network conditions. Overlay networks are responsible for providing a resource location service. Overlay networks can be classified in terms of their degree of centralization and structure. There are three categories (depicted in Figure 1) concerning the centralization issue:

- *Purely Decentralized Architectures*: There is no central coordination point of the distribution activities. Nodes are referred as *servents* due to their dual nature (SERVers+cliENTS). This model is more robust than centralized one because the failure of any particular node does not force the system resulting in high availability of the network (fault tolerance) and reduced costs. Unfortunately, this model presents two mains drawbacks. First, the localization of an object is not guaranteed because of the directory decentralization. Second, the mechanism of research by flooding (set of broadcast) wastes high amounts of network bandwidth. Indeed, the increase of the number of the peers generates an exponential increase of requests what pollute the network, slow down downloads and poses scalability problems.

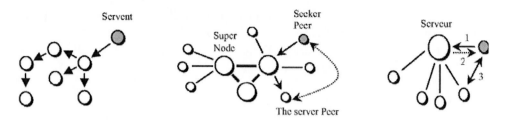

Figure 1. Purely decentralized systems; partially decentralized systems; and hybrid systems (Benayoune and Lancieri, 2004).

- *Partially Centralized Architectures:* Special roles are assumed for some nodes called "supernodes", which carry out special tasks mainly aimed at improving the performance of network routing. However, in case of failures of the primary *Super-node*, others are defined to automatically replace it. Super-Nodes can be elected according to their own capacities, in particular in term of bandwidth and persistence in the system (time of connection) but each user can decide to be or not a Super-Node.

- *Hybrid Decentralized Architectures*: A central server offers the interaction among the nodes, since indexes which support data searches and node identification are centralized, but the data is distributed. P2P indexes for simple key lookup can be assessed, including those based on Plaxton trees, rings, tori, butterflies, de Bruijn graphs and skip graphs. Risson and Moors (2006) explored P2P indexes for keyword lookup, information retrieval and data management. Currently, there are emerging schema-based P2P designs [like that proposed by Nejdl et al. (2003)] with super-node hierarchies and structure within documents. Schema-based P2P designs are quite distinct from the structured DHT proposals. Semantic indexes capture object relationships. While the DHTs methods guarantee that a key can be found if it exists, they do not on their own capture the relationships between the document name and its content or metadata. Semantic P2P designs capture such relationships and are often driven by heuristics. Thus, semantic P2P designs may not guarantee that scarce items will be found. In Hybrid decentralize architectures we have a very efficient way to locate resources and we have a complete view of the network. Even if shared-files are more easily managed, there is a single access point that poses various problems (failure, overload, copyright, security, etc). Moreover, the central server limits the extensibility of the network.

Centralized vs. Decentralized

The P2P overlay can be built via either a centralized scheme or via a decentralized scheme. In a centralized scheme, a central entity (e.g., a *tracker*) maintains information of all peers in the P2P network, and is primarily responsible in making decisions on how the peers are matched. An example of centralized overlay building is BitTorrent. The BitTorrent tracker is a central entity that is responsible for building the overlay. An example of decentralized overlay construction is Gnutella. In Gnutella, there is no central entity. The Gnutella peer discovers and connects to other Gnutella peers through a random walk procedure. Each Gnutella node maintains a neighbourhood table, which contains the IP address and port of known Gnutella nodes. In addition to the pure centralized and pure decentralized overlay building, there are hybrid approaches. For example, in PPLive, the new coming peer first retrieves a list of peers from the tracker. Then, when it connects to other PPLive peers, they further exchange their peer list to discover more peers without involving the tracker.

Tiered Overlay

Tiered overlay is an important method in P2P overlay construction. The supernodes interconnect with the other supernodes and form a supernode overlay, which becomes the core of the P2P network. The client node then picks one or a small number of supernodes to associate with and form the client overlay. During the file sharing session in FastTrack or VoIP session in Skype, two clients may temporarily establish a direct connection between themselves to exchange files or conduct VoIP.

DHT: Distributed Hash Table

DHT is an active area in the distributed system research. The first four DHTs, CAN (Ratnasamy et al., 2001), Chord (Stoica et al., 2001), Pastry (Rowstron and Druschel, 2001) and Tapestry (Zhao et al., 2004), were introduced in 2001. The common approach of the DHT is to use a large key space, and to let each participating node hold an ID in the key space. Each node is then charged with a set of keys in its neighborhood, as a result, the node can be considered as a slot in the hash table formed by the key space. The resultant distributed system is thus called the DHT (distributed hash table). The DHT design philosophy is to develop a distributed system that can scale to a large number of nodes and can handle constant node arrival and failure. DHT schemes usually implement two basic features: *routing and hash table operation*. The DHT routing function can be abstracted to: FindNode(ID, which takes an ID as the input, and finds one or a set of nodes that are in charge of the space covering the ID. Those nodes are usually the nodes closest to ID with some distance measure.

Proximity and Heterogeneity

A key issue in overlay building is to consider the proximity and the heterogeneity of the peers. The heterogeneity concerns the difference of the resource available to a peer, e.g., the upload /download bandwidth, the CPU resource, and the NAT/firewall that the peer is connected to. The proximity concerns the distance between the two peers, e.g., the latency, the throughput and the ISP locality. It is beneficial to link neighbour peers in the overlay, and to use peers with more resource as the hubs in the overlay.

2.2. P2P Scheduling

The P2P scheduling concerns the method for delivering the data from the source to its destinations under a given overlay. A good P2P scheduling algorithm has three aspects. First, it is efficient in utilizing the bandwidth resource available in the P2P network. Second, it is robust in adapting to the changes in the conditions of the peer and the network. Third, the delivery satisfies certain quality of service requirement of the content.

2.2.1. Tree-Based vs. Mesh-Based Delivery

We may roughly classify the P2P content delivery methods into two categories: the tree-based delivery and the mesh-based delivery. The tree-based P2P delivery can be traced back to IP multicast (RFC 3170, 2001), where a single block transmitted from the source is replicated by the routers along a distribution tree rooted at the source node, and is thereby delivered to an arbitrary number of receivers. *IP multicast* is a method of forwarding IP datagrams to a group of interested receivers. PGM (Gemmell et al., 2003) is a reliable multicast protocol using a hybrid mechanism, namely FEC (Forward error correction) with a hierarchical approach and NAK suppression, to achieve scalability. It supports single-source multicast applications. It runs over a best-effort datagram protocol like IP multicast, but also needs router support for constructing hierarchy. Another approach in the category of FEC-based solutions, namely digital fountain (Byers et al., 2002), supports asynchronous reliable multicast for a group of heterogeneous participants. A digital fountain offers participants to retrieve content on their time of demand that is asynchronously. FEC-based erasure codes are used to implement the reliable multicast protocol based on digital fountain approach. In erasure codes, data encoded with the redundant packets are transmitted by the source. Any subset of these encoded packets with length equal to the length of the original data would be enough to reconstruct the data. Thus, in case of data loss at a receiver, redundant packets are used for loss recovery. Since these packets can be utilized by several receivers, this approach can significantly decrease the amount of retransmissions. In the category of scalable overlay multicast protocols offering reliable data dissemination, well-known approaches are Split-Stream (Castro et al., 2003), and Scribe (Castro et al., 2002). Split-Stream addresses the problem of distributing the forwarding load of traditional tree-based overlay multicast among the participating peers evenly. It is a high-bandwidth content distribution system based on end-system multicast, robust to node failures, and can manage peers with different bandwidth capacities. The content to be distributed is striped across multiple multicast trees. This fact increases the resilience to node failures. With suitable data encoding methods such as erasure coding and multiple description coding, applications can achieve data loss recovery in the case of node failures. Split-Stream is built using Pastry, which is a scalable, self-organizing structured P2P overlay network similar to Chord. Scribe is a scalable, self-organizing and fully decentralized overlay multicast approach that offers best-effort reliability. It is built on top of Pastry and uses it for managing group creation, join, building multicast tree and repairing it in the case of a node failure. It uses TCP for reliable delivery of data in the multicast tree and for flow control. The load on participants is balanced, and in comparison to network layer multicast, delay and link stress achieved is acceptable. It is worth mentioning that Hosseini et al. (2007) surveyed and classified application layer overlay multicast protocols.

2.2.2. Pull vs. Push vs. Hybrid Delivery

Depend on whether the sender and/or the receiver take the initiative in moving the blocks, three modes may be used in the P2P delivery. In the *push* mode (also called the *sender-driven delivery* mode), the sender takes the initiative, and pushes the received block to a selected peer. In the *pull* mode (also called the *receiver-driven delivery* mode), the receiver takes the initiative, and pulls the block it wants from its neighbor. In the *hybrid* mode, both the receiver and the sender may take the initiative, and negotiate the block delivery.

2.2.3. Flow Control

The flow control is an essential part of a P2P delivery algorithm. For the sender, the flow control ensures that the upload pipeline is fully utilized. For the receiver, it ensures that a constant stream of blocks is arriving. P2P applications employ different flow control mechanisms.

3. Identifying Non-functional Properties of Content Distribution Systems

The main non-functional characteristics of P2P content distribution systems (CDS) include provisions for security, anonymity, fairness, increased scalability, and performance, as well as resource management, and organization capabilities.

- *Security.* Further analyzed in terms of: *integrity and authenticity.* Safeguarding the accuracy and completeness of data and processing methods. Unauthorized entities cannot change data; adversaries cannot substitute a forged document for a requested one.
- *Privacy and confidentiality.* Ensuring that data is accessible only to those authorized to have access, and that there is control over what data is collected, how it is used, and how it is maintained.
- *Availability and persistence.* Ensuring that authorized users have access to data and associated assets when required. For a peer-to-peer content distribution system this often means always. This property entails stability in the presence of failure, or changing node populations. Availability has a significant influence on popularity. In fact, it is probably the security property that user most worry about. Availability is measured by how often object requests are successfully served, and, in particular, mapping two factors: the number of peers (average node availability) and the number of object replicas (replica storage size).
- *Scalability.* Maintaining the system's performance attributes independent of the number of nodes or documents in its network. A dramatic increase in the number of nodes or documents will have minimal effect on performance and availability.
- *Performance.* The time required for performing the operations allowed by the system, typically publication, searching, and retrieval of documents.
- *Fairness.* Ensuring that users offer and consume resources in a fair and balanced manner. May rely on accountability, reputation, and resource trading mechanisms.
- *Resource Management Capabilities.* P2P content distribution systems mainly allow the publishing, searching, and retrieval of documents. More sophisticated systems

may afford more advanced resource management capabilities, such as editing or removal of documents, management of storage space, and operations on metadata.

- *Semantic Grouping of Information.* An area of research that has attracted considerable attention recently is the semantic grouping and organization of content and information in P2P networks. Various grouping schemes are encountered, such as semantic grouping, based on the content itself; grouping, based on locality or network distance; grouping, based on organization ties, as well as others.

Currently, most P2P applications serve content in a single mode, either in file sharing, in streaming, or in broadcast. However, the system proposed by Huang and Li (2006) supports both file sharing and streaming. A hybrid P2P content delivery application may aggregate resource in the P2P network and improve the QoS for users in the streaming and the broadcast mode. An ideal P2P platform supports file sharing, audio/video conferencing (VoIP), and music/video streaming simultaneously. The user of such P2P platform tends to always be online, as it can be used for so many tasks, and the file sharing task alone can take a long time. This P2P system is capable of diverting the resource of the P2P network to ensure that those peers with stringent QoS demand are met first. It may improve the QoS experience of the users beyond what is capable of by a single mode P2P content delivery system.

65–70% of the Internet backbone traffic can be attributed P2P. If the majority of the P2P applications are agnostic to the Internet architecture, they will quickly overwhelm the Internet. It is crucial to build P2P applications that are aware of the underlying Internet architecture, and are friendly to the ISPs. A few works (Li, 2007; Karagiannis et al., 2005; Huang et al., 2007) have implemented platforms which adopt such an approach. The most popular commercial solution of large scale content delivery is the CDN (content delivery networks). A CDN is a system of computers networked together across the Internet that cooperate transparently to deliver content to end users, most often for the purpose of improving performance, scalability, and cost efficiency. CDN deploy servers in multiple backbones and ISPs, and often in multiple POPs (point of presences) within each ISP. By providing a shared distribution infrastructure, CDNs provide reliable delivery and cost-effective scaling. P2P serves as a natural complement to CDN, with the main difference being that P2P employ user peers not managed by the CDN directly. The concept of using P2P to extend the CDN network has been raised by Pakkala and Latvakoski, (2005) as well as by Xu et al. (2003). Akamai (http://www.akamai.com) expects to combine P2P file management and distribution software with the scalable backend control system and global network of edge servers of Akamai. VeriSign (http://www.verisign.com/), CacheLogic (http://cachelogic.net), Grid Networks and Joost all announce their own P2P CDN service as well. However, none of the existing works analyze the key building blocks of P2P CDN, as well as quantifying the performance difference, in term of latency and throughput, among the P2P, CDN and hybrid P2P-CDN solutions.

4. Conclusions

In this chapter, we surveyed the current state of the art of P2P content delivery. A well-designed P2P system should reliably and efficiently deliver the content and satisfy certain quality of service (QoS) constraint. In P2P file sharing research area, new solutions are required even though existing P2P file sharing applications have demonstrated that they can efficiently and reliably transfer the file in P2P fashion to many users. The problem of efficiently and reliably streaming content in P2P is still not solved even though there many deployed P2P streaming solutions. For example, Hei et al. (2006) made known that PPLive cannot sustain the streaming to all peers without playback stalling. During streaming, the network resource should be used more efficiently, to sustain the streaming rate more robustly in case of peer and network anomaly, and to make sure that the playback does not pause. The research in the P2P broadcast concentrates around tree-based P2P delivery schemes derived from the application layer multicast (ALM) (Banerjee et al., 2002). The best available P2P broadcast systems are not as efficient, as robust, and as scalable compared to solutions in the P2P file sharing and P2P streaming space. It will be interesting to see more works in the P2P broadcast and/or P2P conferencing space. Another interesting research area is the hybrid mode P2P delivery. Research on other aspects and properties of peer-to-peer content distribution systems has taken advantage of knowledge and solutions from numerous scientific fields. Characteristic examples include research on the application of reputation systems in peer-to-peer environments, the semantic organization of information, as well as the use of cryptographic techniques for the protection of data, both stored and in transit through the network. Finally, as peer-to-peer technologies are still evolving, there are a multitude of open research problems, directions, and opportunities. As Li (2008) states future work would focus on extensions to the following items:

- The design of new distributed object location, routing and distributed hash table data structures and algorithms for maximizing performance, security and scalability, both in structured and unstructured network architectures.
- The study of more efficient security, anonymity, and censorship resistance schemes. These features will be critical to the future of P2P systems and their adoption for increasingly more sensitive applications.
- The semantic grouping of information in P2P networks. This direction that has a lot in common with efforts in the semantic Web domain.
- The design of incentive mechanisms and reputation systems that will stimulate the cooperative behavior between the users, and make the overall operation of peer-to-peer networks more fair.
- The convergence of Grid and P2P systems. Research in this direction aims to combine the benefits of the established field of distributed computing (including interoperability standards) with the merits of new peer-to-peer architectures.

References

Androutsellis, T., and Spinellis, D. (2004) A survey of peer-to-peer content distribution technologies, *ACM Computing Surveys*, Vol. 36, No. 4, pp.335-371.

Banerjee, S., Bhattacharjee, B., and Kommareddy, C. (2002) Scalable application layer multicast. In: Proceedings of *ACM SIGCOMM 2002*, pp.205-217, Pittsburgh, PA, August.

Benayoune, F. and Lancieri, L. (2004) Models of cooperation in peer-to-peer networks – A survey. M. Freire et al. (Eds.): *ECUMN 2004, LNCS 3262*, pp.327-336, Springer-Verlag Berlin Heidelberg 2004.

Byers, J.W., Luby, M., and Mitzenmacher, M. (2002) A digital fountain approach to asynchronous reliable multicast, *IEEE Journal on Selected Areas in Communications*, Vol. 20, No. 8, pp.1528–1540.

Castro, M., Druschel, P. Kermarrec, A.M. and Rowstron, A. (2002) SCRIBE: a large-scale and decentralized application-level multicast infrastructure, *IEEE Journal on Selected Areas in Communications*, Vol. 20, No. 8, pp. 1489-1498.

Castro, M., Druschel, P., Kermarrec, A.M., Nandi, A., Rowstron, A., and Singh A. (2003) SplitStream: high-bandwidth multicast in cooperative environments, *ACM SIGOPS Operating Systems Review*, Vol. 37, No. 5, pp.298-313.

Chen, Y., Katz, R., and Kubiatowicz, J. (2000) Scan: A dynamic, scalable and efficient content distribution network. In *Proceedings of International Conference on Pervasive Computing*, pp.145-148.

Clarke, I., Sandberg, O., and Wiley, B. (2000) Freenet: A distributed anonymous information storage and retrieval system. In Proceedings of the *Workshop on Design Issues in Anonymity and Unobservability*, pp.46-66, Berkeley, CA.

Dingledine, R., Freedman, M., and Molnar, D. (2000) The FreeHaven project: Distributed anonymous storage service. In *Workshop on Design Issues in Anonymity and Unobservability*. pp.67-95.

Druschel, P. and Rowstron, A. (2001) Past: A largescale, persistent peer-to-peer storage utility. In Proceedings of the *Eighth Workshop on Hot Topics in Operating Systems*.

Gemmell, J., Montgomery, T., Speakman, T. Crowcroft, J. (2003) The PGM reliable multicast protocol, *IEEE Network*, Vol. 17, No. 1, pp.16-22.

Gnutella (2003) The Gnutella web site: http:// gnutella.wego.com.

Groove (2003) The Groove web site. http://www.groove.net.

Hand, S., and Roscoe, T. (2002) Mnemosyne: Peer-to-peer steganographic storage. In Proceedings of the 1st *International Workshop on Peer-to-Peer Systems* (IPTPS'02). MIT Faculty Club, Cambridge, MA.

Hei, X., Liang, C., Liang, J., Liu, Y., and Ross, KW. (2006) Insights into PPLive: a measurement study of a large-scale P2P IPTV system. In: Workshop *on Internet Protocol TV (IPTV) services over World Wide Web* in conjunction with WWW2006, Edinburgh, Scotland, May.

Hosseini, M., Ahmed, D.T., Shirmohammadi, S., and Georganas, N.D. (2007) A survey of application-layer multicast protocols, *IEEE Communications Surveys & Tutorials*, Vol. 9, No. 3, pp.58-74.

Huang, C., and Li, J. (2006) DISCOVR: distributed collaborative video recorder. 2006 *International Conference on Multimedia & Expo* (ICME'2006), pp.1413-1416, Toronto, Canada, Jul. 9–12.

Huang, C., Li, J., and Ross, K. (2007) Can internet video-on-demand be profitable. Proc. *ACM Sigcomm'07*, pp.133 - 144, Kyoto, Japan, Aug.

Kanellopoulos, D., Kotsiantis, S., and Pintelas, P. (2009) Internet and multimedia communications. In Mehdi Khosrow-Pour (Ed.) *Encyclopedia of Information Science and Technology*. Second Edition. pp.2176-2182, Idea Group Inc(IGI).

Karagiannis, T., Rodriguez, P., and Papagiannaki, K. (2005) Should Internet service providers fear peer-assisted content distribution? In: Proc. Internet Measurement Conference 2005. Berkeley, CA, Oct.

Kazaa (2003) The Kazaa web site. http://www.kazaa.com.

Kubiatowicz, J., Bindel, D., Chen, Y., Eaton, P., Geels, D., Gummadi, S., Weatherspoon, H., Weimer, W., Wells, C., and Zhao, B. (2000) Oceanstore: an architecture for global-scale persistent storage. In *Proceedings of ACM ASPLOS*, pp.190-201.

Li, J. (2007) Locality aware peer assisted delivery: the way to scale Internet video to the world. *16th Packet Video workshop (PV 2007)*, pp.133-142, Lausanne, Switzerland, Nov.

Li, J. (2008) On peer-to-peer (P2P) content delivery, *Peer-to-Peer Networking and Applications*, Vol. 1, No. 1, pp.45-63.

MojoNation (2003) The MojoNation web site. http://www.mojonation.net.

Napster (2002) The Napster Web Site. http://www.napster.com

Nejdl, W Siberski, W., and Sintek, M. (2003) Design issues and challenges for RDF- and schema-based peer-to-peer systems, *ACM SIGMOD Record*, Vol. 32, No. 3, pp.41-46.

Pakkala, D., Latvakoski, J. (2005) Towards a peer-to-peer extended content delivery network. *14th IST Mobile & Wireless Communications Summit*, Dresden, June.

Ratnasamy, S., Francis, P., Handley, M., Karp, R., and Shenker, S. (2001) A scalable content-addressable network. In: *Proceedings of ACM SIGCOMM 2001*. pp.161-172, San Diego, CA, Aug.

RFC 3170 (2001) *IP Multicast Applications: Challenges and Solutions*. Available at: http://www.faqs.org/rfcs/rfc3170.html

Risson J., and Moors, T. (2006) Survey of research towards robust peer-to-peer networks: Search methods, *Computer Networks,* Vol. 50, No. 17, pp.3485–3521.

Rowstron, A., and Druschel, P. (2001) Pastry: scalable, distributed object location and routing for large-scale peer-to-peer systems. *IFIP/ACM International Conference on Distributed Systems Platforms* (Middleware). Heidelberg, Germany, pp. 329–350, November.

Schollmeier, R. (2001) A definition of peer-to-peer networking for the classification of peer-to-peer architectures and applications. Proc. of *1st Intern. Conf. on Peer-to-Peer Computing*, Linkoping, Sweden, pp.101–102, Aug.

Steinmetz, R., and Wehrle, K. (2005) Peer-to-peer systems and applications. *LNCS* Vol. 3485. Springer.

Stoica, I., Morris, R., Karger, D., Kaashoek, M., and Balakrishnan, H. (2001) Chord: A scalable peer-to-peer lookup service for internet applications. In *Proceedings of SIGCOMM 2001,* pp.149-160.

Tran, D., Hua, K., and Do, T. (2003) Zigzag: an efficient peer-to-peer scheme for media streaming. Proc. of INFOCOM 2003, the *22nd Annual Joint Conference of the IEEE Computer and Communications Societies*, San Francisco, CA, Apr.

Waldman, M., and Mazi, D. (2001) Tangler: a censorship-resistant publishing system based on document entanglements. In Proceedings of the *ACM Conference on Computer and Communications Security*, pp.126-131.

Xu, D., Chai, HK., Rosenberg, C., and Kulkami, S. (2003) Analysis of a hybrid architecture for cost-effective streaming media distribution. *SPIE/ACM Conf. on Multimedia Computing and Networking* (MMCN'03). San Jose, CA, Jan.

Zhao, BY., Huang, L., Stribling, J., Rhea, SC., Joseph, AD., and Kubiatowcz, JD. (2004) Tapestry: a resilient global-scale overlay for service deployment, *IEEE Journal on Selected Areas in Communications*, Vol. 22, No. 1, pp.41-53.

In: Peer-to-Peer Networks and Internet Policies
Editors: Diego Vegros and Jaime Sáenz, pp. 205-214

ISBN: 978-1-60876-287-3
© 2010 Nova Science Publishers, Inc.

Chapter 9

THE ETHICS OF ONLINE RESEARCH:
THE NEW CHALLENGES OF NEW MEDIA

Karen Rodham and Jeff Gavin
Department of Psychology, University of Bath, UK

Abstract

As the context and content of psychological research changes, so too do the ethical decisions faced by researchers. The Internet continues to grow in popularity and as it does so, more and more people are turning to it in order to seek information, advice and psychological support (Coulson, Malik, & Mo, 2007). The Internet has therefore become an invaluable resource for recruiting research participants, especially for studies that require recruitment of clinical or hard to find populations. Indeed, the prevalence of topic specific websites, online message boards and e-mail lists, provides researchers with a ready-made sampling frame that they can utilize to access participants who are interested, affiliated and connected to the topic under investigation (Griffiths, 2001; Murray & Fisher, 2002; Szabo, Frenkl, & Caputo, 1996). As in 'offline' research, a range of qualitative approaches can be employed which include: online surveys, online interviews (both 'synchronous' and 'asynchronous'), online focus groups and online observational studies, (whereby the behavior of people using chat rooms or message boards is analysed).

However, the expansion of the online research milieu brings with it new ethical challenges particularly in terms of consent and privacy and confidentiality. As a consequence, a number of authors have written about practical and ethical considerations with regard to online research (Coulson et al., 2007; DeLorme, Zinkhan, & French, 2001; Eysenbach & Till, 2001; Rodham & Gavin, 2006). Furthermore, the British Psychological Society (2007) has recently published guidelines for conducting research online which are intended to be a supplement to the existing ethical code of conduct for British psychologists, whereas other professional bodies specifically mention the issue of online research within their statement of ethical practice (e.g., British Sociological Association, 2002). The British Psychological Society (BPS) guidelines, however, do not address the ethical and methodological challenges posed by so-called Web 2.0. How do researchers deal with the changing trends in Internet use, which now include multi-author and multi-media sites such as Facebook, Myspace and Youtube? How can decisions about public and private spaces, informed consent, or anonymity be addressed in online environments containing several layers of text, image and audio-visual input from multiple sources across multiple, linked sites?

Over the last few years, we have built up a body of research utilising the Internet as a means of collecting data (e.g. Adams, Rodham & Gavin, 2005; Hadert & Rodham, 2008; Rodham, Gavin & Miles, 2007; Gavin, Duffield, Brosnan, M., Joiner, Maras, & Scott, 2007; Gavin, Rodham & Poyer, 2008; Rodham, McCabe & Blake, 2009; Whitty & Gavin, 2001). We draw upon our experience as online qualitative researchers and offer a commentary on the ethics of conducting online research.

Introduction

"Responsible and ethical research is not a matter of codes, policy or procedure. Rather, responsible and ethical research centres on a commitment to protect the participants of one's study from potential harm. Such a commitment necessitates a keen eye on the impact of research on participants, the context of the situation, the interpersonal dynamics of the group and the implicit as well as explicit, structure of group interaction." (Waskul & Douglass, 1996).

Whilst written nearly 15 years ago, the sentiments expressed in this extract are just as important, if not more important in today's growing cyber-society. In the time since Waskul and Douglass (1996) wrote this paper, there have been few changes to the way psychology thinks about ethics. In the same time however, there have been important shifts in the way that humans think, interact and communicate with each other. These changes are a result of the now ubiquitous position of the Internet in Western societies and of its status as a taken-for-granted part of everyday life.

Several years ago, in an earlier think-piece, we reviewed the state of ethical guidelines as they apply to the practice of psychological research online (Rodham & Gavin, 2006). In our paper we outlined three approaches to online data collection, and focused specifically on the issues of consent and anonymity of participants. We concluded that ethical issues raised when planning and implementing online data collection were no different to those raised by more traditional approaches to data collection. Whilst it is taken for granted that online interviews, experiments and focus groups must conform to traditional ethical guidelines (White, 2002) the focus of this chapter is on pre-existing data, such as online forums, message boards, blogs, and online profiles. The ethical issues surrounding this naturally occurring data are less clear cut, and a critical discussion of these issues highlights many of the ethical ambiguities encountered when researching 21st century online social practices.

Here, we revisit our original conclusions in light of recent changes to technology and concomitant changes in the way in which we communicate online. We offer an overview of the standard ethical tenets of psychological research: consent and anonymity. We then reconceptualise these tenets in the light of the increasingly blurred boundaries between what is considered to be public and what is considered to be private. We consider the extent to which relevant professional bodies have attempted to deal with the evolving nature of the Internet. Finally, we discuss the ethical challenges for the future in terms of Web 2.0, where self-presentation and expression are increasingly decentred and dispersed across multiple users and domains.

Rethinking Consent and Anonymity

As the context and content of psychological research changes, so too do the ethical decisions facing researchers. The Internet continues to grow in popularity and as it does so, more and more people are turning to it in order to seek information, advice and psychological support (Coulson, Malik, & Mo, 2007), as well as to maintain and extend more general social networks. The Internet has therefore become an invaluable source of data, especially as it pertains to clinical or hard to find populations. Furthermore, the prevalence of topic specific websites, online message boards and e-mail lists, provides researchers with a ready-made sampling frame that they can utilize to access participants who are interested, affiliated and connected to the topic under investigation (Griffiths, 2001; Murray & Fisher, 2002; Szabo, Frenkl, & Caputo, 1996).

Like us, White (2002) distinguishes between pre-existing data and data generated by the researcher. However, unlike White, we believe it is too simplistic to treat the former as outside of the realm of human subjects research. We agree with Capurro and Pingel (2002, p189) that "being human is becoming more and more a matter of being online." As psychologists we must take account of the human behind the text, and the expansion of online research opportunities therefore brings with it ethical challenges. The tension between the expansion of opportunity in conjunction with ethical challenges has resulted in academics being 'simultaneously concerned *and* excited about how accessible material is on the Internet' (White, 2002, p252). As a consequence, a number of authors have written about practical and ethical considerations with regard to online research with a particular focus on the issues of informed consent and anonymity (Coulson et al., 2007; DeLorme, Zinkhan, & French, 2001; Eysenbach & Till, 2001; Rodham & Gavin, 2006; see Madge (2007) for an excellent review of these issues).

Public or Private? The Ambiguous Status of Online Data?

Previously, the issues of consent and anonymity have both been discussed with reference to the nature of how public or how private the online research setting is considered to be. The level of 'public-ness' (both acknowledged and perceived) will vary for different environments and will therefore have different implications for the issue of gaining informed consent. It is therefore important to point out that although online venues may appear private and encourage the disclosure of personal thoughts, they are often, in reality public domains that are relatively easy to access and afford little guarantee of absolute confidentiality or anonymity (Murray and Fisher, 2002). This is even more salient when research is being conducted via more closed fora, and when asking participants for their consent, the 'public/private paradox' should be highlighted in order that participants can make an informed decision as to whether or not they wish to take part. However, the dichotomy of public and private is no longer something which is as straightforward as once appeared. Previously a distinction has been made concerning how public an Internet location was, in other words, if anyone who had access to the Internet could view the content of 'open message boards' or post messages on them, the venue was considered to be in the public domain and consequently not subject to the requirement that the researcher obtains informed consent prior to using data collected from such environments. The 'open message board' is therefore considered to be both a public domain, as well as an environment where those posting and/or replying to posts would expect to be observed by others. Now there is a need to acknowledge both the perceived and the acknowledged privacy of the particular (in this case, Internet) environment being targeted for research.

The terms 'publicly private' and 'privately public' have been used to highlight that private interactions 'persist in spite of public accessibility' (Waskul & Douglass, 1996, p.129). Online data need to be judged in terms of both how much information a person reveals about their identity and how widely accessible the content is. In addition, recognition should be given to the fact that in online settings data can be 'publicly private' or 'privately pubic' (Lange, 2008). For example, an online message board can be public in the sense that participants reveal identifying information, but private in the sense that it is password protected or accessible by invitation only (that is, publicly private). On the other hand, an online forum might contain little identifying information about its members but be accessible by all Internet users (that is, privately public). In terms of published research (including our own research; see Gavin, Rodham & Poyer, 2007; Gavin, Duffield, Brosnan et al., 2007; Hadert & Rodham, 2008, Rodham, Gavin & Miles, 2007; Rodham, McCabe & Blake, 2009; Whitty & Gavin, 2001), the rule of thumb seems to be that collecting data that is privately public is compatible with ethical guidelines, while publicly private data is ethically off-limits. The former would often necessitate deception (e.g., joining a group under false pretences) or subterfuge (e.g., creating a pseudonym for the purposes of creating a password), thereby violating several ethical principles. The Internet experience therefore can only be fully understood through detailed analysis of the context in which it happens (Mantovani, 1996), as the public/private distinction shows this context can vary from site to site, and person to person. Such subtleties are not acknowledged by ethical guidelines published by the major relevant professional bodies, which on the whole, provide scant guidance for the practicalities of online research.

Keeping Pace with the Cyber World: The Challenge for Professional Bodies

As we have outlined above, the notion of conducting online research in an ethical manner is not as straightforward as might at first be thought. Indeed, we highlight in our introductory paragraph that the continued growth and development of the Internet has led to us rethinking the conclusions we drew three years ago; namely that ethical issues for online research were no different to those raised by more traditional approaches to data collection (Rodham & Gavin, 2006). Professional bodies are likewise struggling to produce guidelines that keep abreast of the fast-paced changing nature of the online world. As a consequence, some professional bodies appear to have decided that rather than attempting to keep pace with the fast moving field, the onus should be firmly placed on their members to familiarise themselves with, and conform to, the current debates relating to online research. For example, the British Sociological Association (2004: p5-6) states that:

> "Members should *take special care* when carrying out research via the Internet. Ethical standards for Internet research are *not well developed* as yet...... Members who carry out

research online should ensure that they are *familiar with ongoing debates* on the ethics of Internet research...." (our emphasis).

Similarly, although the American Psychological Association (APA, 2002) does not explicitly mention online research in their ethics code, they take a comparable approach: "*In emerging areas in which generally recognised standards for preparatory training do not yet exist* psychologists nevertheless take reasonable steps to ensure the competence of their work and to protect [participants]......from harm." Therefore in this case, online research is covered by the umbrella category 'emerging area without recognised standards'.

In contrast, the British Psychological Society has produced a set of guidelines which explicitly focus on the ethical practice of conducting psychological research online (BPS, 2007). In the body of these guidelines, it is acknowledged that online research is considered to involve the same ethical considerations that should be given to all participants taking part in research, with the inclusion of some 'additional ethical issues'. These additional issues include the absence of physical contact between researcher and participant and the consequent need for careful consideration of the 'design of stimulus materials required' (BPS, 2007: p1). With no direct contact between the researcher and the researched, it is difficult to identify whether the experience of taking part in the research is distressing or detrimental to the participant, and consequently it is hard to ensure that participants' wellbeing is attended to. It is clear however that these aspects of the guidelines, relating to researcher-led activities such as online experiments or surveys, do not apply to the study of pre-existing online data. In this regard, the BPS ethical guidelines concerning the protection of participants' anonymity should be more relevant.

We agree that it is important when engaging in the practice of 'harvesting' (collecting the words of others) from 'open' sites that both the composers of the words and the name of the site hosting the message board itself should be given pseudonyms in the write up of the research. Such practices do serve to protect the anonymity of those whose words are being quoted and of the site concerned. However, the BPS (2007:1) highlights that researchers should be aware that the author of online quotations can sometimes be identified by the use of a search engine. This is an issue which is also explored by Kraut et al (2004) who formed the Board of the Scientific Affairs Advisory Group on the Conduct of Research on the Internet. Kraut et al (2004) suggested that researchers should go one step further and in addition to providing pseudonyms should also alter quoted text. Whilst taking such a precaution would indeed prevent someone from tracing the original quote by inserting it into a search engine, such a step also moves away from the principles of sound, high quality qualitative research and could in itself be considered unethical. Qualitative researchers analyse what people say or write, and how this is said or written. Changing the words used results in changes to the meaning, references made and context of the quote and so negates the raison d'être of qualitative research.

The Association of Internet Researchers (AoIR, 2002), an international committee, has produced the document entitled 'Ethical decision-making and Internet Research' which was intended to become a resource bringing together 'current discussion of important ethical issues in the field'. As of February 2009 this document had not been updated and so its claims to present a 'current discussion' can be questioned. However, what is more interesting it that the AoIR directs researchers to turn to their own professional body guidelines in the first instance, with the remainder of the AoIR document tending to focus on reproducing ethical approaches to traditional research and applying them to the Internet. This instruction therefore results in a 'Catch-22' scenario where a researcher who is looking for guidance on conducting online research in an ethical manner, turns to the Association for Internet Research, who refer him back to his discipline specific principles and practices of research. As English speaking practising psychologists ourselves, in searching for discipline specific principles, we restricted our search to the UK and US psychology professional bodies. We also included the British Sociological Society guidelines in order to have a point of comparison with an alternative branch of the social sciences. With the exception of the British Psychological Society, explicit guidelines are lacking and it is very much left to the individual researcher to make themselves familiar with the current debates concerning online research.

Negotiating Ethics in a Multi-site, Multi-authored Social World

Even where guidelines have been explicitly related to the needs of online researchers (e.g., BPS, 2007), these guidelines have nevertheless failed to keep pace with changes to the Internet itself. So far, we and most other theorists of online ethics have addressed only the issues facing researchers of first generation web technologies, such as email, online chat, online forums, message boards and threaded discussions. Indeed, to date these have been the technologies and environments most often researched and utilised within psychological online research. However, there is now an emerging research interest in second generation, or Web 2.0, technologies; a research arena which is likely to expand with the current boom in such technologies and the social transformations thus underway.

The Internet is fast becoming an interactive, participatory, and multi-authored medium (Treese, 2006), and Web 2.0 refers to the technologies that have enabled these changes. Web 2.0 allows multiple users to author, modify, record, and delete data, including text-based, audio, video, and externally linked information. It encompasses social networking sites (SNS) such as Facebook, Myspace and Youtube, as well as well as collaborative sites such as Wikipedia, and interactive blogs. These sites combine instant web publishing, social networking tools, user-generated content, and communal tagging, rating and commenting (Thacker & Dayton, 2008) in ways that challenge the notions of the single author and autonomous self-presentation occurring in a clearly delineated space.

Alexander (2008) illustrates the complexities of Web 2.0 by way of an anecdote. A blogger mentions a film, and includes in his blog entry: a link to the film on GoogleVideo, a commentary on the film, and a sample of the content (embedded as a still image until clicked). Readers then comment on this content, the blog entry is subsequently discovered by other bloggers through social aggregators and search services. These people add comments to the original blog entry (which they might link to from their own blog), view the video, and add comments on GoogleVideo; thereby intensifying and contributing further to a networked discussion across multiple sites, with multiple authors, and text, hyper-text and audio-visual content. If a researcher were to study this discussion whose consent would be sought? Whose right to anonymity needs protecting? If only one link in this network of sites is considered 'private', does that render the whole exchange private? Or does a 'private' user linking and contributing to this multi-site discussion render his or her contributions public?

Given that the BPS and other professional ethical bodies have barely begun to address the ethical and methodological challenges posed by first generation web technologies, it is not surprising that current guidelines are ill-prepared to address the issues of the second generation. Crucially, how can decisions about public and private spaces, informed consent, or anonymity be addressed in online environments containing several layers of text, image and audio-visual input from multiple sources and authors across multiple, linked sites? These are not simply rhetorical or hypothetical questions. There is now a growing body of research examining self-presentation, social networks and support, and identity management in SNS.

For example, Zhao et al. (2008) recently conducted a content analysis of 63 Facebook accounts. Included in the analysis were users' profiles, contact information, social networks and self-descriptions. The 'participants' were chosen from a list of students who responded to a student survey conducted by the administration of a large university in a north eastern US city. These students did not, however, indicate their consent to take part in the Facebook study. Data collection excluded Facebook accounts that were 'blocked to the public'. The remainder, however, while not blocked to the public, presumably required a user account to access, and although no information is provided, it is likely that the researchers who downloaded the data were members of the university network to which the students belonged. Does this breach ethical guidelines? What is the public/private status of this data, and what are the subsequent obligations with respect to consent and anonymity? On the one hand, the data are 'private' in the sense that they are open to only those people belonging to a particular university network; albeit a network to which any academic or researcher with a university email address may legitimately belong. On the other hand, the data might be considered 'public' in the sense that a typical university network will have many thousands of members. (The University of Bath network, a relatively small university network to which one of the authors belongs, contains over 15,000 members, and London, his regional network, contains nearly 3.5 million). In their analysis of MySpace profiles, Magnusson and Dundas (2008) side-stepped the issue of 'privacy' and inaccessible profiles by analysing only those profiles accessible to the lead researcher through her 'primary network'; that is, they analysed only the profiles of her friends and her extended network (friends of friends). This approach, however, if widely adopted by online researchers would severely limit the scope of psychological research. How far can psychology progress, and to what extent can findings be generalised, if we study only our friends and extended networks? It also raises the issue of anonymity. In Facebook for example, the default privacy setting makes ones friends visible even to non-friends.

These issues can of course be circumvented through different research designs, albeit within different psychological paradigms. Lab-based studies have used experimental designs with mock profiles (e.g., Walther et al, 2008), while more radical approaches have used participant-observer methodologies (Glaser, Dixit & Green, 2002). Other approaches have examined large-scale patterns using anonymised data gathered through automated collection techniques or data sets provided by SNS companies. Golder, Wilkinson and Huberman (2007) for example, used such techniques in their analysis of social network structures, analysing 362 million anonymised messages exchanged by over 4 million Facebook users. All three approaches have their strengths, although none allow unfettered in-depth access to naturalistic SNS activities in the same way that earlier first generation studies have had in relation to online forums or message boards.

Conclusion

The Internet is a fast changing environment which has increasingly blurred boundaries between what is considered to be public and what is considered to be private. With the advent of Web 2.0, self presentation and expression online are increasingly decentred and dispersed across multiple users and domains. These changes bring with them challenges for researchers who have responsibilities to conduct research in an ethically mindful manner. Increasingly, professional bodies are finding it difficult to keep pace with the developments in the cyberworld and the concomitant implications these bring. Indeed, as we have noted, the stance taken by some professional bodies is rather than issue guidelines, to place the onus on individual researchers to familiarise themselves with current debates relating to online research. Whilst much research conducted online can be covered by existing ethical guidelines, the blurred public/private boundary brings with it particularly difficult ethical dilemmas. We did not set out to address the ethical chasm created by the gap between existing guidelines and the reality of the ever changing cyberworld, but we did aim to begin to map out the territory, to tease out those issues which require particularly careful ethical consideration. We therefore suggest that traditional ethical approaches to research are now in many instances incommensurate with recent developments in the ways that humans communicate and interact on the Internet, and with transformations to the Internet itself.

The need now is to produce a set of more flexible guidelines; ones that pay greater attention to the context and intentions of Internet users. There is a need to update not only the guidelines themselves, but the language used to frame these guidelines. Perhaps we need to do away with terms such as 'anonymity', 'consent' and 'privacy', and start thinking in terms of 'open' or closed networks', public and private 'target audiences', and 'implied consent'. Most importantly, the relevant professional bodies need to respond more quickly to the changing ethical dilemmas faced by present-day researchers in a way that gives researchers the flexibility to adapt to the guidelines as required by the changing evolving online research context.

References

Adams, J., Rodham, K. & Gavin, J. (2005). Investigating the 'self' in deliberate self-harm. *Qualitative Health Research,* **15** (10), 1293-1309.

Alexander, B. (2008). Web 2.0 and emergent multiliteracies. *Theory Into practice*, **47**(2), 150-160.

American Psychological Association (2002). *The ethical principles of Psychologists and Code of Conduct.* Accessed from: http://www.apa.org/ethics/code2002.html on 25th November 2008.

Association of Internet Researchers (2002). *Ethical decision making and Internet Research: Recommendations from the AoIR Ethics working Committee.* Accessed from: http://aoir.org/reports/ethics.pdf on 25th November 2008

Balakrishna, K. (2006). Facebook becomes tool for employers. *Yale Daily News.* Accessed from http://www.yaledailynews.com/articles/priontarticle/16696 on 11th February 2009.

British Psychological Society (2006). *Code of Ethics and Conduct.* Accessed from: http://www.bps.org.uk/the-society/ethics-rules-charter-code-of-conduct/code-of-conduct/ethical-principles-for-conducting-research-with-human-participants.cfm   on Friday 2nd June 2006.

British Psychological Society (2007). *Report of the working party on conducting research on the Internet: Guidelines for ethical practice in psychological research online.* British Psychological Society: Leicester. Accessed from http://www.bps.org.uk/the-society/code-of-conduct/code-of-conduct_home.cfm on 25th November 2008.

British Sociological Association (2002). Statement of Ethical Practice for the British Sociological Association, accessed from http://www.britsoc.co.uk/equality/ Statement%20Ethical%20Practice on 25th November 2008.

Capurro, R. & Pingel, C. (2002). Ethical issues of online communication research. *Ethics and Information Technology,* **4** (3), 189-194.

Coulson, N., Malike, S. & Mo, P.K.H. (2007). Researching virtual communities and electronic support groups: Some practical and ethical considerations on the use of message boards. *Health Psychology Update,* **16**(3), 3-6.

DeLorme, D.E., Zinkhan, G.M. & French, W. (2001). Ethics and the Internet: Issues associated with qualitative research. *Journal of Business Ethics,* **33** (4), 271-286.

Eysenbach, G., Till, J.E. (2001). Ethical issues in qualitative research on Internet communities. *British Medical Journal,* **323**(7321), 1103-1105.

Gavin, J., Duffield, J., Brosnan, M., Joiner, R., Maras, P. & Scott, A. (2007). Drawing the net: Internet identification, Internet use, and the image of Internet users. *CyberPsychology & Behavior.* **10**(3), 478-481

Gavin, J., Rodham, K. & Poyer, H. (2008). The presentation of 'pro-anorexia' in online group interactions, *Qualitative Health Research,* **18**(3), 325-333.

Glaser, J., Dixit, J., & Green, D. (2002). Studying hate crime with the Internet: what makes racists advocate racist violence? *Journal of Social Issues,* **58**(1), 177-193.

Golder, S.A. Wilkinson, D., & Huberman, B.A. (2007). Rhythms of social interaction: Messaging within a massive online network. In C. Steinfeld, B. Pentland, M. Ackerman, & N. Contractor (Eds.), *Proceedings of Third International conference on Communities and technologies* (pp. 41-66). London: Springer.

Griffiths, M. (2001). Sex on the Internet: Observations and implications for Internet sex addiction. *Journal of Sex Research,* **38**(4), 333-342.

Hadert, A. & Rodham, K. (2008). The invisible reality of arthritis: A qualitative analysis of an online message board. *Musculoskeletal Care,* 6(3), 181-196

Kraut, R., Olson, J., Banaji, M., Bruckman, A., Cohen, J. & Couper, M. (2004). Psychological Research Online: Report of Scientific Affairs' Advisory Group on the Conduct of Research on the Internet. *American Psychologist,* **59**(2), 105-117.

Lange, P.G. (2008). Publicly private and privately public: Social networking on YouTube. *Journal of Computer-Mediated Communication,* **13**(1), 361-380.

Madge, C. (2007). Developing a geographers' agenda for online research ethics. *Progress in Human Geography,* **31**(5), 654-674

Magnuson, M.J., & Dundes, L. (2008). Gender differences in 'social portraits' reflected in MySpace profiles. *CyberPsychology and Behavior,* **11**(2), 239-241.

Mantovani, G. (1996). *New communication environments: From everyday to virtual.* London: Taylor & Francis

Murray, M. & Fisher, JD. (2002).The Internet: A virtually untapped tool for research: *Journal of Technology in Human Services,* **19**(2/3), 5-18.

O'Connor, H. & Madge, C. (2001). Cyber-mothers: Online synchronous interviewing using conference software. *Sociological Research Online,* **5**(4).

Rodham, K. & Gavin, J. (2006). The ethics of using the Internet to collect qualitative research data, *Research Ethics Review* **2**(3), 83-116.

Rodham, K., Gavin, J. & Miles, M. (2007). I hear, I listen and I care: A qualitative investigation into the function of a self-harm message board. *Suicide and Life Threatening Behaviour,* **37**(4), 422-430.

Rodham, K., McCabe, C., & Blake, D. (2009). Seeking support: An Interpretative Phenomenological Analysis of an Internet message board for people with Complex Regional Pain Syndrome, *Psychology and Health,* **24**(6), 619-634.

Szabo, A., Frenkl, R. & Caputo, A. (1996). Deprivation feelings anxiety and commitment in various forms of physical activity: A cross-sectional study on the Internet. *Psychologia,* **39**(4), 223-230.

Thacker, C. & Dayton, D. (2008). Using Web 2.0 to conduct qualitative research: A conceptual model. *Technical Communication,* **55**(4), 383-391.

Treese, W. (2006). Web 2.0: Is it really different? *netWorker,* **10**(2), 15-17.

Walther, J.B., Van Der Heide, B., Kim, S-Y., Westerman, D., & Tong, S.T. (2008). The role of friends' appearance and behaviour on evaluations of individuals on Facebook: Are we known by the company we keep? *Human Communication Research,* **34**(1), 28-49.

Waskul, D. & Douglass, M. (1996). Considering the electronic participant: Some polemical observations on the ethics of on-line research. *The Information Society,* **12**(2), 129-139.

Waskul, D. & Douglass, M. (1997). Cyberself: The emergence of Self in On-Line Chat. *The Information Society,* **13**(4), 375-397.

White, M. (2002). Representations or people? *Ethics and Information Technology,* **4**(3), 249-266.

Whitty, M. & Gavin, J. (2001). Age/sex/location: Uncovering the social cues in the development of on-line relationships. *Cyber-Psychology and Behaviour,* **4**(5), 623-630.

Zhao, S., Grasmuck, S., & Martin, J. (2008). Identity construction on Facebook: digital empowerment in anchored relationships. *Computers in Human Behaviour,* **24**(5), 1816-1836.

In: Peer-to-Peer Networks and Internet Policies   ISBN: 978-1-60876-287-3
Editors: Diego Vegros and Jaime Sáenz, pp. 215-221   © 2010 Nova Science Publishers, Inc.

Chapter 10

PHENOMENOLOGY OF INTERNET ADDICTION

Caroline Gresle and Michel Lejoyeux[*]

Department of Psychiatry. Hopital Bichat-Claude Bernard,
AP-HP. Paris, France

Introduction

Internet is one of the major inventions of 20th century. For most users, Internet is at the same time a way of communication, a convivial and powerful workspace and a recreational activity. Internet therefore became essential to the daily lives of more than one billion people [1]. In 1982, the word *Internet* made its appearance and the web became accessible to the public in the 90's. Its almost unlimited possibilities, in the field of the communication and the diffusion of knowledge, make it a very popular tool. Internet quickly rapidely became essential in the professional sphere as a powerful tool of transferring and sharing data and in the privacy of homes as an essential need to open up to the world and knowledge. A majority of specialists estimates that between 6% and 8% of Internet users would be dependent. Nevertheless, as the phenomenon is still too recent, the national and world prevalence of cyber addiction still seems difficult to quantify [2].

Whereas the benefits are undeniable, some people to suffer the consequences of excessive use. This problem is often underestimated but some of them swear by the web. These compulsive Internet users can be described as "'connection addicts'". Their abusive use of Internet is at the origin of a new disease called the cyber addiction. Other subjects do not have an addictive relation to the web but suffer from an excessive involvement in the cyber life. They reduce their interest for relations in the "real world" and prefer on-line activities. Their abuse of the web leads them to a new form of "cocooning". Cocooning can be described as the feeling of being so well at home that one hardly wants to go out even for vital needs.

---

[*] E-mail address: michel.lejoyeux@bch.aphp.fr. Phone : 33 1 40 25 82 62; Fax : 33 1 40 25 67 80; Corresponding Author: Michel Lejoyeux. Department of Psychiatry. AP-HP, Hopital Bichat Claude Bernard. 75 877 Paris Cedex 18 and Hôpital Maison Blanche. France.

Since the 80's, psychologists have warned that fragile consumers could substitute reality for the virtual world of Internet. With the help of psychiatrists and sociologists, they tried to describe as precisely as possible this new form of dependence and to understand its implications. In 1995, Ivan Goldberg was the first to suggest the term of Internet addiction. It draws a descriptive picture of the disorder of Internet addiction based on the DSM-IV-R criteria for alcohol or drug dependence. The expression was used again in 1996 by the psychologist Kimberley Young, during a conference of the American Psychological Association in Toronto. As a pioneer of this new field of addiction, she defined Internet addiction by borrowing the criteria used for compulsive gambling [3, 4]. Her definition was to be widely used in future literature.

Cyber addiction shares some characteristics with the other forms of dependence i.e. loss of control, inability to reduce addictive consumption and feeling of intense pleasure. The criteria proposed for cyber addiction are [4, 5]:

- *Excessive use* of Internet, often associated with a loss of the sense of time,
- *A feeling of craving* when connection is stopped,
- *Withdrawal symptoms*, with a feeling of tension and/or depression
- A phenomena of *tolerance*, which tends to increase connection time even more.
- *Relapse*, a tendency for earlier patterns of earlier addictive activity to recur.

This new form of dependency has taken various names: cyber addiction, addiction to Internet, pathological or problematic use of Internet, etc. Whatever word is employed, the definition is the same: it corresponds to a relation of dependency on computers and Internet. By extension, it involves a dependency on network games, chat rooms, on-line pathological gambling or compulsive buying on web sites devoted to buying.

Prevalence, Risk Factors and Psychiatric Co-morbidities

Prevalence

In 1998, Young estimated that between 5 and 10% of Net surfers show Internet dependency. One year later, a large survey on this topic, coordinated by David Greenfield estimated that 6% of Americans are cyber addicts. Elias Aboujaoude found lower rates for prevalence of Internet addiction. He estimated that only 1% of the American population is concerned with dependence to Internet. According to Block, 9 million of Americans could be dependent on Internet or may be at risk [6]. For Block (2007) the precise evaluation of the disorder remains largely marked by a lack of data. Furthermore, he suspects a minimization of the phenomenon in the United States, caused by shame, denial and the under-recognition of the disorder and its complications [7].

Other assessments were undertaken in Asia. The majority of works were published in South Korea [7]. They suggest that this area of the world is statistically the most exposed to Internet addiction. However a number of other countries have not undertaken national studies on web addiction yet and may ignore or underestimate the impact of this addiction. Following single cases of deaths which occurred due to a prolonged and intensive use of Internet, South Korea considered that addiction to Internet was a serious public health problem. In 2006, its government estimated that approximately 210,000 children aged 6 to 19 (20.1%), were dependent or had a problematic use of Internet [7]. According to Ahn (2007), 80% of these children would need psychotropic treatment, while 20 to 24% would require hospitalization. South-Koreans students spend on average 23 hours a week on Internet games [7]. These surprising estimates are unfortunately the same as in many countries where Internet is extremely popular among young people [5, 7].

China belongs to the countries also exposed to a pathological use of Internet. As it is the most populated country in the world, it also has the greatest number of Web surfers - 298 million at the end of 2008. According to the Chinese Internet Network Information Centre, this estimate increased by approximately 42% en une année préciser SVP. Officially, Internet addiction is not recognized in China. yet [8]. In 2008, J Block, quoted Tao Ran who estimated that approximately 13.7% of Chinese teenagers were Internet dependent– i.e. 10 million.

In France, Internet met with the same scepticism concerning its addictiveness. However the number of psychiatric consultations for cyber addiction has not ceased to increase in recent years. In 2004, the phenomenon concerned 150.000 French. In 2008, A. Grossokst and P. Jeanneteau, two deputies, wrote a report to establish the extent of the problem. According to their estimates, 3 to 4% of the French (600 to 800,000 people) would be dependent on Internet via an excessive use of on-line video games. Only 10% of these Internet addicts consult a specialist. These figures are all the more overpowering, as they do not take into account the full extent of the phenomenon of cyber addiction: chat- rooms, online gambling, cyber pornography, E-mails … More worrying still, the reported estimates mainly relate to young people aged from 13 to 25.

Risk Factors – Co-morbidity

The pathological use of Internet is more frequent: after an early experimentation, for socially isolated and young people. Men are more exposed to Internet addiction [5, 9, 10, 11, 12,]. Yang and Tung (2004) studied the prevalence of Internet addiction in Taiwanese teenagers from 17 to 19 years. Among the addicts identified, men were overrepresented (ratio of 3 boys for 1 girl). Cao and Lu (2006) came to the same conclusion: 83% of Chinese teenage cyber addicts were boys versus 11% of girls. If most studies seem to agree on the relationship between gender and the risk for Internet addiction, few works have found no relationship between gender and web addiction [13].

Interpersonal factors are important for initiation of Internet dependence. Psychiatric disorders increase the risk for Internet addiction. Web surfers having a predisposition to mood disorders [5, 14], anxiety - social phobia – [5, 15], depression [5, 14, 15, 16,] or low self-esteem [5, 15], are more at the risk to develop cyber addiction. Links between suicide and Internet addiction were also shown. Among cyberaddicts, this last correlation is more important in girls [15].

Conversely, the mode of use of Internet seems predictive of Internet dependence [5, 12]. Subjects using Internet for its social functions are more exposed to addiction [5, 12]. Web surfers at risk for dependence mainly use Internet to meet people [17] and spend more and more time on these sites to maintain these numerous virtual relationships.

Many complications affect consumers who misuse Internet. Most frequent damages include sleep and sight problems [15], migraines, back and cervical pains and carpal tunnel syndrome. Sleep is disturbed and can no longer play its repairing role. The pathological use of Internet is also marked by food disorders [4], lack of hygiene and in the most extreme cases, death [7]. On a psychological level, one finds, a reduced interest in everything with does not concern the object of dependence. The importance attached to Internet influences almost all thoughts of the users who misuse it. It causes anxiety and maladaptive cognitions according Davis (2001) [18]. In this article, Davis was tracked it two types: thought about the self of the kind "I am only good on the internet" and thought about the world of the style "Internet is the only place I am respected" This exclusiveness influences the feelings and attitudes by altering, for example, the initiation of behaviours related to socialisation [16]. This involves an impoverishment of affective life, both relational and intellectual [16]. Addicts have numerous problems in daily life [5]. They neglect family and friends and spend more time connected to internet than in "real" life [15]. Addicts can be more inclined to divorce, lose their employment more easily, encounter educational difficulties and give up school or university.

Treatments for Cyber Addiction

The treatment of cyber addicts calls principally upon psychotherapeutic treatments which can be supplemented by pharmacological treatments. In most cases, cyber addiction is treated only with psychotherapy. In the same way as with other addictive disorders, motivational counselling is an essential precondition which aims at initiating behavioural change by helping the patients to solve their problems and to explore their ambivalence. Before undertaking any therapy, it is necessary to inform the patients about the pathological use of Internet, to give him a definition and to outline consequences of the disorder. Above all, it is essential to alert patients of the addictive characteristic of their behaviour. Like in almost all other forms of addiction, the most difficult stage for success remains the recognition of the dependence.

Among the therapies used, that of psycho-analytical inspiration seems most adapted in the getting cyber addicts to assume responsibility. They mainly use verbal language in order to rehabilitate the expressive function of thought. Cyber addicts do not lack the capacity to think but they lack the capacity to express themselves.

Support therapies: The cyber addict learns how to manage his behaviour by becoming aware of factors which make him an addict. Among these therapies: "Web counselling" is a kind of virtual clinic and group therapies. There are also Internet Relay Chat Rooms (IRC), developed by ex-cyber addicts or their entourage. Particularly developed in the US these help-lines facilitate verbal expression and then later encourage the cyber addict to engage in "a true" dialogue face-to-face. Groups of mutual aid, like Anonymous Net surfers, copied the therapeutic program developed by Alcoholics Anonymous which includes twelve stages. In these groups, the addict admits the reality of his addiction to Internet.

Cognitive and behavioural therapies have also been offered to web addicts. Cognitive-behavioural model of cyber addiction highlights the role of unsuited cognitions and dysfunctional behaviour [18]. It identifies two types of unsuited cognitions specific to the individuals having a problematic use of Internet: erroneous cognitions about the patient and of the world around him. Among false cognitions reported by Davis can be found: "I am weak when I am not connected, but online I am somebody"; "I am a failure when I am not connected" [18]. Goal of the cognitive treatments includes a cognitive reorganisation of these distorted thoughts. This work supposes that the patient recognizes his false cognitions and accepts to cure them [18, 19]. False cognitive distortions are associated with addictive behaviours. Other behavioural approachs can be offer to web addicts are: techniques of relaxation, keeping a diary which evaluates automatic thoughts. *Behavioral Approach* [18, 19], aims at a tangible modification of relation to the web.

Several techniques are reported such as:

- modifying the sighting of the computer,
- changing times of connections,
- practising activities incompatible with Internet,
- learn relaxation.

The patient is encouraged to practice activities unrelated to Internet such as sport, socialising, cultural activities or hobbies, outings during the week.

Prevention of Internet Addiction

The cyber addiction is a true society' problem whose frightening consequences led many countries to work out a prevention of the risks. Among the projects of prevention in progress, can be cited the publicity campaigns informing on French television on the dangers of Internet. Even if they do not immediately target the problem of cyber addiction, these campaigns have the merit to alert parents on the unsuited contents that circulate on the web for their children and teenagers. These spots which put in scene a mother opening her front door and inviting in avatars of violence (Skinheads, destroying robots), or in an other one, avatars of pornography and paedophilia, conclude on these words: "don't let danger come in your home!". These campaigns are interesting insofar as they really say something to the parents and the families on the danger that Internet's contents can represent. By alienating a parental control on the contents diffused by Internet, the parents keep an eye on what their children use Internet for.

Public awareness campaigns on the addictive use of Internet should be carried out in the next years. They aim at informing the adults on the phenomenon of cyber addiction, knowing the risks and locating the symptoms. In parallel, prevention campaigns early targeting young people may inform them on the dangers of a too regular use of Internet and video games.

Beginning again what had been made already elsewhere as regards prevention against the dangers of alcohol, one will find in the commercials the diffusion of medical messages. These messages will informe on the dangers of an intensive use of any support related to data processing, Internet or video games. Such as for the anti-tobacco campaigns, of the warning messages, as "an excessive use is harmful for health" or "to play takes time", would come to supplement the descriptive PEGI (Side-European Range Information) on packing of any data-processing apparatus: computers, consoles, video games…

Within the framework of a more active prevention, it is planned to interfere directly on the game itself in various ways:

- A visible clock on the screens would indicate the time spent in front of a game and could even flicker after three to four hours of consecutive play. It would be relayed by warning messages posted regularly beyond excessive time of use of the game.
- A non playable psychological character is also considered. He would intervene in the game to< invite the player to make a pause or to encourage it to reflect over time that he passes on the game.
- Another more active measurement would consist in tiring the avatars of the players by reducing their power and thus obliging the players to make a pause long enough in the game in order to restore the energy of their character.

Conclusion

Internet is an incontestably amazing communication tool that is bound to occupy an increasingly dominating place in our lives. It is important that all the protagonists, Net surfers, doctors, psychologists, legislators, become aware of the potential dangers that can involve cyber-dependency. Far from demonising the use, it appears necessary today to take the measurement of the drifts which result from this.

References

[1] Internet World Stats. http://www.internetworldstats.com/stats.htm , view on the January 27th 2009.

[2] Dell'Osso, B., Altamura, A., Allen, Marazziti, D., & Hollander, E. (2006). Epidemiologic and clinical updates on impulse control disorders: A critical review. *European Archives of Psychiatry and Clinical Neuroscience*, **256**, 464-475.

[3] Young, K., (1996). Psychology computer use: XL. Addictive use of the internet: a case that breaks the stereotype. *Psychological Rep*, **79**, 899-902.

[4] Young, K., (1998). Caught in the Net: How to Recognize the Signs of Internet Addiction -- and A Winning Strategy For Recovery, Wiley, New York.

[5] Yang, S. & Tung, C. (2007). Comparison of Internet addicts and non-addicts in Taiwanese high school. *Computer in Human Behavior*, **23** (1), 79-96.

[6] J., Fitzgerald (2008). Internet Addiction: Recognition and Interventions. *Archives of Psychiatric Nursing*, Vol.22, N°2.

[7] Block, J., (2008). Issue for DSM-V: Internet Addiction, *American Journal of Psychiatry*, mars, 165-3.

[8] Wu, H. & Zhu, K. (2004) Path analysis on related factors causing internet addiction disorder in college students. *Chinese Journal of Public Health*, **20**, 1363-1634.

[9] Morahan-Martin, J. & Schumacher, P., (2000). Incidence and correlates of pathological internet uses among college students, *Computer in Human Behavior*, **16**, 13-29.

[10] Wang, W., (2001). Internet dependency and psychosocial maturity among college students, *International Journal of Human-Computer Studies*, **55**, 919-938.

[11] Cao, F. & Su, L. (2006). Internet addiction among Chinese adolescents: prevalence and psychological features. *Child: care, health and development*. **33**, 3, 275-281.

[12] Li, S. & Chung, T. (2006). Internet function and Internet addictive behaviour. *Computer in human Behavior*, **22**, 1067-1071.

[13] Hall, A. &Parsons, J. (2001). Internet addiction: College case study using vest practices in cognitive behavior Therapy. *Journal of mental Health Counseling*, **23**(4), 312-328.

[14] Shapira, N., Goldsmith, T., Keck, P., Khosla, U. & Mc Elroy, S. (2000). Psychiatry features of individuals with problematic internet use. *Journal of Affective Disorders*, **57**, 267-272.

[15] Kim, K., Ryu, E., Chon, M., Yeun, E., Choi, S., Seo, J., & Nam, B., (2005). Internet addiction in Korean adolescents and its relation to depression and suicidal ideation: A questionnaire survey. *International journal of nursing studies*, **43**(2), 185-192

[16] Baruch, Y. (2001). The autistic society. *Information and management*, **38**, 129-136.

[17] Ju, M. (2000). *Research on personal characteristics, the behavior of using Internet and Internet addiction for Taiwanese college study*. Master thesis. Taiwan.

[18] Davis, R. (2001). A cognitive-behavioral model of pathological Internet use. *Computer in Human Behavior*, **17**; 187-195.

[19] Caplan, S. (2002). Problematic Internet use ad psychosocial well-being: development of theory-bases cognitive-behavioral measurement instrument. *Computer in Human Behavior*, **18**; 553-575.

Chapter 11

Leveraging Peer-to-Peer Networks for Effectively Managing Computing Resources

Chetan Kumar[*]

Department of Information Systems and Operations Management,
College of Business Administration, California State University San Marcos,
San Marcos, CA, USA

Abstract

Peer-to-Peer (P2P) network based technologies facilitate a distributed community of users to share their digital or computer processing resources. Every node, or peer, that is a part of the network can potentially contribute resources to other peers. Consequently P2P networks have many advantages over centralized networks, such as: (a) inherent scalability, (b) no single point of failure, and (c) self-administration capabilities. P2P technology-based applications have recently become increasingly popular with both businesses and individual users in the Internet era. Some common P2P applications include content delivery networks (CDN) such as Amazon Cloud Front (http://aws.amazon.com/cloudfront/), collaboration technologies such as Groove (www.groove.net), digital content distribution services such as Joost (www.joost.com), among others. Many of the largest IT companies including HP, Microsoft, and IBM have invested considerable resources in such P2P applications. In this article we review some related research on P2P networks and discuss its characteristics and applications. Given the inherent advantages of decentralized P2P networks, we believe that it provides a useful methodology for organizations to effectively manage their computing resources.

Introduction

Peer-to-Peer (P2P) networks facilitate operation of connected computing resources without necessary use of dedicated or centralized servers. This is a novel aspect of P2P

---

[*] E-mail address: ckumar@csusm.edu; Phone: (760) 477-3976; Fax: (760) 750-4250

networks compared to traditional client-server networks [9]. P2P network based technologies permit a distributed community of users to share their digital or computer processing resources. Every node, or peer, that is a part of the network can potentially contribute resources to other peers. Consequently P2P networks have many advantages over centralized networks, such as: (a) inherent scalability, (b) no single point of failure, and (c) self-administration capabilities [10]. According to Informationweek.com, businesses value P2P networking as a useful methodology to manage their computing resources, as discussed in following report extract [11].

> "The potential benefits (of P2P networks) are so great that Hewlett-Packard, IBM, and Intel now want to standardize and commercialize the technology. They, along with several startups (and other industry and research institutions), have launched the Peer-to-Peer Working Group (P2Pwg), a consortium whose goal is to give businesses the benefits of peer-to-peer computing (HTTP://P2P.INTERNET2.EDU/)" [11].

Figure 1 demonstrates an example of a P2P network that can be utilized for sharing distributed computing resources. Every node can communicate with other peers in the network. A job or task that is required by one peer can potentially be allocated to other nodes, consequently allowing the peers to pool their resources. As P2P system users can share their resources, the P2P network may be considered as a "public good" or shared utility [9]. Interestingly in a P2P environment, unlike traditional public good examples, any peer can impact other peers in the network both positively and negatively. This externality effect that individuals have on others has been empirically observed in P2P file sharing networks [1]. A greater number of peers can increase congestion that increases network latency or delays. At the same time each peer may potentially contribute their own resources that benefit other users in the network. As a result we can substantially reduce the "Tragedy of the Commons," where individuals over utilize shared resources, for P2P networks by providing incentives for individual users to utilize the system responsibly [4].

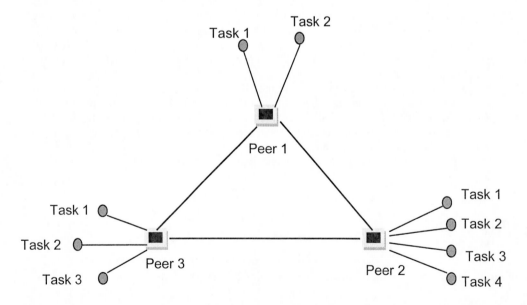

Figure 1. A P2P network for sharing distributed computing resources (adapted from: Kumar et al. [6]).

P2P technology-based applications have recently become increasingly popular with both businesses and individual users in the Internet era [14]. Other than the well known P2P file sharing networks of questionable legality such as Kazaa, the first version of Napster, and Limewire, P2P technologies are used in a wide variety of business settings [5,11]. Some common P2P applications are as follows: content delivery networks (CDN) such as Amazon Cloud Front (HTTP://AWS.AMAZON.COM/CLOUDFRONT/), collaboration technologies such as Groove (WWW.GROOVE.NET), Internet discussion forums such as Usenet (HTTP://EN.WIKIPEDIA.ORG/WIKI/USENET), proxy cache networks such as IRCache (WWW.IRCACHE.NET), digital content distribution services such as Joost (WWW.JOOST.COM), knowledge management, etc. (HTTP://EN. WIKIPEDIA.ORG/ WIKI/PEER-TO-PEER). Many of the largest IT companies including HP, Microsoft, and IBM have invested considerable resources in such P2P applications [14]. For numerous organizations their ability to effectively deliver digital content and services to end users is critically dependent on how well they manage their computer networks. In addition for firms providing physical goods their computer networks are crucial for managing their supply chains and for disseminating information. However as congestion on the Internet grows we can experience increased waiting time for computer network users [3,7]. P2P based technologies have enormous potential for helping organizations manage their computer resources effectively. In this article we review related research on P2P networks and discuss the P2P based mechanism of Kumar et al. [6].

Related Literature and Discussion

There are numerous studies focused primarily on performance analysis of computer networks and systems [8,15]. The classical work of Mendelson [12] was one of the first to look at control and management issues related to a single-server computer system. It provides a microeconomic analysis that incorporates queuing effects and incentive issues. One of the key results of the study, which considers transfer pricing for a single-server system, is that the marginal job should be priced at the level of congestion it imposes on all the jobs in the system. Mendelson and Whang [13] extend the model for the case of jobs with multiple priorities and heterogeneous sizes. The main concern of the Kumar et al. [6] paper is to study the pricing issue for congestible resources from a broader perspective of a P2P system. This involves examining a multiple-server computer system in an organization, which may be located at different coordinates, behave as peers that can share their computing resources. The original Mendelson [12] model thus becomes a special single-server case of the general Kumar et al. [6] model.

Though the concept of P2P based applications have gained popularity Information Systems (IS) literature in that area is scarce due to its relative novelty. Li et al. [10] demonstrate the advantages of scalability of P2P networks compared to centralized networks. Krishnan et al. [9] identify the special characteristic of P2P file sharing networks versus other public goods or shared utilities. Asvanund et al. [1] empirically demonstrate the presence of both positive and negative network externalities in P2P music sharing networks. Bhattacharjee et al. [2] study the effect of digital sharing technologies on survival of music albums on ranking charts. The focus of the earlier studies was the popular P2P file sharing networks. Some file sharing networks have subsequently run into legal issues [5]. However

P2P based applications has a wide variety of applications and is being increasingly adopted by businesses [14]. Given the inherent advantages of decentralized networks, P2P based mechanisms provide a beneficial method for organizations to better utilize and share their resources.

A Mechanism for Resource Allocation in P2P Networks

Kumar et al. [6] develop a mechanism utilizing P2P networks for managing computing resources within a firm. In the base case of their model they derive an expression for the optimal incentive-compatible transfer price that any arriving job at a node pays at the steady state. They consider a P2P network of queues where every location observes a fixed exogenous arrival rate of jobs. A pricing scheme is developed where every individual user makes a decision whether or not to join the system on the basis of a posted price. A job may be executed either at the location where it has arrived, or it may be allocated to a neighbor location that is connected by a direct link. Under the net value maximization objective of peers, the optimal price p_j^* for executing a job at location j is given by

$$p_j^* = v\Gamma_j^* \left(\partial W_j / \partial \Gamma_j^*\right),$$ where $\partial W_j / \partial \Gamma_j^*$, the incremental delay added to waiting time W_j

at j as a result of an incremental arrival Γ_j^*, is evaluated at the optimal arrival rate of Γ_j^*. The optimal price p_j^* is equal to the externality cost, which is the expected delay cost per unit time inflicted on the rest of the system by an infinitesimal increase in job flow. Therefore the optimal price for executing any job is essentially equal to the marginal delay cost it imposes on all current jobs in the system. With this pricing scheme no individual user has an incentive to overutilize the system. Consequently it can be used to mitigate the "Tragedy of the Commons" for P2P networks. Note that every node j has a specific price p_j^* for executing jobs that arrive at it. This is a generalization of the original Mendelson [12] model that does not consider multiple server locations. The result is along lines of Mendelson and Whang [13] that consider additional factors such as multiple priorities and heterogeneous sizes. Kumar et al. [6] then extend their model to consider the case where every peer in the network has a maximum permissible queue length constraint. This would correspond to having a quality of service (QoS) guarantee since user delays would now be limited by a specific queue length. We can then use this model extension for the case where any server has the ability to outsource a job to a third party when the utilization level at that server reaches a certain point. Interested readers are referred to Kumar et al. [6] for a detailed discussion of their mechanism.

Conclusion

P2P based technologies have enormous potential for helping organizations manage their computer resources effectively. For instance, using the Kumar et al. [6] mechanism organizations can decide how to price and allocate the jobs such that, given the objective of the peers, the outcome is optimal for the network. In addition they can manage the network to provide a guaranteed level of QoS to users. Given these properties, and merits of other P2P applications discussed in Asvanund et al. [1] and Ottolenghi [14], P2P based mechanisms provide a useful methodology for organizations to better utilize and share their computing resources. Some of the largest IT companies including HP, Microsoft, and IBM have invested considerable resources in different P2P applications [11,14]. Based on these factors we believe that P2P networks are an important area for IS research.

Acknowledgments

This article includes a review of the discussion of Kumar, C., Altinkemer, A., and De, P. "A Mechanism for Pricing and Resource Allocation in Peer-to-Peer Networks," Working paper, 2008; among other sources. Interested readers are referred to Kumar et al. [6], Asvanund et al. [1], and Ottolenghi [20] for a detailed discussion on P2P networks and their applications for managing computer resources.

References

Asvanund, A., Clay, K., Krishnan, R., Smith, Michael D. "An Empirical Analysis of Network Externalities in Peer-to-Peer Music-Sharing Networks," *Information Systems Research*, **15**, 2, 155–174, 2004.

Bhattacharjee, S., Gopal, R. D., Lertwachara, K., Marsden, J. R., Telang, R. "The Effect of Digital Sharing Technologies on Music Markets: A Survival Analysis of Albums on Ranking Charts," *Management Science*, **53**, 9, 1359–1374, 2007.

Datta, A., Dutta, K., Thomas, H., and VanderMeer, D. "World Wide Wait: A Study of Internet Scalability and Cache-Based Approaches to Alleviate It," *Management Science*, **49**, 10, 1425-1444, 2003.

Hardin, G., "The Tragedy of the Commons," *Science*, **162**, 3859, 1243-1248, 1968.

Jones, K.C., "International Dragnet Targets Illegal Music File-Sharing," http://www.informationweek.com/showarticle.jhtml?articleid=184428675, April 4, 2006.

Kumar, C., Altinkemer, A., and De, P. "A Mechanism for Pricing and Resource Allocation in Peer-to-Peer Networks," *Working paper*, 2008.

Kumar, C., and Norris, J.B. "A New Approach for a Proxy-Level Web Caching Mechanism," *Decision Support Systems* **46** (2008) 52-60.

Kleinrock, L., *Communication Nets*, Dover, New York, 1964.

Krishnan, R., Smith, M.D., and Telang, R., "The Economics of Peer-to-Peer Networks," *JITTA : Journal of Information Technology Theory and Application,* **5**, 3, 2003.

Li, Y., Tan, Y., and Zhou, Y., "On the Scale of Peer-to-Peer Networks," *Proceedings of Workshop on Information Technology and Systems*, Barcelona, Spain, 2002.

McDougall, P., "The Power of Peer-to-Peer," www.informationweek.com/801/peer.htm, August 2000.

Mendelson, H., "Pricing Computer Services: Queuing Effects," *Comm. ACM*, **28**, 3, 312-321, 1985.

Mendelson, H. and Wang, S., "Optimal Incentive Compatible Priority Pricing for the M/M/1 Queue," *Operations Research*, **38**, 5, 870-883, 1990.

Ottolenghi, L., "The Future of Peer-to-Peer (P2P) Technology," Report to United States Senate Subcommittee on Competition, Infrastructure, and Foreign Commerce, http://commerce.senate.gov/pdf/ottolenghi062304.doc, 2007.

Tanenbaum, A.S., *Computer Networks*, Fourth Edition, Prentice-Hall, Englewood Cliffs, NJ, 2003.

In: Peer-to-Peer Networks and Internet Policies   ISBN: 978-1-60876-287-3
Editors: Diego Vegros and Jaime Sáenz, pp. 229-25 © 2010 Nova Science Publishers, Inc.

Chapter 12

NCTUns Tool for Evaluating the Performances of Real-Life P2P Applications

Shie-Yuan Wang, Chih-Che Lin and Chao-Chan Huang
Department of Computer Science,
National Chiao Tung University, Hsinchu, Taiwan

Abstract

This chapter presents the NCTUns simulation/emulation tool for researchers to evaluate the performances of real-life P2P applications such as BitTorrent. By using a unique simulation methodology, NCTUns directly uses the real-life network protocol stacks in the Linux operating system for realistic network simulations and enables any real-life network application to be executed on a node in a simulated network. These unique capabilities enable researchers to evaluate the performances of real-life P2P applications such as BitTorrent on accurately-simulated networks. In this chapter, we present the architecture of NCTUns, its simulation methodology, its unique capabilities, its detailed usages, and its scalability in real-life P2P application researches. More information about NCTUns is available at http://NSL.cs.nctu.edu.tw/nctuns.html.

1. Introduction

In this decade, peer-to-peer (P2P) applications have emerged as popular tools for sharing data. Such P2P applications build an overlay network on top of existing wired and wireless infrastructure networks and can disseminate and share data in a peer-to-peer manner. P2P applications have also gained much attention in the network research community due to its complicated behaviors. In the literature, several previous studies have shown that the performances of P2P applications strongly depend on the link conditions of the underlying infrastructure networks [1]. As a result, a high-fidelity packet-level P2P network simulator is highly desired in the P2P research community to study the relationship between the performances of P2P applications and the conditions of the underlying infrastructure networks.

However, developing such a packet-level network simulator from scratch is time-consuming and requires a great amount of effort to validate its correctness. Therefore, instead of developing a new packet-level network simulator for P2P researches, researchers prefer to use existing network simulators that have been well developed and carefully validated. To satisfy such needs, in this chapter we introduce a high-fidelity packet-level network simulation/emulation tool, called the NCTUns network simulator and emulator [2][3], for readers.

NCTUns is a powerful research tool for studying and developing P2P protocols. It has two unique features that are difficult to be achieved by traditional network simulators such as ns-2 [4] and OPNET modeler [5]. The first feature is that it uses the real-life Linux-kernel TCP/UDP/IP protocol stack to conduct simulations. This feature allows it to generate high-fidelity simulation results with a realistic transport-layer and network-layer protocol suite that have been widely used and tested in the world. The other feature is that NCTUns can run real-life application programs on simulated nodes during simulation. This feature allows it to generate simulation results using traffic generated by real-life application programs. With these two unique features, NCTUns can "run" real TCP/UDP/IP protocols and user applications in a simulated network and generate more accurate simulation results than other network simulators.

In addition to introducing NCTUns, in this chapter we illustrate the steps of using NCTUns to conduct P2P network simulations and emulations. To demonstrate the capability of NCTUns as a valuable research tool, we also present a performance study on a *real-life* BitTorrent (BT) protocol implementation under various network conditions simulated by NCTUns.

2.   Introduction to NCTUns

In this section, we briefly explain the architecture and simulation methodology of NCTUns for readers. As shown in Fig. 1, NCTUns is mainly composed of six components: 1) Graphical User Interface (GUI); 2) Dispatcher; 3) Coordinator; 4) simulation engine; 5) application programs; and 6) patches to the kernel TCP/UDP/IP protocol stacks. The main functions of these components are explained below.

1) **GUI**

NCTUns provides a front-end GUI program (called "nctunsclient" in its package), which provides useful facilities for users to efficiently create simulation and emulation cases. According to users' common needs, it groups the operations of generating a simulation/emulation case into four modes, which are briefly introduced here.

a) **The "Draw Topology" mode**:

In this mode, one can insert network nodes, create network links, and specify the locations and moving paths of mobile nodes. In addition, the GUI program provides a complete tool kit for users to construct road networks, which is fundamental to wireless vehicular network simulations, where many P2P researchers are proposing to run P2P applications.

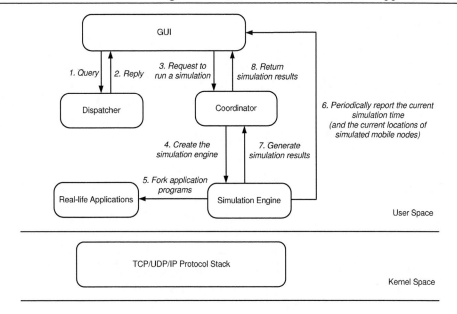

Figure 1. The architecture of NCTUns.

b) **The "Edit Property" mode**:

In this mode, one can double-click the icon of a network node to configure its properties (e.g., the network protocol stack used in this node, the applications to be run on this node, and other parameters).

c) **The "Run Simulation" mode**:

In this mode, the GUI program provides users with a complete set of commands to **start/pause/stop** a simulation. One can easily control the progress of a simulation by simply pressing a button on the GUI control panel.

d) **The "Play Back" mode**:

After a simulation is finished, the GUI program will automatically switch itself into the "Play Back" mode and read the packet trace file generated during the simulation. In this mode, one can use the GUI program to replay a node's packet transmission/reception operations in an animated manner.

2) **Dispatcher**

NCTUns provides a flexible simulation architecture, by which the GUI program and the simulation engine program can be run on different machines. In NCTUns, the GUI program need not find a simulation server to run the simulation engine program for a simulation. Instead, it sends the Dispatcher program an inquiry message to know which simulation server is currently available. (The details of the handshake protocol used by these components are explained later.) The Dispatcher program is responsible for monitoring the statuses of the simulation servers that it manages and selecting an available simulation server (if one exists) to serve the simulation request issued from the GUI program.

3) Coordinator

The Coordinator program has the following four tasks: 1) processing the commands sent from Dispatcher; 2) forking (creating) a simulation engine process to perform a simulation; 3) reporting the status of the created simulation engine process to the Dispatcher program; and 4) collecting the simulation results produced by its created simulation engine process and sending them to the GUI program. Before starting any simulation on a simulation server, one should first run up a Coordinator program on it.

4) Simulation Engine

The simulation engine program is composed of a set of various protocol modules and an event scheduler. The former is responsible for simulating protocol behaviors while the latter is responsible for scheduling events in a non-decreasing order based on their timestamps. In addition, during simulation the simulation engine process will periodically report the current simulation time to the GUI program.

5) Application Program

Application programs are responsible for generating network traffic in a simulated network. Most real-life application program can be directly run up on a node simulated by NCTUns to generate realistic network traffic.

6) Kernel Patches

NCTUns uses the real-life Linux network protocol stack to "simulate" transport-layer and network-layer protocols, such as TCP, UDP, IP, and ICMP. Minor modifications to Linux kernel timers are required so that the timers used by the in-kernel protocol stack of each simulated node can advance their times based on the simulated clock (controlled by NCTUns) rather than the real-world clock.

In the following, we explain how NCTUns performs a simulation in detail. Suppose that one has finished specifying his simulation case. By clicking the "Run" command (on the GUI control panel), one can trigger the GUI program to start a simulation. The GUI program first inquiries the Dispatcher program whether any simulation server is now available. If not, the Dispatcher program returns a "No servers are available" message to the GUI program. Otherwise, the Dispatcher program picks an available simulation server and then sends the GUI program the IP address of the chosen simulation server.

After receiving the IP address of the chosen simulation server, the GUI program sends a simulation request (with the files describing the simulation case to be run) to the Coordinator program running on the chosen simulation server. After receiving such a request, the Coordinator program forks a simulation engine process to run the received simulation case. (To save space, in the following we will simply use "simulation engine" to refer to "simulation engine process.") The tasks of the simulation engine process are explained below.

The simulation engine first constructs the topology of the simulated network, sets up global data structures used for the simulation, and creates/initializes the protocol stack of each simulated node. It then initializes the simulation clock to zero, inserts "Create Application" events (explained below) into the event scheduler, and finally starts the simulation.

A "Create Application" event is used to notify the simulation engine of when and which application should be created (forked) during simulation. When the simulation clock advances to the time specified by a "Create Application" event, the simulation engine will fork the application program specified by that event (to generate traffic). Note that the timers of an application process forked by the simulation engine are controlled by the virtual clock of NCTUns. That is, when an application process invokes library calls, such as gettimeofday(), sleep(), and alarm(), these library calls will be triggered based on the virtual clock of NCTUns. This is achieved by modifying time-related system calls in the kernel.

During simulation, the simulation engine periodically reports the current simulation time to the GUI program to show the progress of the simulation. After the simulation is done, the Coordinator program will collect and pack all the log files generated during simulation and then transmit them back to the GUI program for further processing and display.

2.1.   Simulation Methodology of NCTUns

NCTUns uses an innovative kernel re-entering methodology to perform network simulations. Detailed information about this methodology can be found in [3]. To help readers quickly understand how NCTUns integrates user-level application programs, the kernel-level TCP/UDP/IP protocol stacks, and various protocol modules (compiled and linked with the simulation engine) into a complete simulation environment, in this section we use a simple example case to briefly explain the simulation methodology of NCTUns.

NCTUns uses a pseudo network device driver (called the tunnel device driver in Linux) to virtualize the function of a Network Interface Card (NIC). A pseudo network device driver is a set of standard driver functions, such as open(), read(), write(), close(), etc., that do not perform any real packet transmission/reception operations and are not associated with any real NIC. A pseudo network device driver contains a packet output queue, which is used by NCTUns to temporarily store packets to be transmitted. By properly configuring the IP address and routing entries associated with a pseudo network device driver, NCTUns makes the Linux kernel think that a pseudo network device driver created by NCTUns is a **"real"** NIC device driver that controls a real NIC.

Consider a simple network scenario shown in Fig. 2(a), where a UDP sender program wants to transmit data to a UDP receiver program. These two programs are run on two different machines, which are connected via a wired link. As shown in Fig. 2(b), before starting the simulation, NCTUns first creates two tunnel device drivers to represent the NICs of the sending node and the receiving node, respectively. It then sets up the IP addresses of these two tunnel devices. Suppose that the IP address of tunnel device 1 (which is on the sending node) is set to 1.0.1.10 and that of tunnel device 2 (which is on the receiving node) is set to 1.0.1.20, respectively. The next step is to add proper routing entries into the kernel routing table so that the Linux kernel will enqueue packets that are originated from 1.0.1.10 and destined to 1.0.1.20 into the output queue of tunnel device 1 for transmission.

After being forked, the UDP receiver process first uses standard socket APIs, such as socket() and bind(), to create a socket structure that is associated with the IP address of

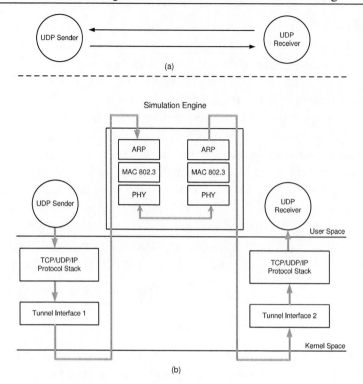

Figure 2. The simulation methodology of NCTUns.

tunnel device 2 (i.e., 1.0.1.20). It then uses the recvfrom() call to wait for packets destined to the IP address 1.0.1.20. On the other hand, after being forked, the UDP sender process first uses the socket() call to create a socket structure and then uses the sendto() call to write a segment of data into the socket send buffer, which is in the kernel space. The written data segment will then pass through (be processed by) the UDP/IP protocol stack and be encapsulated into an IP packet, which will then be placed in the output queue of tunnel device 1.

Later on, the simulation engine reads these packets out from the output queue of tunnel device 1 and simulates the processing of the ARP, MAC-layer, and physical-layer protocols on node 1. After finding the MAC address for the IP address of the packet's destination node, the ARP module fills out the Ethernet header of the packet and sends it down to the MAC module. Such a "sending down" process repeats until the packet reaches the PHY module, which simulates the transmission/reception behavior of a packet over a wired link. Finally, the PHY module of node 1 delivers the packet to the PHY module of node 2.

Upon receiving the packet, the PHY module of node 2 first simulates the reception of this packet. If it receives any other packet during the reception of this packet, it drops these two packets because they are collided with each other. Otherwise, after the reception of this packet has elapsed, the node 2's PHY module delivers it up to the MAC module, which performs the MAC-layer processing for this packet. Similar to the "sending down" process on the transmitting node, such a "sending up" process on the receiving node repeats until the received packet reaches the ARP module, where the simulation engine writes the packet into tunnel device 2. After this operation is performed, the Linux kernel invokes the IP-layer receiving routines to process this packet as if this packet was received from a real NIC. Following the normal processing for an incoming IP packet, this packet is then dispatched to the UDP layer. The UDP-layer receiving routines then enqueue this packet into the socket-layer receive buffer (which stores the packets destined to the socket created by the UDP receiver process). Upon detecting the arrival of this packet at the socket receive buffer, the Linux kernel then wakes up the UDP receiver process, which then copies the data carried by this packet to its own memory space (i.e., return from the recvfrom() call).

As one sees, by using this methodology the UDP sender and receiver programs used in an NCTUns-simulated network are real-life application programs and the TCP/UDP/IP protocol stacks used to process their packets are the real-life protocol stacks in the Linux kernel. These two unique properties are very important to P2P researchers as now they can evaluate the performances of many real-life P2P network applications (such as BitTorrent) on accurately-simulated networks.

3.   The Operation of the BitTorrent Protocol

In this chapter, we choose the BitTorrent (BT) protocol, one of the most widely used P2P communication protocols in the Internet, to demonstrate the usages of NCTUns in P2P researches. Before going into the configuration details, we provide some background knowledge about the BT protocol for readers. With the provided background knowledge, one can more easily understand the context to be presented. The BT protocol described in this section is the basic BT protocol. Although there have been many extensions to the basic BT protocol, because the objective of this chapter focuses on how to use NCTUns to conduct P2P network simulations and emulations, we do not explain the details of the extensions here.

As shown in Fig. 3, the BT protocol is composed of three types of nodes: 1) tracker server, 2) seeder, and 3) client. The tracker server maintains the list of active clients that are uploading and downloading files to be shared. The seeder is a client that possesses complete copies of files to be shared. The seeder that owns the first copy of the shared file is called the initial seeder. The last type is the client, which denotes the nodes that do not possess the shared file and want to download that file.

Initially, before the P2P communication takes place, the initial seeder should divide the file to be shared into several blocks of the same size. It then generates a torrent file that stores the meta information of the file to be shared. Such meta information includes the descriptions about the division of the shared file, the checksum value of each divided file block (explained later), and the IP address of the tracker server that is chosen by this initial seeder to maintain the list of active clients that are uploading/downloading the file.

After generating the torrent file, the initial seeder then computes a checksum value for each divided file block using a specific hash function (e.g., SHA-1 [6]). Such a checksum value is stored in the torrent file of the shared file and used by a downloading client to examine whether a received file block is correct or not. After receiving a complete file block, a downloading client first computes the checksum value of the received file block using the same hash function. It then compares the computed checksum value with the one stored in the torrent file. If these two values are the same, it means that the received file

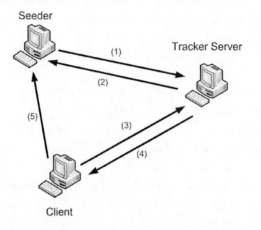

Figure 3. The operation of the BT protocol.

block is correct. Otherwise, the received file block is corrupted and the downloading client should re-download it for the integrity of the whole file.

Later on, the initial seeder should release the torrent file that it created (e.g., publish it at a third-party website) so that other clients have a chance to obtain the torrent file. Meanwhile, the initial seeder should start seeding the file. This is done by transmitting a control message to the tracker server that it specifies in the torrent file. After receiving a control message from the initial seeder, the tracker server sends back the seeder a list of clients that are currently uploading and downloading the file to be shared. (It is obvious that the initial active client list contains only the initial seeder itself.)

For a client that intends to download the shared file, it should first obtain the torrent file of the shared file (e.g., by downloading the torrent file from the website where the initial seeder published the torrent file). After obtaining the torrent file, it transmits a control message to the tracker server specified in the torrent file to obtain the active client list. By using the information in the active client list, the client then tries to connect to other active clients that are uploading/downloading the same shared file. After establishing connections with those clients, the client can obtain the blocks of the shared file from the connected clients in a peer-to-peer manner. Each client should periodically send the tracker server a control message to indicate its existence. If the tracker server does not receive such a renewal control message from a client within a pre-defined period, the tracker server will remove the client from the active client list.

4.   Build a P2P Network Simulation Case over NCTUns

In this section, we illustrate how to use NCTUns to conduct a P2P network simulation case. We used the "bittorrent" package included in the Fedora 9 Linux distribution to generate P2P network traffic. The "bittorrent" package is composed of three programs. The first is the "maketorrent-console" program, which is used to generate a torrent file of a shared file; the second is the "bittorrent-tracker" program, which implements the function of a tracker server; and the last one is the "bittorrent-console" program, which is a text-mode bittorrent client program. The detailed usages of these programs can be found in

Linux manual pages and in this section we only show the commands required to start these programs in our simulation case.

In the following, we present the steps to run up the bittorrent package over an NCTUns-simulated network:

1) **Create a symbolic link in the "/usr/local/nctuns/tools" directory for each application program that is to be run in simulations** (e.g., the bittorrent-tracker and bittorrent-client programs). The "/usr/local/nctuns/tools" directory stores the programs that can be forked by the simulation engine during simulation. Thus, one should place all application programs to be run during simulation in this directory before the simulation starts. One way to achieve this is to simply copy all programs to be run during simulation into the "/usr/local/nctuns/tools" directory and the other way is to create symbolic links in the "/usr/local/nctuns/tools" directory pointing to these programs. In this example case, we use the latter way to achieve this goal.

Suppose that the programs of the bittorrent package are installed on the "/usr/bin/"directory. The detailed commands to create symbolic links for them are shown below:

    a) cd /usr/local/nctuns/tools

    b) ln -s /usr/bin/bittorrent-tracker bt _tracker

    c) ln -s /usr/bin/bittorrent-console bt _client

(Note: In this example, the link name of the bittorrent-tracker program is chosen to be "bt_tracker" and that of the bittorrent-console program is chosen to be "bt _client.")

2) **Specify the network topology.** One can use the GUI program to specify the network topology in an intuitive manner. With its aid, one can save much time on creating and editing a simulation case. For example, as shown in Fig. 4, when switching into the "Edit Property" mode, the GUI program can automatically generate proper IP addresses for all simulated nodes, which is a tedious and error-prone task if it is manually done by a user. To see the IP address assigned to a simulated node, one can move the mouse cursor onto the icon of a simulated node, which will show up the IP address assigned to this simulated node.

3) **Generate a torrent file.**

Suppose that the file to be shared in this example network is named "test.avi" and placed in the /root/ directory, and the tracker server is to be run at TCP port number 6969 on node 1 during simulation. (Note that the IP address automatically assigned by the GUI program to node 1 is 1.0.1.1.) To generate a torrent file required by the BT protocol, one needs to perform the "maketorrent-console http://1.0.1.1:6969/announce test.avi" command, which will generate a torrent file named "test.avi.torrent" in the directory where the maketorrent-console command is executed.

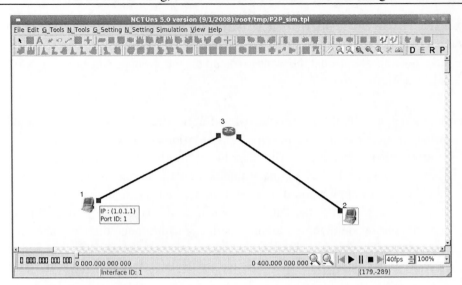

Figure 4. The network topology used in the simulations.

4) Specify the execution of the tracker server program

The next step is to configure the execution of the tracker server program. To achieve this, we first switch the GUI program to the "Edit Property" mode. We then double-click the icon of node 1 to pop up its dialog box. As shown in the left part of Fig. 5, by clicking the "Add" button on the **Application** tab, the dialog box for setting up traffic generator programs to be run on node 1 will show up.

One can specify the start time, the stop time, and the complete command to launch a program in this dialog box. Assume that we start the tracker server program at the 2nd second of the simulated time and stop it at the 400th second of the simulated time. Further assume that the TCP port number used by the tracker server program is 6969 and the tracker server program stores the active client information in the /root/dtate file. As shown in the right part of Fig. 5, the complete command to run a tracker server program with these settings is "bt_tracker --port 6969 --dfile /root/dtate."

5) Specify the execution of a seeder program

Because NCTUns treats both a seeder (client) program and a tracker server program as user-level application programs, the ways to specify the commands for launching these two programs are the same. Assume that the seeder program is to be run on node 1, starts at the 4th second of the simulated time, and stops at the 400th second of the simulated time. To set up it in NCTUns, one should first invoke node 1's dialog box and click the "Add" button on the **Application** tab. On the traffic dialog box, one can specify the start and stop times of this seeder program. The command to run this seeder program is "bt_client --save_as /root/upload/test.avi /root/upload/test.avi.torrent," where "/root/upload/test.avi" and "/root/upload/test.avi.torrent" specify the locations of the test.avi file and its corresponding torrent file, respectively.

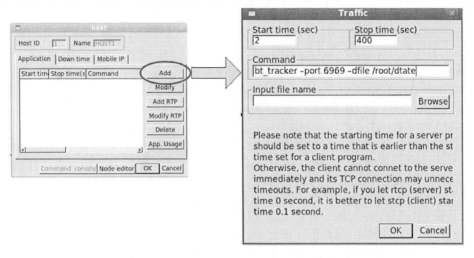

Figure 5. The dialog box for setting up a BT tracker program.

6) **Specify the execution of a client program**

Assume that the client program is to be run on node 2 during simulation, starts at the 10th second of the simulated time, and stops at the 400th second of the simulated time. The command used to specify this client program is "bt_client --save_as /root/download/test.avi /root/download/test.avi.torrent," where "/root/download/test.avi" and "/root/download/test.avi.torrent" specify the locations to store the received test.avi file and its corresponding torrent file, respectively.

Note that, because a seeder program is essentially a client program that already possesses the shared file, the commands to run these two programs are the same. Upon initializing itself, a client program first examines whether the file specified in the command line (to download) exists or not. If the file exists, the client program then further examines whether it is complete or not. If the file is complete, the client program will run as a seeder (i.e., solely upload possessed file blocks). Otherwise, the client program will run as a normal client.

7) **Start Simulation**

After setting up the simulation case, one can switch the operating mode of the GUI program to the "Run Simulation" mode. This can be done by pressing the "R" button on the top-right control panel of the GUI program. In the "Run Simulation" mode, one can start/pause/stop a simulation by using the commands provided in the "Simulation" function list. The detailed usages of these commands can be found in [7].

5. Build a P2P Network Emulation Case over NCTUns

In addition to performing network simulations, NCTUns can perform network emulations in an easy and intuitive way. By using its innovative kernel re-entering methodology, NCTUns can seamlessly connect a simulated network with a real-life network, which means that hosts in the real world can communicate (i.e., transmit/receive packets) with those in a simulated network over NCTUns. This feature is useful for P2P researchers due to the following reasons.

First, by using emulations, various network devices (e.g., host, laptop, PDA, etc.) using different operating systems (e.g., Windows XP/Vista, Symbian, Sun Solaris, FreeBSD, etc.) can communicate with the nodes simulated in NCTUns. With this capability, one can easily test and evaluate the performances of P2P application programs running on non-Linux platforms under various network conditions without the need to port them to Linux.

Second, P2P application programs are usually memory-intensive because they require a large amount of memory to temporarily store received file blocks. If one runs P2P simulations using these real-life P2P application programs, all of such memory-intensive programs need to be run up on the same machine. In such a condition, these memory-intensive programs may exhaust the main memory of the simulation machine. As one knows, when the physical memory is exhausted, the operating system will use the secondary storage, such as hard disks, to store data that are not currently used. (This operation is called "swap out.") Later on, if the "swapped out" data are needed by some processes, the operating system will move them back into the main memory by reading the data from the secondary storage. (This operation is called "swap in.") However, the access time of the secondary storage device is hundred thousand times slower than that of main memory. For this reason, network simulations that involve with memory swapping in/out operations are very time-consuming.

To overcome this problem, NCTUns emulations can be used. By using the emulation approach, such memory-intensive P2P application programs can be run on different machines, which distributes the memory load over multiple machines and thus alleviates the memory shortage problem on each machine. As a result, using NCTUns emulations can allow more P2P application programs to be run and tested in a case.

In this section, we use a simple network case to demonstrate how to conduct an emulation using NCTUns. As shown in Fig. 6, suppose that an emulated network comprises three external (real) hosts, which are connected together via a simulated switch node and these hosts use IP addresses 10.0.0.1, 10.0.0.2, and 10.0.0.3, respectively. We show the detailed steps to configure this emulation case below.

The steps for configuring an emulation case is the same as those for configuring a simulation case, except that in an emulation case one should add **external nodes** into the working field of the GUI program, while in a simulation case one should add **simulation nodes** into the working field of the GUI program. In an emulated network, each external node is a representative of an external (real) machine. Adding an external node into a network case is simple — first click an external node icon (which is on the node list panel of the GUI program) and then click anywhere on the working field of the GUI program.

After switching into the **"Edit Property"** mode, the GUI program will automatically assign virtual IP addresses to all simulated and emulated nodes. In this example, external hosts 1, 2, and 3, are assigned the IP addresses 1.0.1.1, 1.0.1.2, and 1.0.1.3, respectively. One should then click the icon of each external node on the GUI program to invoke its configuration dialog box. By filling in the information required by the configuration dialog box and following its instructions, one can easily configure an external node. The detailed steps are explained below.

As shown in Fig. 7, the dialog box of an external node is composed of three text fields and two buttons. The first text field shows the IP address that is automatically assigned to

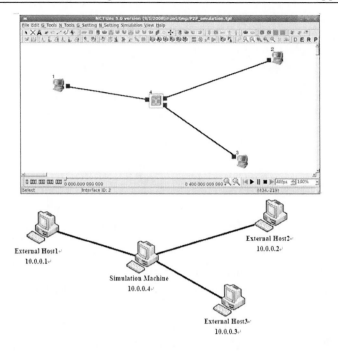

Figure 6. The topology of the example emulated network.

this node by the GUI program. One should fill in the second and third text fields with the external node's real IP address (i.e., the IP address associated with the NIC on the external machine) and the IP address of the simulation machine's NIC (i.e., the IP address associated with the NIC that is on the simulation machine and connects with the external machine), respectively. Note that if the simulation machine has multiple real NICs, one should use the IP address of the NIC that connects with this external machine. Otherwise, the GUI program may calculate incorrect routing entries to forward packets from/to this external machine.

After providing the IP addresses of the external and simulation machines, one has to properly configure the routing table of the external machine so that packets transmitted by the external machine can be correctly received by the NCTUns simulation machine and vice versa. To help users correctly do this task without mistakes, the GUI program can automatically generate correct routing commands for an emulation case. This is done by pressing either the "for Linux" button or the "for FreeBSD" button, depending on which kind of operating systems is used on the external machine. After pressing either button, the GUI program will show up the complete "route-add" command for users to set up the routing table of the external machine. One can directly copy the shown "route-add" command and execute it on the external machine, which will add a proper routing entry into the routing table of the external machine.

After finishing configuring an emulation case, one can switch the GUI program to the "Run Simulation" mode and start the emulation. (Note that, application programs need not be specified before the emulation starts. Instead, they can be run up on external machines after the emulation starts.) The operation to start/stop an emulation is the same as that used

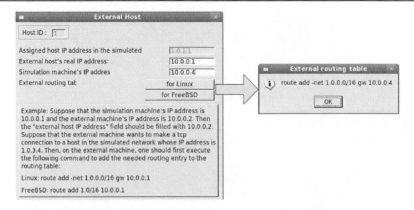

Figure 7. The dialog box used to configure an external node.

to start/stop a simulation and is thus omitted here to save space. After starting the emulation, one should manually run up application programs on external machines to generate network traffic. In this emulation example case, we first ran the tracker server program and the seeder program on external machine 1 and then ran two client programs on external machines 2 and 3, respectively. The commands to run these application programs on external machines are the same as the commands to run them on NCTUns-simulated nodes, which have been presented in Section 4. and are not shown again here.

One issue that should be noticed is that, when making a torrent file, one should use the virtual IP address of external host 1 (i.e., 1.0.1.1 in this example case) to specify the IP address of the tracker server, rather than use the real IP address of external host 1 (i.e., 10.0.0.1 in this example case). This is because, when a real-life packet (coming from an external machine) enters the NCTUns machine, NCTUns will automatically replace its original (real) source and destination IP addresses with their corresponding virtual IP addresses assigned by the GUI program. That is, in the core emulated network NCTUns forwards packets based on virtual IP addresses. For this reason, to correctly forward packets destined to the tracker server, the IP address of the tracker server specified in a torrent file should be the virtual IP address assigned to the external machine where the tracker server is run.

To increase the number of external machines that connect to the NCTUns simulation machine, a high-performance switch with many ports can be used. For example, a 24-port Ethernet switch can be used. The NCTUns machine and all external machines can connect to this switch to exchange their packets. To increase the number of P2P application programs participating in an emulation case, multiple P2P application programs can be run up on each external machine. For example, if 20 external machines are connected to the NCTUns machine and on each of them 50 P2P application programs are run up, in total 1,000 real-life P2P application programs can participate in a P2P emulation case.

6.   Performance Study of BT-based P2P Networks over NCTUns

In this section, we first present the simulation performances of NCTUns under different P2P traffic load conditions in Section 6.1. and then study the performances of the BT protocol under different network conditions in Section 6.2.. The parameter settings used in our

Table 1. The parameter settings used in the simulations

Parameter Name	Value
CPU Model	Intel Dual-Core 3.0 GHz
Main Memory	3 GBytes
Simulated Time (s)	10000
Traffic Type	BitTorrent
Interface Output Queue Length (pkts)	50
Link Bandwidth (Mbps)	0.1, 0.5, 1, 5, 10
Link Delay (μs)	1
The Size of the File to be Shared (MB)	100
File Block Size (KB)	256
File Block Number of the File to be Shared	400
Rarest-first Threshold Value	0, 4, 100, 200, 300, 400

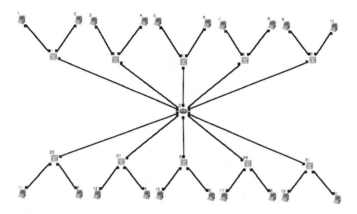

Figure 8. The star topology used in the simulations.

simulations are shown in Table 1.

As shown in Fig. 8, we created a star topology where 20 hosts are grouped into 10 subnets (with two hosts in each subnet) that are connected to the same router via wired links. We used the real-life "bittorrent" package, which has been introduced in Section 4., to generate network traffic. During simulation, each simulated host node runs a bt_client program on it. The BT tracker server program is run on node 1. The initial seeder is chosen to be the bt_client program running on node 1 and has possessed a copy of the file to be shared before the simulation starts. If the number of initial seeders N_{sd} is more than 1 in a simulation, we randomly chose ($N_{sd} - 1$) bt_client programs run on other nodes to be initial seeders. In each simulation case, the routes are pre-determined using Dijkstra's shortest path algorithm. Each point plotted in the following figures is the average across three simulation runs.

6.1. Simulation Performances of NCTUns under Different P2P Traffic Loads

Fig. 9 shows the time required by NCTUns to finish a simulation case over different numbers of initial seeders. One sees that, as the number of initial seeders increases, the time required to finish a simulation case decreases. This phenomenon is expected and explained here. The way we added an extra initial seeder is by making one more client

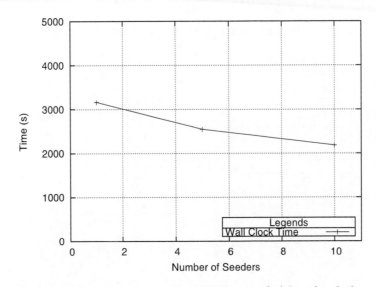

Figure 9. The time required by NCTUns to finish a simulation.

possess a copy of the whole file to be shared. This means that adding one extra initial seeder into the network will reduce the number of clients that need to download the shared file by one. Therefore, increasing the number of initial seeders in this way will result in the decrease of the total number of file blocks that need to be transmitted in the simulated network. Because shared file blocks are transmitted using packets, which are simulated by events, the total number of events that need to be simulated by NCTUns in a simulation case is thus reduced. In such a condition, the time required by NCTUns to finish a simulation case will be decreased because it has fewer events to simulate.

Fig. 10 shows the amount of memory consumed by NCTUns simulation over different numbers of downloading nodes (i.e., clients) in the simulated network. In this series of simulations, we fixed the number of initial seeders to 1 and added extra clients into the network. Such extra clients were evenly added into different subnets. The simulated time of each simulation is set to 600 seconds. We logged the maximum amount of memory used by the NCTUns simulation engine and all clients during each simulation. Before a simulation starts (i.e., after the operating system just boots up), the testing machine has already consumed 410 MB of main memory. The memory usage results show that the amount of memory used by NCTUns simulation is proportional to the number of clients. This phenomenon is explained below.

During simulation, each client program needs a certain amount of memory space to temporarily store the received file blocks. We logged the memory usage of each client program during the simulations and found that in these 600-second simulation cases a client program maximally required about 31 MB memory space to store its received file blocks. These results show that most main memory used in these simulations is consumed by client programs rather than the simulation engine of NCTUns. As discussed in Section 5., if the memory resource of the simulation machine cannot accommodate the whole simulation case, NCTUns emulations can be used instead.

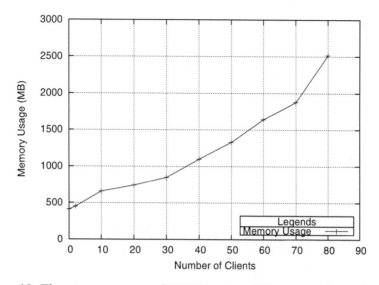

Figure 10. The memory usage of NCTUns over different numbers of clients.

6.2. Performances of the BT Protocol under Different Network Conditions

In this section, we studied the performances of the BT protocol under different network conditions and protocol designs. In addition to the star topology, which has been previously used, in this suite of simulations we created a ring topology and a mesh topology to study the impacts of different network topologies on the BT protocol. As shown in Fig. 11, the used ring topology is composed of 20 hosts, which is further grouped into 10 subnets. Each subnet has its own router and each router is connected with its two neighboring routers via wired links to form a ring topology. The created mesh topology is shown in Fig. 12, where the core twelve routers are deployed to form the grid. Each router is connected to its respective vertical and horizontal neighboring routers to form a mesh network. In the following simulations, if the number of initial seeders is not varied, it is set to 1 by default; if the link bandwidth is not varied, it is set to 1 Mbps by default.

Fig. 13 shows the average simulated time required for all clients to finish downloading the shared file over the evaluated topologies under different numbers of seeders. There are two findings about this figure. The first finding is that the trends of the required download times over three different topologies are similar — when the number of initial seeders increases, the time required for all clients to download the shared file decreases. This phenomenon can be explained from two aspects.

First, when the number of initial seeders increases, clients can choose from more seeders to download the shared file. In such a condition, a client can download required file blocks from seeders that are closer to itself. This means that the transmitted file blocks can travel fewer hops (i.e., forwarded by fewer intermediate routers) before arriving at the client. This reduces the bandwidth needs of this P2P file sharing and lessens the network congestion level. Therefore, a client can more quickly get the shared file.

Second, because each client now can download file blocks from the seeders that are closer to it, the traffic load of seeders can be more uniformly distributed, resulting in a better load balancing. This further decreases the time required for all clients to download

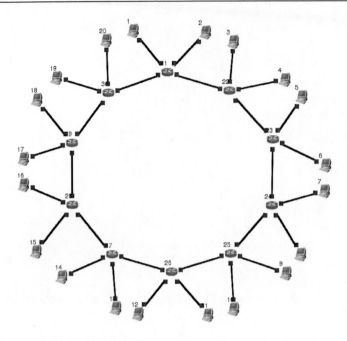

Figure 11. The ring topology used in the simulations.

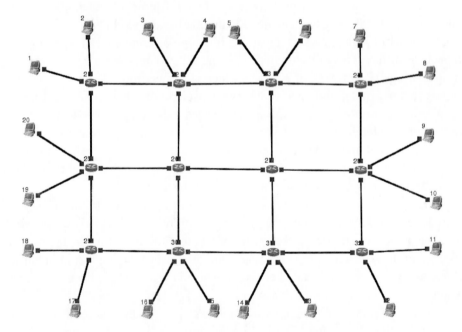

Figure 12. The mesh topology used in the simulations.

the shared file.

The second finding is that the mesh topology greatly outperforms the star and ring topologies on the time required for all clients to download the shared file. This is because nodes in the mesh topology have more links to transmit packets to other nodes than those in

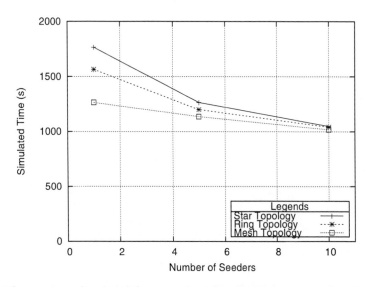

Figure 13. The average simulated time required for all clients to download the shared file.

the other two topologies. Since the aggregate link bandwidth is higher in the mesh topology, clients in this topology can download the shared file more quickly.

Fig. 14 shows the Average Download Rate of All BT Clients (denoted as ADR-ABC for brevity) under different link bandwidths. ADR-ABC is defined as follows:

$$ADR = \frac{\sum_{i=1}^{n} ADRN_i}{n}, \tag{1}$$

where $ADRN_i$ (Average Download Rate of Node i) denotes the average download rate of node i during the period when it downloads the shared file and n is the number of clients in the simulated network, which is set to 20 in our simulations.

As one sees, when the link bandwidth is below 1 Mbps, the average download rates of clients in the three evaluated topologies are similar. This is because initially only one node (i.e., the only initial seeder) possesses the file to be shared in the network. This means that all clients have to download file blocks from the same node at the beginning. Therefore, the download rates of clients are mainly bounded by the bandwidth of the initial seeder's outgoing link. When the link bandwidth is large (e.g., over 1 Mbps), the uploading rate of the initial seeder increases so that the blocks of the shared file can be more quickly distributed to other clients. In such a condition, clients can download required file blocks from nodes that are closer to them, thus increasing their download rates. In addition, because the mesh topology has the largest number of links among the three evaluated topologies, clients in it can achieve the highest file download rate.

We finally studied whether the file block selection algorithm used in the BT protocol can affect the downloading performances of clients. The bittorrent client program uses the rarest-first algorithm to determine the downloading preference of each file block. This algorithm is briefly explained below.

This algorithm initially selects file blocks to be downloaded in a random manner and uses a parameter "rarest-first threshold" to control when to select file blocks to be downloaded in a rarest-first manner. A "rarest-first threshold" value x means that, after x blocks

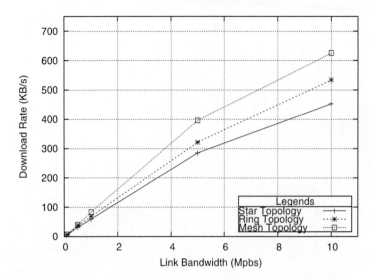

Figure 14. The ADR-ABC values over different link bandwidths.

of the shared file have been downloaded, the algorithm should start to download the remaining blocks of the shared file in the order based on their rareness. That is, the file block of the shared file that is possessed by the fewest clients should be downloaded first.

The default value of the "rarest-first threshold" parameter used in the bittorrent client program is 4. We changed this value from 1 to 400[1] and conducted a suite of simulations to observe the impacts of this value on the downloading performances of the BT protocol. The results are plotted in Fig. 15, which shows the total time needed for all clients to download the shared file over different "rarest-first threshold" values. As one sees, the "rarest-first threshold" value is insignificant to the downloading performances of BT in the three evaluated topologies. The phenomenon can be attributed to the following reason: In this suite of simulations there is only one initial seeder in the network. In such a condition, the effect of randomly choosing file blocks is similar to that of choosing the rarest file blocks.

7.   Related Work

In the literature, P2P network simulators can be roughly divided into two categories. One is the packet-level network simulator, which aims to simulate P2P networks with the details of underlying network protocols (e.g., the behaviors of the transport layer, the network layer, etc.). This type of P2P network simulator simulates the communication network at a fine-grain level; thus, the simulation speed and simulation scalability of a packet-level P2P network simulator is limited.

One representative of the packet-level P2P network simulator is the ns-2 network simulator [4], which is an open-source network simulator written in C++ and has been widely

---

[1]The shared file is divided into 400 blocks; thus, setting the "rarest-first threshold" to 400 is equivalent to making the rarest-first algorithm always download file blocks in a random manner.

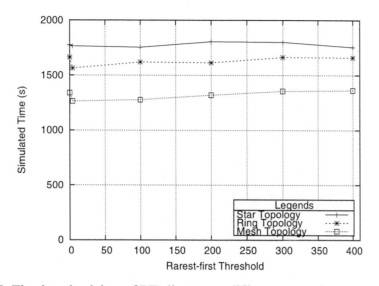

Figure 15. The download time of BT clients over different rarest-first threshold values.

used in the network research community. In 2004, the PDAS research group at Georgia Institute of Technology proposed an extension to ns-2, called Parallel/Distributed NS (PDNS) [8], to increase the simulation scalability of ns-2. PDNS uses a conservative approach to synchronize multiple ns-2 instances on different machines (each simulating a part of the whole simulated network) to collaboratively complete a simulation task. Using this distributed simulation architecture, PDNS can increase the number of nodes that can be simulated by ns-2 in a simulated network.

NCTUns also falls in the packet-level P2P network simulator category. However, as described in Sections 1. and 2., by using the innovative kernel re-entering methodology, NCTUns enables a simulation user to use real-life P2P application programs and real-life Linux protocol stacks to conduct realistic P2P network simulation. This unique capability cannot be easily achieved by other network simulators.

The other P2P network simulator category is the message-level P2P network simulator, which virtualizes the communication details between peer nodes and generates simulation results mainly based on messages generated by the top-level P2P protocols. Many message-level P2P network simulators have been proposed, such as P2PRealm [9], NeuroGrid [10], P2PSim [11], PeerSim [12], QueryCycle [13], 3LS [14], GPS [15], Oversim [16], etc.

The main objective of these message-level P2P network simulators is to conveniently observe and evaluate the behaviors and performances of P2P protocols in a large-scale network, rather than to observe the relationship between P2P protocol performances and various network conditions and settings. Because the design goals and applications of such message-level P2P network simulators greatly differ from and are less relevant to those of NCTUns, to save space we do not explain in detail the designs and implementations of these message-level P2P network simulators here.

Another track of P2P network simulation is combining the packet-level P2P network simulator with the message-level P2P network simulator. In [1], the authors proposed a framework that can integrate a message-level P2P network simulator and a packet-level network simulator into a compound P2P network simulation platform. By using the APIs provided by the proposed framework, messages generated by the message-level simulator can be properly injected into the sockets simulated by the underlying packet-level network simulator and vice versa.

Such a framework allows one to conduct simulations using different underlying packet-level network simulators without modifications to the used message-level simulator and application code. Therefore, it provides users with simulation flexibility to some extent. For example, depending on his needs, one can control the degree of packet transmission and reception simulations by choosing an appropriate packet-level network simulator. However, like other traditional packet-level network simulators, this simulation framework still uses fake P2P application program to generate simulated network traffic and uses abstracted network protocol stacks to simulate the processings of packet transmission and reception. Therefore, the fidelity of the simulation results generated by this simulation framework is still limited.

8. Conclusion

In this chapter, we introduce the NCTUns network simulator, which is open-source and uses real-life applications and real-life network protocol stacks to conduct simulations and emulations. Such features are very unique and helpful to P2P network researches. We illustrated how to use NCTUns to conduct P2P network simulations and emulations step by step, which can be good references and tutorials for P2P network researchers to conduct their own P2P network simulations/emulations over NCTUns. We also showed a case study on the performances of BitTorrent-based P2P networks using NCTUns. In this study, we used real-life BitTorrent package to generate P2P network traffic and evaluated the average download rates of BitTorrent clients under various network conditions. Finally, we tested and presented the simulation performances of NCTUns over different P2P workloads. The maximum number of BT clients that can participate in a NCTUns simulation is mainly limited by the amount of main memory on the simulation machine. According to our measurements, a BT client consumes about 31 MB during simulation. Therefore, on a PC with 4 GB main memory, about 100+ BT clients can participate in a NCTUns simulation. Beyond this number, NCTUns emulations can be used to utilize multiple machines at the same time to overcome this memory space limitation problem.

References

[1] Q. He, M. Ammar, G. Riley, H. Raj, R. Fujimoto, "Mapping peer behavior to packet-level details: a framework for packet-level simulation of peer-to-peer systems," *Proceedings of the 11th IEEE/ACM International Symposium on Modeling, Analysis and Simulation of Computer Telecommunications Systems, 2003 (MASCOTS 2003)* , p.p. 71-78, Oct. 12-15, 2003, Orlando, Florida, USA.

[2] S.Y. Wang, C.L. Chou, C.H. Huang, C.C. Hwang, Z.M. Yang, C.C. Chiou, and C.C. Lin, "The Design and Implementation of the NCTUns 1.0 Network Simulator," *Computer Networks*, Vol. 42, Issue 2, June 2003, pp. 175-197.

[3]   S.Y. Wang, C.L. Chou, and C.C. Lin, "The Design and Implementation of the NCTUns Network Simulation Engine", *Elsevier Simulation Modelling Practice and Theory* , 15 (2007), p.p. 5781.

[4]   The official website of the ns-2 network simulator *"http://www.isi.edu/nsnam/ns/"* .

[5]   The official website of the OPNET Modeler *"http://www.opnet.com/"*.

[6]   National Institute of Standards and Technology (NIST), a revision to the Federal Information *Processing Standard issued as "FIPS PUB 180-1,"* 1995.

[7]   S.Y. Wang, C.L. Chou, and C.C. Lin, "The GUI User Manual for the NCTUns 5.0 Network Simulator and Emulator." (available for download at http://nsl10.cs.nctu.edu.tw/.)

[8]   The official website of the Parallel/Distributed NS (PDNS) *"http://www.cc.gatech.edu/computing/compass/pdns/index.html"* .

[9]   N. Kotilainen, M. Vapa, T. Keltanen, A. Auvinen, J. Vuori, *"P2PRealm — peer-to-peer network simulator,"* Proceedings of the 11th Intenational Workshop on Computer-Aided Modeling, Analysis and Design of Communication Links and Networks, 2006, (CAMAD 2006), p.p. 93-99, June 8-9, Trento, Italy.

[10] Sam Joseph, *"An Extensible Open Source P2P Simulator,"* P2P Journal, 2003.

[11] The official website of the P2PSim network simulator *"http://pdos.csail.mit.edu/p2psim/index.html"* .

[12] The official website of the PeerSim network simulator *"http://peersim.sourceforge.net/"* .

[13] Mario T. Schlosser, Tyson E. Condie, Ar D. Kamvar, *"Simulating a P2P file-sharing network,"* Proceedings of the first Workshop on Semantics in P2P and Grid Computing, 2002.

[14] N.S. Ting, R. Deters, *"3LS — a peer-to-peer network simulator,"* Proceedings of the 3rd International Conference on Peer-to-Peer Computing , 2003. (P2P 2003), p.p. 212-213, 1-3 Sept, 2003, Linkping, Sweden.

[15] W Yang, N Abu-Ghazaleh, *"GPS: a general peer-to-peer simulator and its use for modeling BitTorrent,"* Proceedings of the 13th International Symposium on Modeling, Analysis, and Simulation of Computer and Telecommunication Systems , 2005, (MASCOTS 2005), pp. 425-432, Sept. 27-29, Atlanta, Georgia, USA.

[16] *The official website of the OverSim network simulator "http://www.oversim.org/" .*

INDEX

G

H

I

N

O

P

T